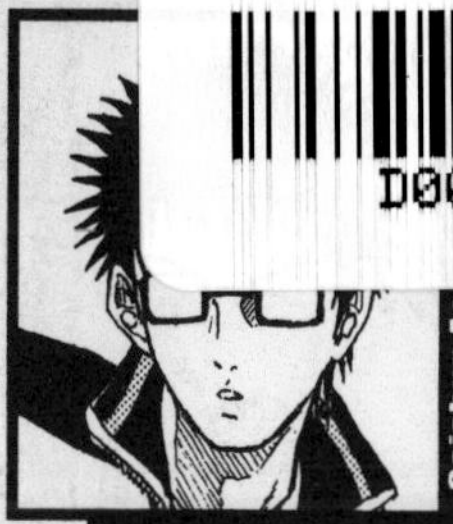

Seishun Ac
Tennis Team (9

Sadaharu Inui

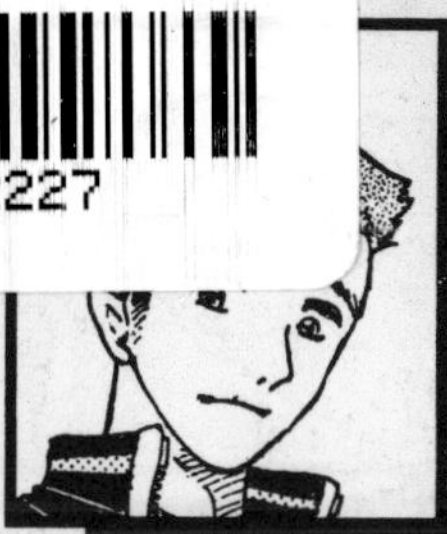

Seishun Academy
Tennis Team (9th Grade)

Takashi Kawamura

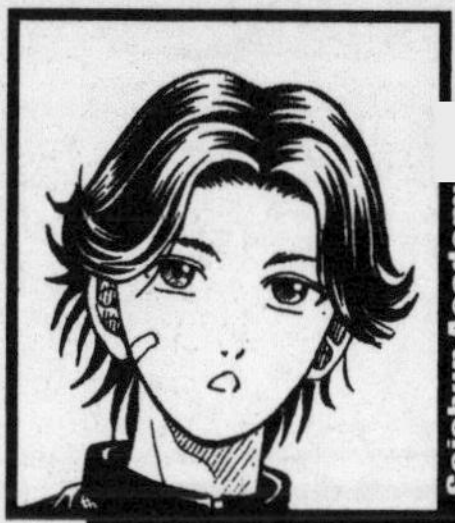

Seishun Academy
Tennis Team (9th Grade)

Eiji Kikumaru

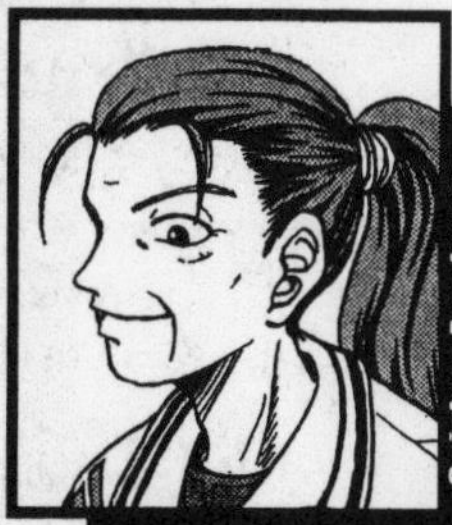

Seishun Academy
Tennis Team (Coach)

Sumire Ryuzaki

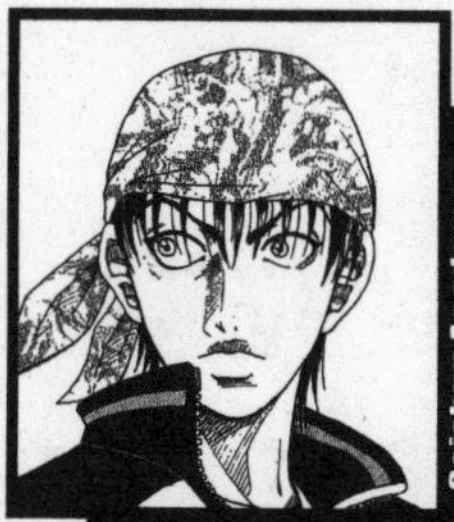

Seishun Academy
Tennis Team (8th Grade)

Kaoru Kaido

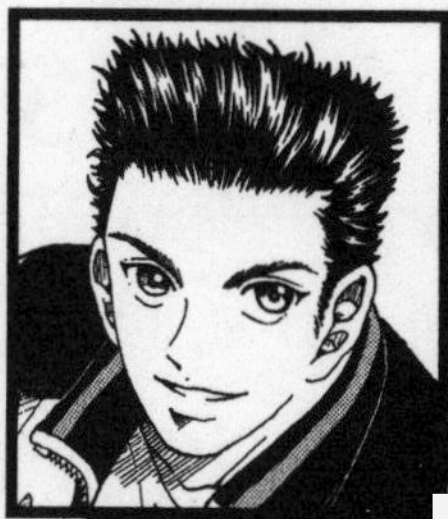

Seishun Academy
Tennis Team (8th Grade)

Takeshi Momoshiro

Ryoma Echizen, a tennis prodigy and winner of four U.S. Junior tournaments, has returned to Japan and enrolled at Seishun Academy Junior High. To everyone's astonishment, he becomes a starter in the District Preliminaries while still in the 7th grade and helps Seishun earn a berth in the City Tournament. Seishun advances easily until they meet St. Rudolph Academy, but at the end of the No. 2 Doubles match, they find themselves with one win and one loss. But at last, with Ryoma's victory over Shusuke's younger brother, Yuta, in No. 3 Singles, Seishun makes it through the semifinals!

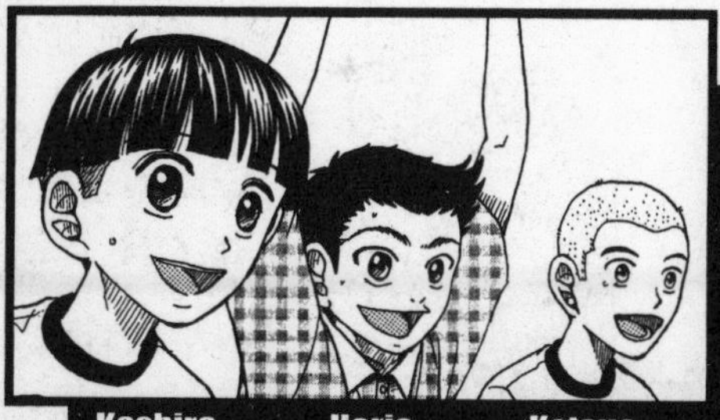

Kachiro Horio Katsuo
Seishun Academy Tennis Team (7th Grade)

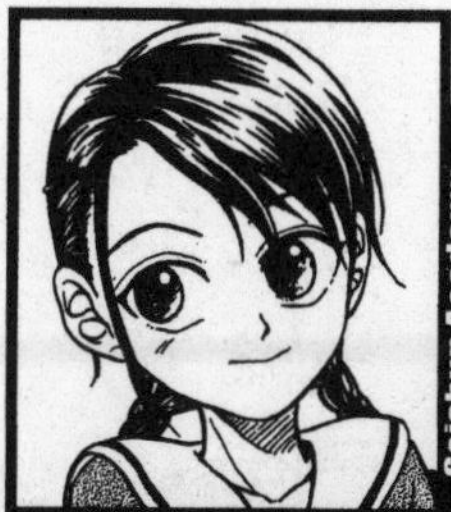

Seishun Academy
Tennis Team (7th Grade)

Sakuno Ryuzaki

CONTENTS Vol. 10
Seize the Moment!

THE PRINCE OF TENNIS

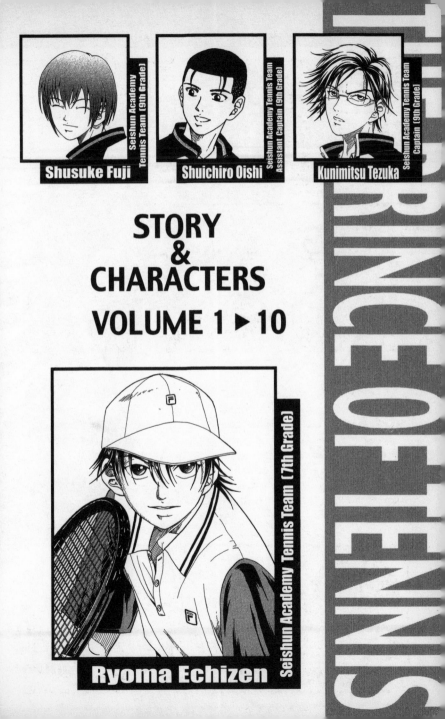

Shusuke Fuji
Seishun Academy Tennis Team (9th Grade)

Shuichiro Oishi
Seishun Academy Tennis Team Assistant Captain (9th Grade)

Kunimitsu Tezuka
Seishun Academy Tennis Team Captain (9th Grade)

STORY & CHARACTERS VOLUME 1 ▶ 10

Ryoma Echizen
Seishun Academy Tennis Team (7th Grade)

Shonen Jump Manga

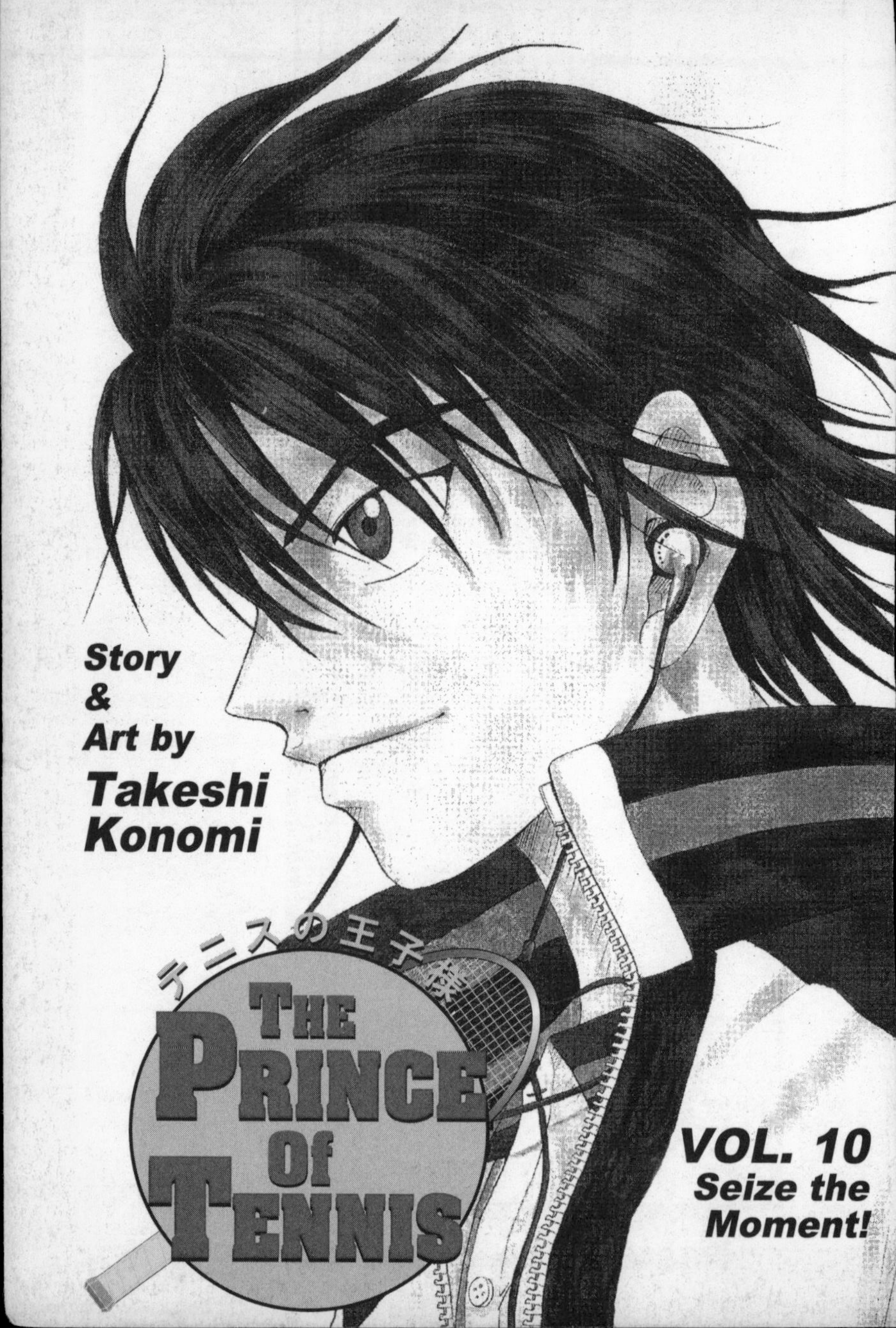

Story & Art by Takeshi Konomi

テニスの王子様

THE PRINCE OF TENNIS

VOL. 10

Seize the Moment!

THE PRINCE OF TENNIS
VOL. 10
The SHONEN JUMP Manga

**STORY AND ART BY
TAKESHI KONOMI**

English Adaptation/Gerard Jones
Translation/Joe Yamazaki
Touch-up Art & Lettering/Andy Ristaino
Cover Design/Terry Bennett
Interior Design/Janet Piercy
Editor/Michelle Pangilinan

Editor in Chief, Books/Alvin Lu
Editor in Chief, Magazines/Marc Weidenbaum
VP of Publishing Licensing/Rika Inouye
VP of Sales/Gonzalo Ferreyra
Sr. VP of Marketing/Liza Coppola
Publisher/Hyoe Narita

Printed in the U.S.A.

Published by VIZ Media, LLC
P.O. Box 77010
San Francisco, CA 94107

SHONEN JUMP Manga Edition
10 9 8 7 6 5 4 3 2
First printing, October 2005
Second printing, November 2007

PARENTAL ADVISORY
THE PRINCE OF TENNIS is rated A and is suitable for readers of all ages.
ratings.viz.com

THE WORLD'S
MOST POPULAR MANGA
www.shonenjump.com

www.viz.com

Recently, I played tennis for the first time in seven years. Sure enough, I was sore the next day and painfully found out I don't move my body enough. I hope to use this as an opportunity to exercise more. Perhaps a tennis tournament with all of you would be nice.

– Takeshi Konomi, 2001

About Takeshi Konomi

Takeshi Konomi exploded onto the manga scene with the incredible **THE PRINCE OF TENNIS**. His refined art style and sleek character designs proved popular with **Weekly Shonen Jump** readers, and **THE PRINCE OF TENNIS** became the No. 1 sports manga in Japan almost overnight. Its cast of fascinating male tennis players attracted legions of female readers even though it was originally intended to be a boys' comic. The manga continues to be a success in Japan. A hit anime series was created, as well as several video games and mountains of merchandise.

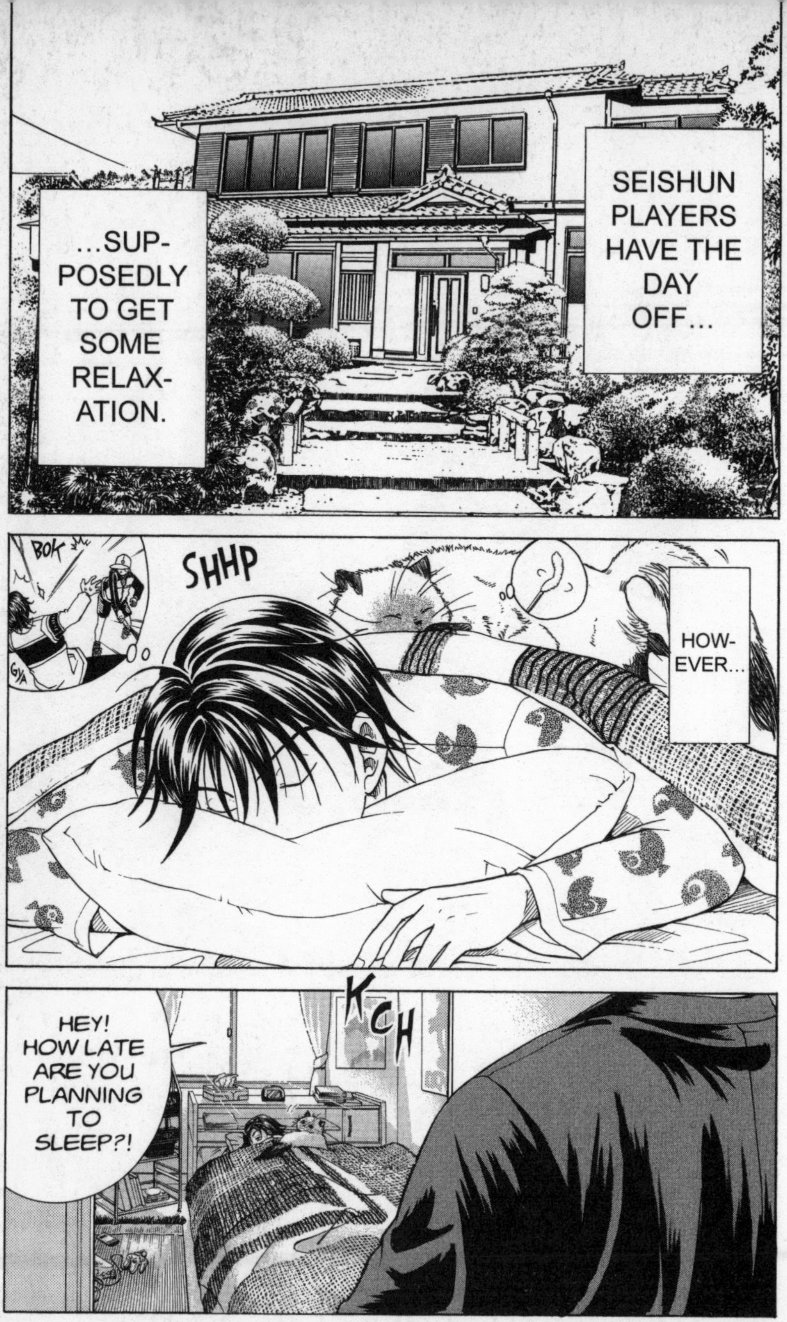
SEISHUN PLAYERS HAVE THE DAY OFF…
…SUP-POSEDLY TO GET SOME RELAX-ATION.
HOW-EVER…
SHHP
BOK
GYA
KCH
HEY! HOW LATE ARE YOU PLANNING TO SLEEP?!

GENIUS 79: SWEET TOOTH

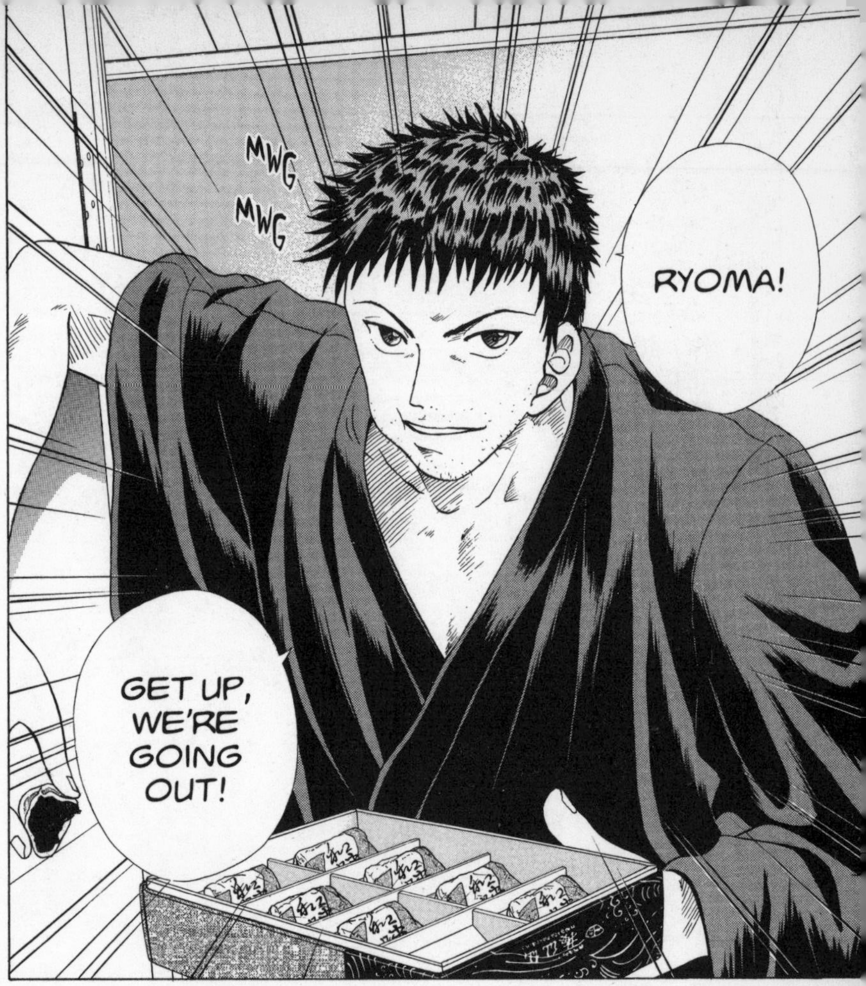
RYOMA!
MWG MWG
GET UP, WE'RE GOING OUT!

GENIUS 79:

SWEET TOOTH

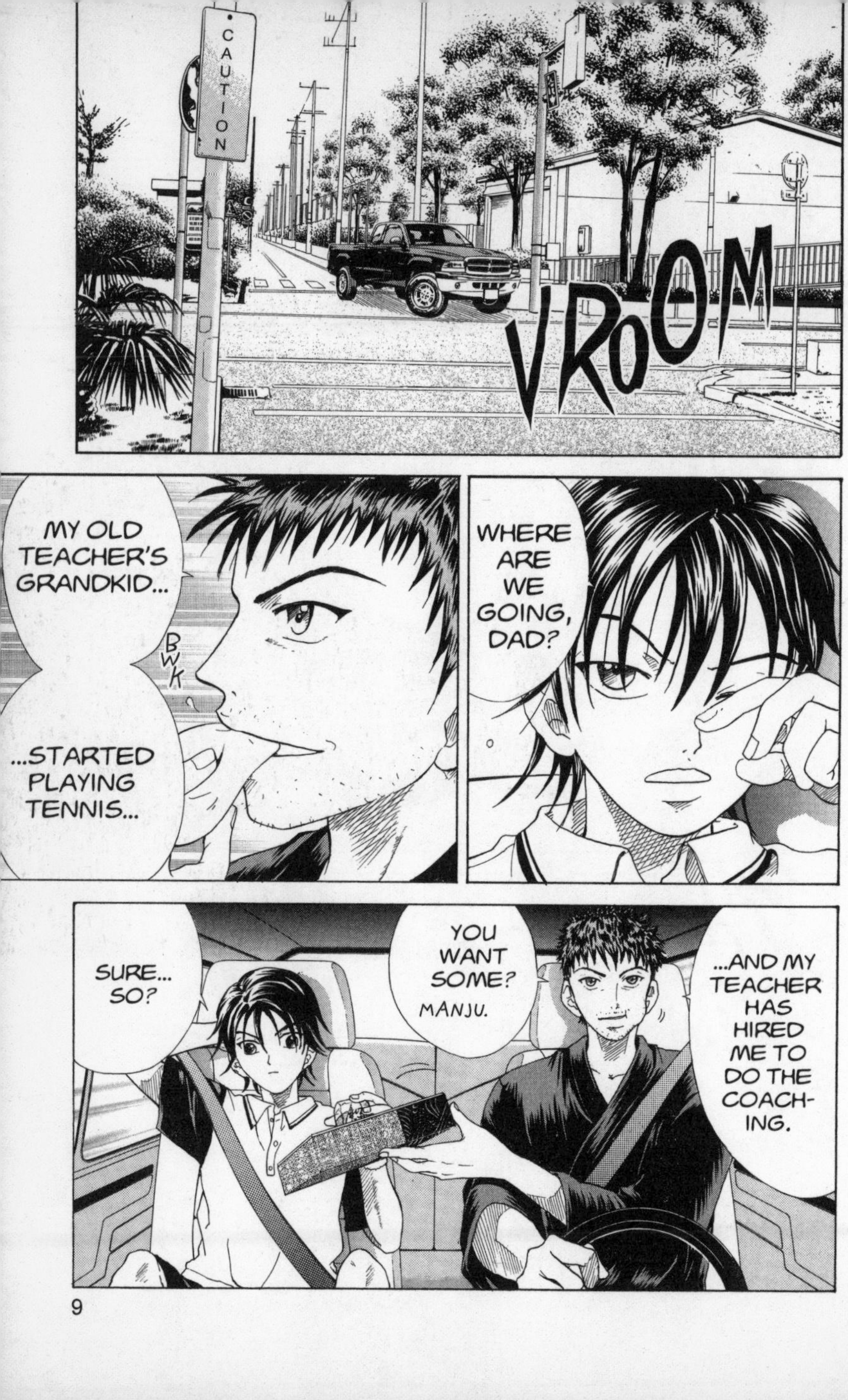
CAUTION
VROOM
WHERE ARE WE GOING, DAD?
MY OLD TEACHER'S GRANDKID...
BWK
...STARTED PLAYING TENNIS...
...AND MY TEACHER HAS HIRED ME TO DO THE COACH-ING.
YOU WANT SOME?
MANJU.
SURE... SO?

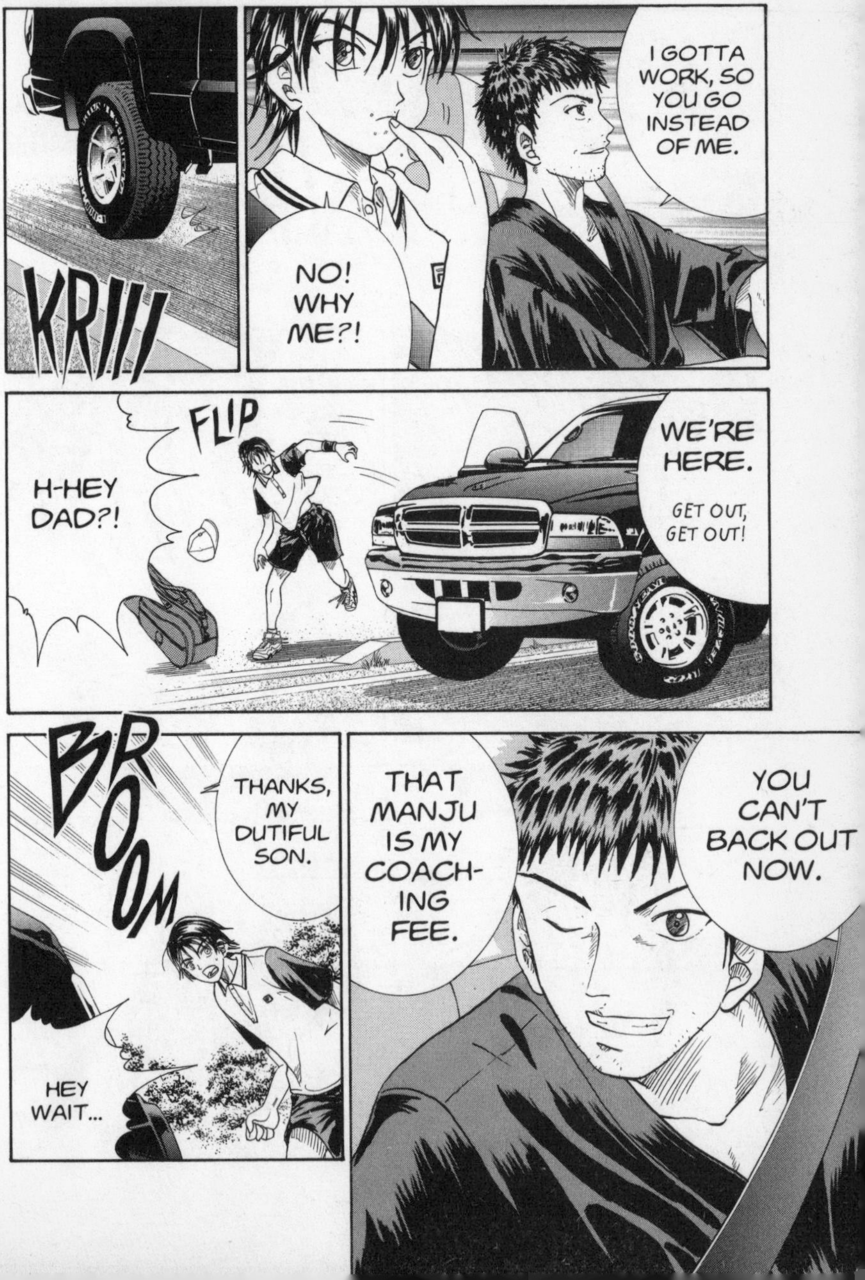
I GOTTA WORK, SO YOU GO INSTEAD OF ME.
NO! WHY ME?!
KRIII
WE'RE HERE.
GET OUT, GET OUT!
FLIP
H-HEY DAD?!
YOU CAN'T BACK OUT NOW.
THAT MANJU IS MY COACH-ING FEE.
BROOOM
THANKS, MY DUTIFUL SON.
HEY WAIT...

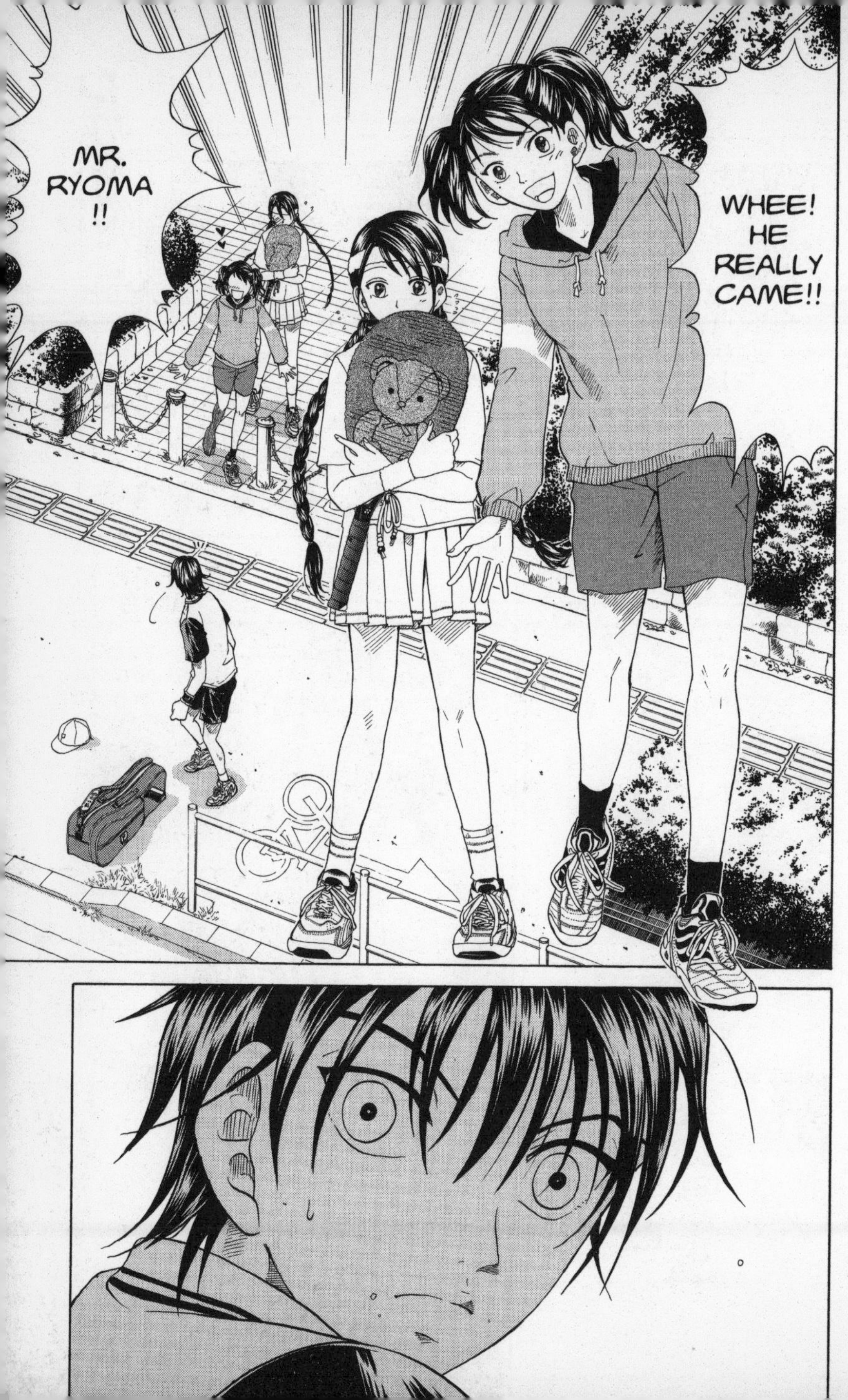
WHEE! HE REALLY CAME!!
MR. RYOMA !!

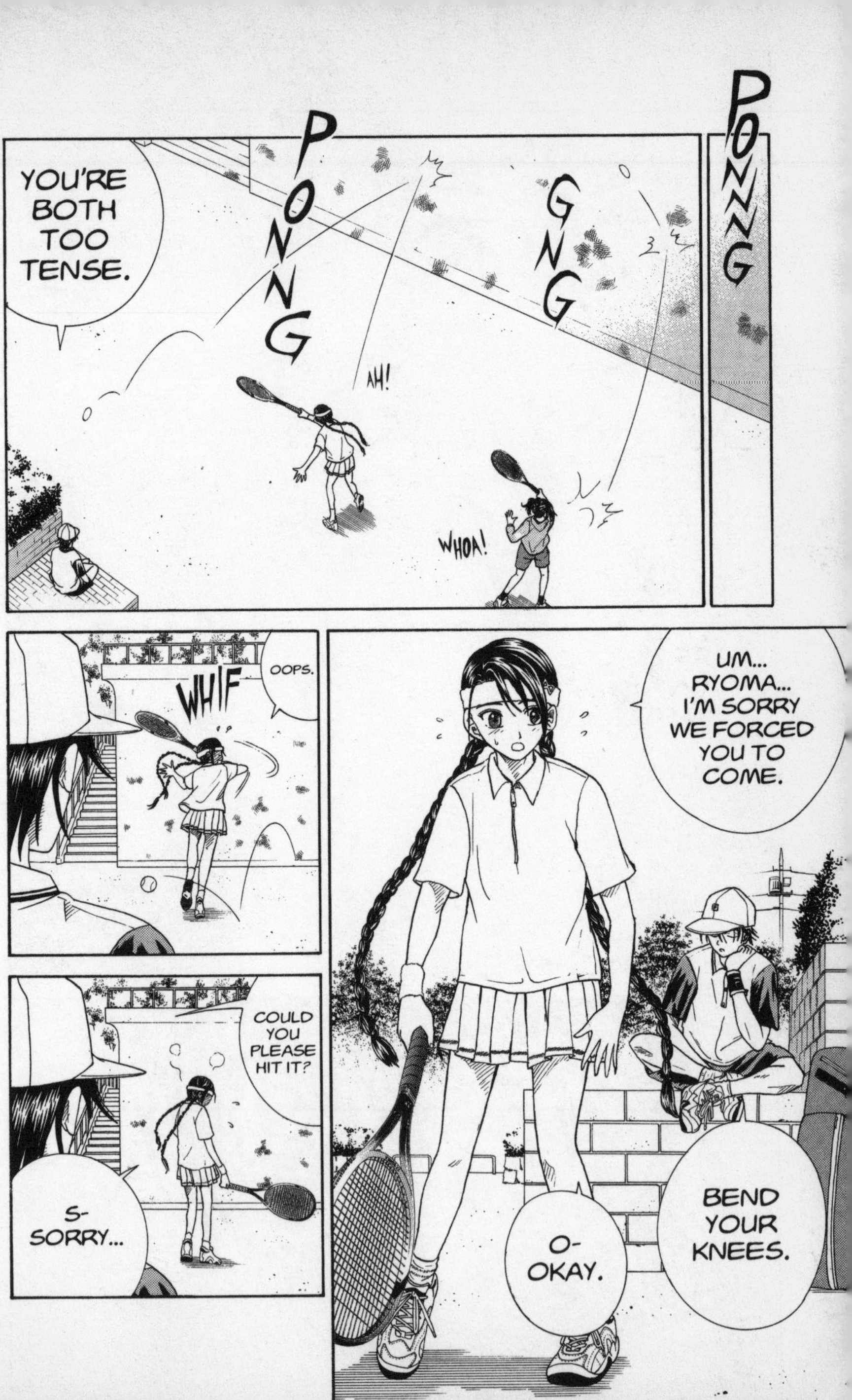
PONNG
GNG
PONNG
YOU'RE BOTH TOO TENSE.
AH!
WHOA!
UM... RYOMA... I'M SORRY WE FORCED YOU TO COME.
BEND YOUR KNEES.
O- OKAY.
OOPS.
WHIF
COULD YOU PLEASE HIT IT?
S- SORRY...

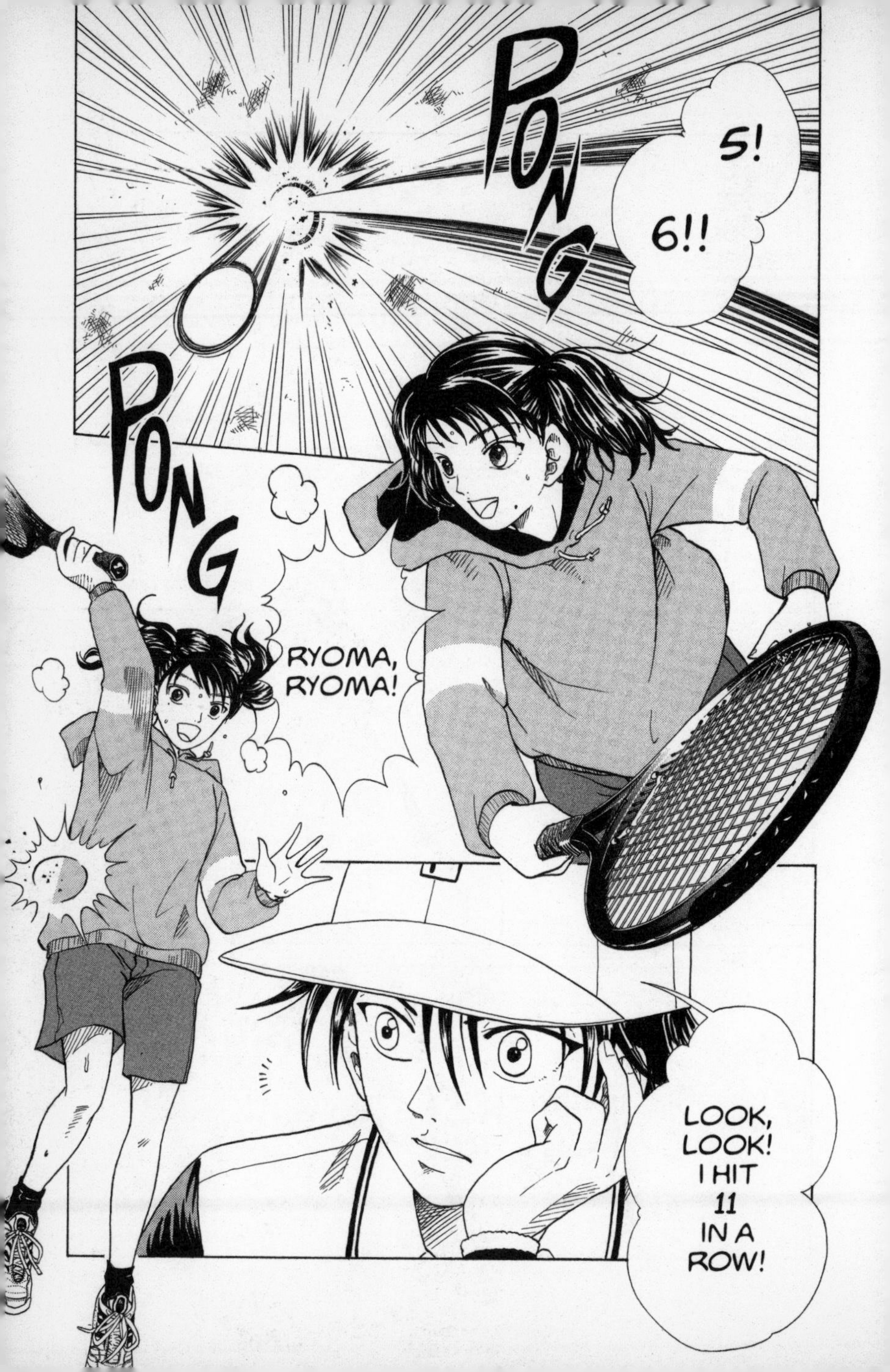
PONG
5!
6!!
PONG
RYOMA, RYOMA!
LOOK, LOOK! I HIT 11 IN A ROW!

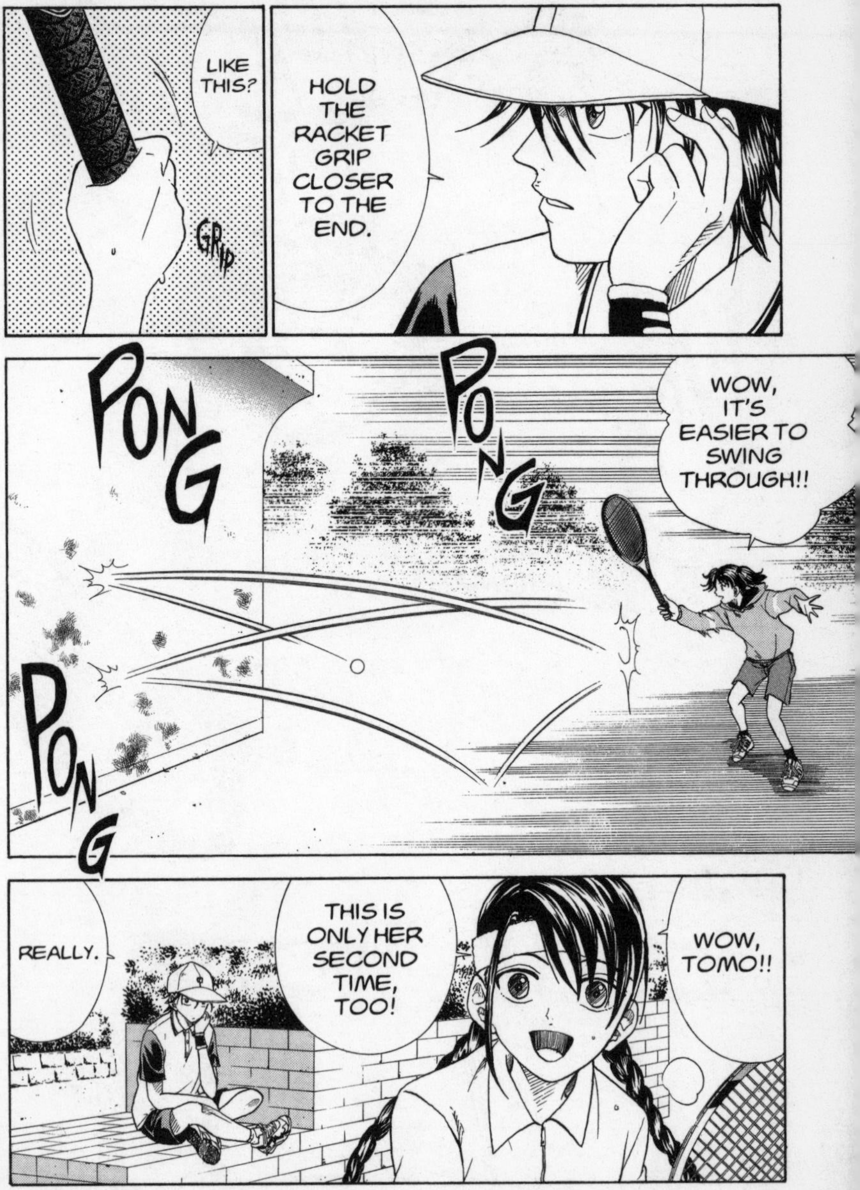
HOLD THE RACKET GRIP CLOSER TO THE END.
LIKE THIS?
GRIP
WOW, IT'S EASIER TO SWING THROUGH!!
PONG
PONG
PONG
WOW, TOMO!!
THIS IS ONLY HER SECOND TIME, TOO!
REALLY.

READ THIS WAY

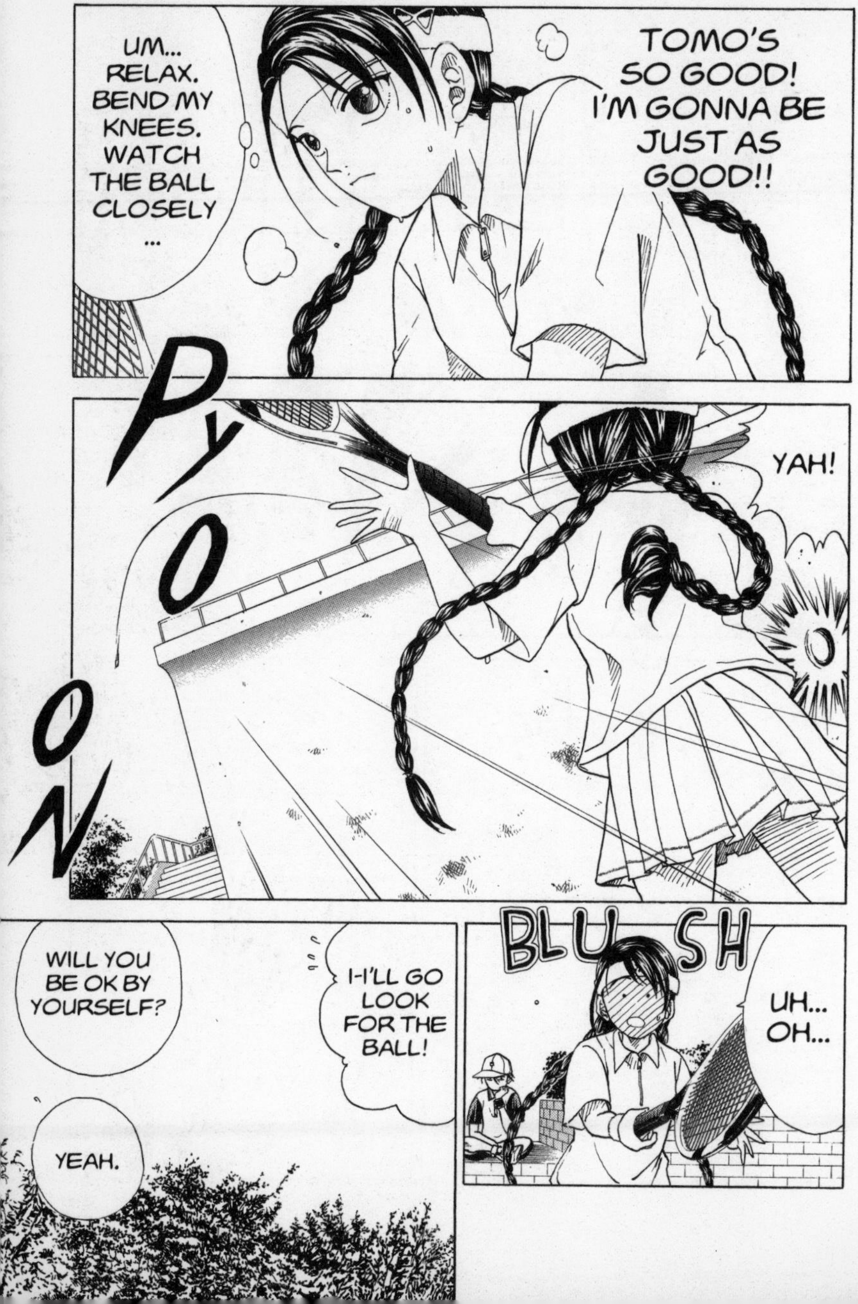
TOMO'S SO GOOD! I'M GONNA BE JUST AS GOOD!!
UM... RELAX. BEND MY KNEES. WATCH THE BALL CLOSELY ...
YAH!
PYOON
BLUSH
UH... OH...
I-I'LL GO LOOK FOR THE BALL!
WILL YOU BE OK BY YOURSELF?
YEAH.

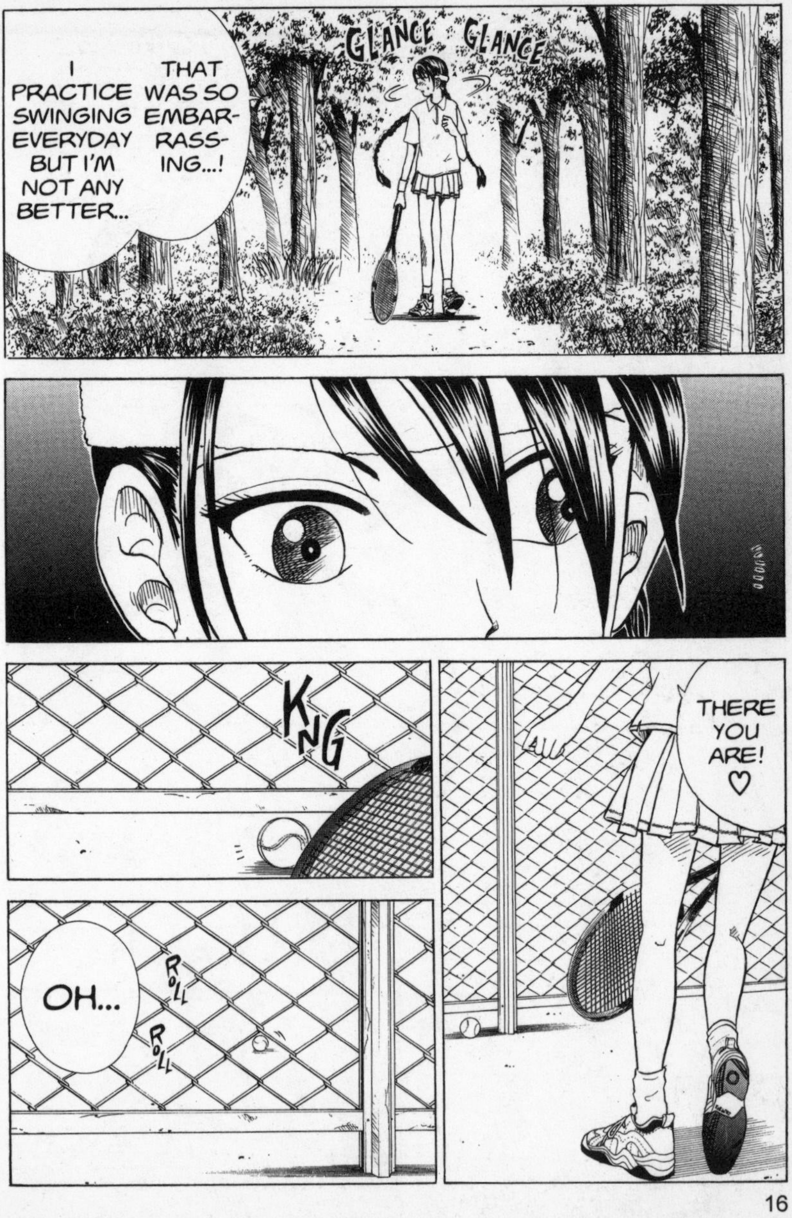
GLANCE GLANCE
THAT WAS SO EMBAR-RASS-ING...!
I PRACTICE SWINGING EVERYDAY BUT I'M NOT ANY BETTER...
THERE YOU ARE! ♡
KNG
OH...
ROLL
ROLL

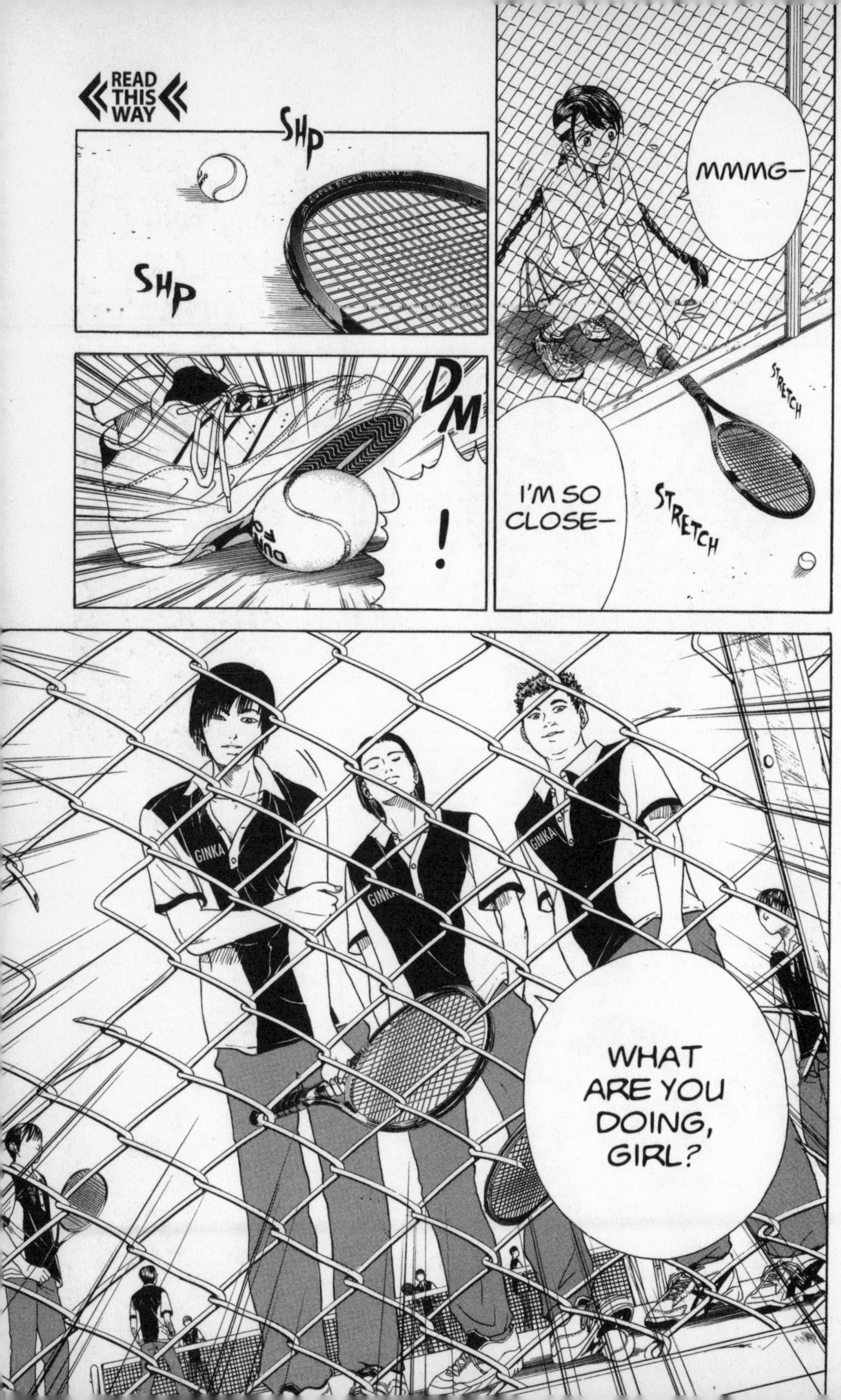
READ THIS WAY
MMMG-
STRETCH
I'M SO CLOSE-
STRETCH
SHP
SHP
DM
!
WHAT ARE YOU DOING, GIRL?

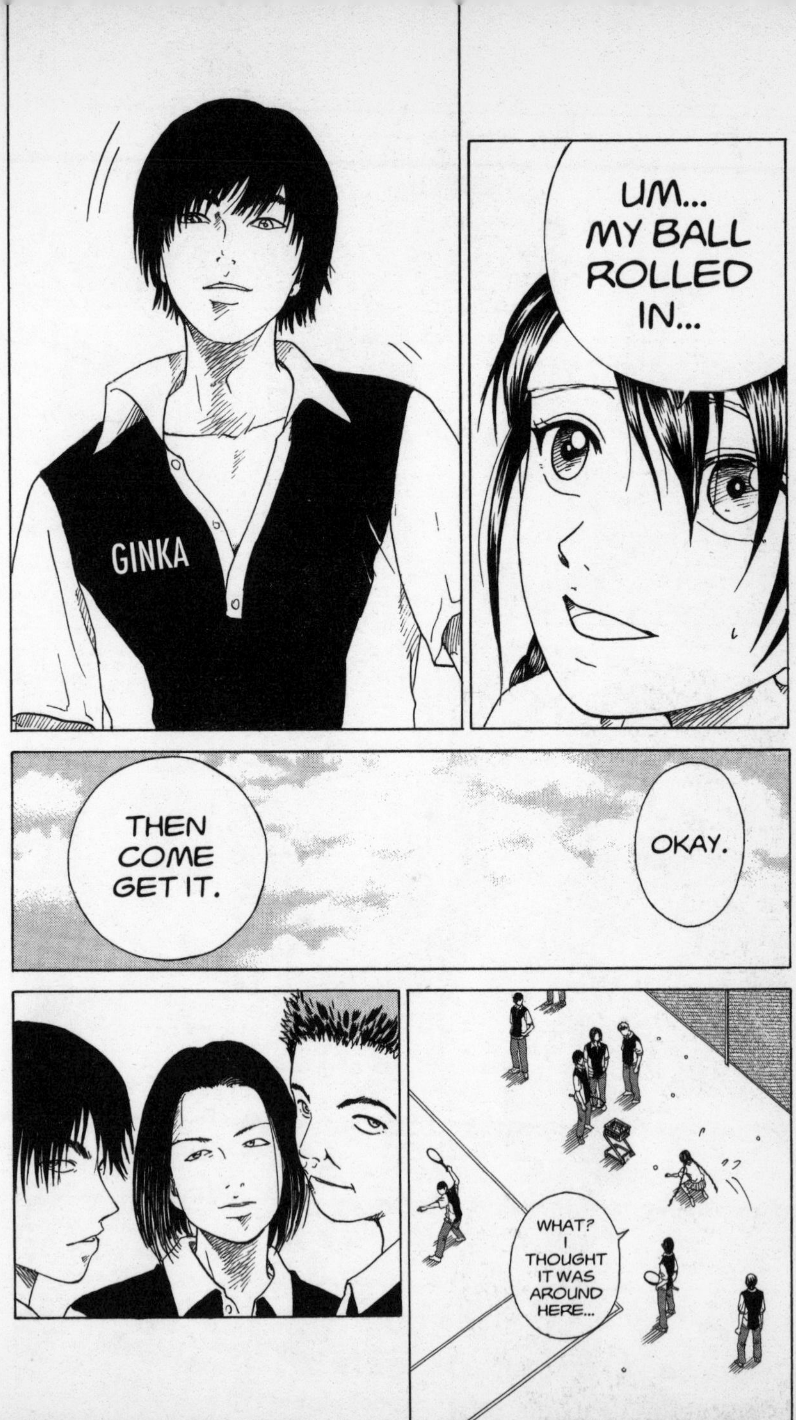
UM... MY BALL ROLLED IN...
GINKA
THEN COME GET IT.
OKAY.
WHAT? I THOUGHT IT WAS AROUND HERE...

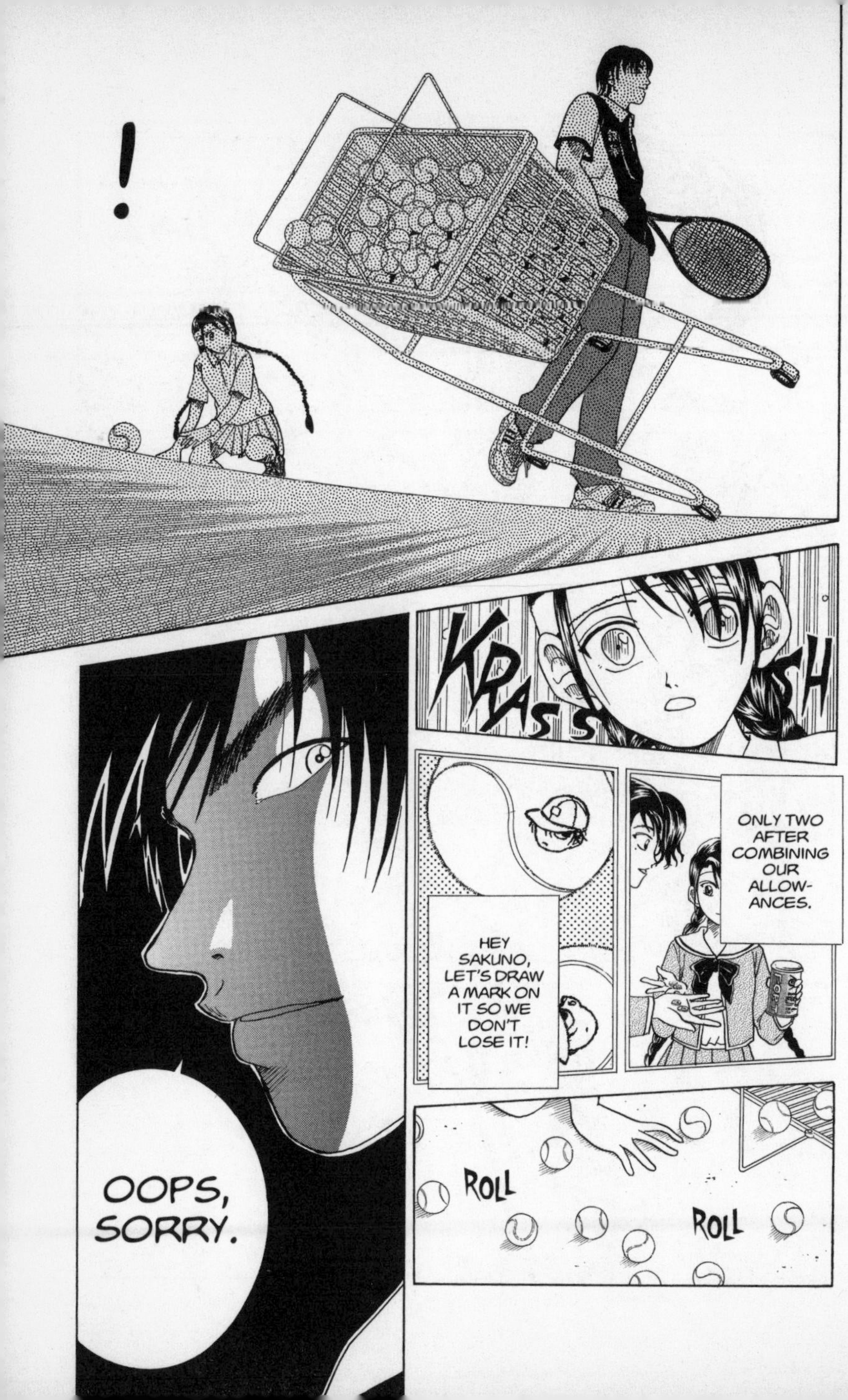
!
KRASSSH
ONLY TWO AFTER COMBINING OUR ALLOW-ANCES.
HEY SAKUNO, LET'S DRAW A MARK ON IT SO WE DON'T LOSE IT!
ROLL
ROLL
OOPS, SORRY.

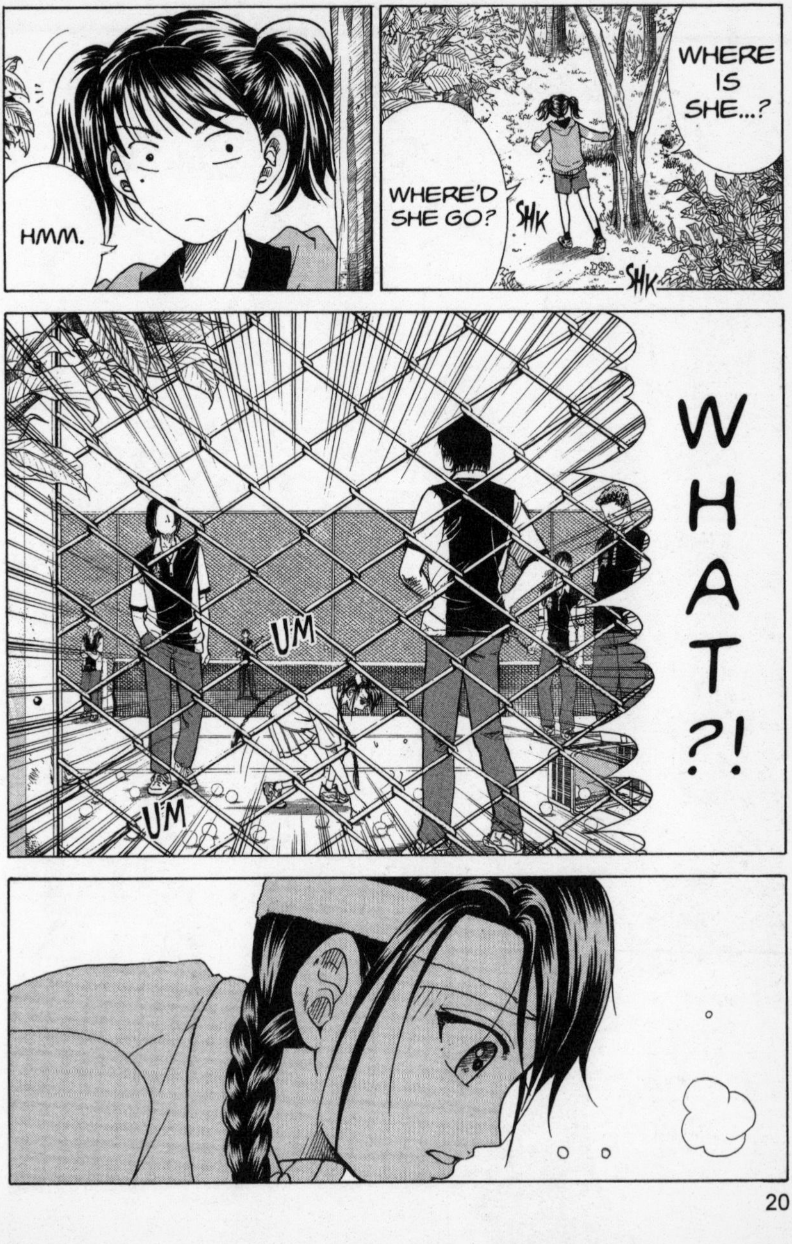
WHERE IS SHE...?
WHERE'D SHE GO?
SHK
SHK
HMM.
WHAT?!
UM
UM

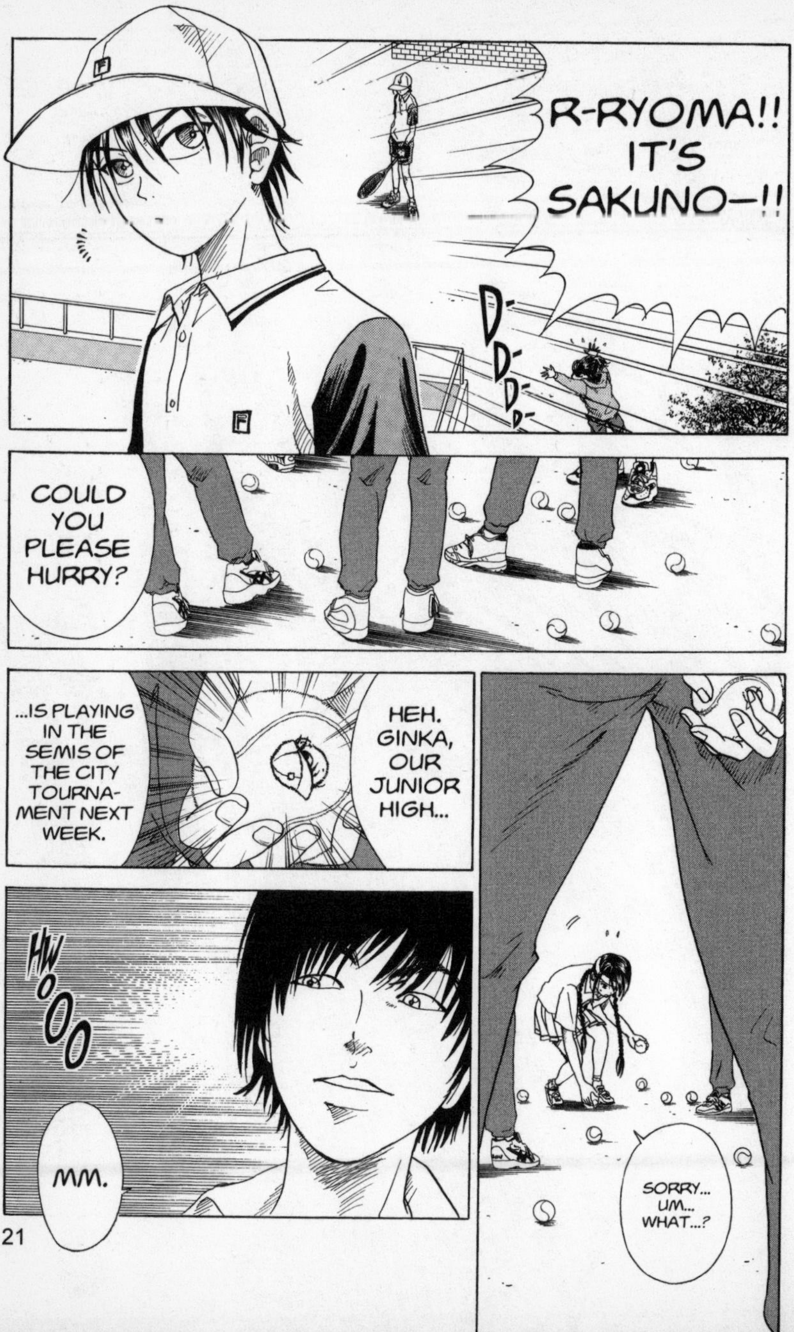
R-RYOMA!! IT'S SAKUNO—!!
D-D-D-D-
COULD YOU PLEASE HURRY?
SORRY... UM... WHAT...?
HEH. GINKA, OUR JUNIOR HIGH...
...IS PLAYING IN THE SEMIS OF THE CITY TOURNAMENT NEXT WEEK.
HWOOO
MM.

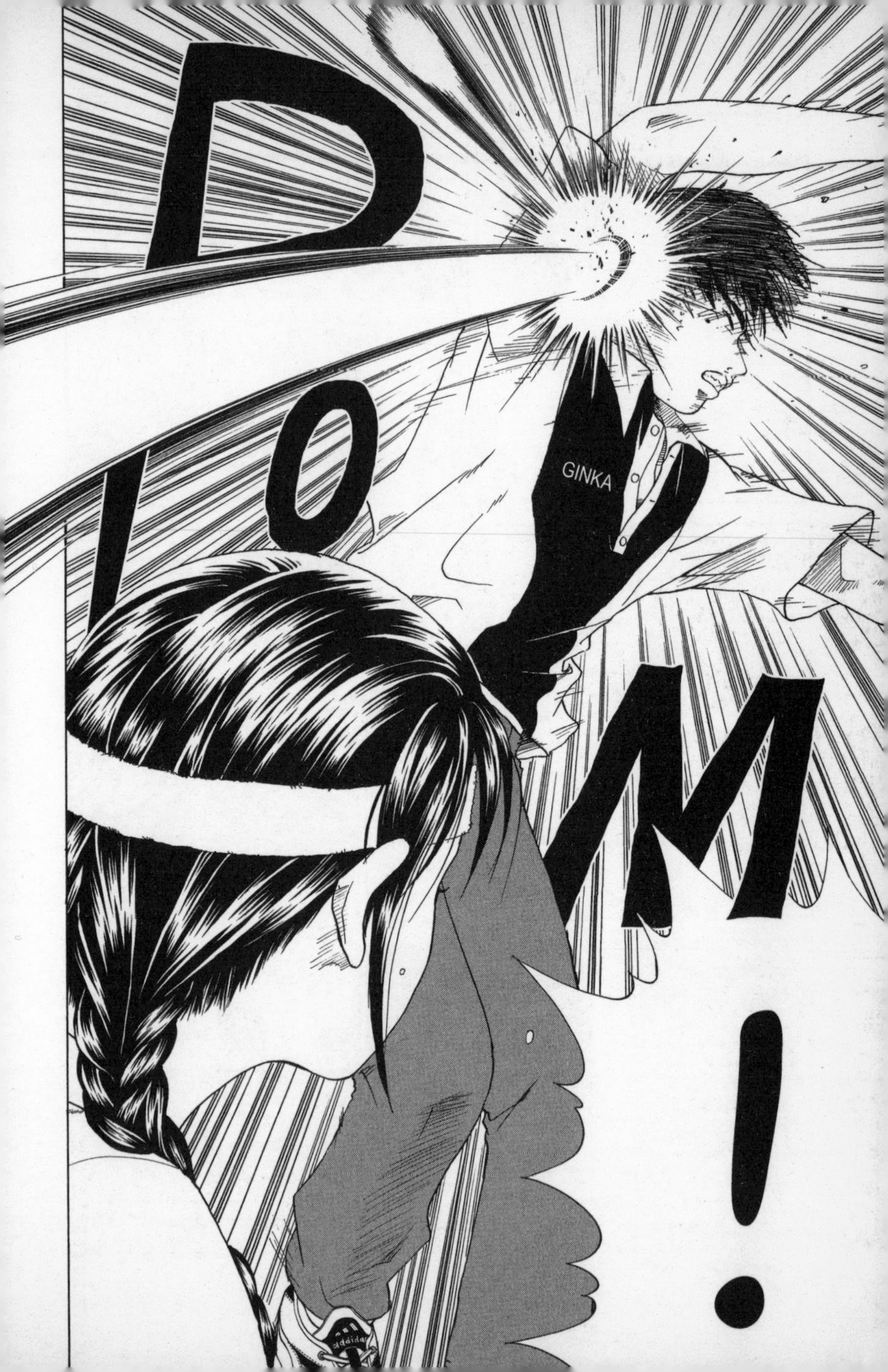
DOOM!
GINKA

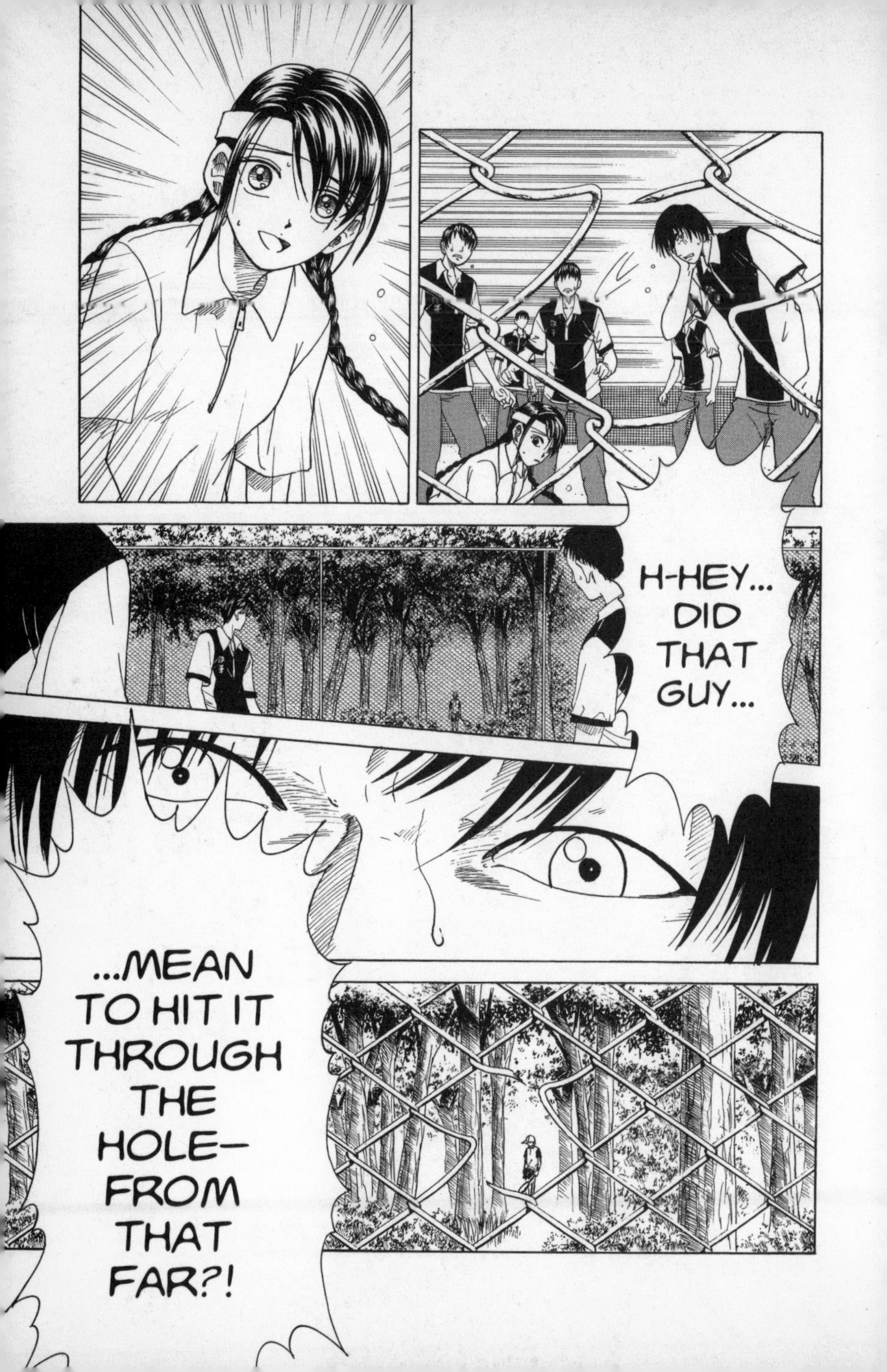
H-HEY... DID THAT GUY...
...MEAN TO HIT IT THROUGH THE HOLE—FROM THAT FAR?!

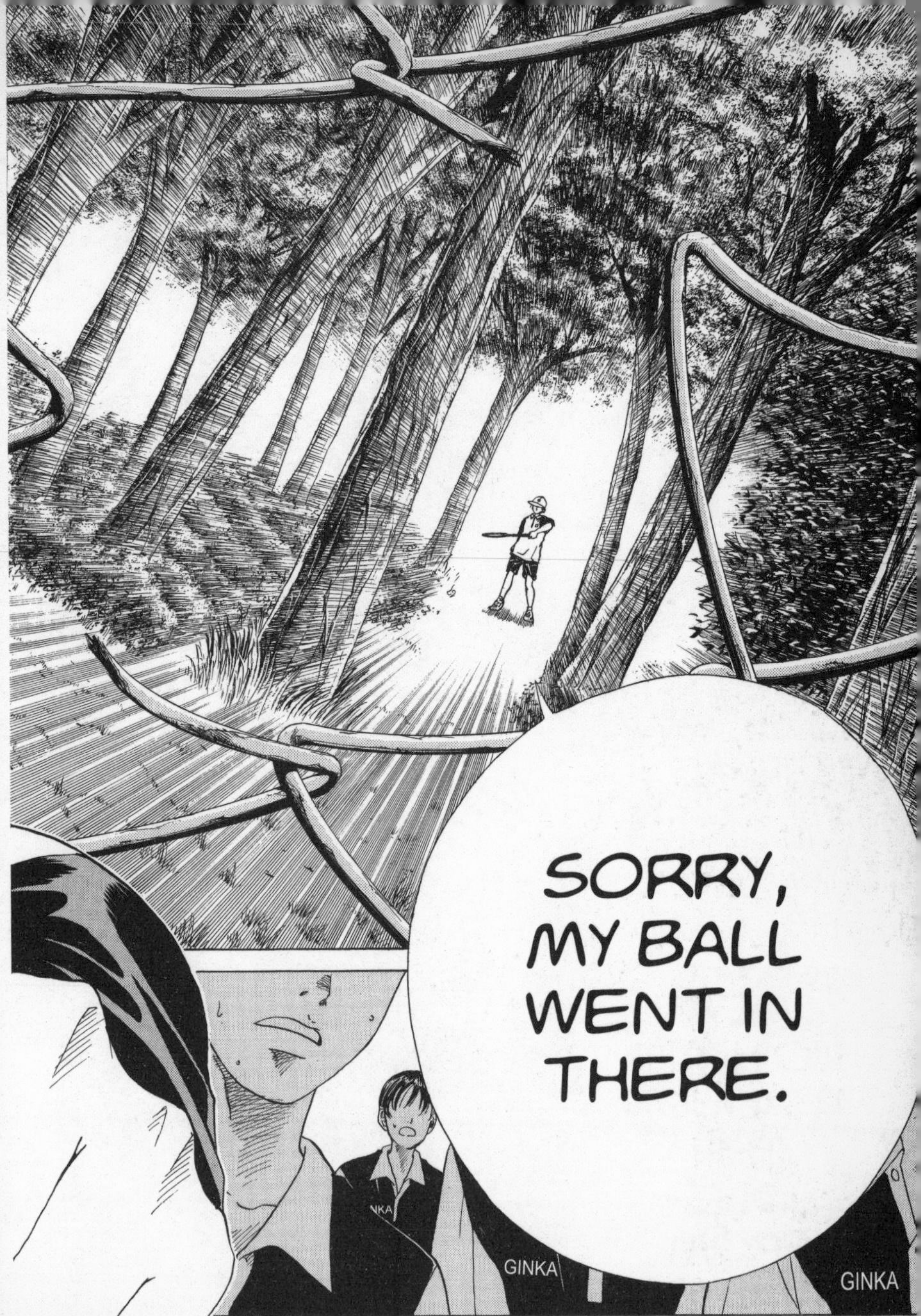
SORRY, MY BALL WENT IN THERE.
GINKA
GINKA

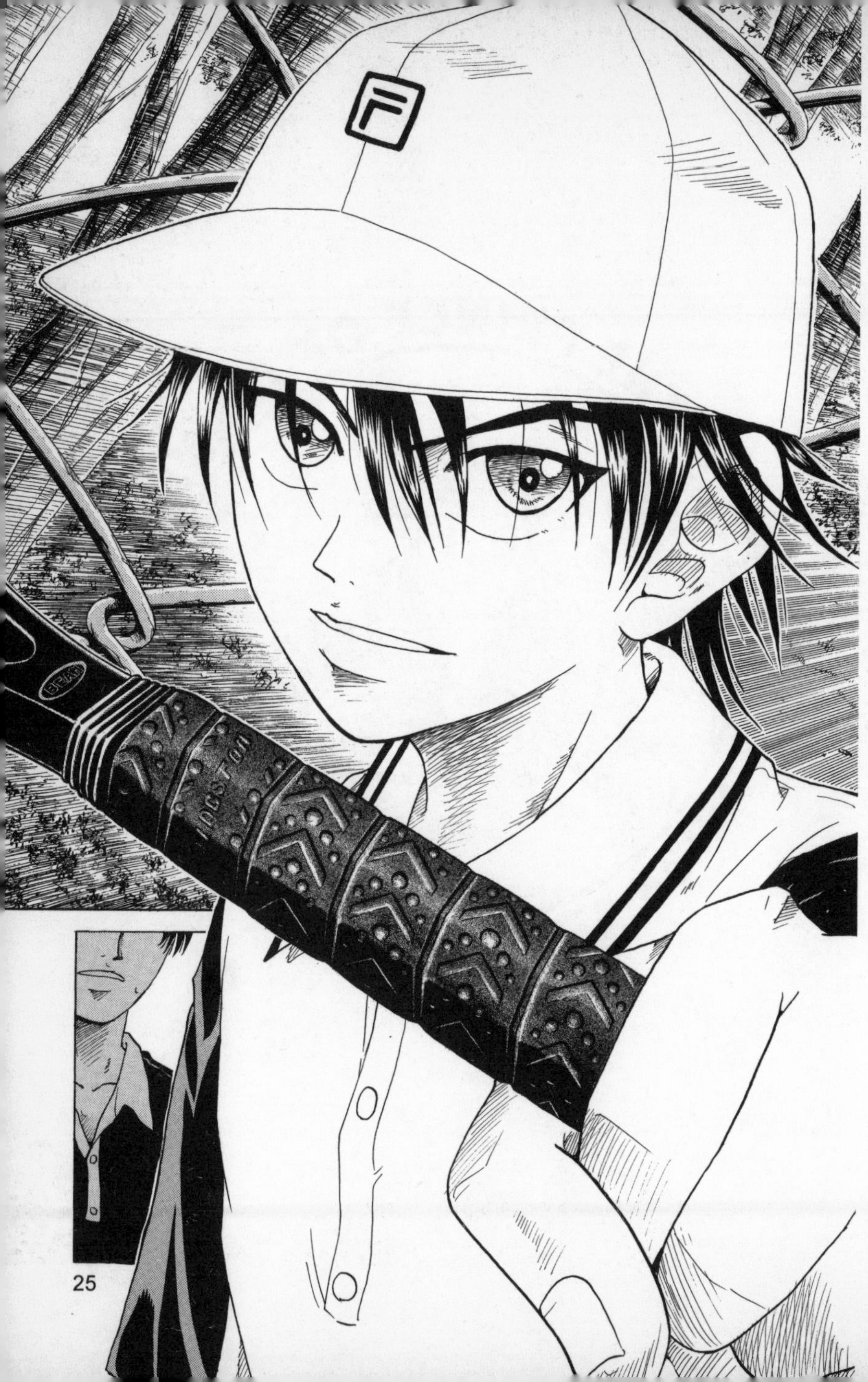

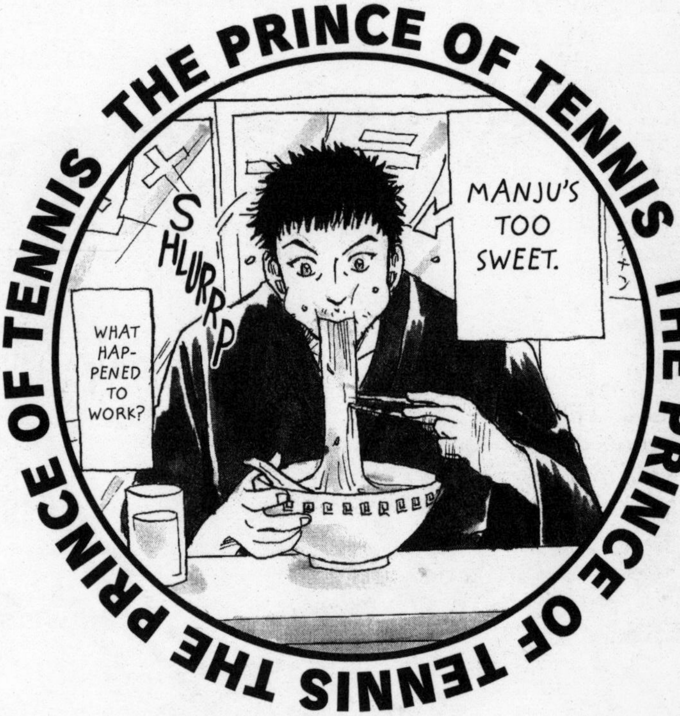
THE PRINCE OF TENNIS THE PRINCE OF TENNIS THE PRINCE OF TENNIS
MANJU'S TOO SWEET.
SHLURRP
WHAT HAP-PENED TO WORK?

GENIUS 80: TARGET

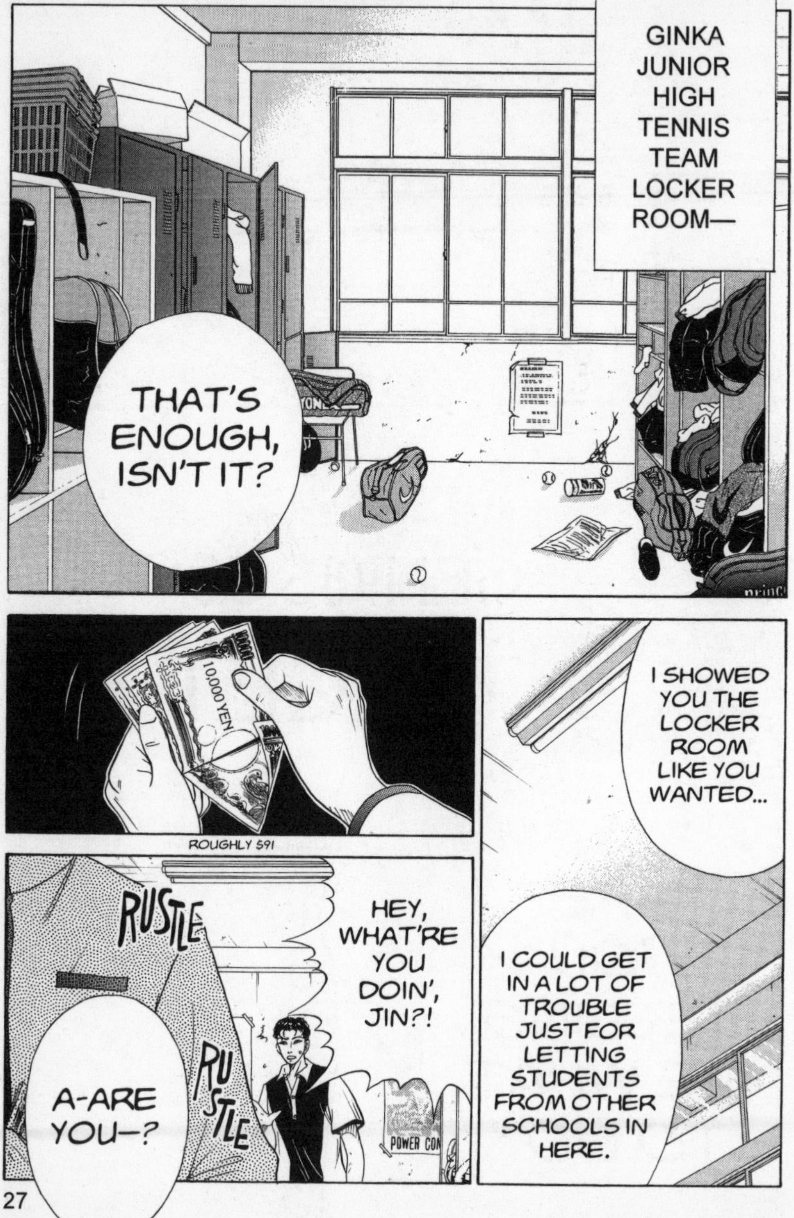
GINKA JUNIOR HIGH TENNIS TEAM LOCKER ROOM—
THAT'S ENOUGH, ISN'T IT?
I SHOWED YOU THE LOCKER ROOM LIKE YOU WANTED...
I COULD GET IN A LOT OF TROUBLE JUST FOR LETTING STUDENTS FROM OTHER SCHOOLS IN HERE.
10,000 YEN
ROUGHLY $91
HEY, WHAT'RE YOU DOIN', JIN?!
RUSTLE
RUSTLE
A-ARE YOU—?

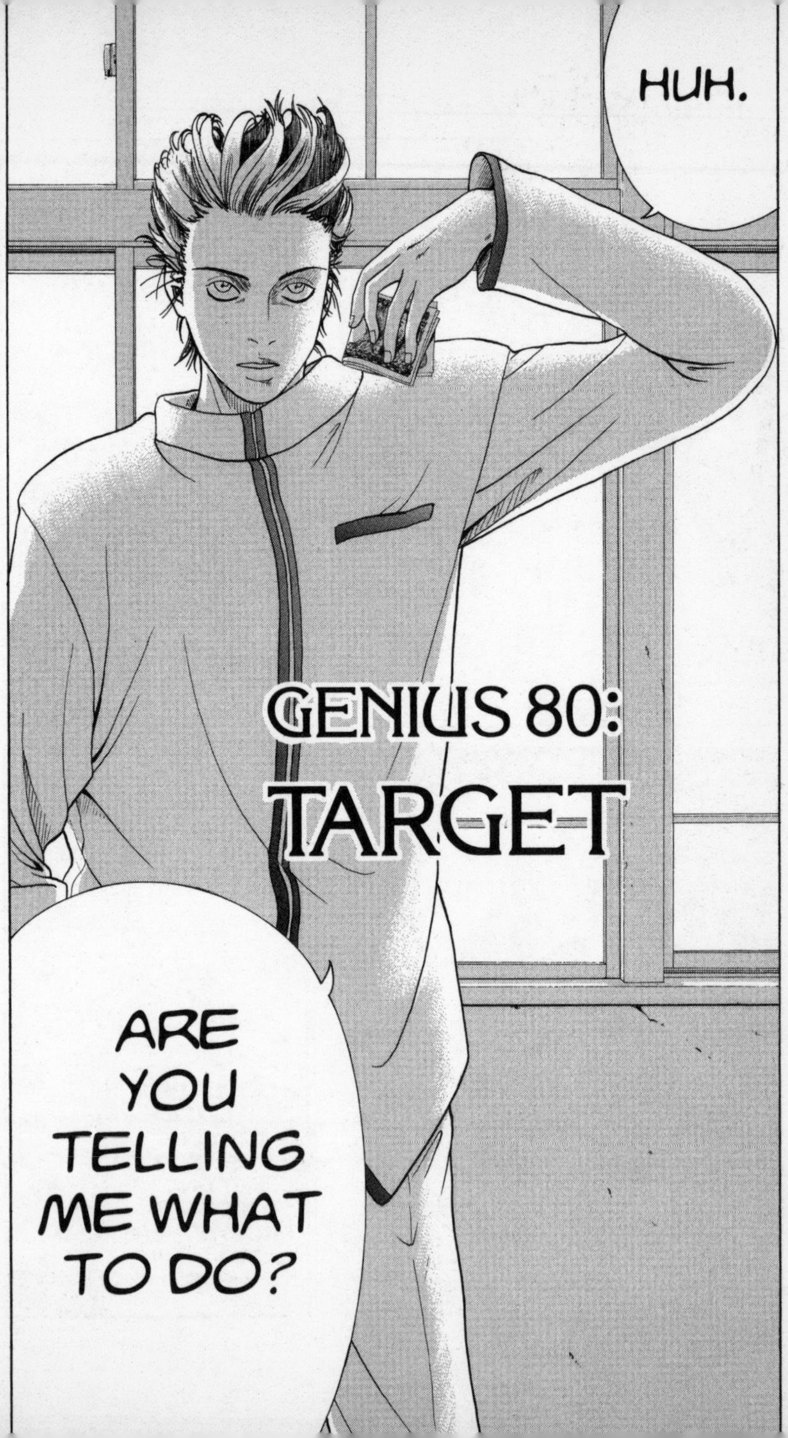
HUH.
GENIUS 80:
TARGET
ARE YOU TELLING ME WHAT TO DO?

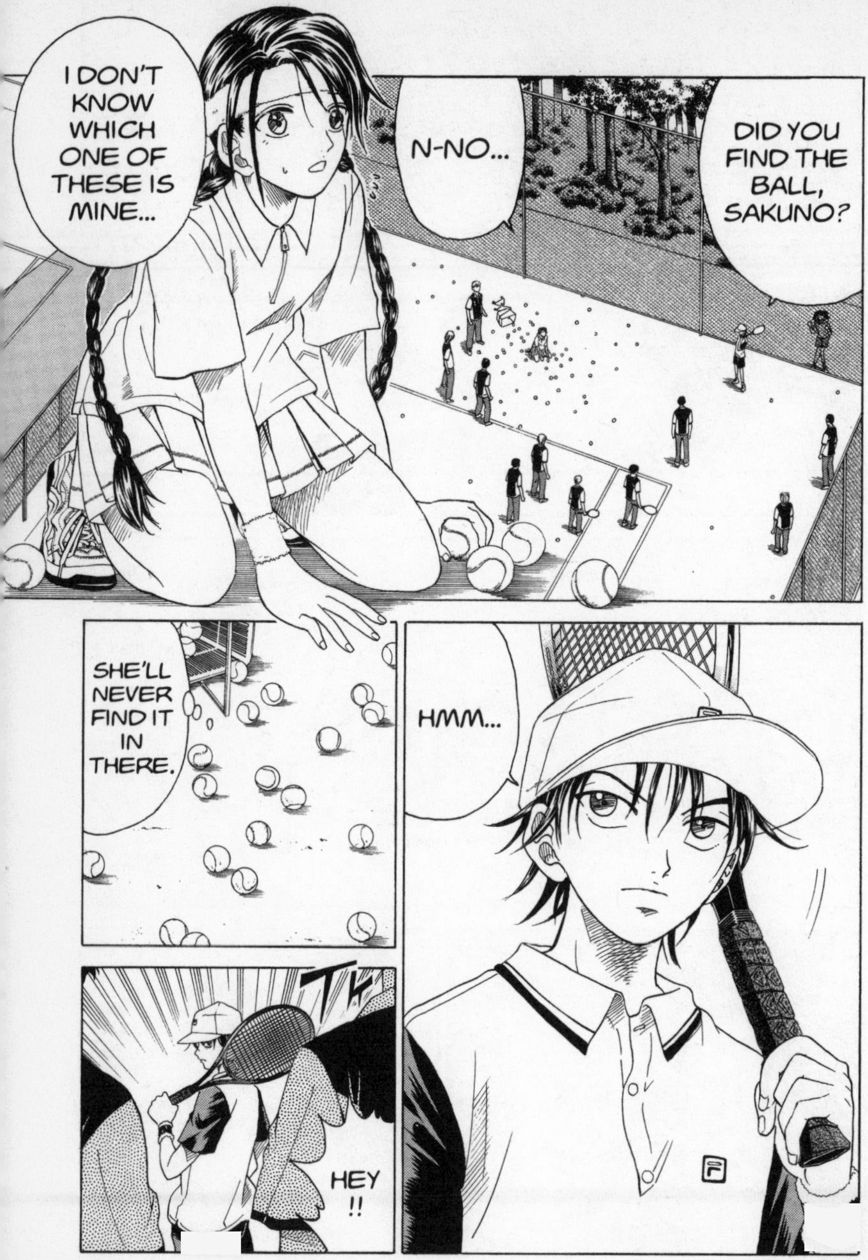
DID YOU FIND THE BALL, SAKUNO?
N-NO...
I DON'T KNOW WHICH ONE OF THESE IS MINE...
HMM...
SHE'LL NEVER FIND IT IN THERE.
TH
HEY !!

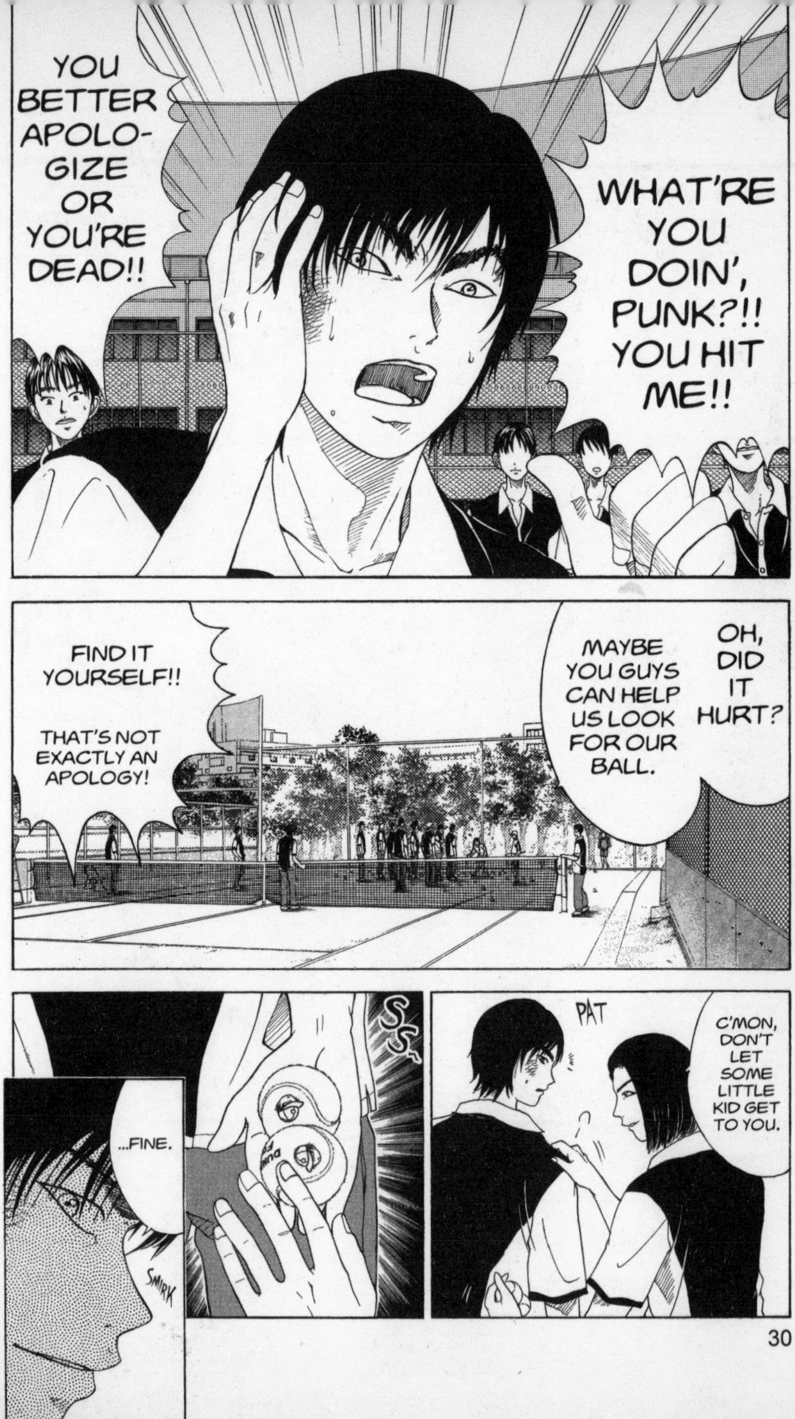
WHAT'RE YOU DOIN', PUNK?!! YOU HIT ME!!
YOU BETTER APOLOGIZE OR YOU'RE DEAD!!
OH, DID IT HURT?
MAYBE YOU GUYS CAN HELP US LOOK FOR OUR BALL.
FIND IT YOURSELF!!
THAT'S NOT EXACTLY AN APOLOGY!
PAT
C'MON, DON'T LET SOME LITTLE KID GET TO YOU.
SS
...FINE.
SMIRK

READ THIS WAY

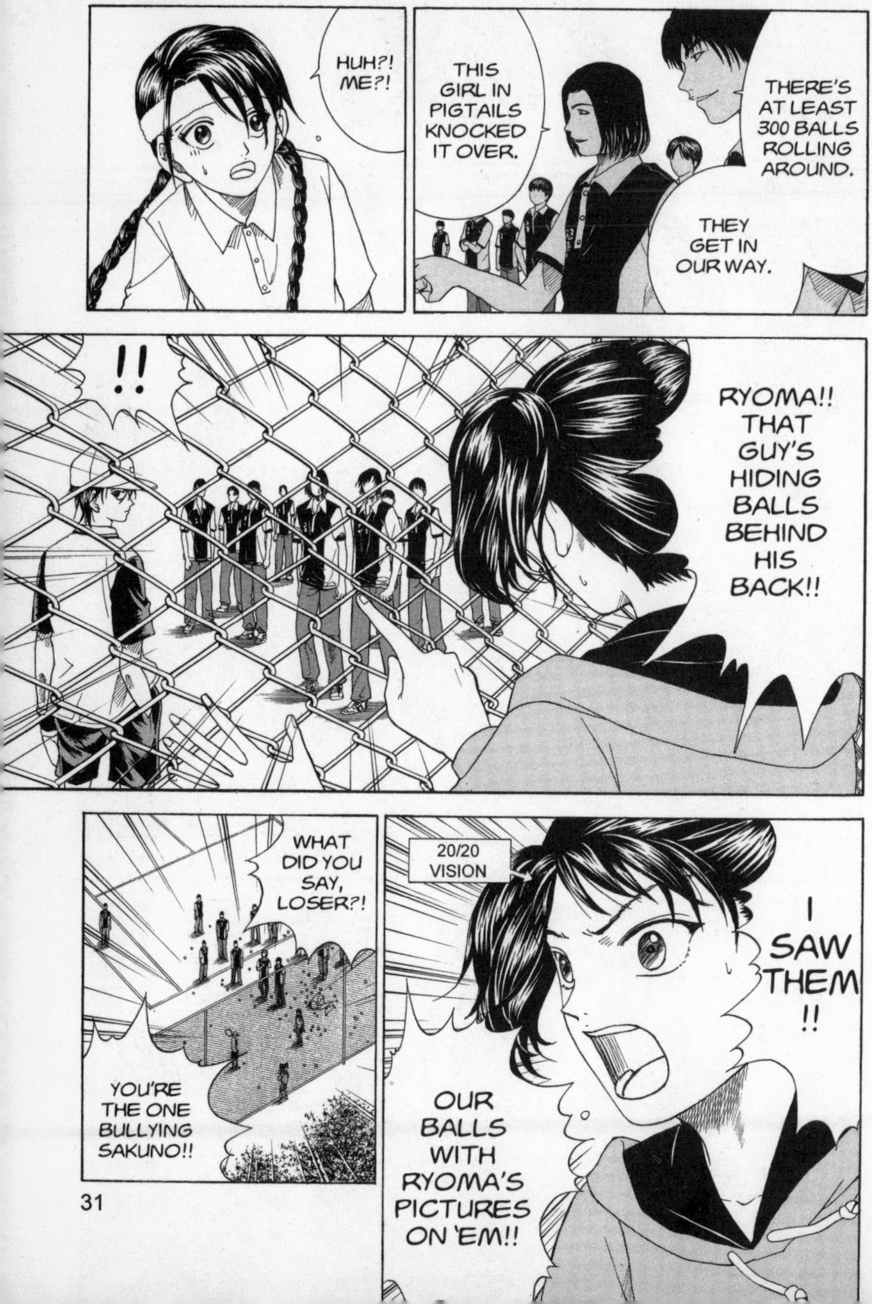

THERE'S AT LEAST 300 BALLS ROLLING AROUND.
THEY GET IN OUR WAY.
THIS GIRL IN PIGTAILS KNOCKED IT OVER.
HUH?! ME?!
RYOMA!! THAT GUY'S HIDING BALLS BEHIND HIS BACK!!
!!
20/20 VISION
I SAW THEM!!
OUR BALLS WITH RYOMA'S PICTURES ON 'EM!!
WHAT DID YOU SAY, LOSER?!
YOU'RE THE ONE BULLYING SAKUNO!!

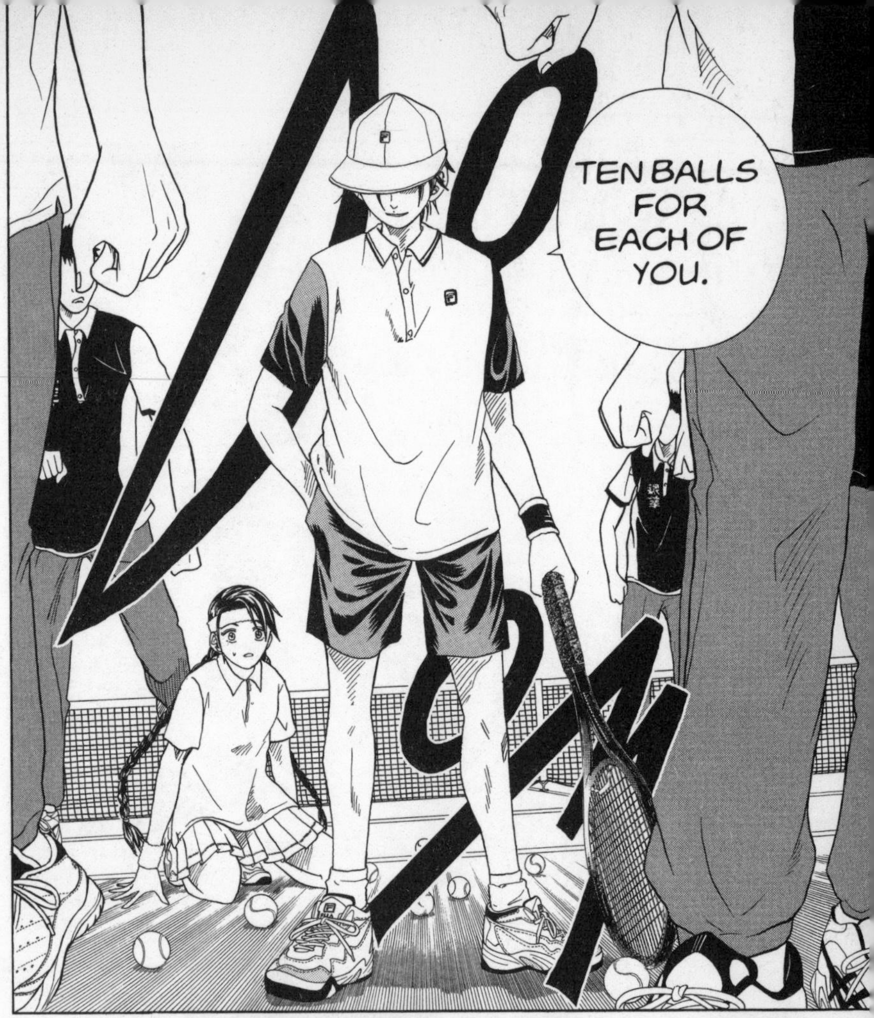
TEN BALLS FOR EACH OF YOU.

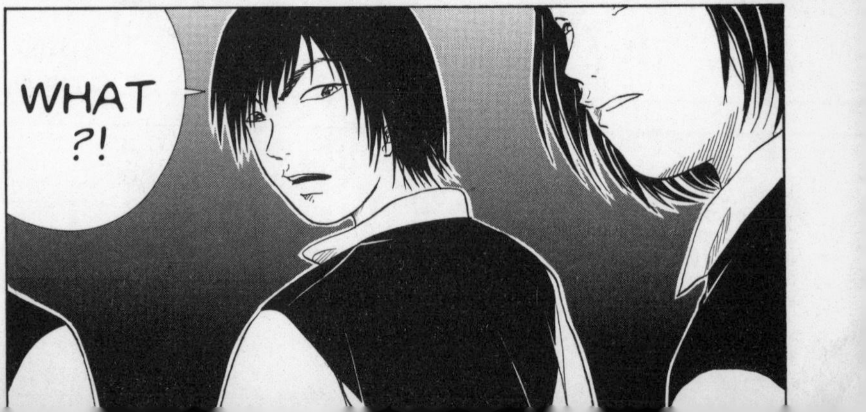
WHAT ?!

READ THIS WAY

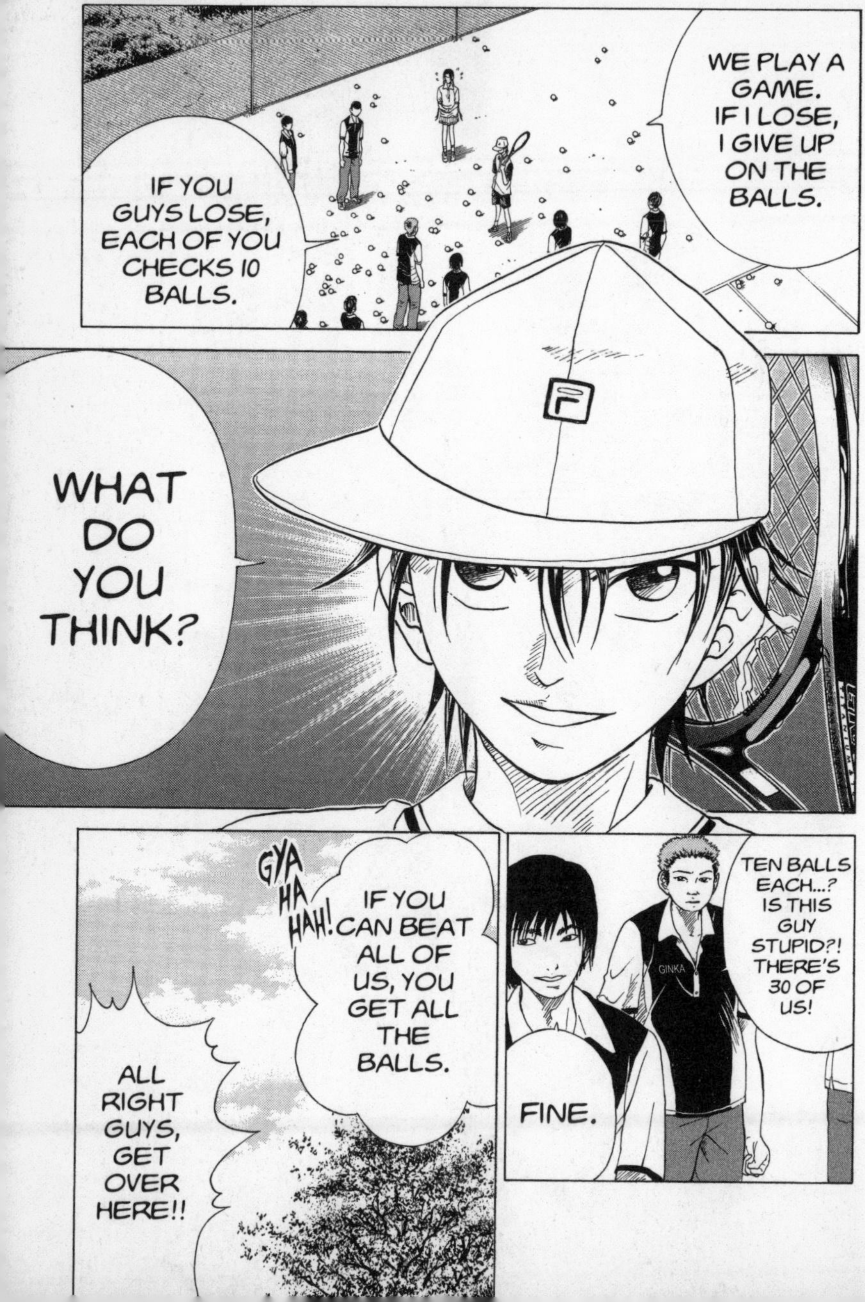
WE PLAY A GAME. IF I LOSE, I GIVE UP ON THE BALLS.
IF YOU GUYS LOSE, EACH OF YOU CHECKS 10 BALLS.
WHAT DO YOU THINK?
TEN BALLS EACH...? IS THIS GUY STUPID?! THERE'S 30 OF US!
GINKA
FINE.
GYA HA HAH!
IF YOU CAN BEAT ALL OF US, YOU GET ALL THE BALLS.
ALL RIGHT GUYS, GET OVER HERE!!

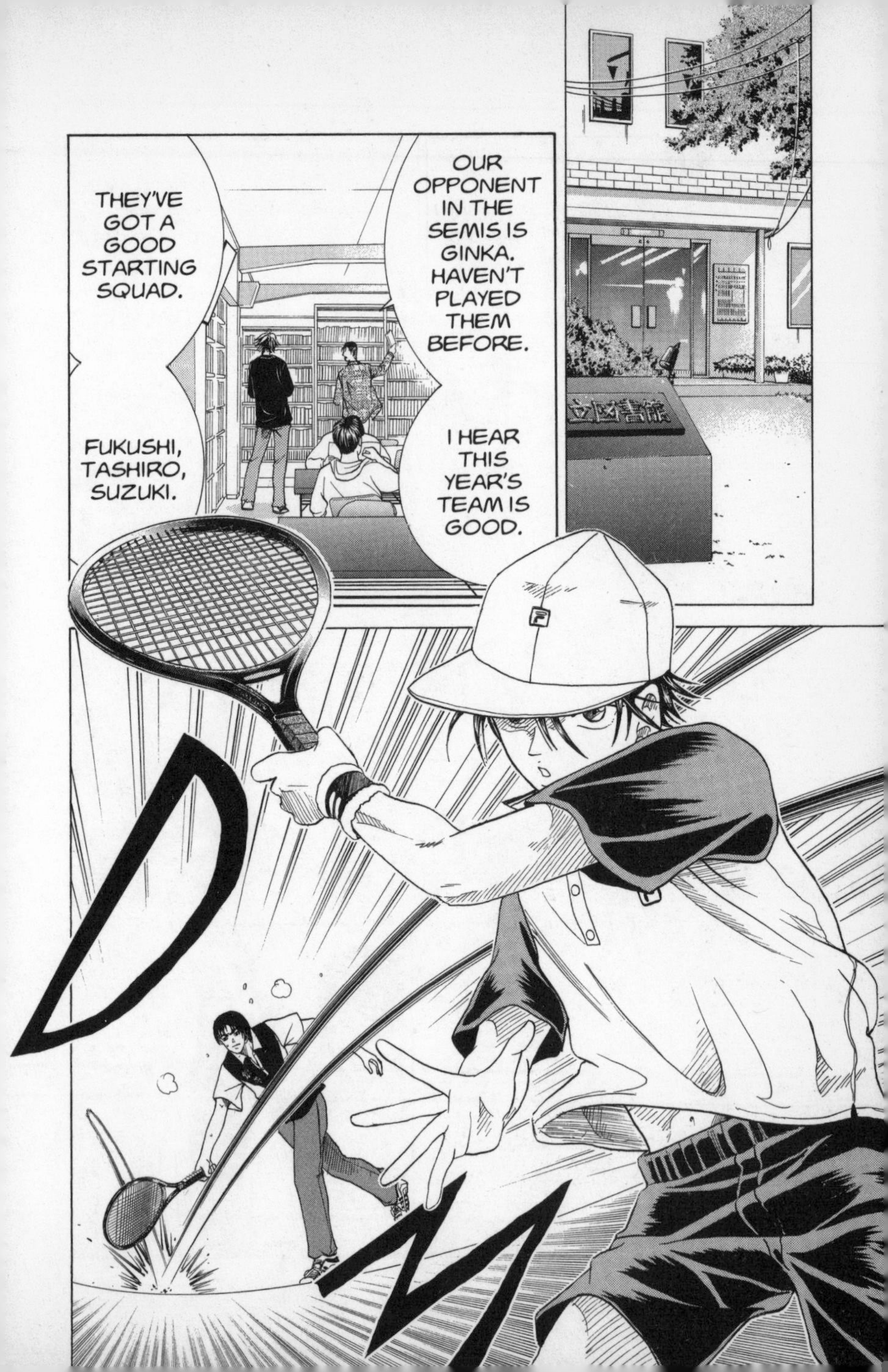
OUR OPPONENT IN THE SEMIS IS GINKA. HAVEN'T PLAYED THEM BEFORE.
I HEAR THIS YEAR'S TEAM IS GOOD.
THEY'VE GOT A GOOD STARTING SQUAD.
FUKUSHI, TASHIRO, SUZUKI.
D
M

READ THIS WAY

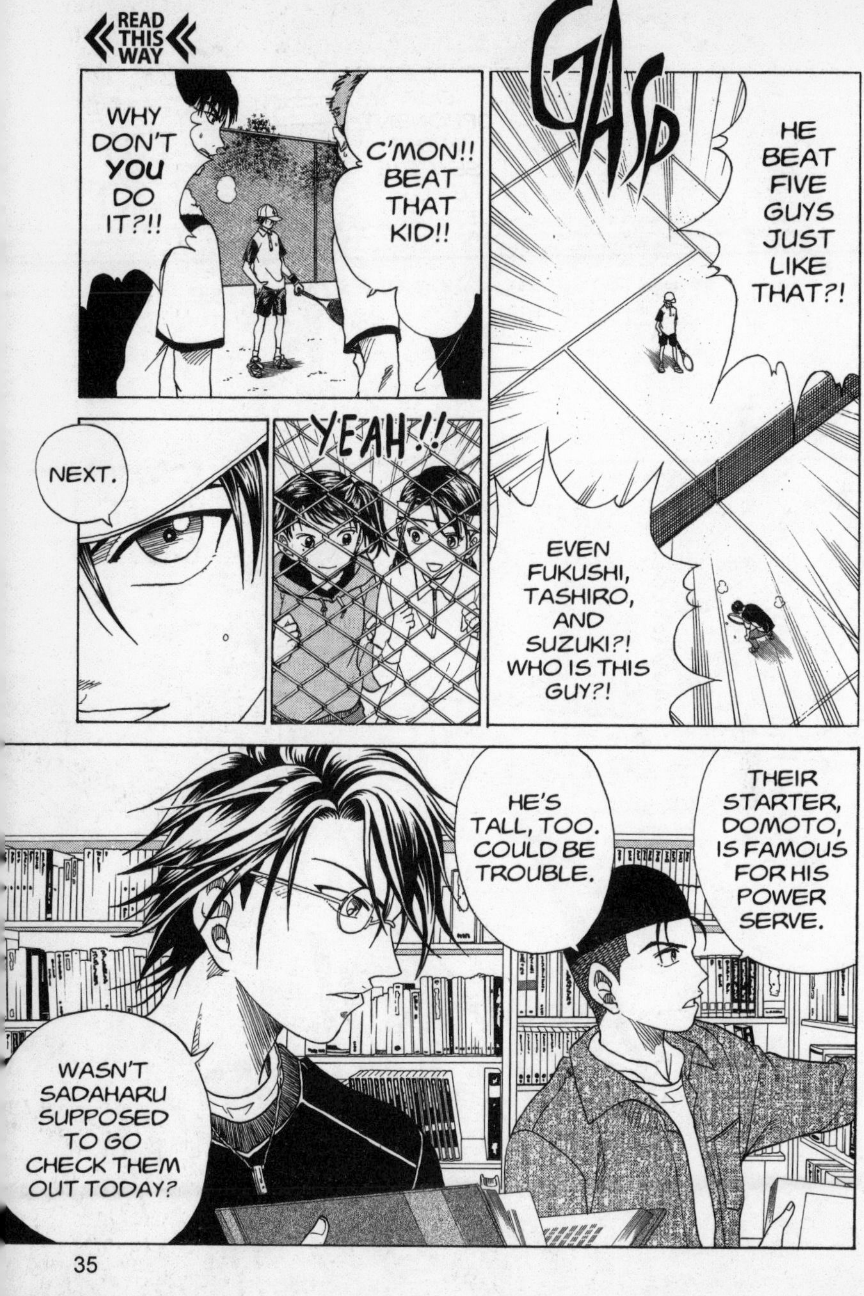
GASP
HE BEAT FIVE GUYS JUST LIKE THAT?!
EVEN FUKUSHI, TASHIRO, AND SUZUKI?! WHO IS THIS GUY?!
C'MON!! BEAT THAT KID!!
WHY DON'T YOU DO IT?!!
YEAH!!
NEXT.
THEIR STARTER, DOMOTO, IS FAMOUS FOR HIS POWER SERVE.
HE'S TALL, TOO. COULD BE TROUBLE.
WASN'T SADAHARU SUPPOSED TO GO CHECK THEM OUT TODAY?

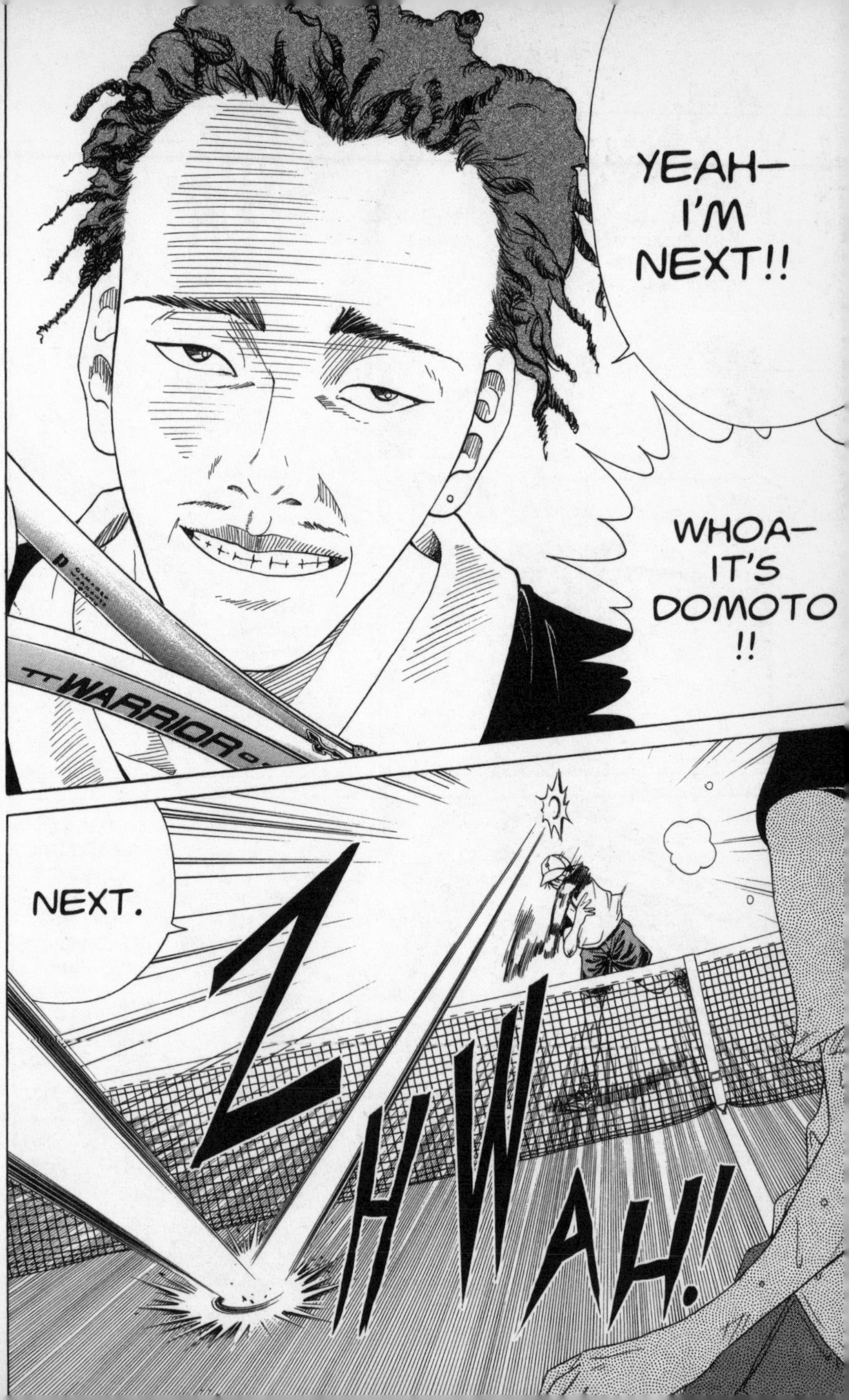
YEAH— I'M NEXT!!
WHOA— IT'S DOMOTO !!
WARRIOR
NEXT.
ZHWAH!

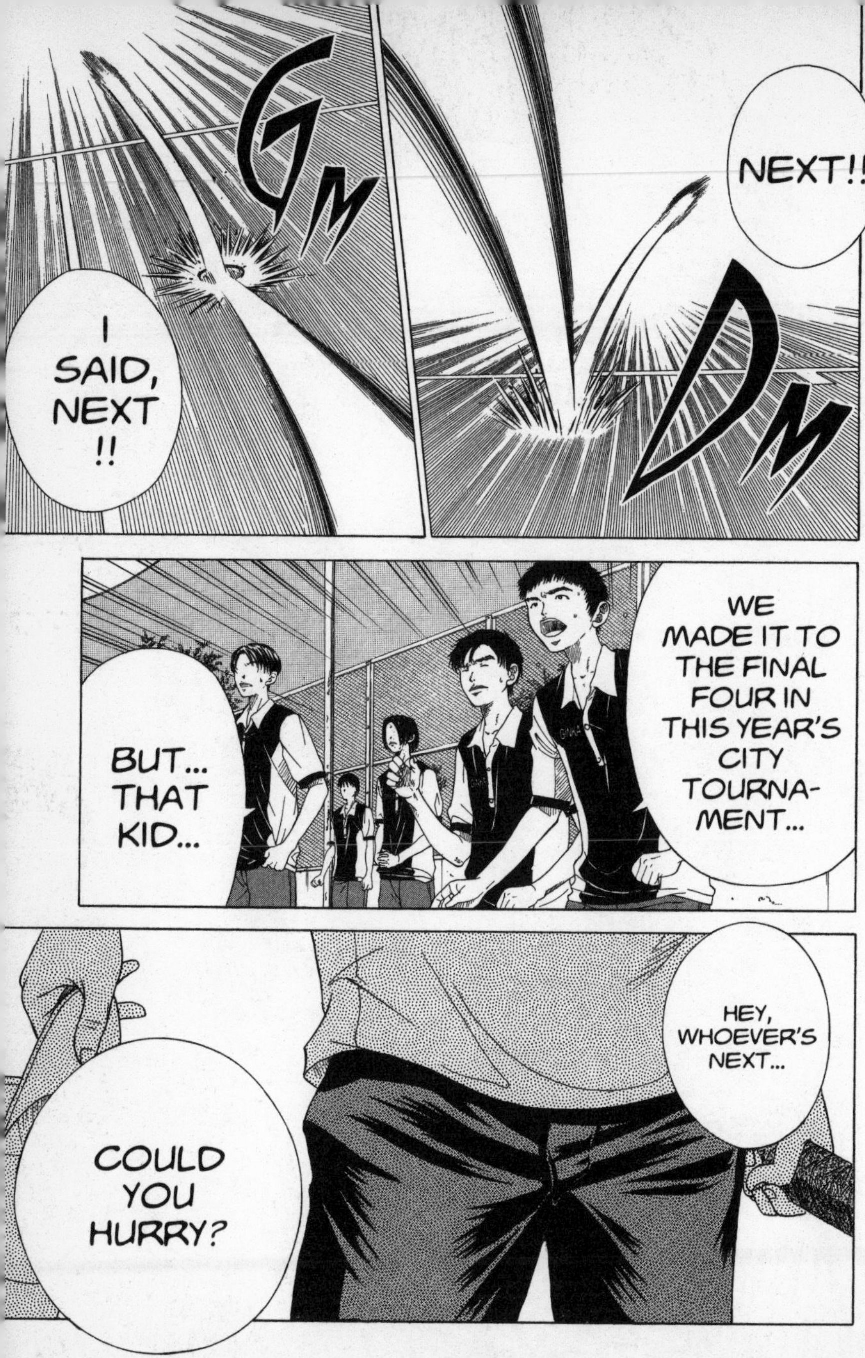
NEXT!!
DM
GM
I SAID, NEXT !!
WE MADE IT TO THE FINAL FOUR IN THIS YEAR'S CITY TOURNA-MENT...
BUT... THAT KID...
HEY, WHOEVER'S NEXT...
COULD YOU HURRY?

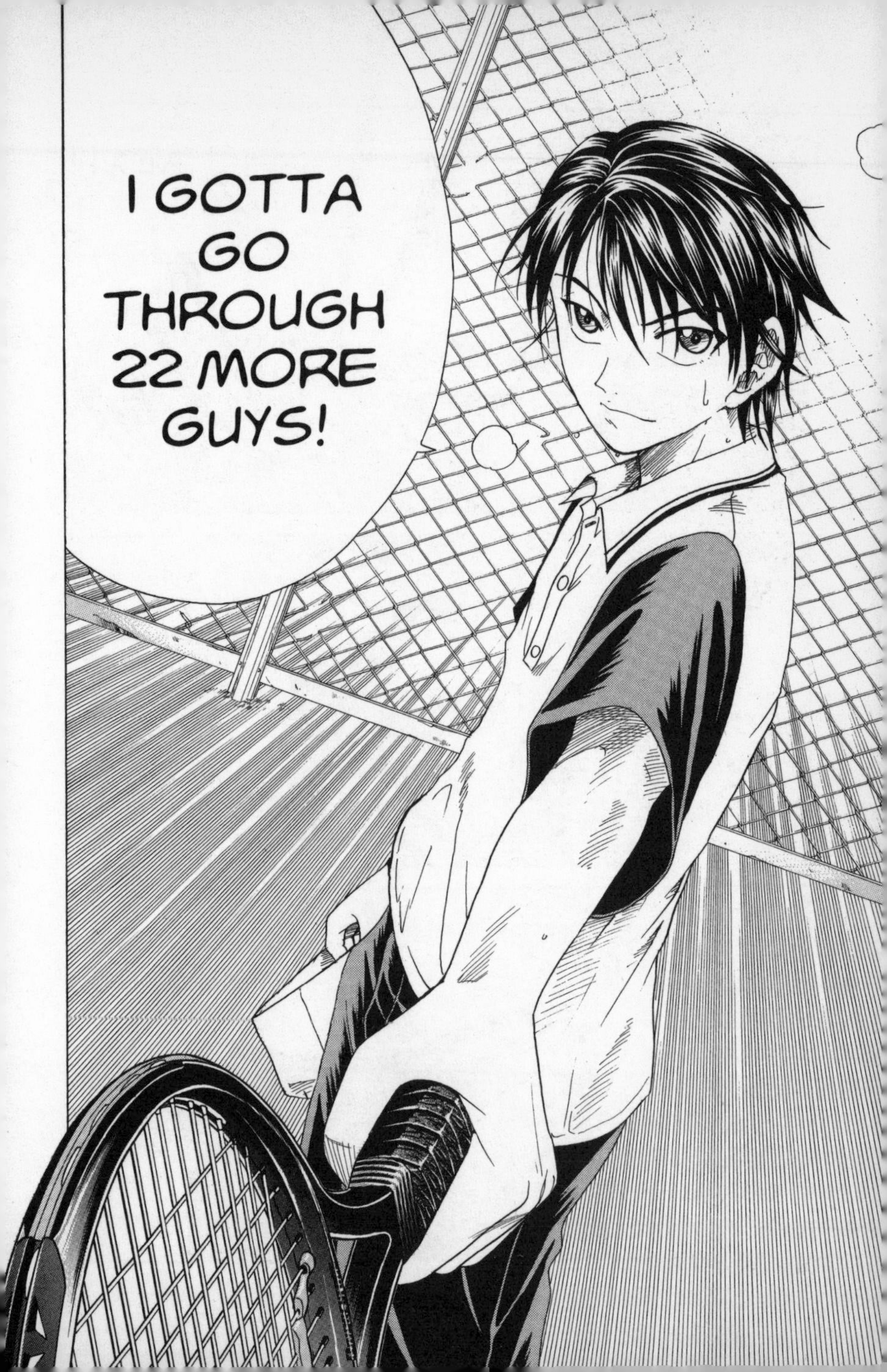
I GOTTA GO THROUGH 22 MORE GUYS!

READ THIS WAY

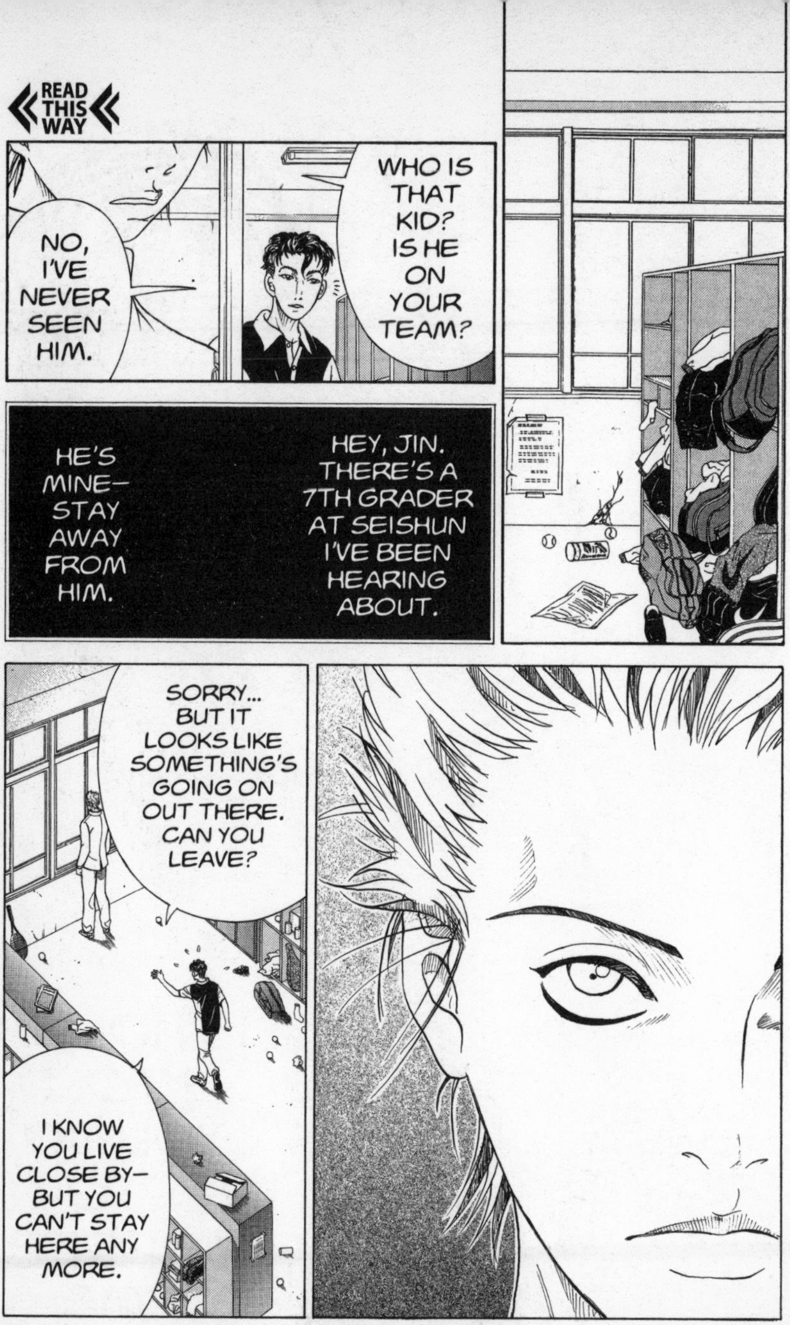

WHO IS THAT KID? IS HE ON YOUR TEAM?
NO, I'VE NEVER SEEN HIM.
HEY, JIN. THERE'S A 7TH GRADER AT SEISHUN I'VE BEEN HEARING ABOUT.
HE'S MINE—STAY AWAY FROM HIM.
SORRY... BUT IT LOOKS LIKE SOMETHING'S GOING ON OUT THERE. CAN YOU LEAVE?
I KNOW YOU LIVE CLOSE BY—BUT YOU CAN'T STAY HERE ANY MORE.

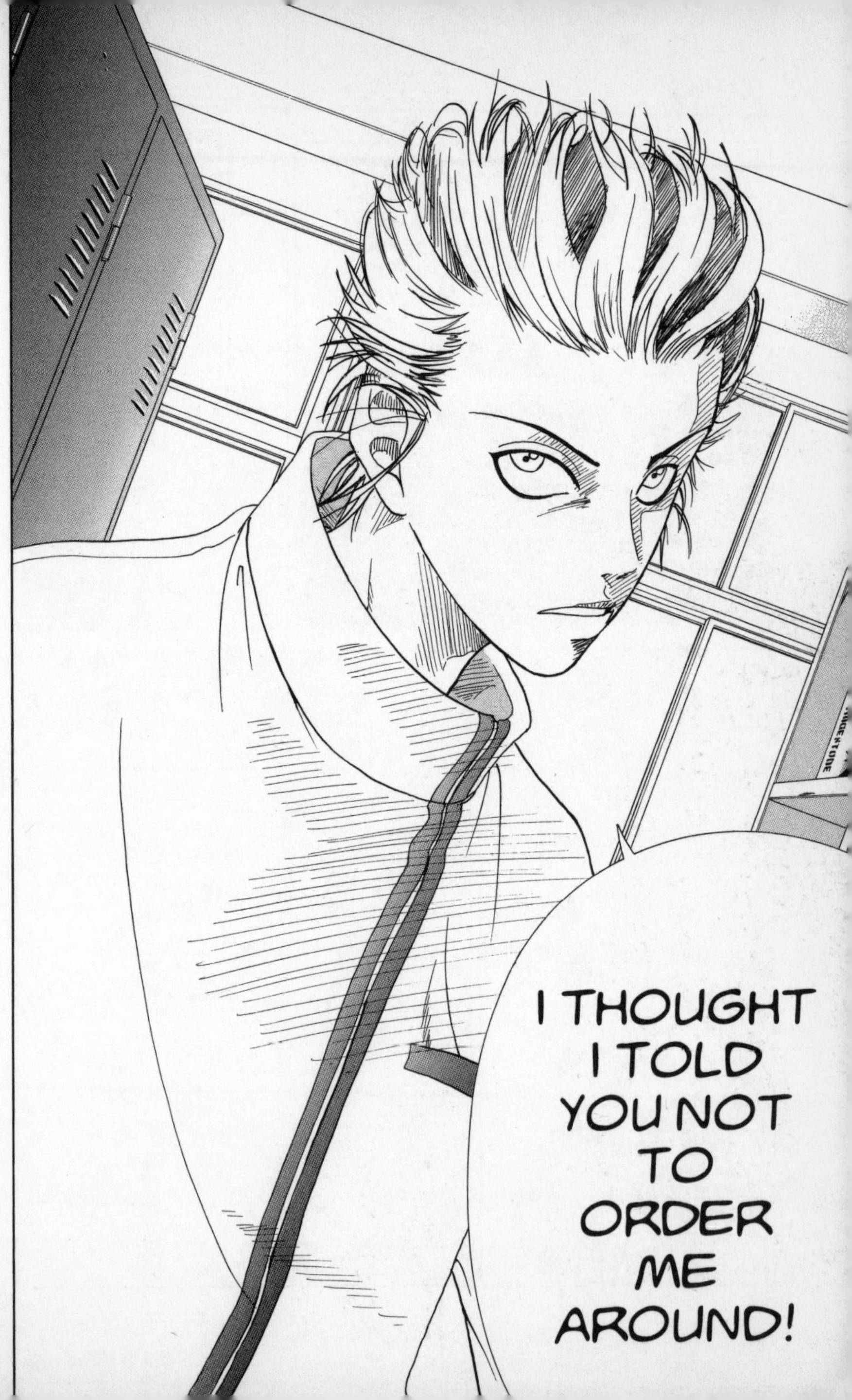
I THOUGHT I TOLD YOU NOT TO ORDER ME AROUND!

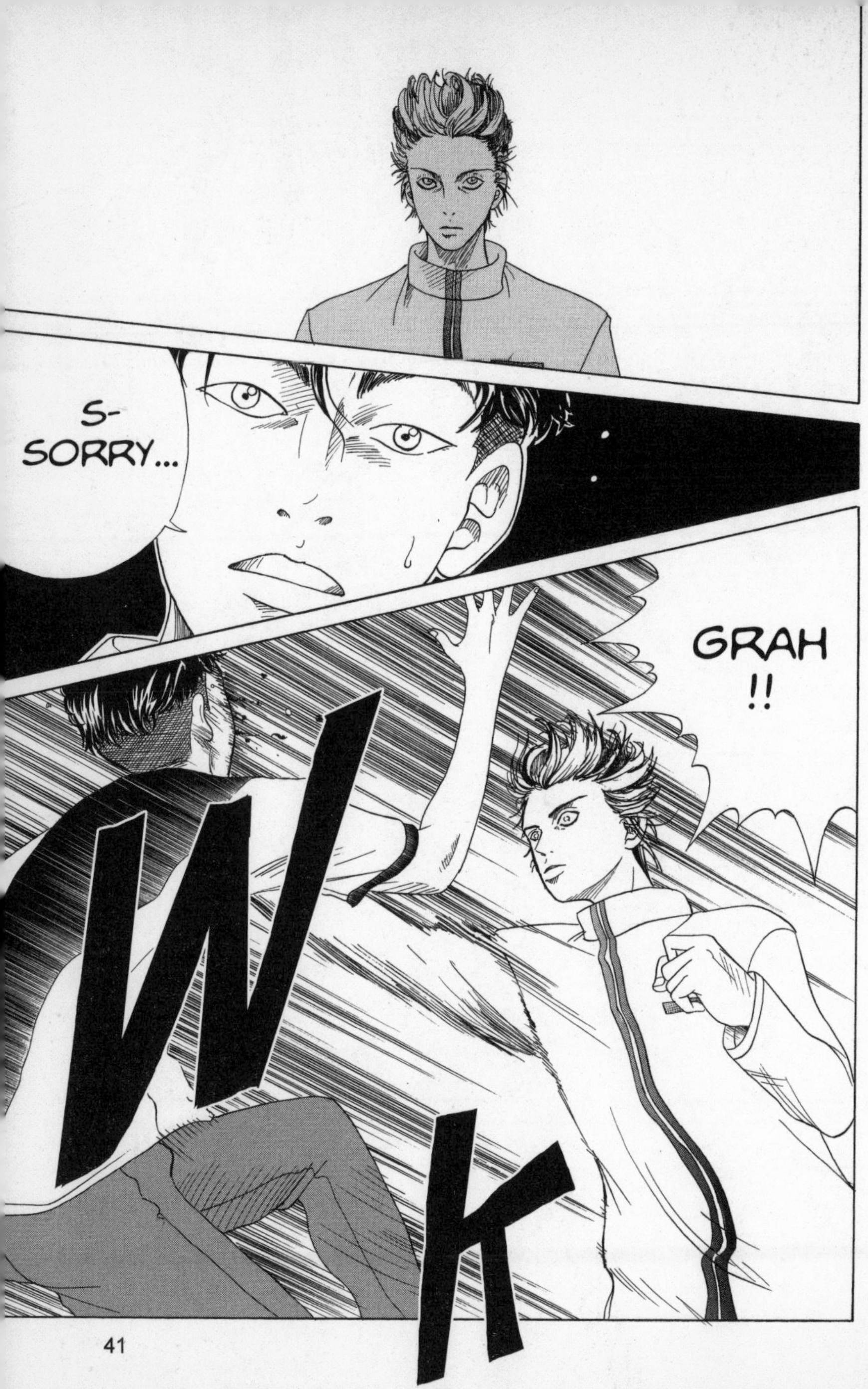
S-
SORRY...
GRAH
!!
WK

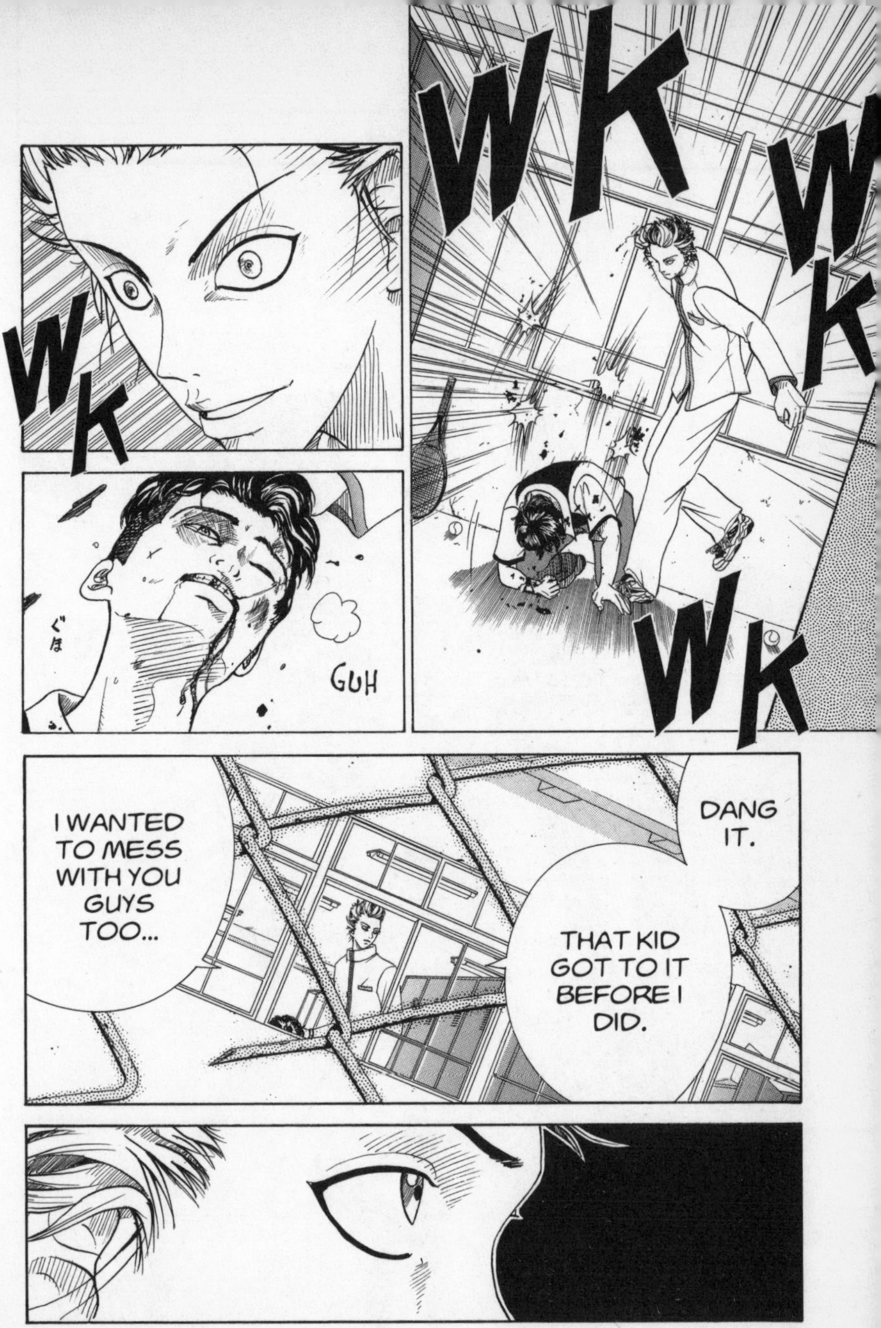
WK
WK
WK
WK
ぐは
GUH
DANG IT.
THAT KID GOT TO IT BEFORE I DID.
I WANTED TO MESS WITH YOU GUYS TOO...

READ THIS WAY

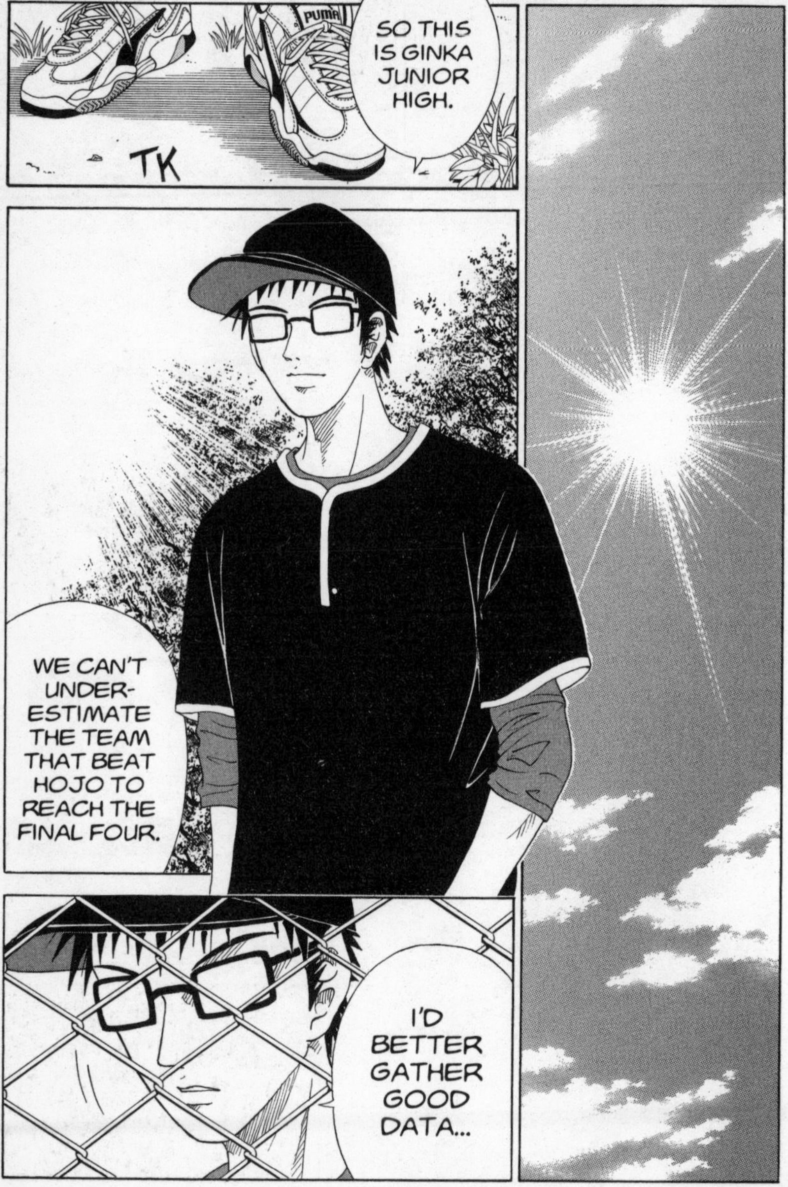
SO THIS IS GINKA JUNIOR HIGH.
TK
WE CAN'T UNDER-ESTIMATE THE TEAM THAT BEAT HOJO TO REACH THE FINAL FOUR.
I'D BETTER GATHER GOOD DATA...

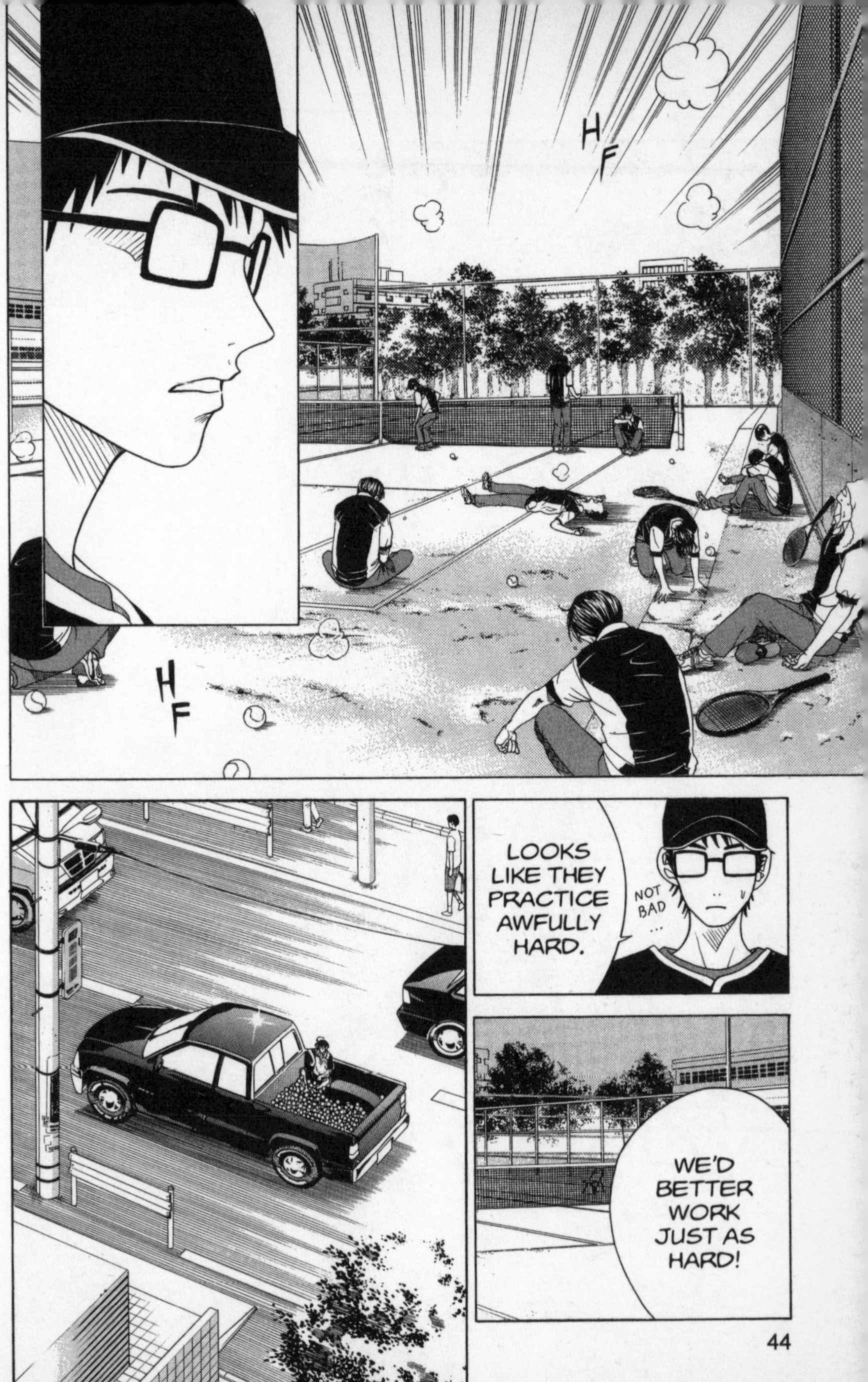
HF
HF
LOOKS LIKE THEY PRACTICE AWFULLY HARD.
NOT BAD ...
WE'D BETTER WORK JUST AS HARD!

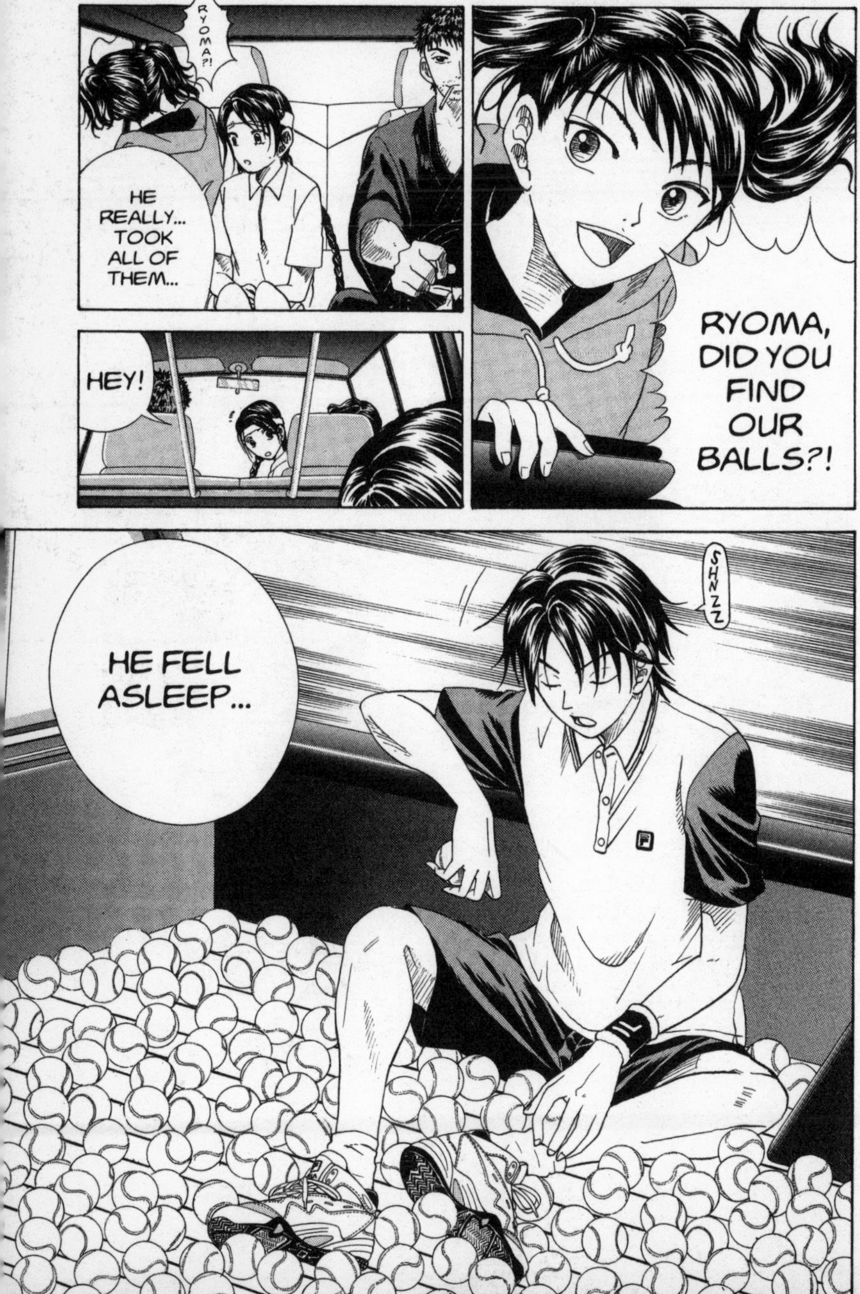
RYOMA, DID YOU FIND OUR BALLS?!
RYOMA?!
HE REALLY... TOOK ALL OF THEM...
HEY!
SHNZZ
HE FELL ASLEEP...

テニスの王子様
THE PRINCE OF TENNIS

The Scene Again!!

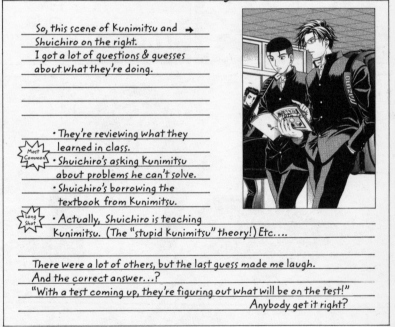

So, this scene of Kunimitsu and → Shuichiro on the right.
I got a lot of questions & guesses about what they're doing.

Most Common

- They're reviewing what they learned in class.
- Shuichiro's asking Kunimitsu about problems he can't solve.
- Shuichiro's borrowing the textbook from Kunimitsu.

Long Shot

- Actually, Shuichiro is teaching Kunimitsu. (The "stupid Kunimitsu" theory!) Etc....

There were a lot of others, but the last guess made me laugh.
And the correct answer...?
"With a test coming up, they're figuring out what will be on the test!"
Anybody get it right?

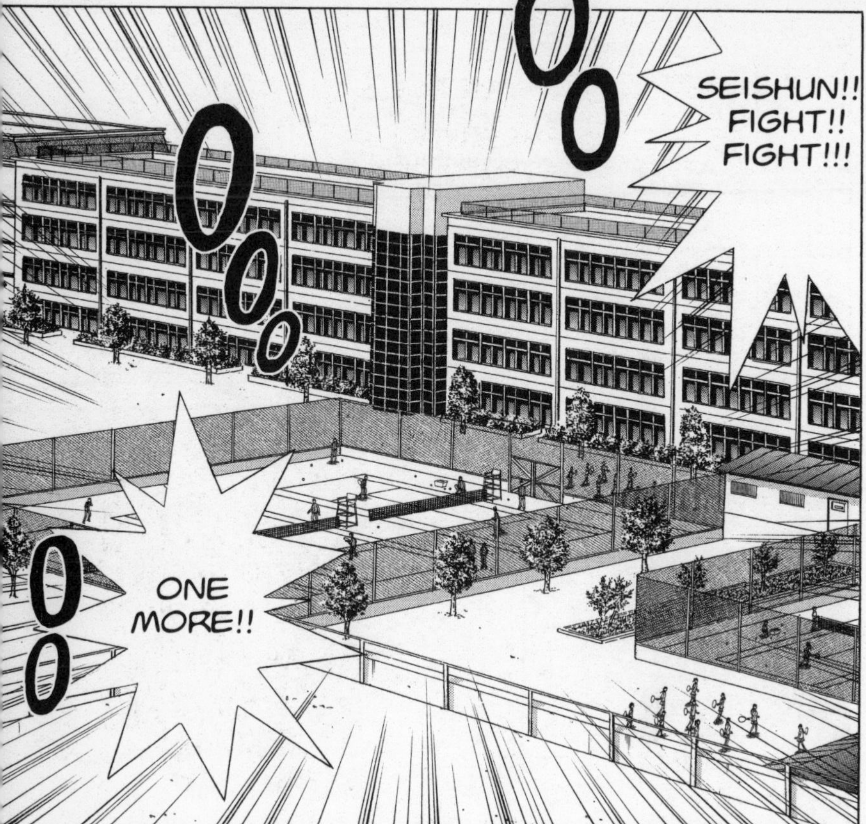
SEISHUN!! FIGHT!! FIGHT!!!
ONE MORE!!

GENIUS 81: SELF-INTRODUCTION (PART 1)

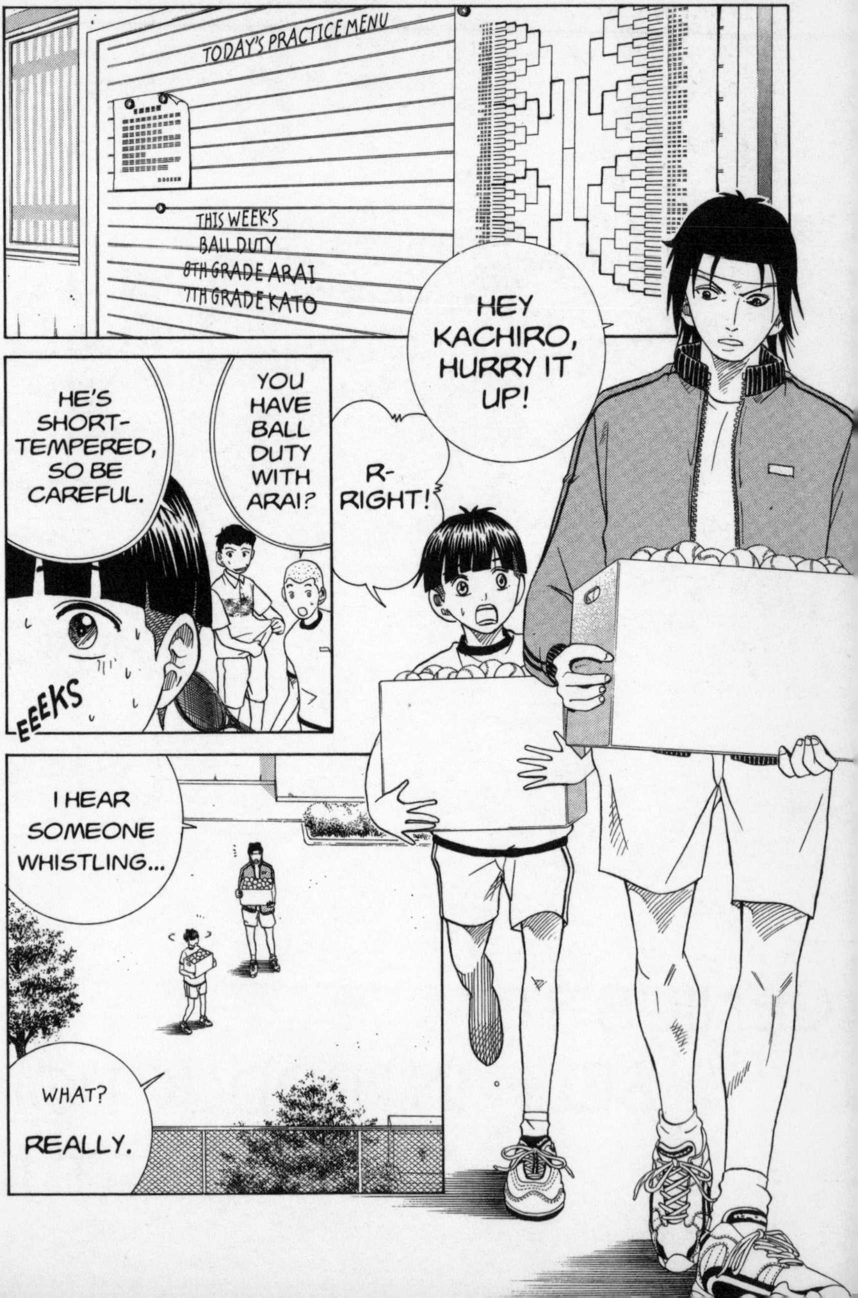
TODAY'S PRACTICE MENU
THIS WEEK'S BALL DUTY 8TH GRADE ARAI 7TH GRADE KATO
HEY KACHIRO, HURRY IT UP!
R-RIGHT!
YOU HAVE BALL DUTY WITH ARAI?
HE'S SHORT-TEMPERED, SO BE CAREFUL.
EEEKS
I HEAR SOMEONE WHISTLING...
WHAT?
REALLY.

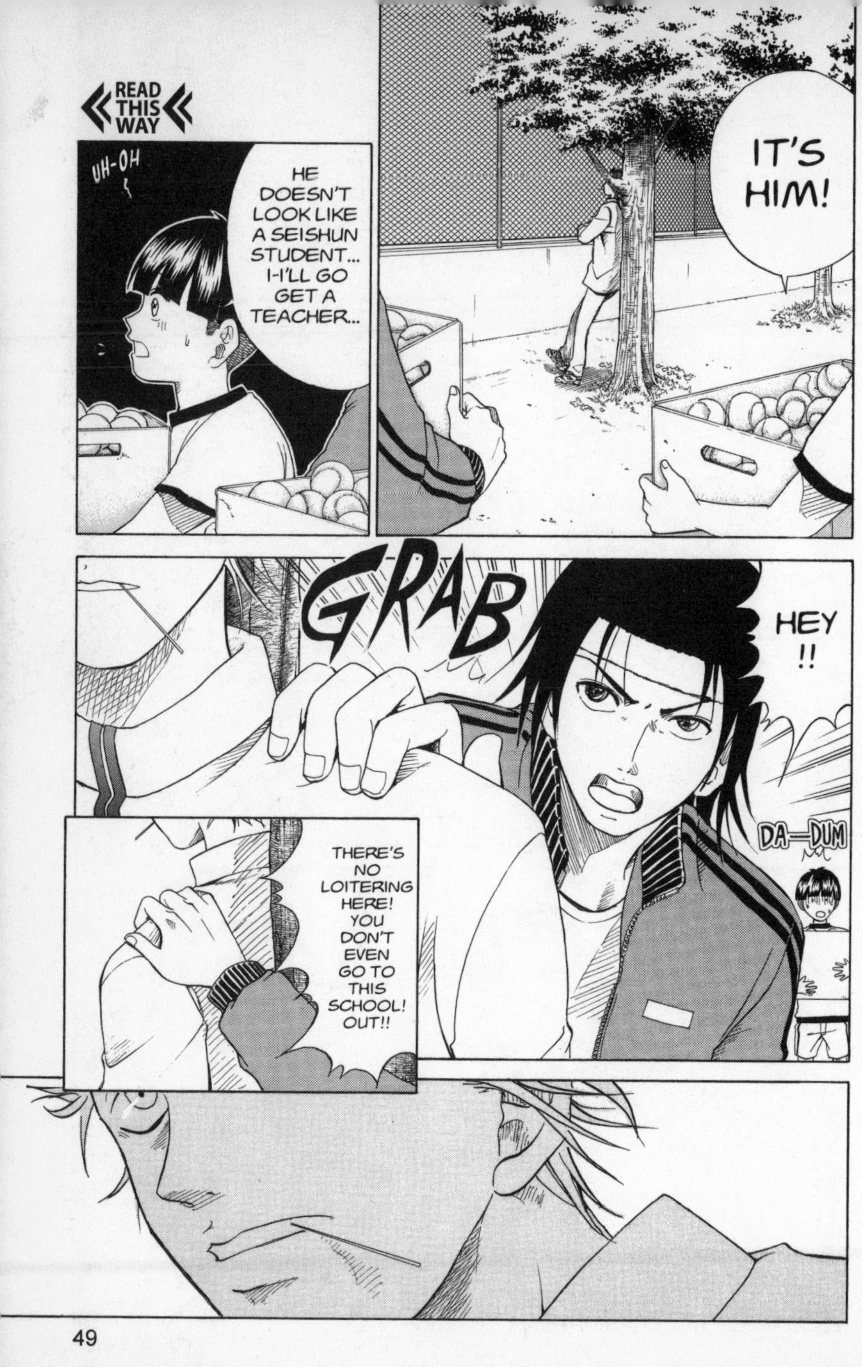
READ THIS WAY
IT'S HIM!
UH-OH
HE DOESN'T LOOK LIKE A SEISHUN STUDENT... I-I'LL GO GET A TEACHER...
GRAB
HEY !!
DA-DUM
THERE'S NO LOITERING HERE! YOU DON'T EVEN GO TO THIS SCHOOL! OUT!!

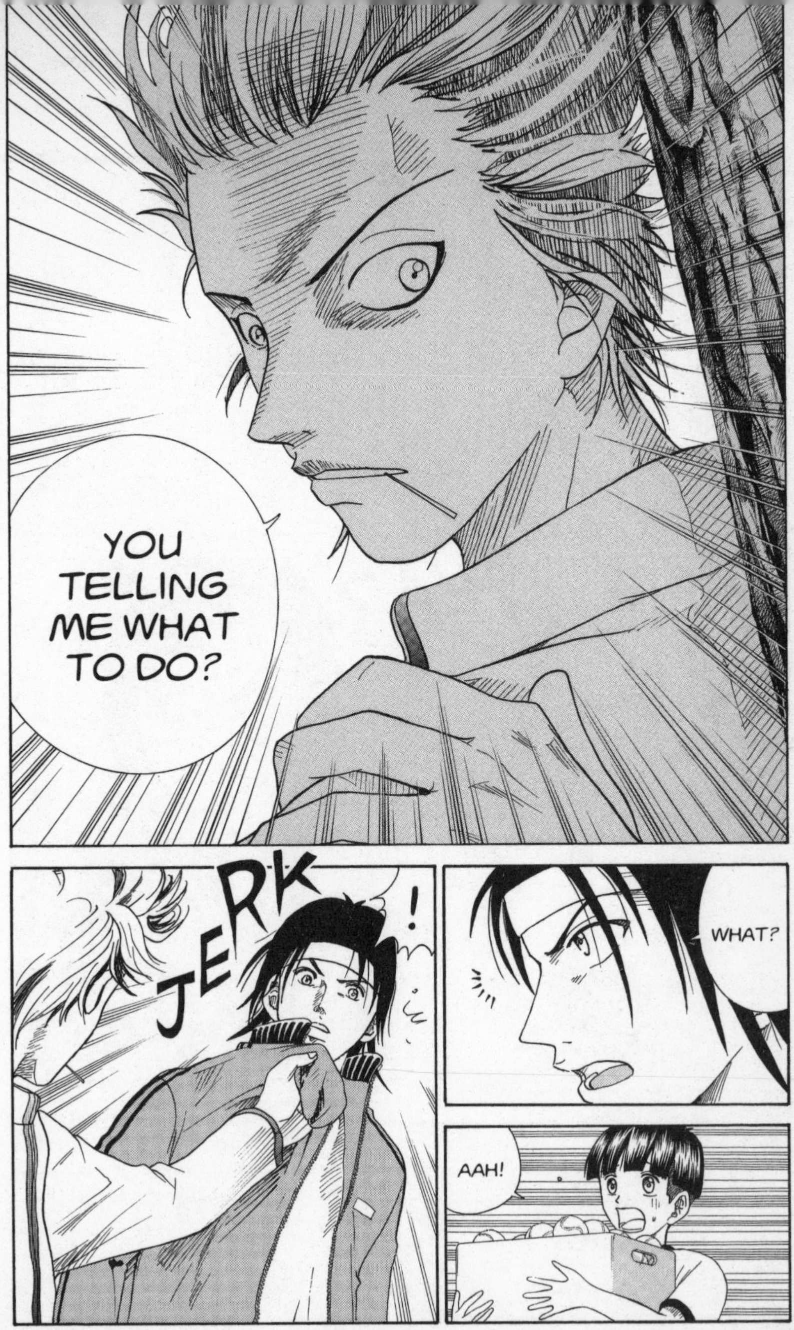
YOU TELLING ME WHAT TO DO?
WHAT?
AAH!
JERK
!

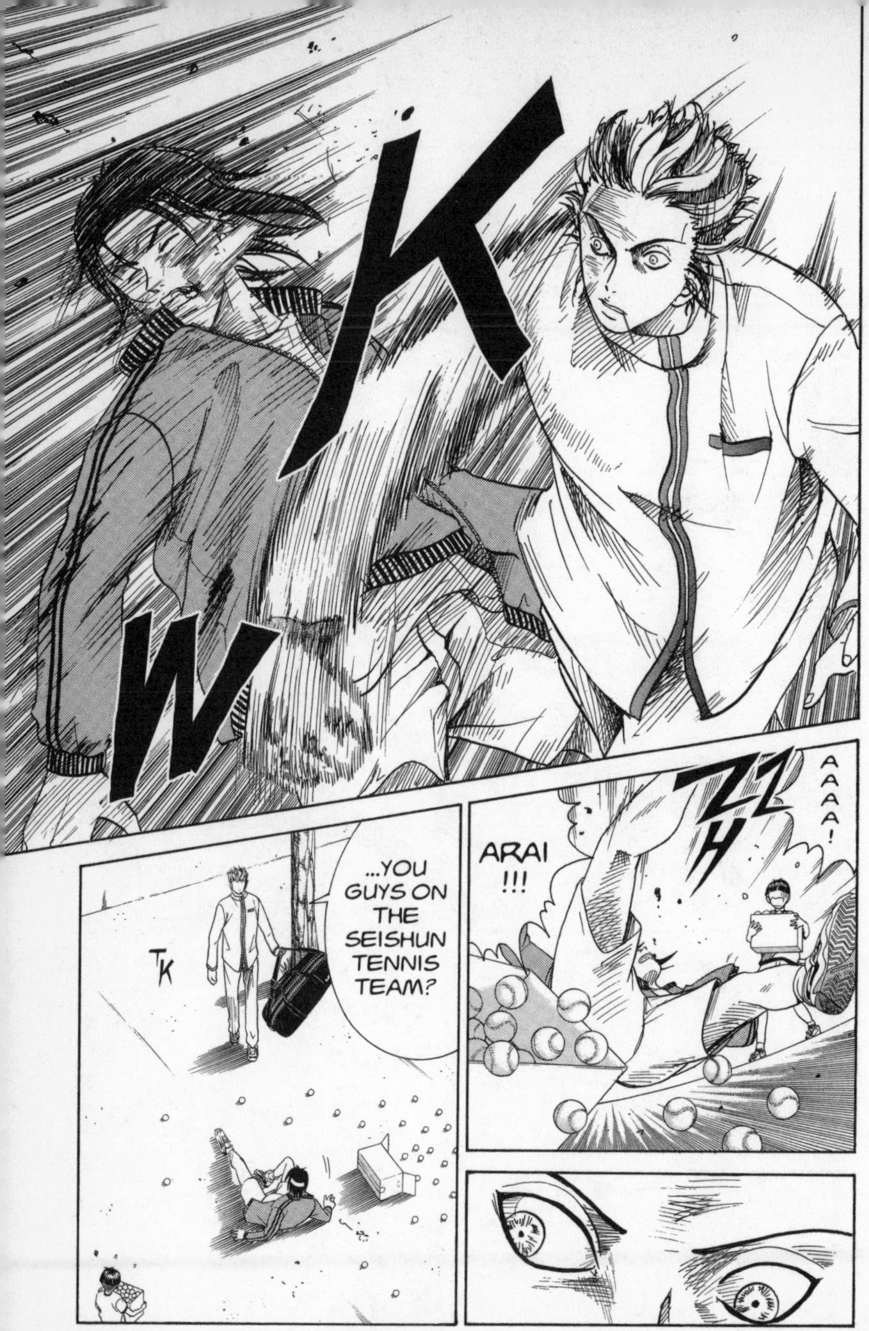
K
W
AAAA!
ZZH
ARAI !!!
...YOU GUYS ON THE SEISHUN TENNIS TEAM?
TK

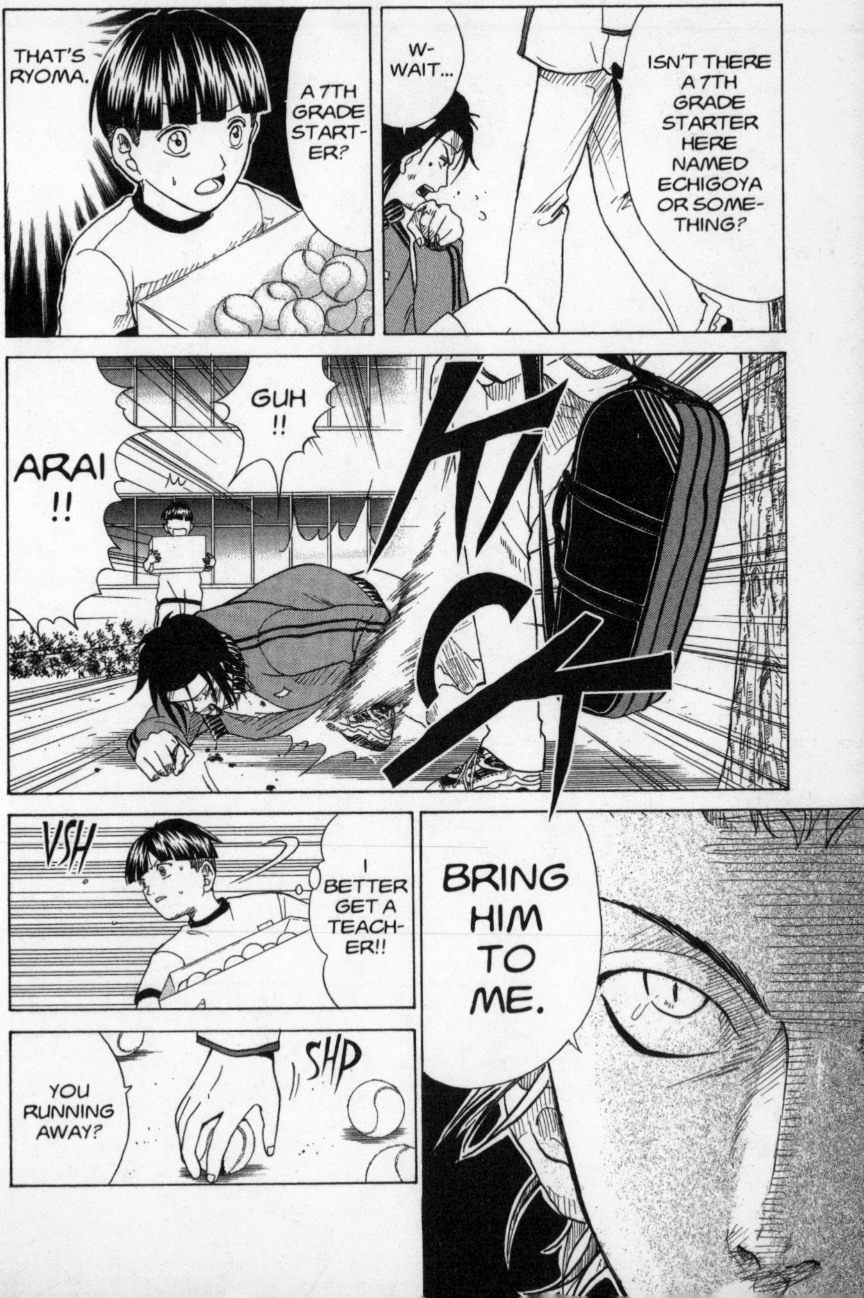
ISN'T THERE A 7TH GRADE STARTER HERE NAMED ECHIGOYA OR SOMETHING?
W-WAIT...
A 7TH GRADE STARTER?
THAT'S RYOMA.
KICK
GUH !!
ARAI !!
BRING HIM TO ME.
I BETTER GET A TEACHER!!
VSH
SHP
YOU RUNNING AWAY?

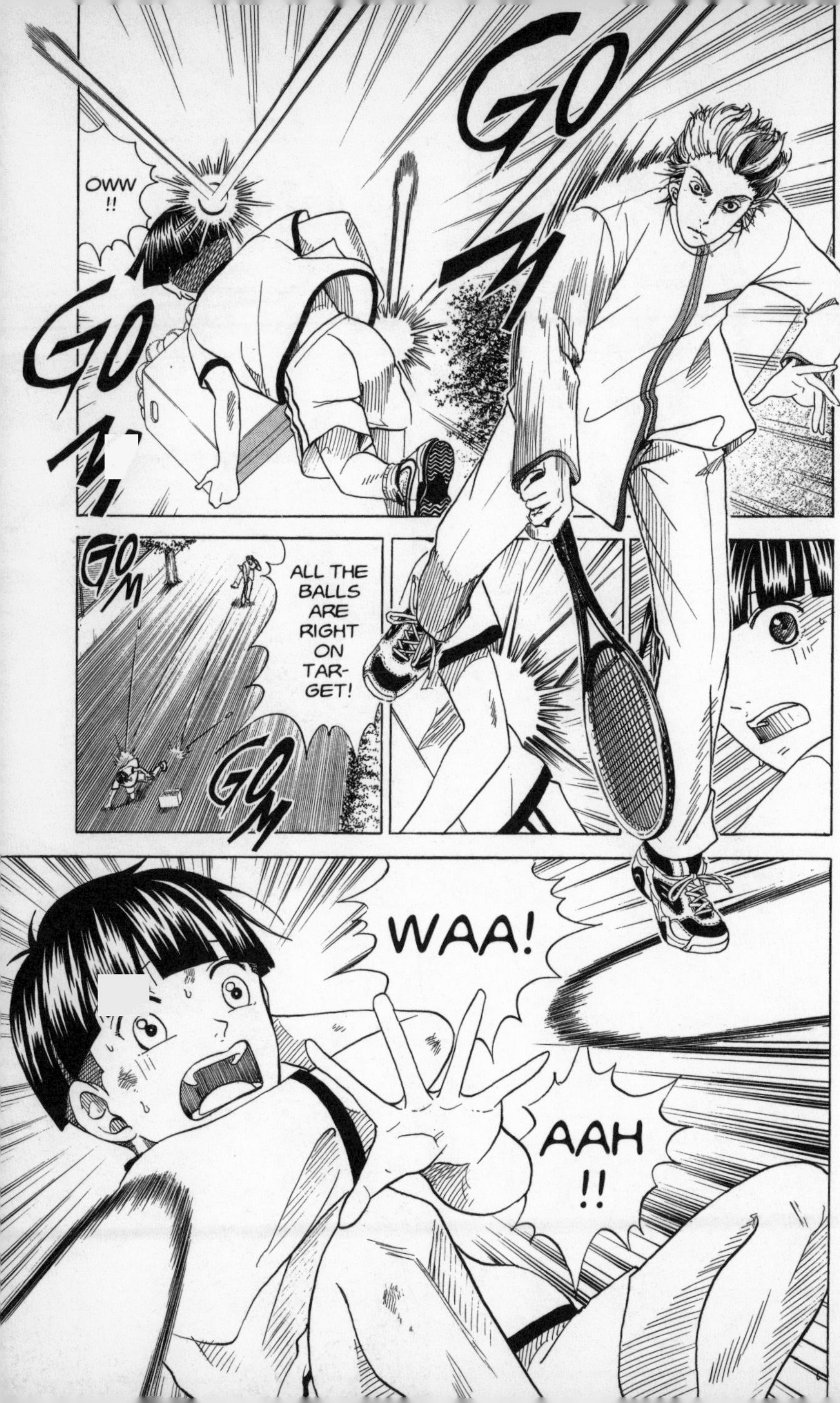
GOM
OWW !!
GOM
GOM
ALL THE BALLS ARE RIGHT ON TAR- GET!
GOM
WAA!
AAH !!

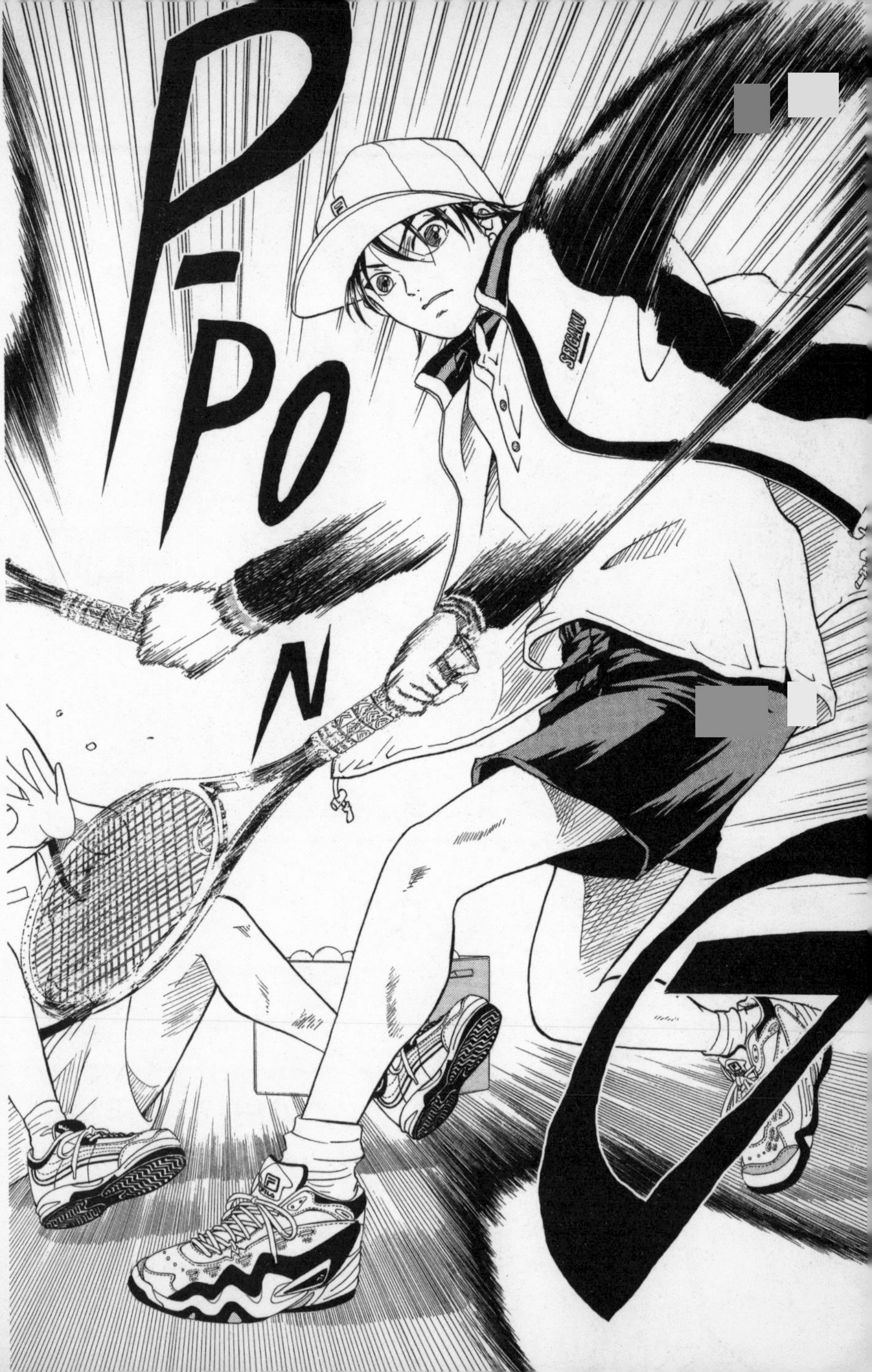
P-PON
SEIGAKU

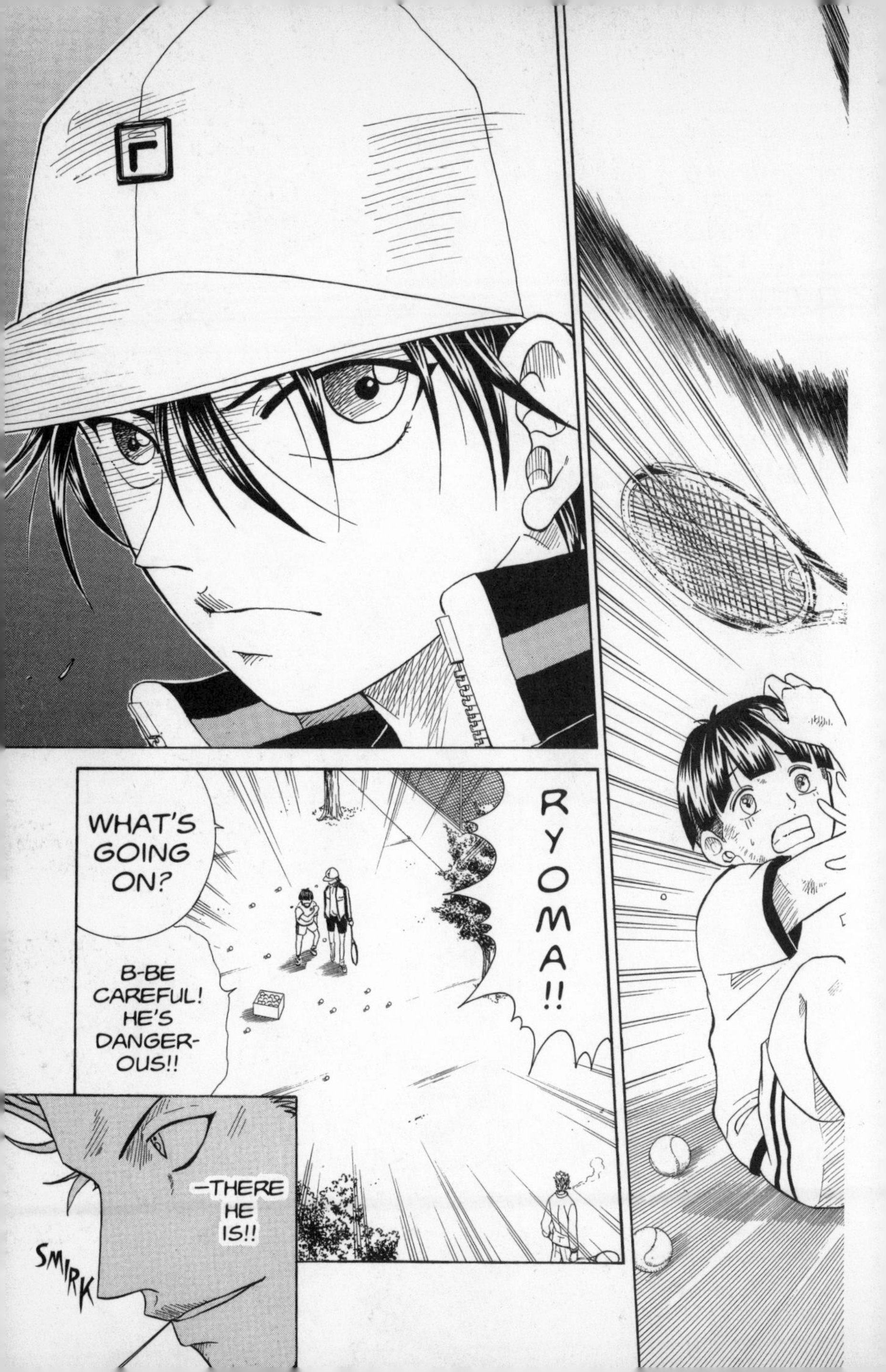
RYOMA!!
WHAT'S GOING ON?
B-BE CAREFUL! HE'S DANGER-OUS!!
—THERE HE IS!!
SMIRK

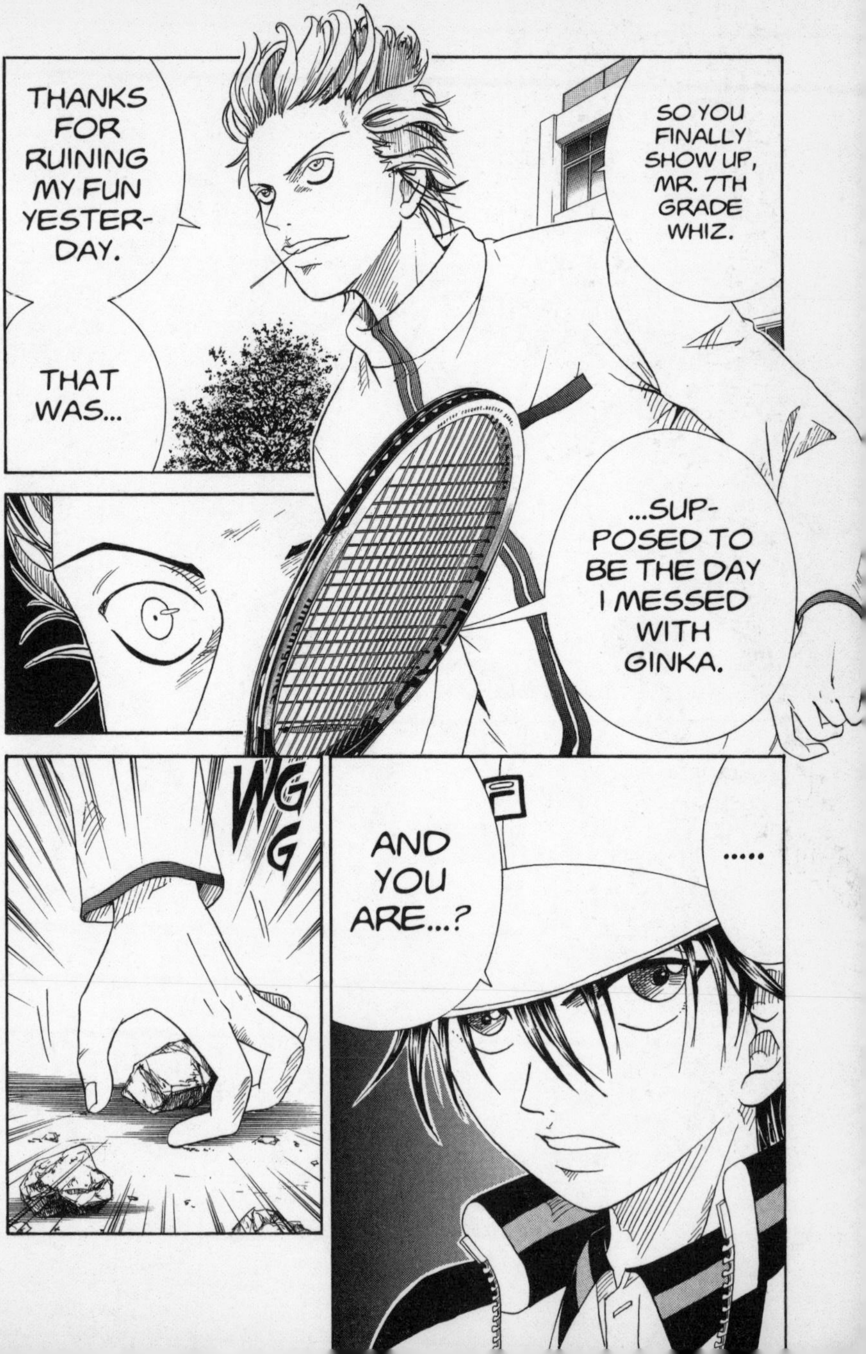
SO YOU FINALLY SHOW UP, MR. 7TH GRADE WHIZ.
THANKS FOR RUINING MY FUN YESTER-DAY.
THAT WAS...
...SUP-POSED TO BE THE DAY I MESSED WITH GINKA.
.....
AND YOU ARE...?
WGG

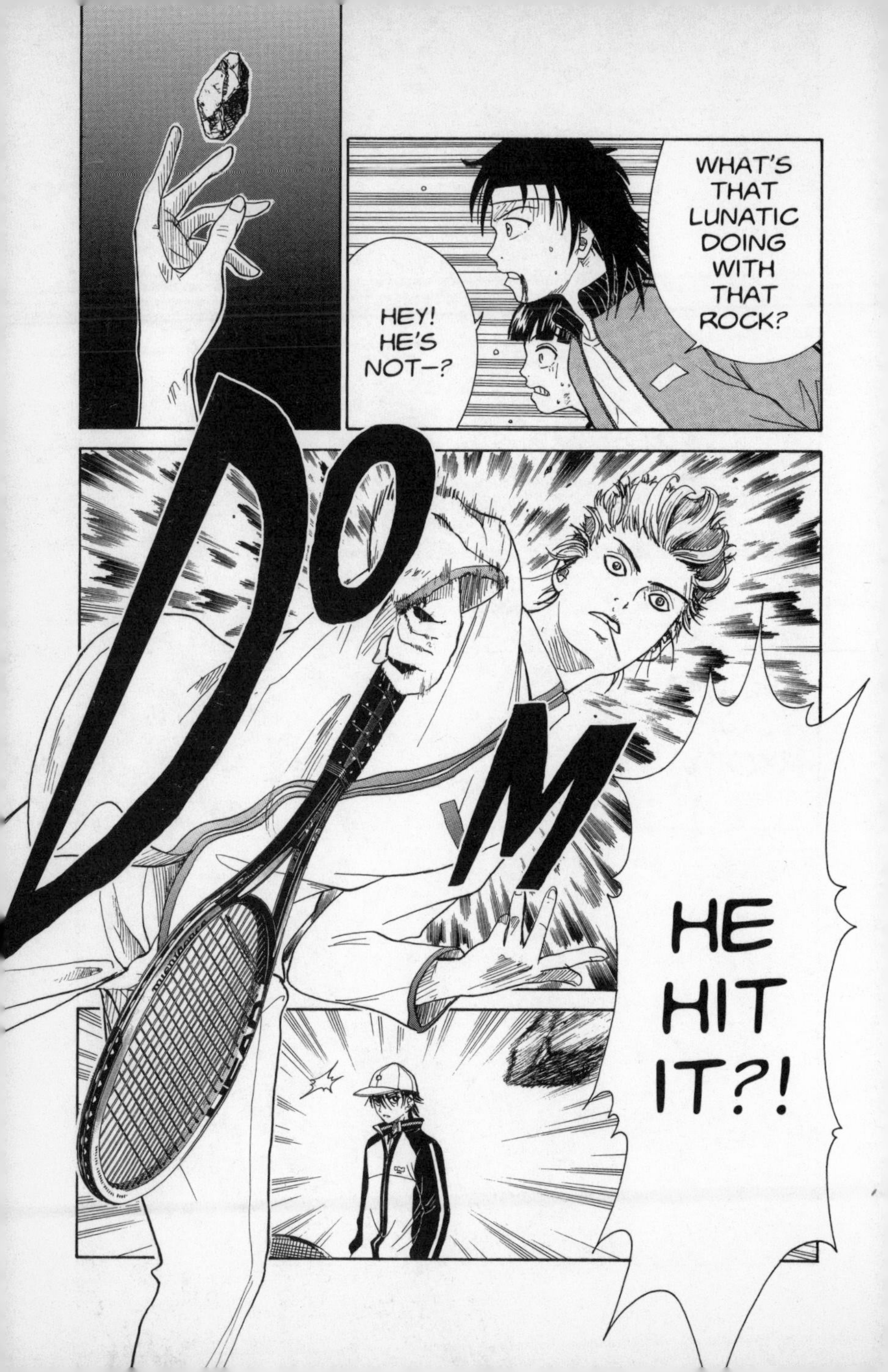
WHAT'S THAT LUNATIC DOING WITH THAT ROCK?
HEY! HE'S NOT—?
DOM
HE HIT IT?!

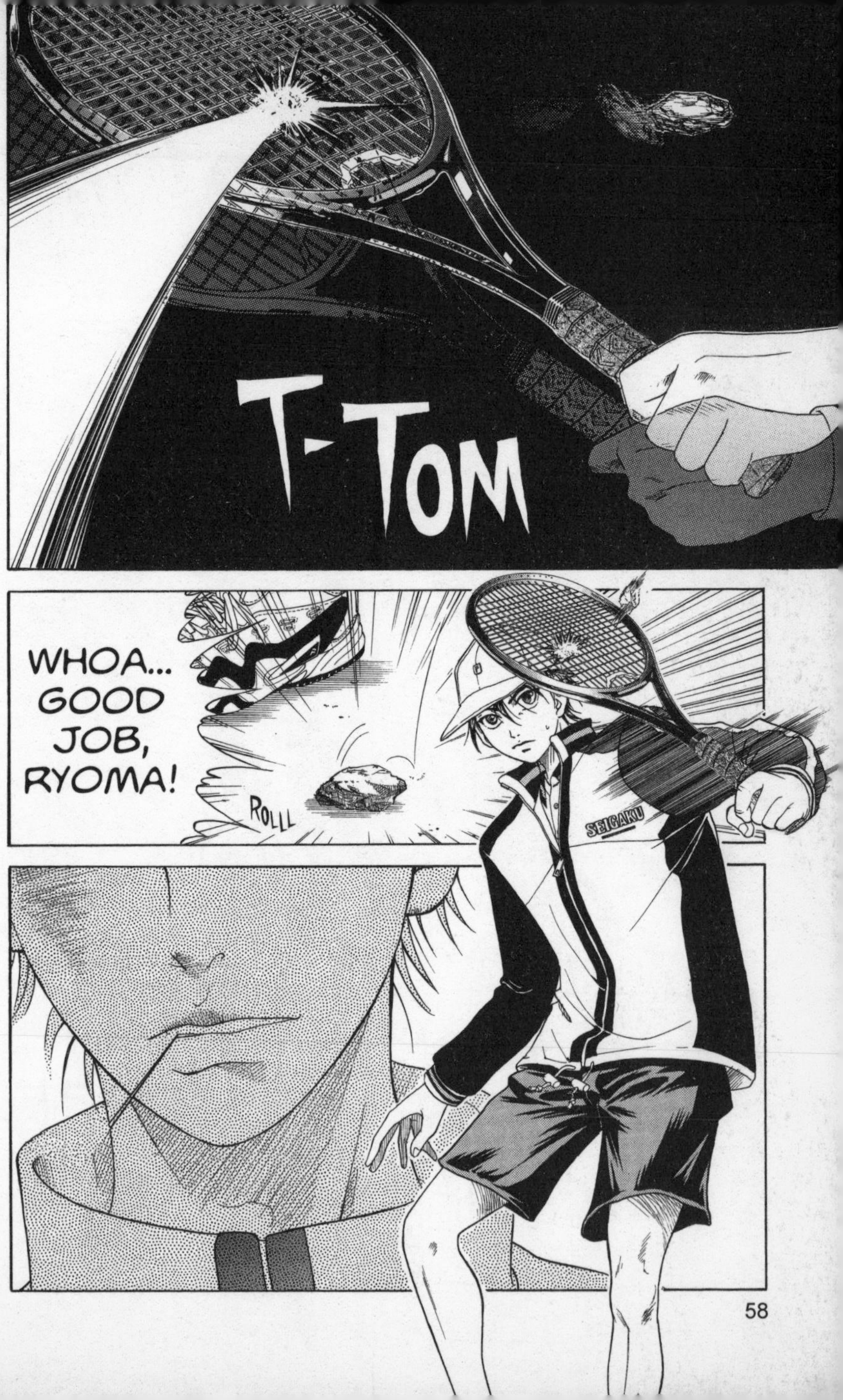
T-TOM
WHOA... GOOD JOB, RYOMA!
ROLLL
SEIGAKU

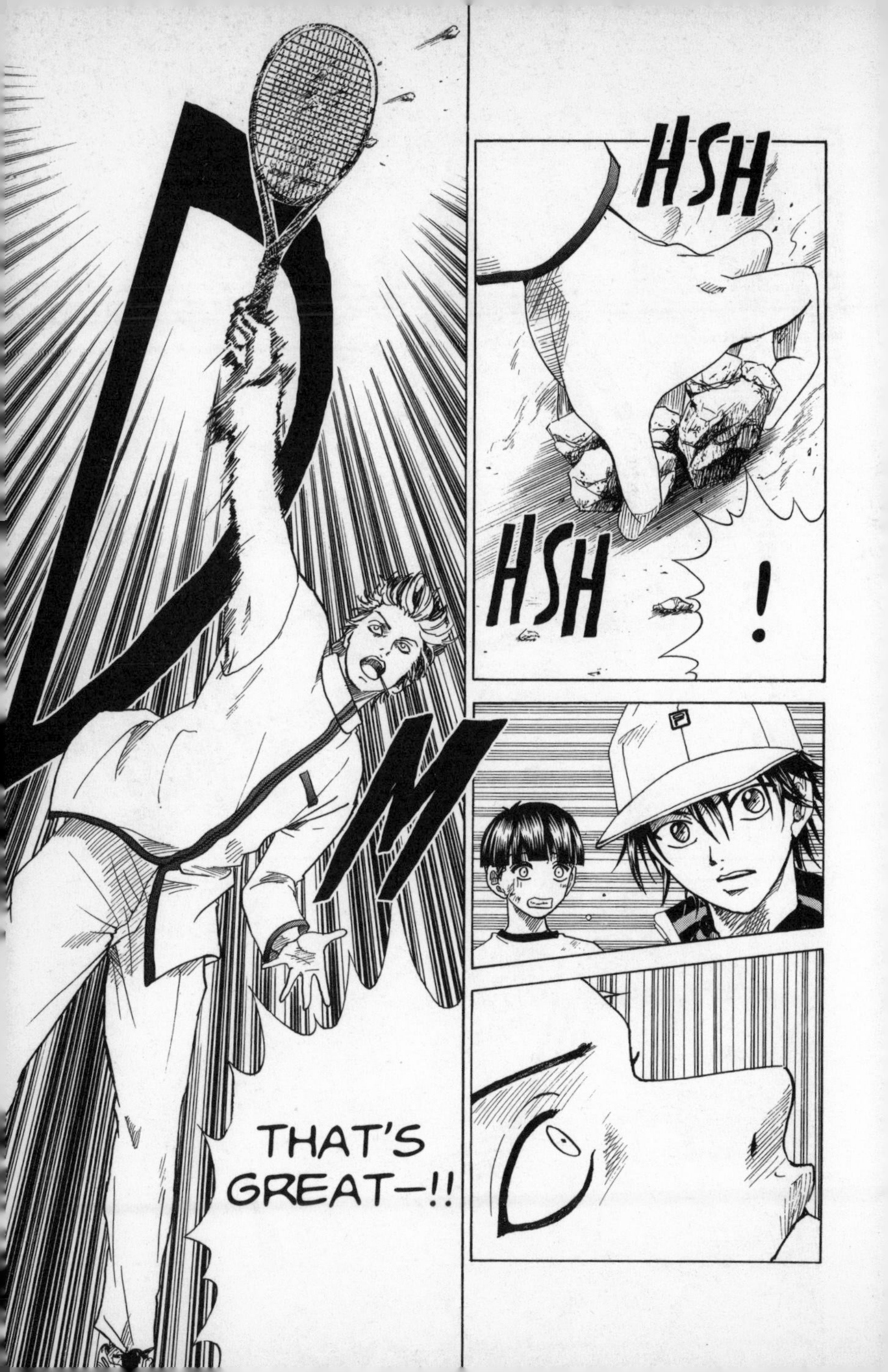
HSH
HSH
!
DM
THAT'S GREAT—!!

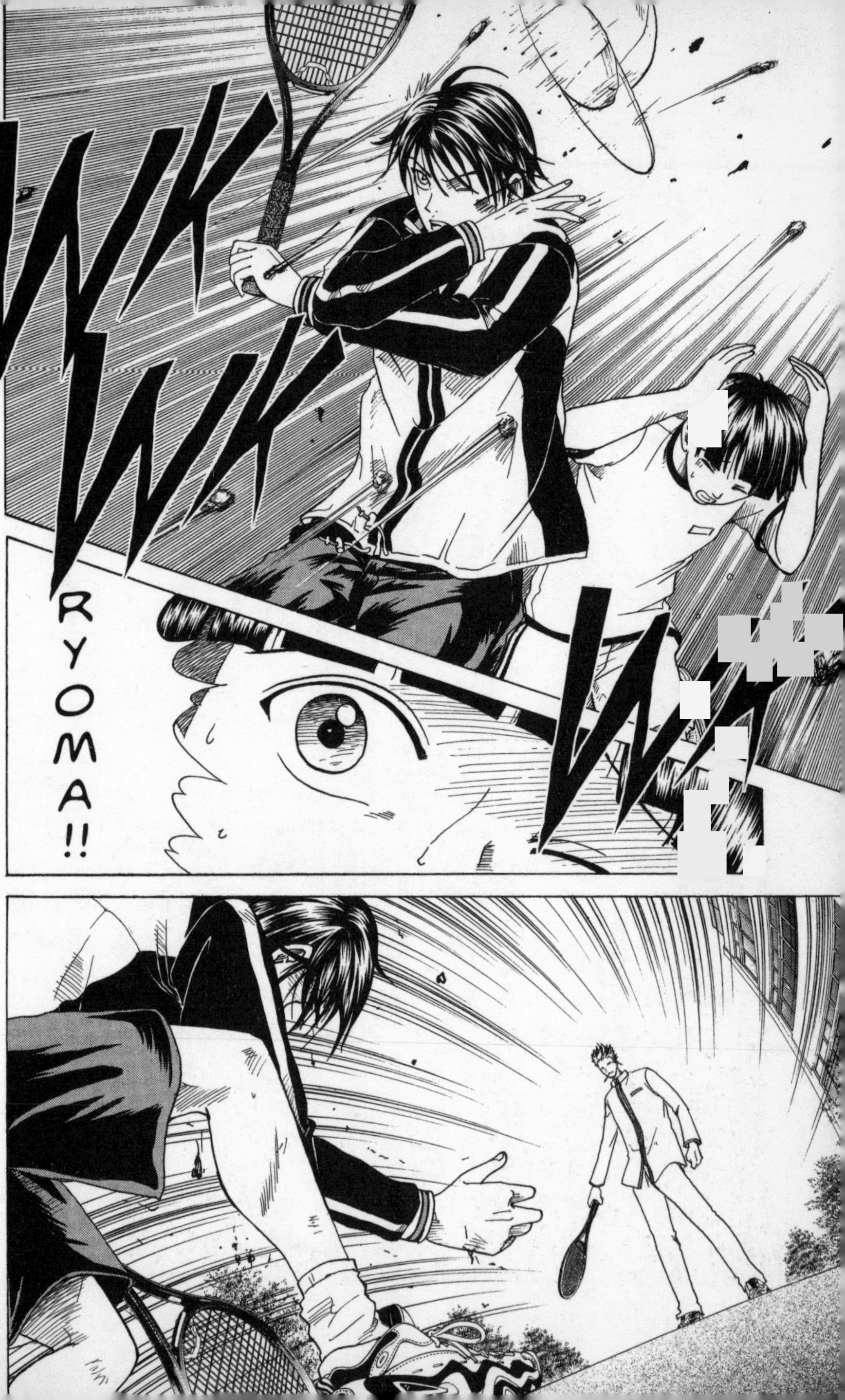
WK WK
WK
RYOMA!!

READ THIS WAY

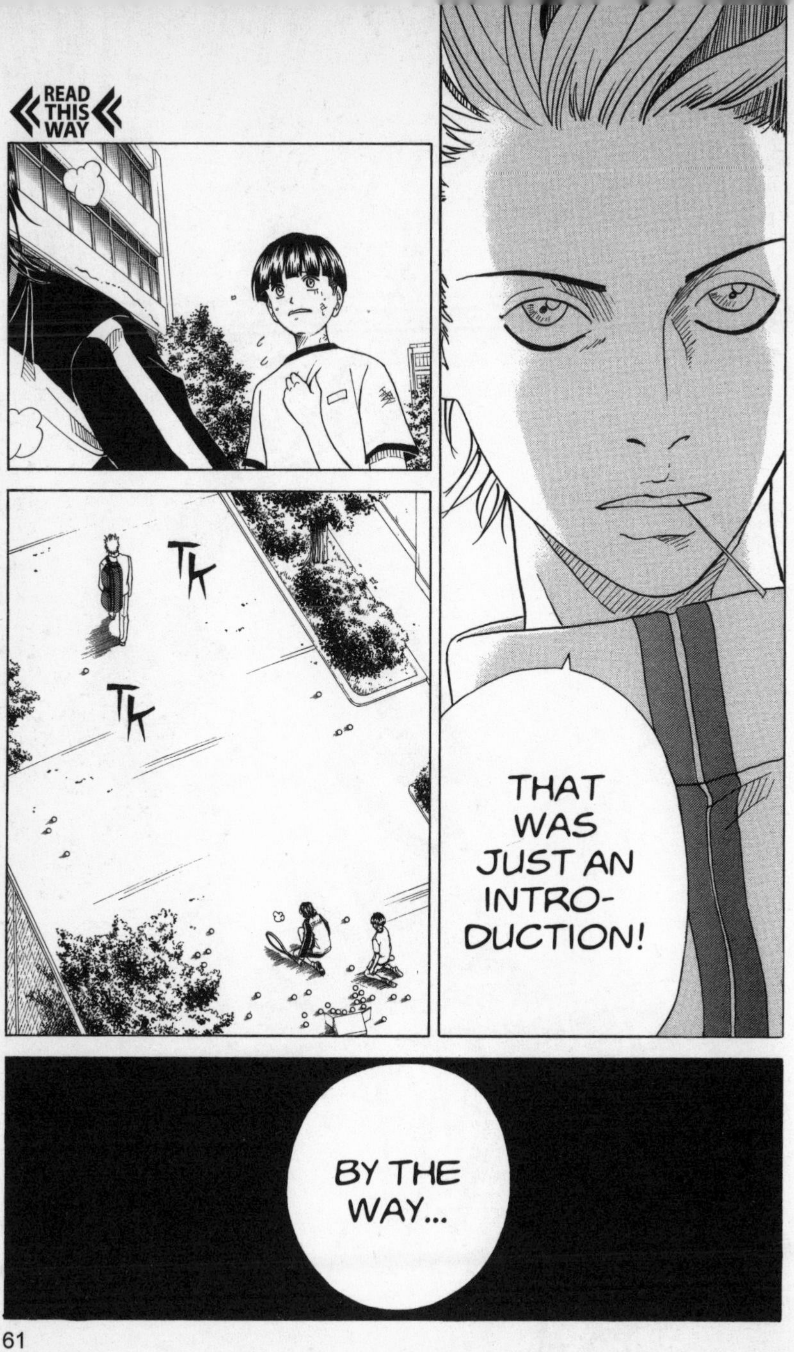
THAT WAS JUST AN INTRO-DUCTION!
TK
TK
BY THE WAY...

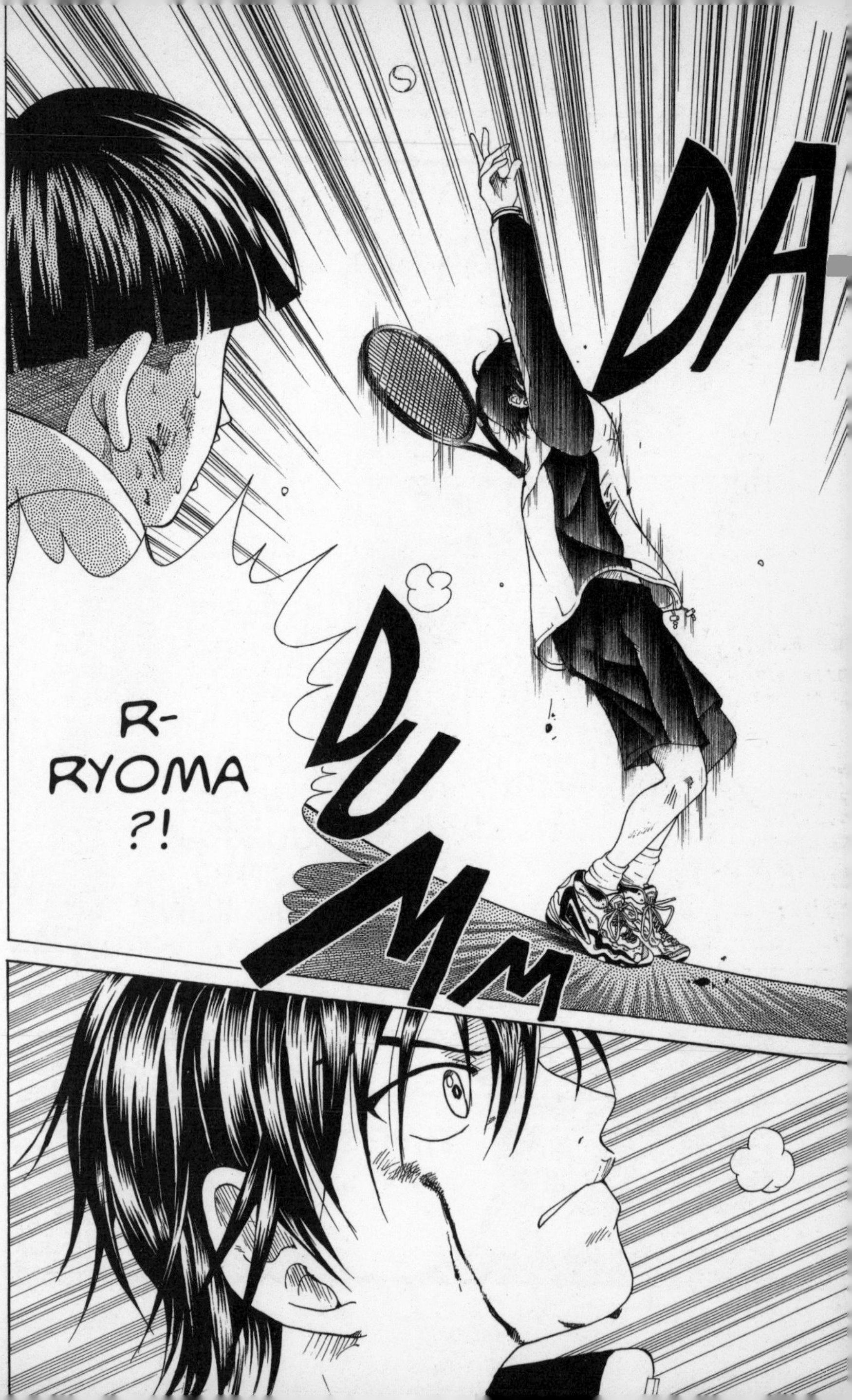
DA
DUMM
R-
RYOMA
?!

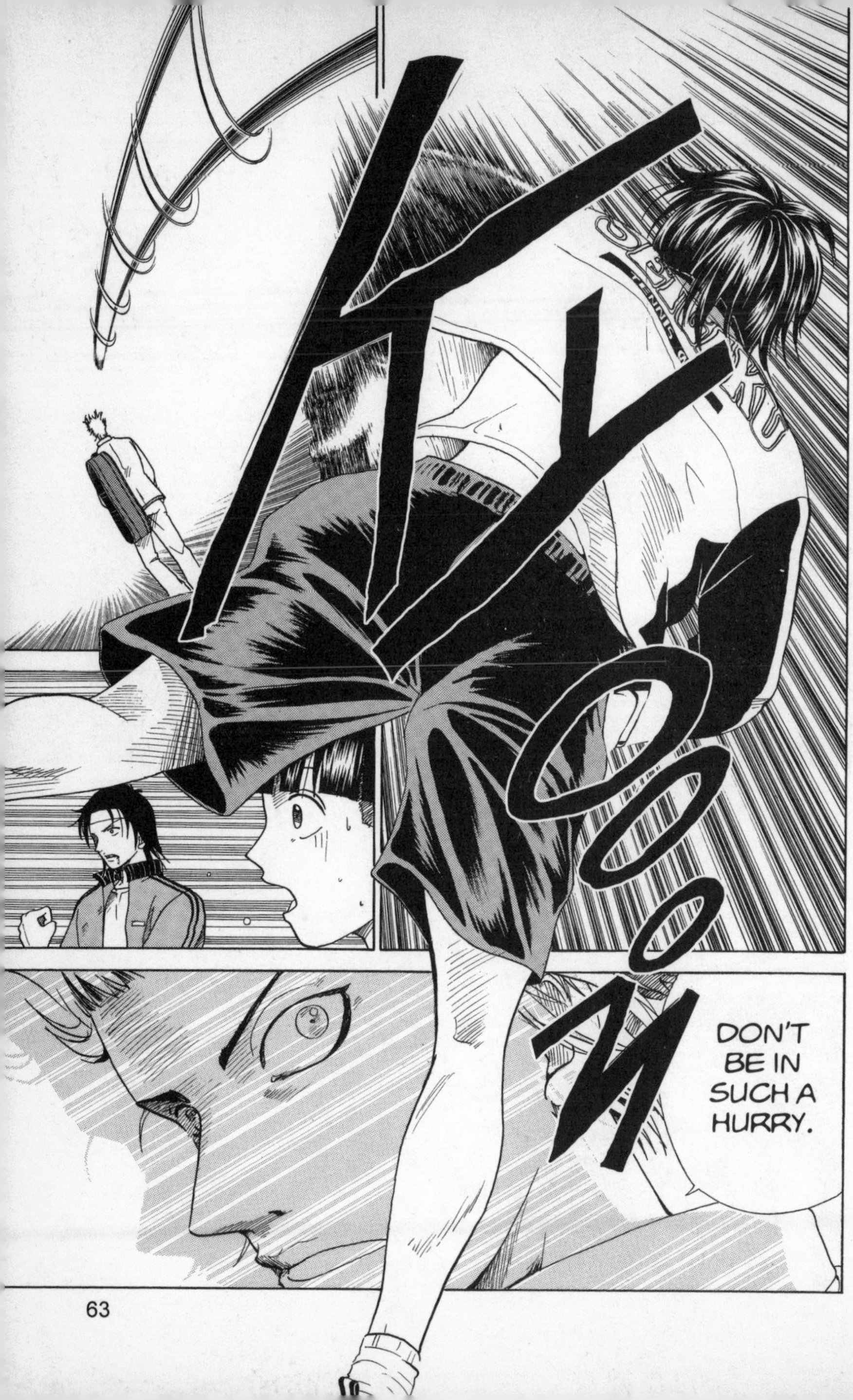
DON'T BE IN SUCH A HURRY.

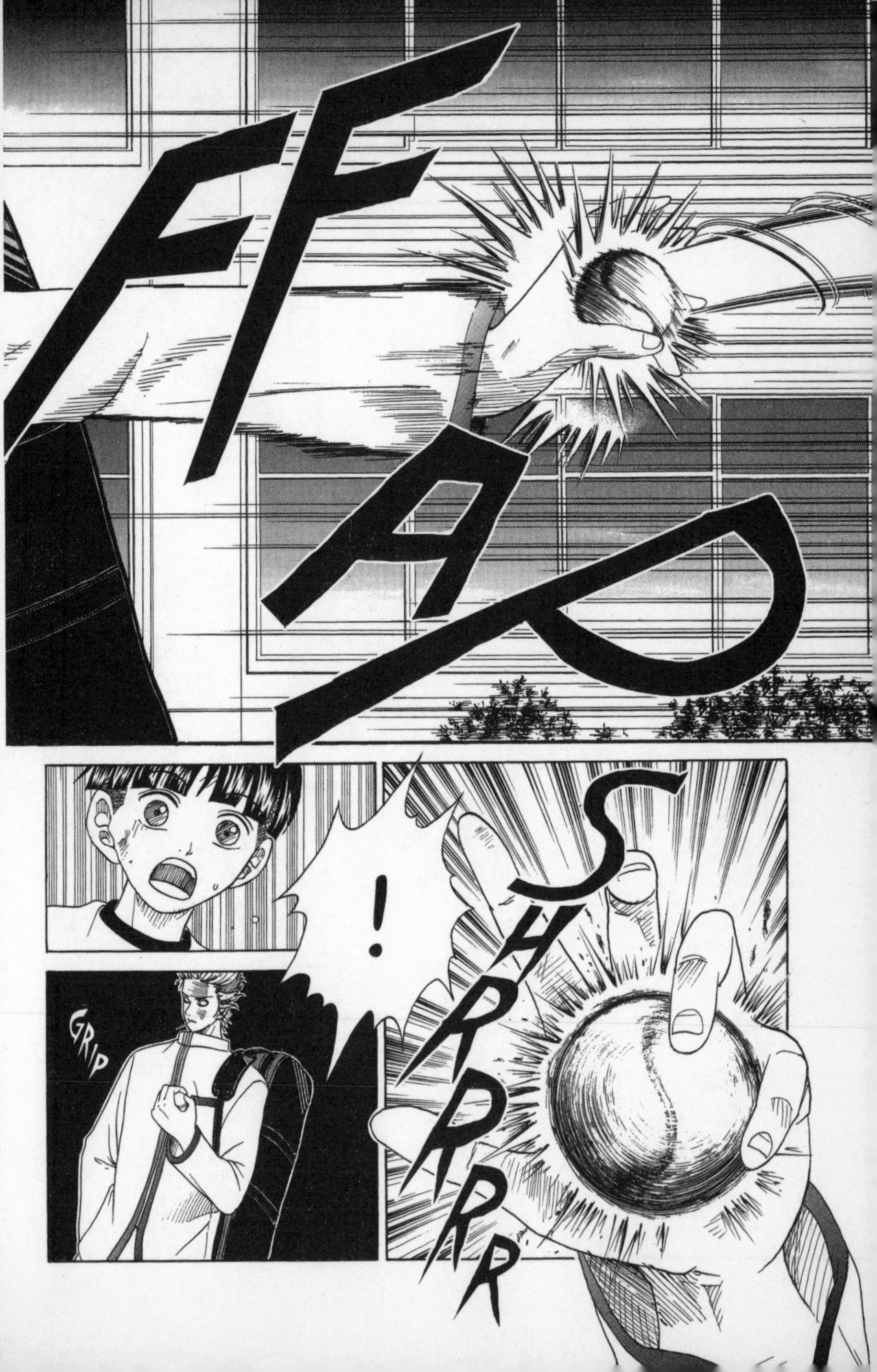
FFAP
SHRRRRR
!
GRIP

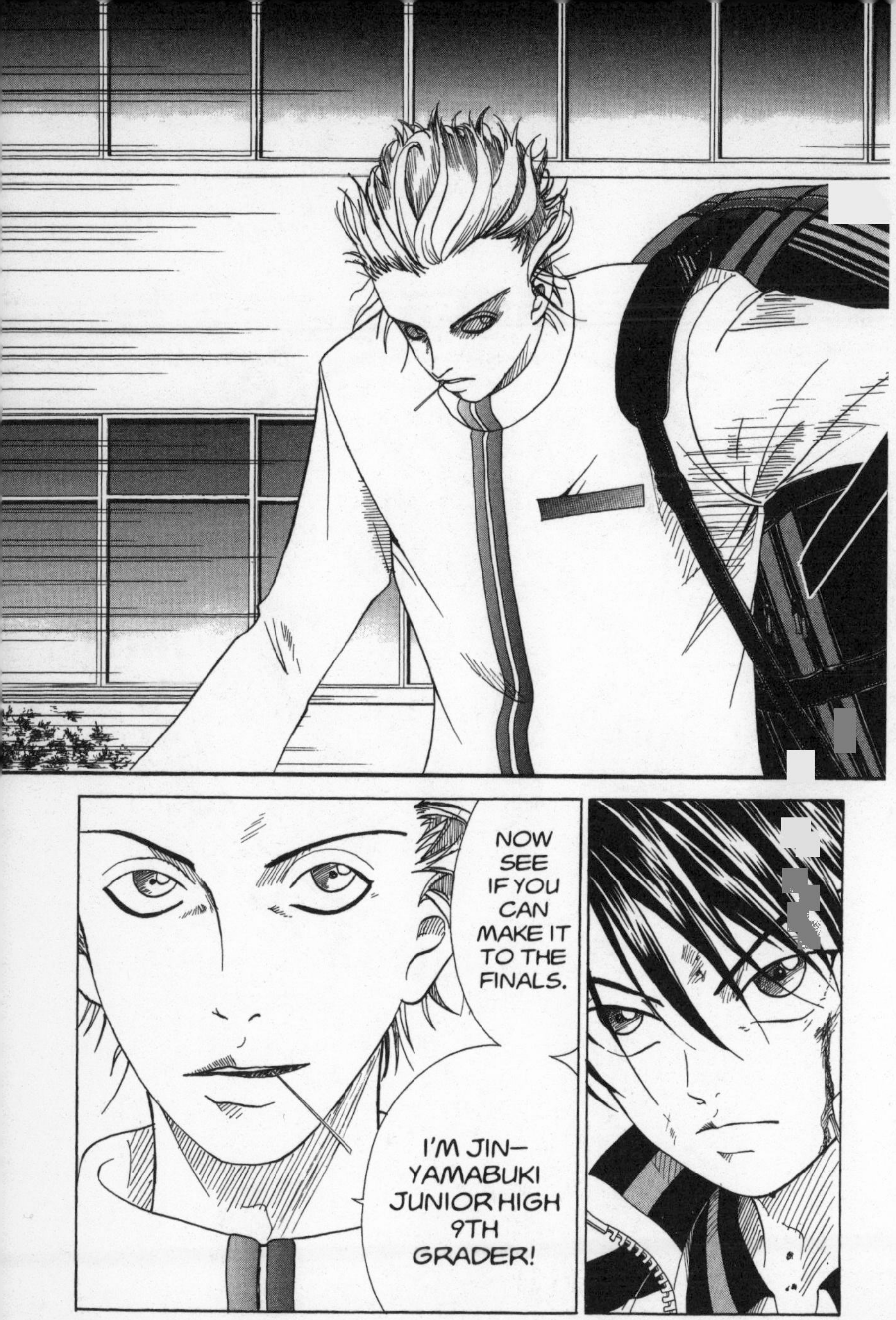
NOW SEE IF YOU CAN MAKE IT TO THE FINALS.
I'M JIN— YAMABUKI JUNIOR HIGH 9TH GRADER!

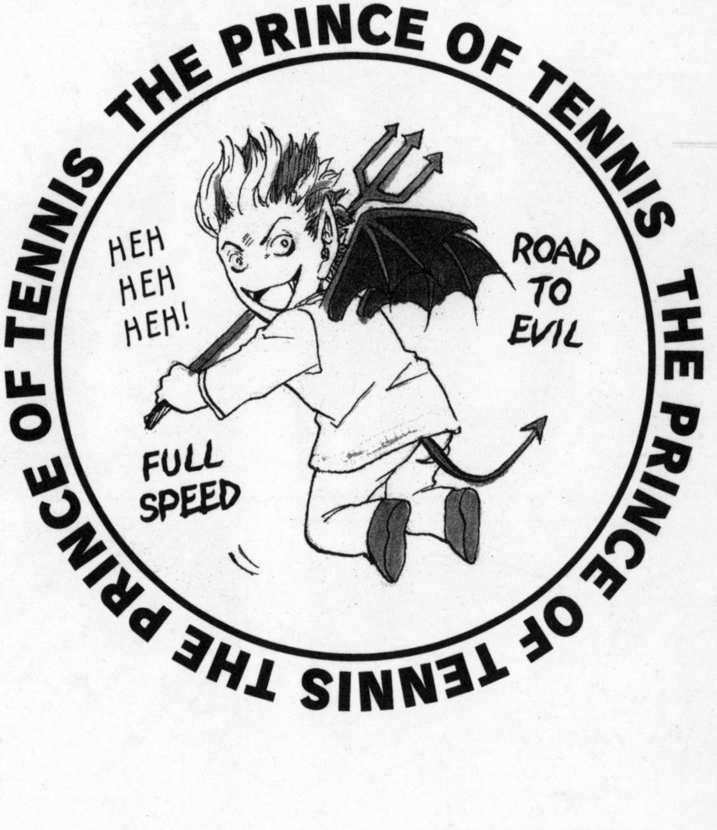
THE PRINCE OF TENNIS THE PRINCE OF TENNIS THE PRINCE OF TENNIS
HEH HEH HEH!
ROAD TO EVIL
FULL SPEED

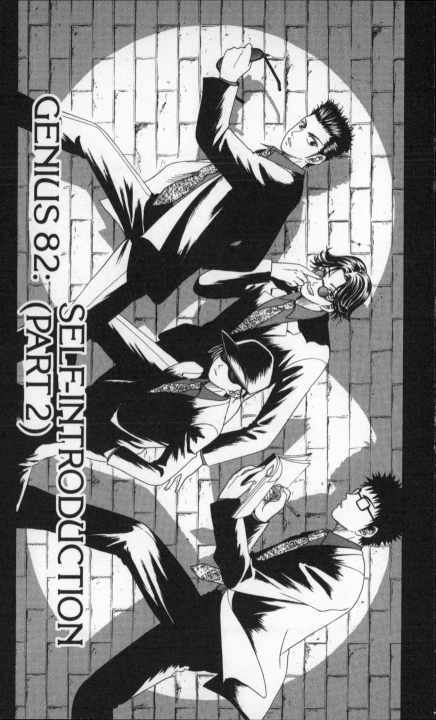

GENIUS 82: SELF-INTRODUCTION (PART 2)

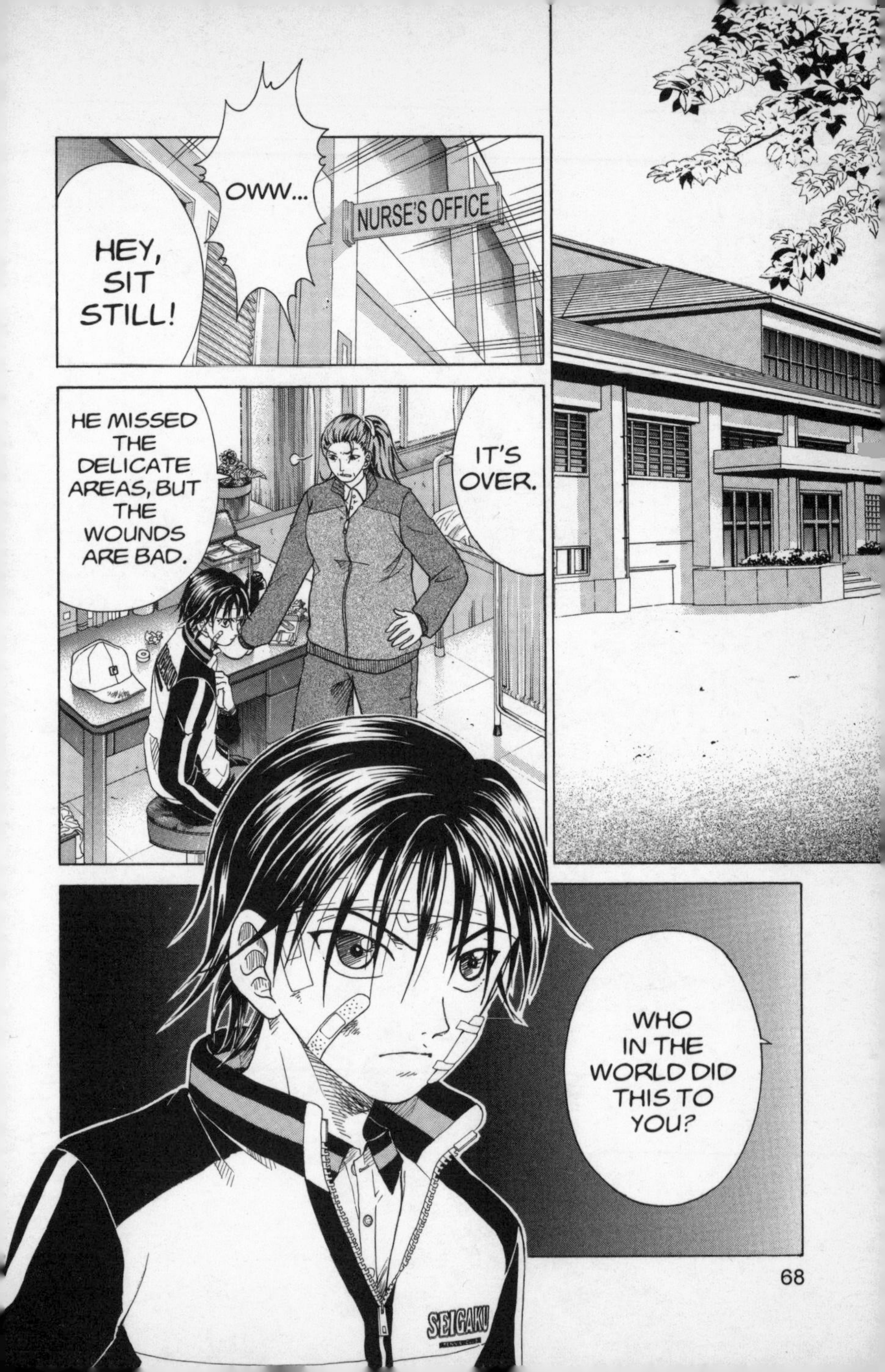
OWW...
NURSE'S OFFICE
HEY, SIT STILL!
IT'S OVER.
HE MISSED THE DELICATE AREAS, BUT THE WOUNDS ARE BAD.
WHO IN THE WORLD DID THIS TO YOU?
SEIGAKU

READ THIS WAY

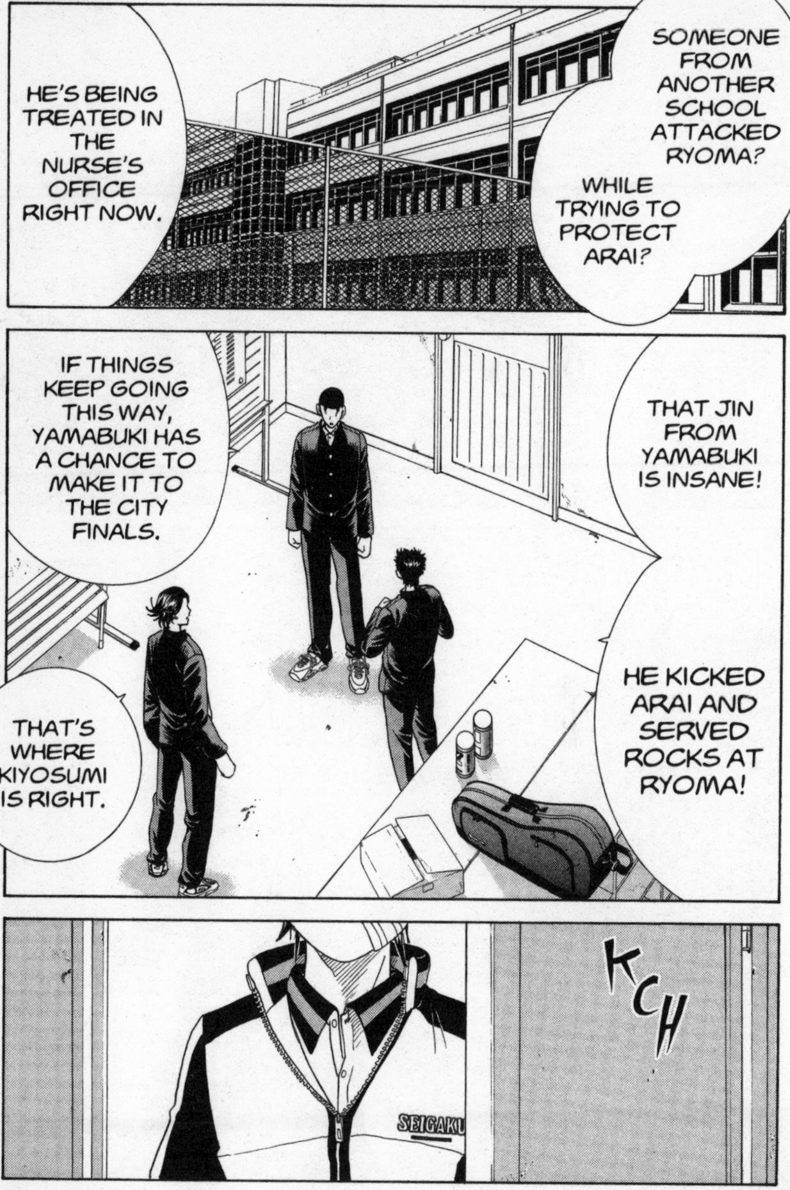
SOMEONE FROM ANOTHER SCHOOL ATTACKED RYOMA?
WHILE TRYING TO PROTECT ARAI?
HE'S BEING TREATED IN THE NURSE'S OFFICE RIGHT NOW.
THAT JIN FROM YAMABUKI IS INSANE!
HE KICKED ARAI AND SERVED ROCKS AT RYOMA!
IF THINGS KEEP GOING THIS WAY, YAMABUKI HAS A CHANCE TO MAKE IT TO THE CITY FINALS.
THAT'S WHERE KIYOSUMI IS RIGHT.
KCH
SEIGAKU

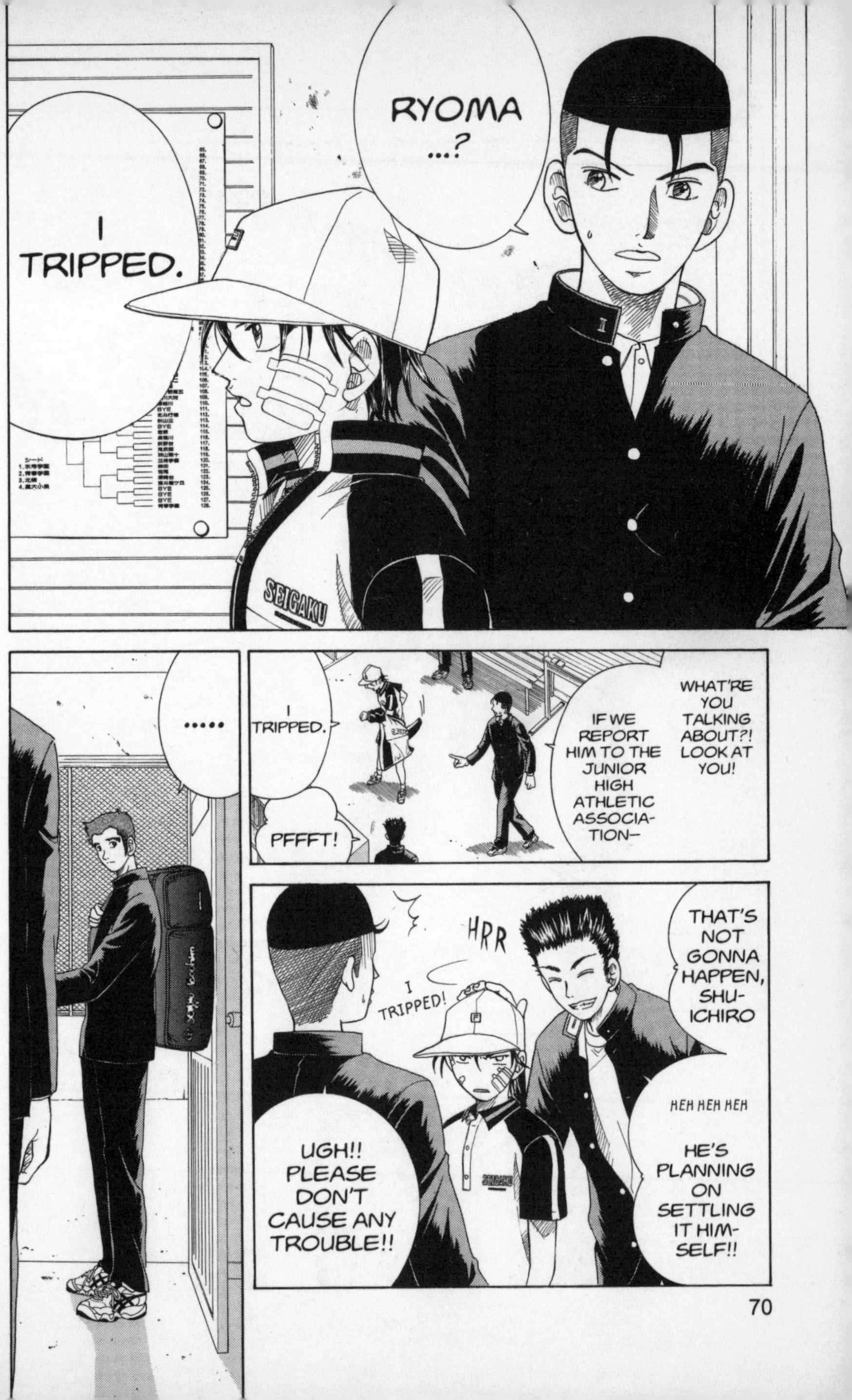
RYOMA ...?
I TRIPPED.
SEIGAKU
WHAT'RE YOU TALKING ABOUT?! LOOK AT YOU!
IF WE REPORT HIM TO THE JUNIOR HIGH ATHLETIC ASSOCIA-TION–
I TRIPPED.
PFFFT!
THAT'S NOT GONNA HAPPEN, SHU-ICHIRO
HEH HEH HEH
HE'S PLANNING ON SETTLING IT HIM-SELF!!
HRR
I TRIPPED!
UGH!! PLEASE DON'T CAUSE ANY TROUBLE!!
SEIGAKU
.....

READ THIS WAY

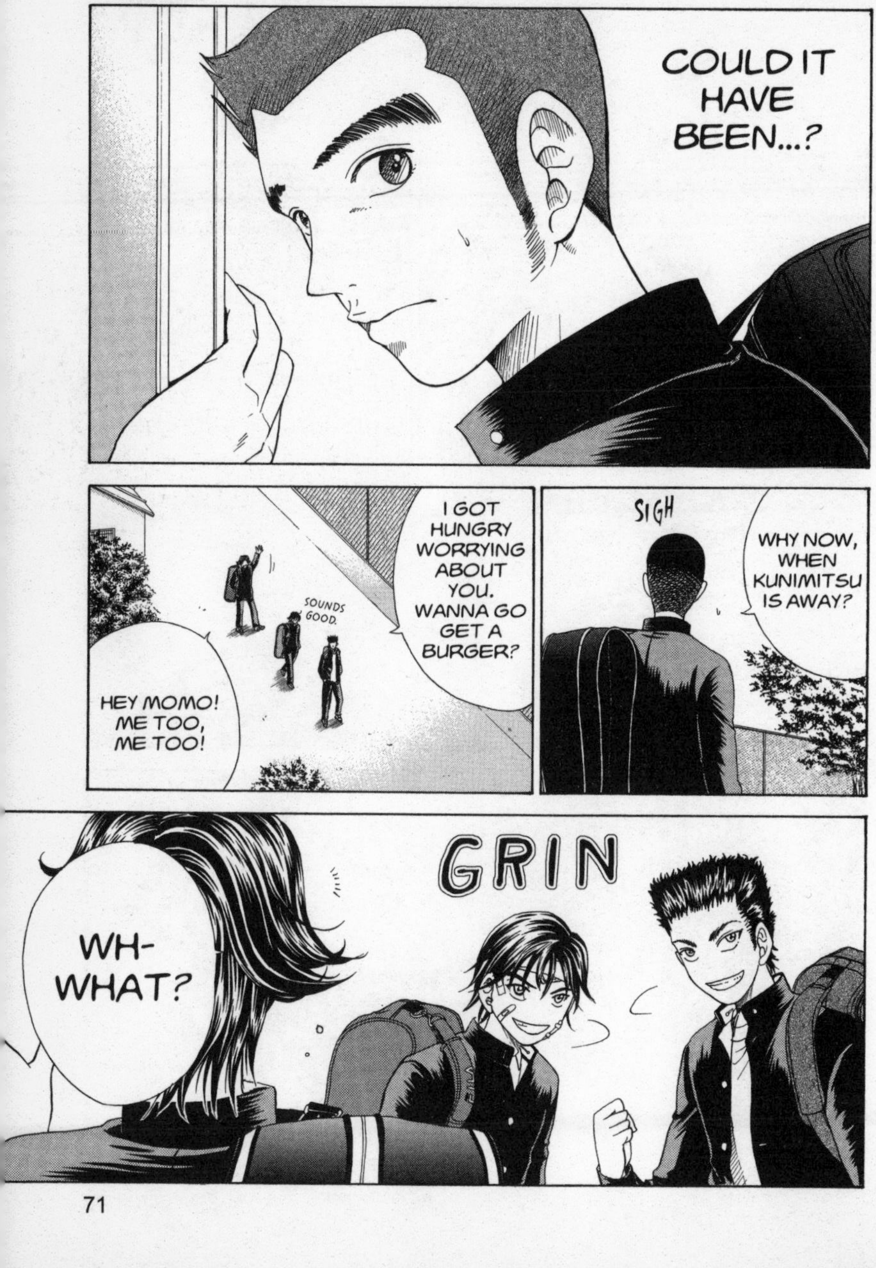
COULD IT HAVE BEEN...?
SIGH
WHY NOW, WHEN KUNIMITSU IS AWAY?
I GOT HUNGRY WORRYING ABOUT YOU. WANNA GO GET A BURGER?
SOUNDS GOOD.
HEY MOMO! ME TOO, ME TOO!
GRIN
WH-WHAT?

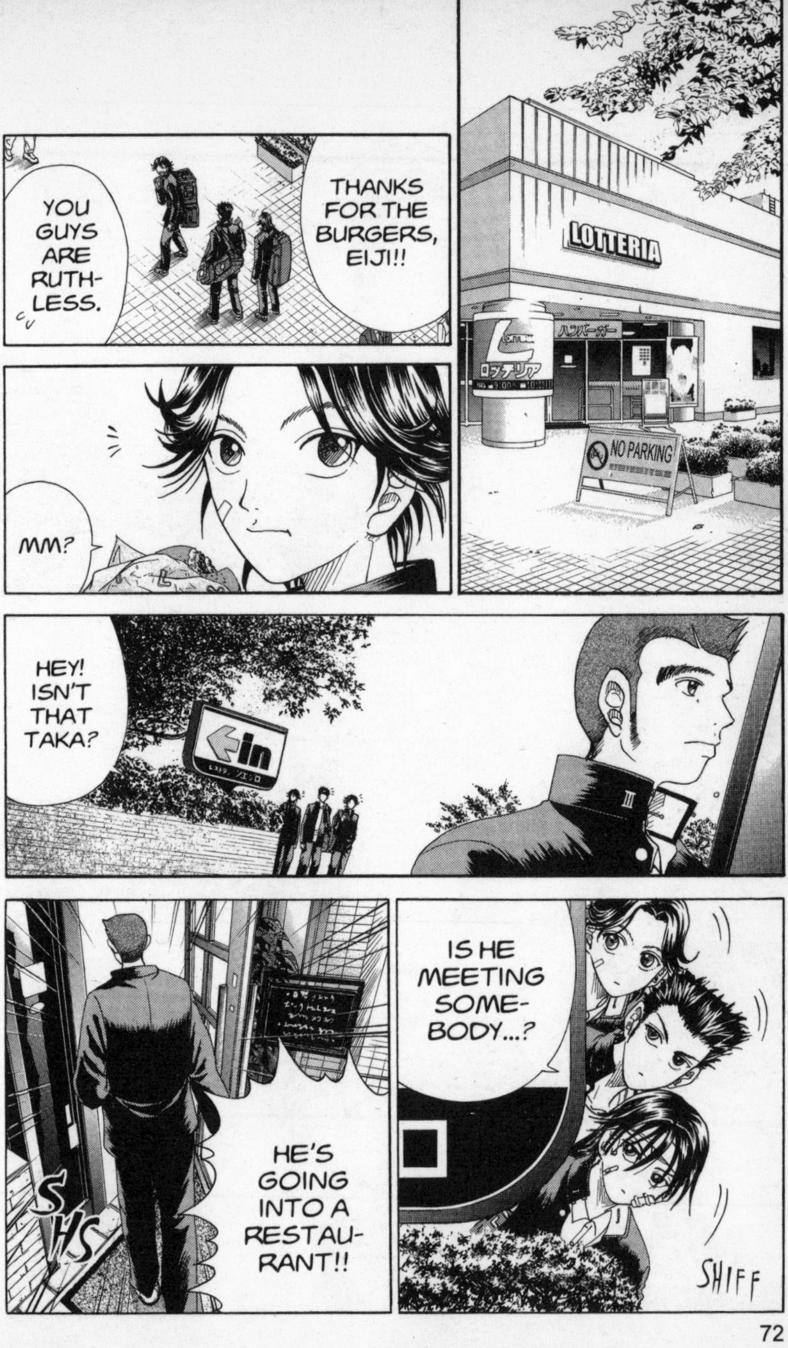
LOTTERIA
NO PARKING
THANKS FOR THE BURGERS, EIJI!!
YOU GUYS ARE RUTHLESS.
MM?
HEY! ISN'T THAT TAKA?
in
IS HE MEETING SOMEBODY...?
SHIFF
HE'S GOING INTO A RESTAURANT!!
SHS

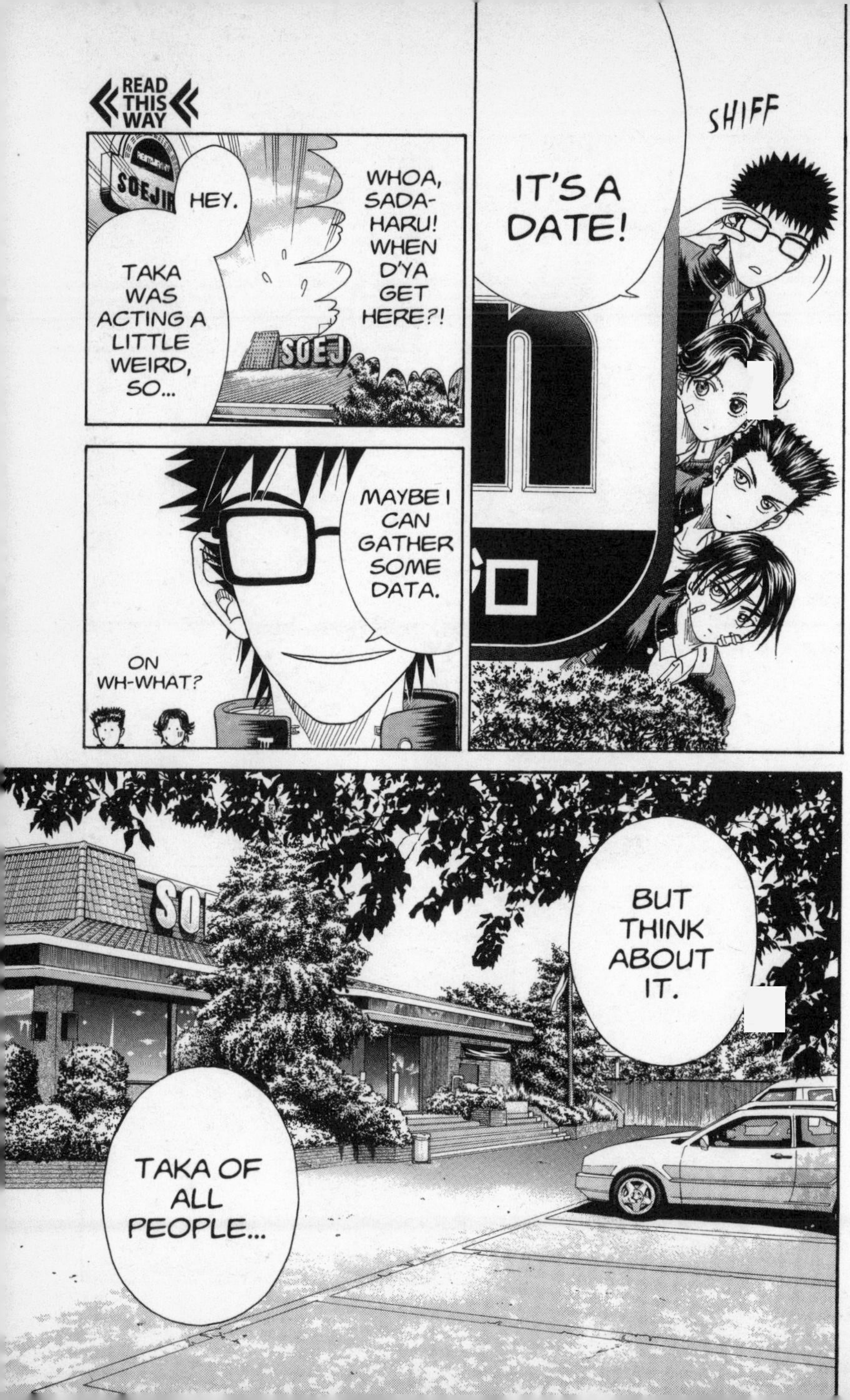
READ THIS WAY
IT'S A DATE!
SHIFF
WHOA, SADAHARU! WHEN D'YA GET HERE?!
HEY.
TAKA WAS ACTING A LITTLE WEIRD, SO...
MAYBE I CAN GATHER SOME DATA.
ON WH-WHAT?
BUT THINK ABOUT IT.
TAKA OF ALL PEOPLE...

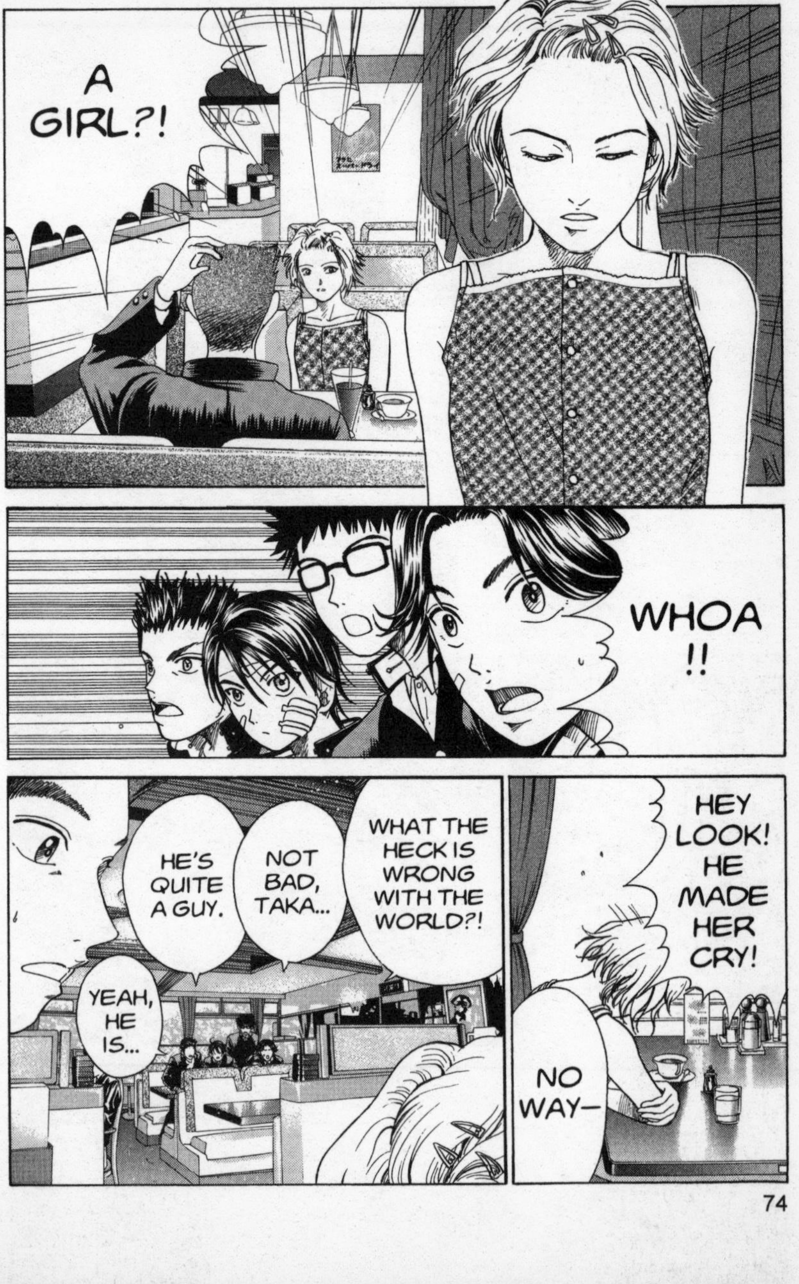
A GIRL?!
WHOA !!
HEY LOOK! HE MADE HER CRY!
NO WAY—
WHAT THE HECK IS WRONG WITH THE WORLD?!
NOT BAD, TAKA...
HE'S QUITE A GUY.
YEAH, HE IS...

READ THIS WAY

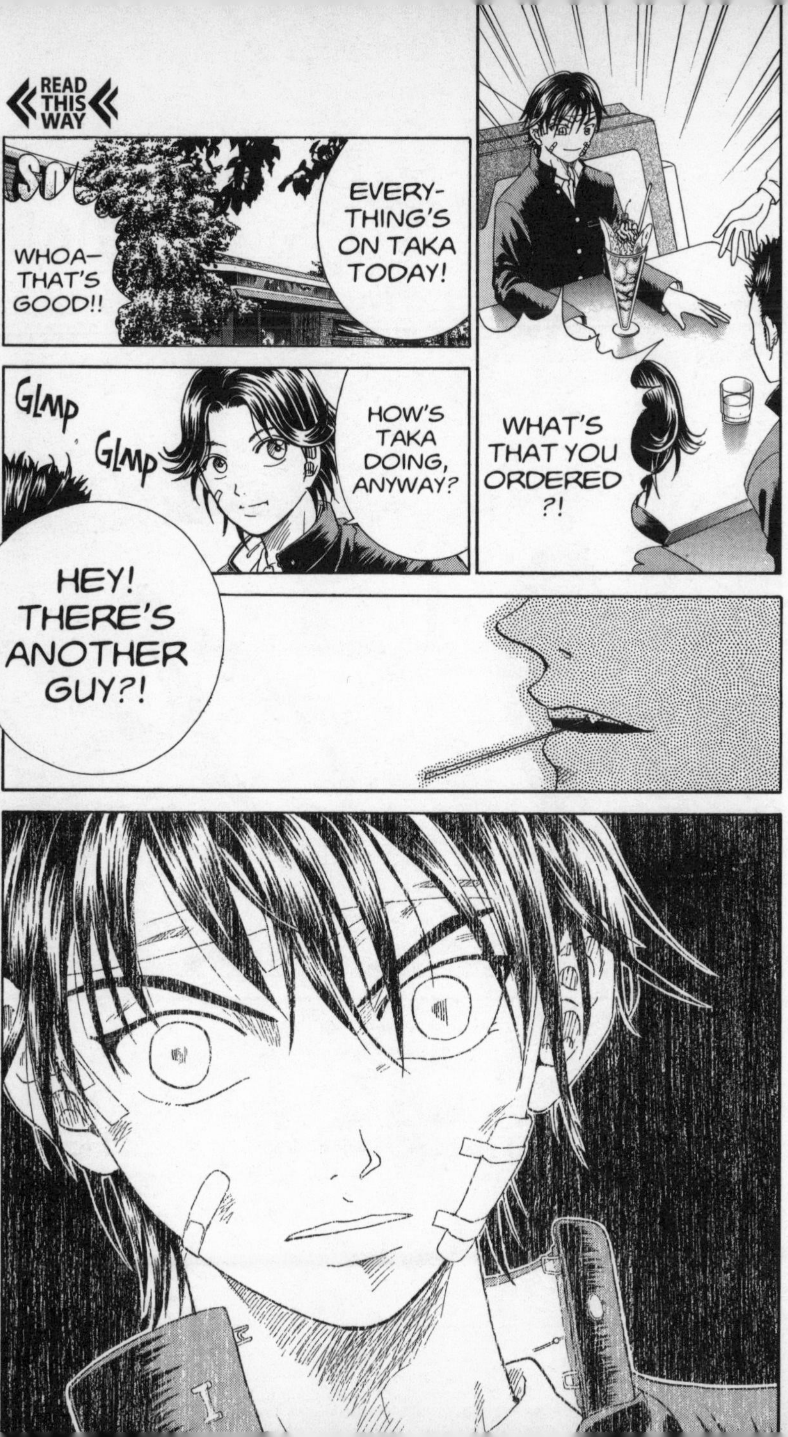

WHAT'S THAT YOU ORDERED ?!
EVERY-THING'S ON TAKA TODAY!
WHOA—THAT'S GOOD!!
HOW'S TAKA DOING, ANYWAY?
GLMP
GLMP
HEY! THERE'S ANOTHER GUY?!

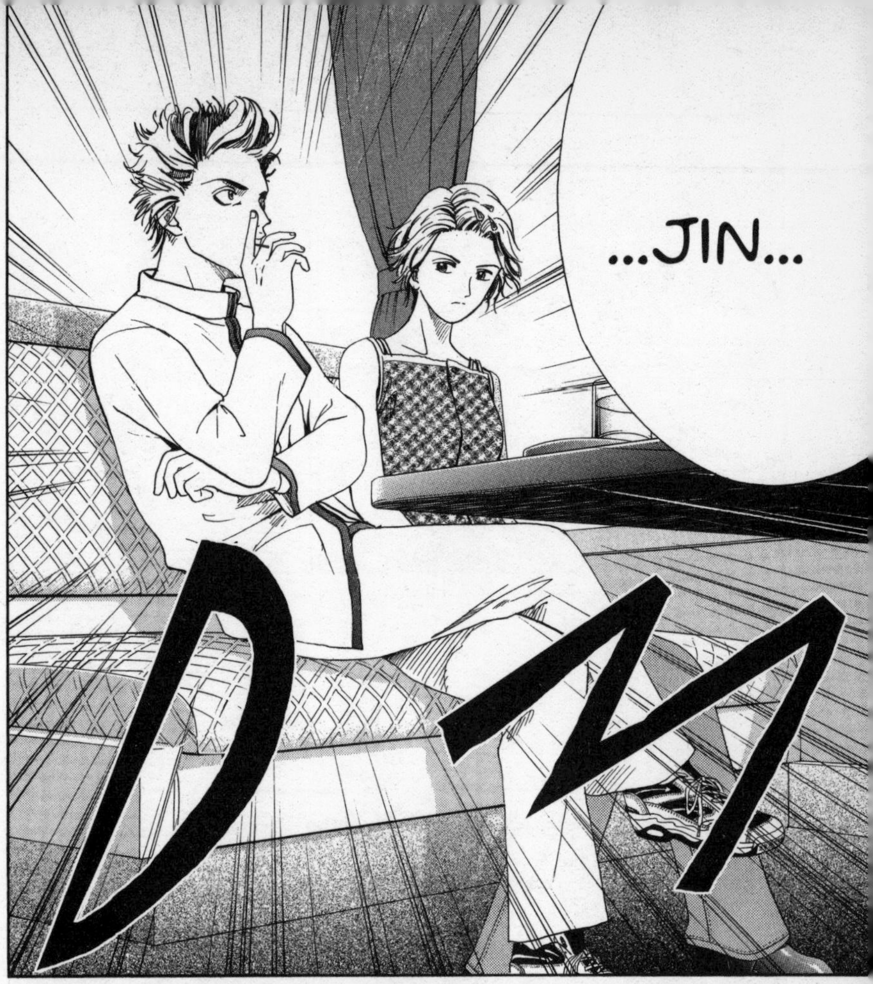
...JIN...

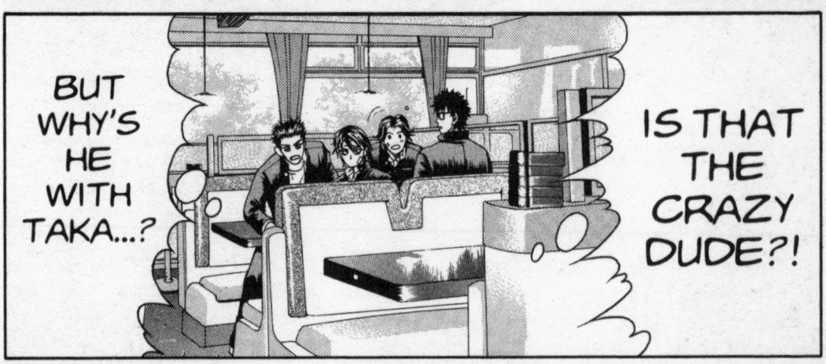
IS THAT THE CRAZY DUDE?!
BUT WHY'S HE WITH TAKA...?

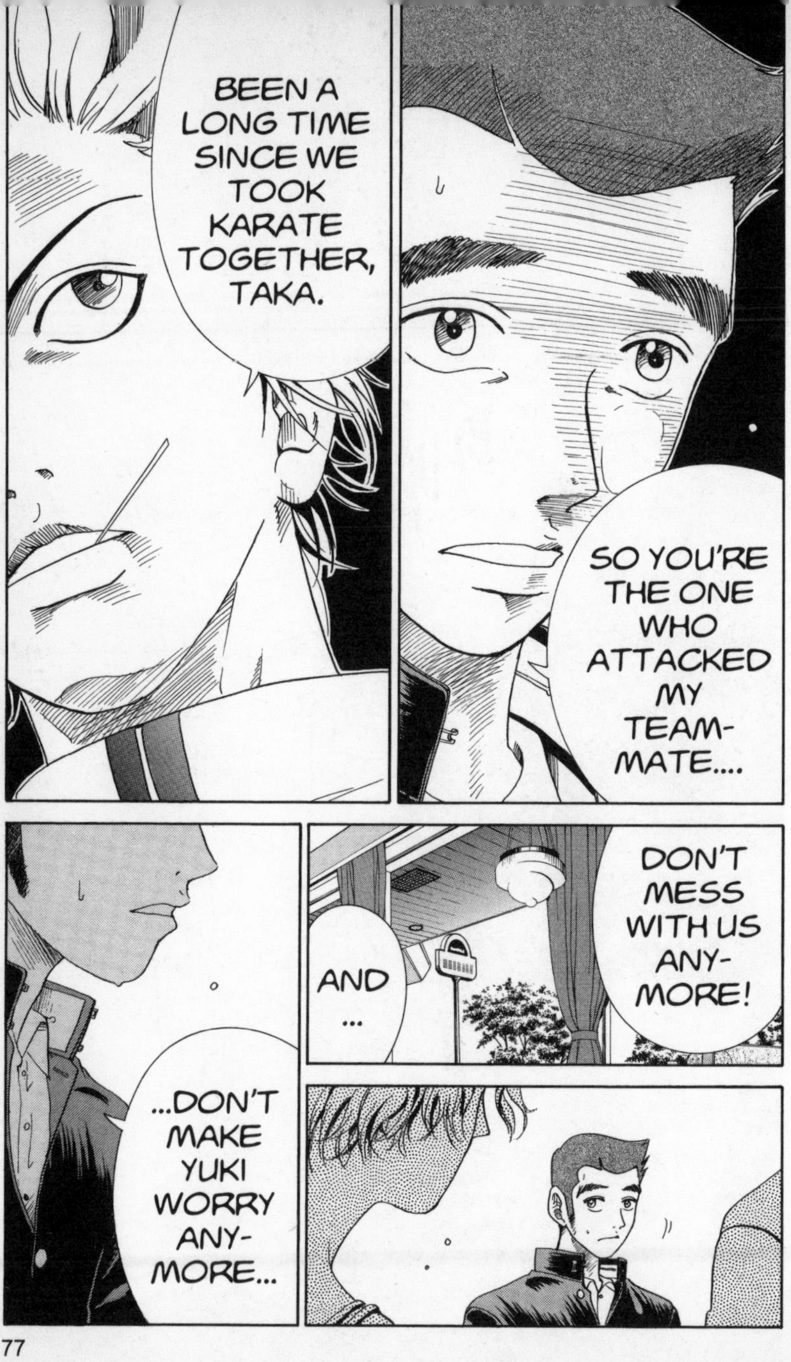
SO YOU'RE THE ONE WHO ATTACKED MY TEAM-MATE....
BEEN A LONG TIME SINCE WE TOOK KARATE TOGETHER, TAKA.
DON'T MESS WITH US ANY-MORE!
AND ...
...DON'T MAKE YUKI WORRY ANY-MORE...

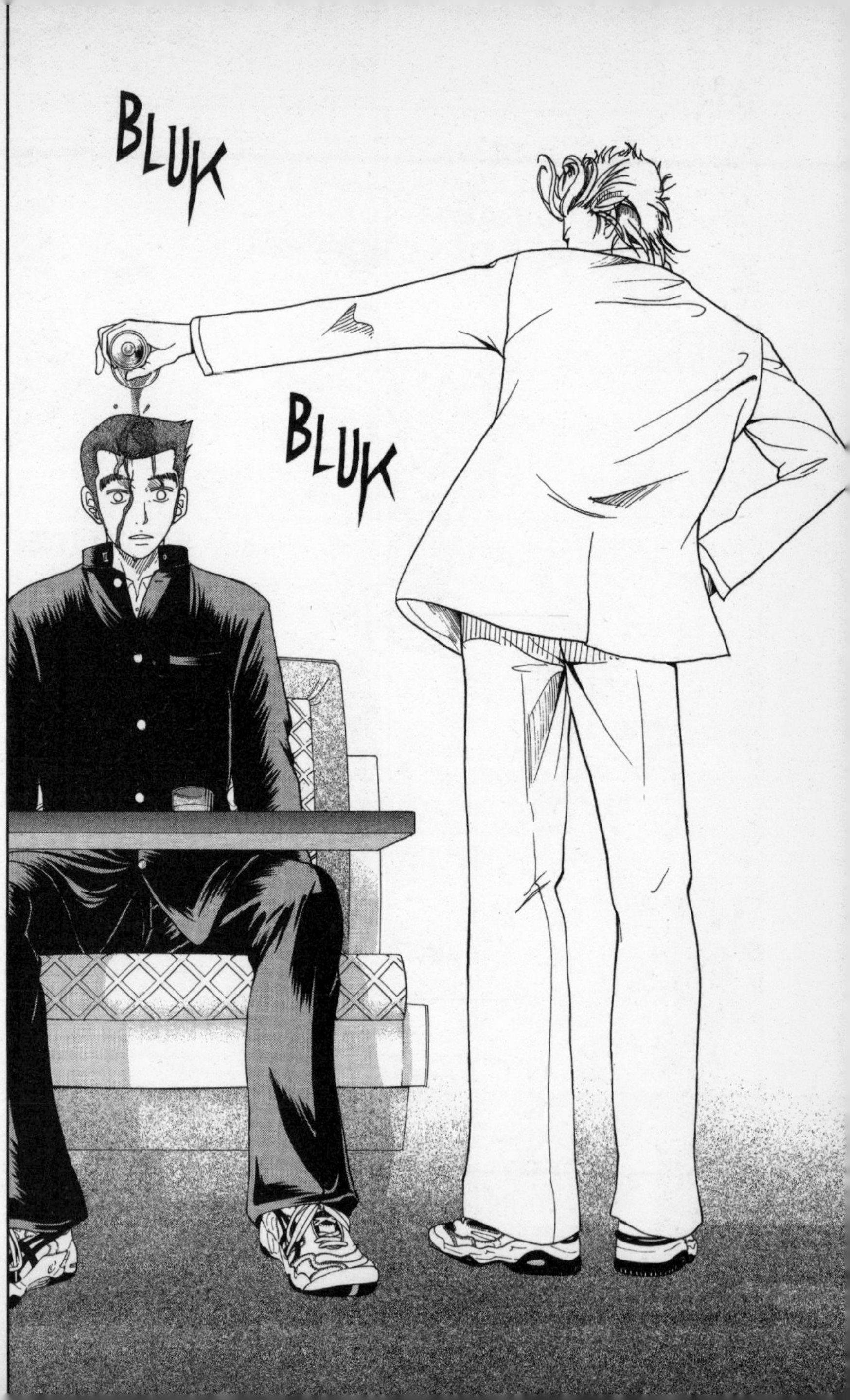
BLUK
BLUK

READ THIS WAY

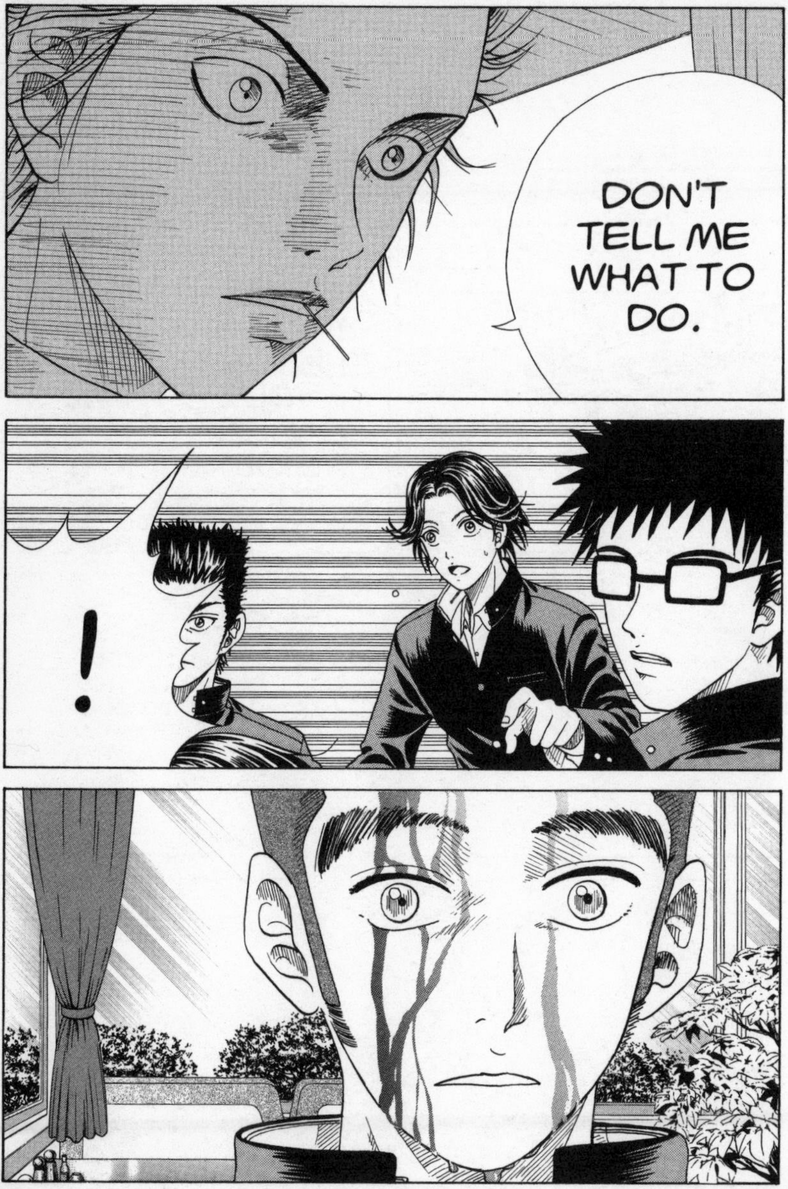
DON'T TELL ME WHAT TO DO.
!

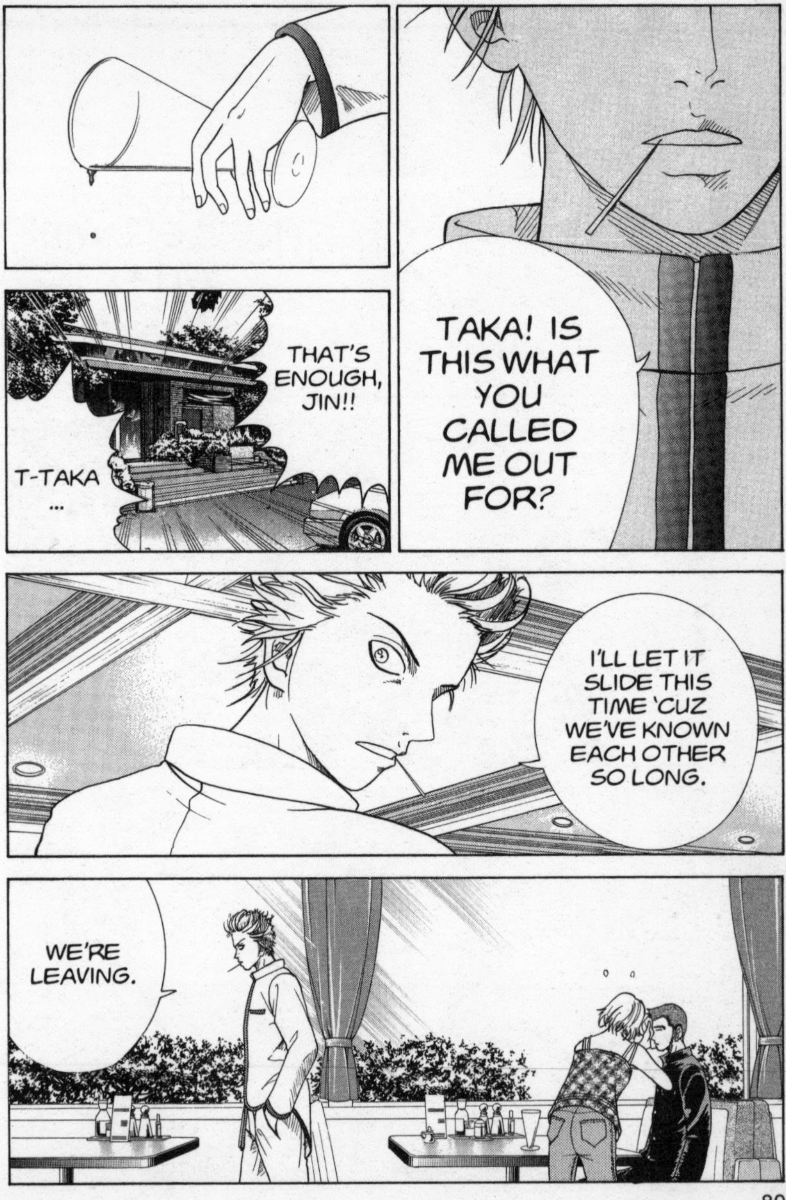
TAKA! IS THIS WHAT YOU CALLED ME OUT FOR?
THAT'S ENOUGH, JIN!!
T-TAKA ...
I'LL LET IT SLIDE THIS TIME 'CUZ WE'VE KNOWN EACH OTHER SO LONG.
WE'RE LEAVING.

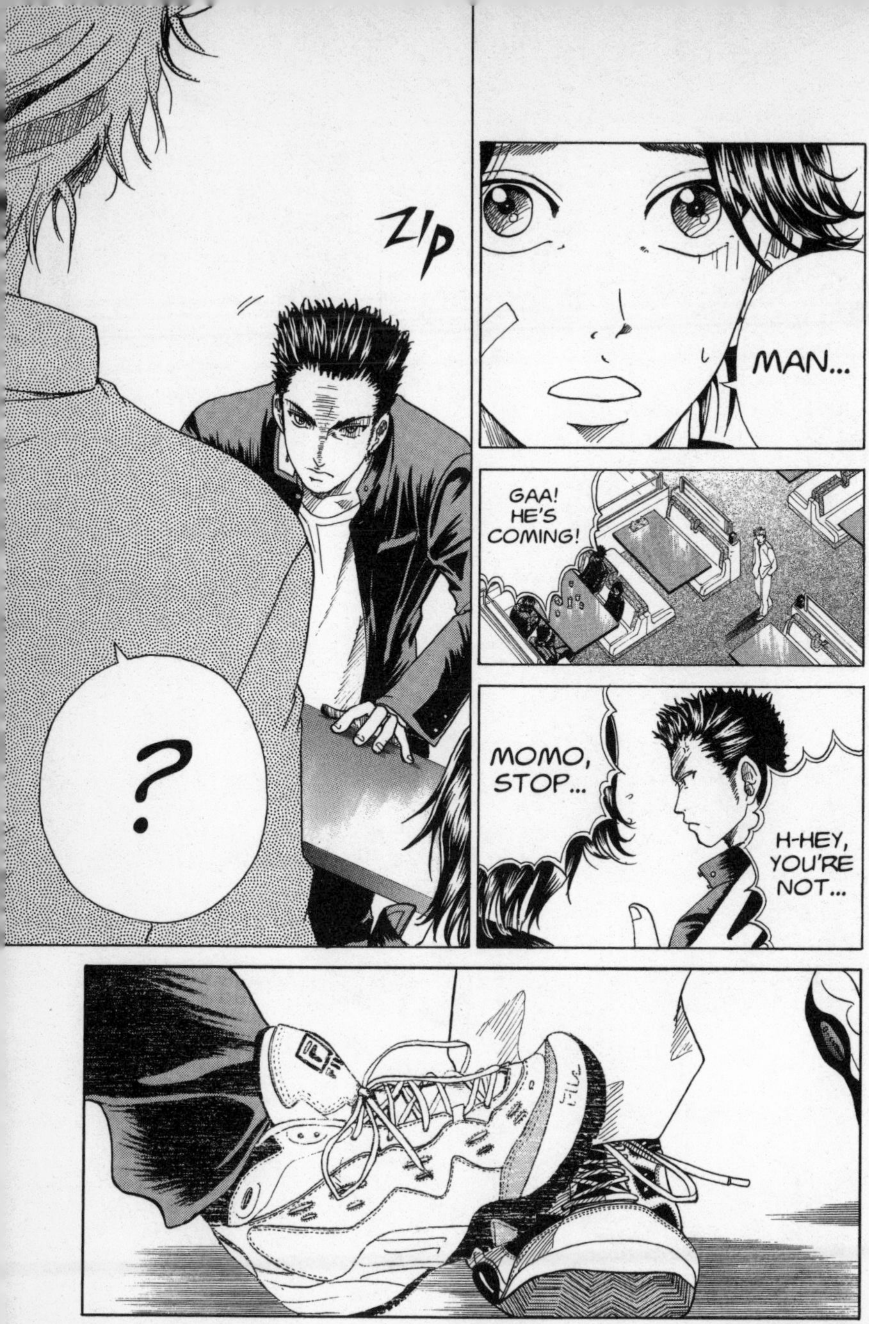
ZIP
MAN...
?
GAA! HE'S COMING!
H-HEY, YOU'RE NOT...
MOMO, STOP...

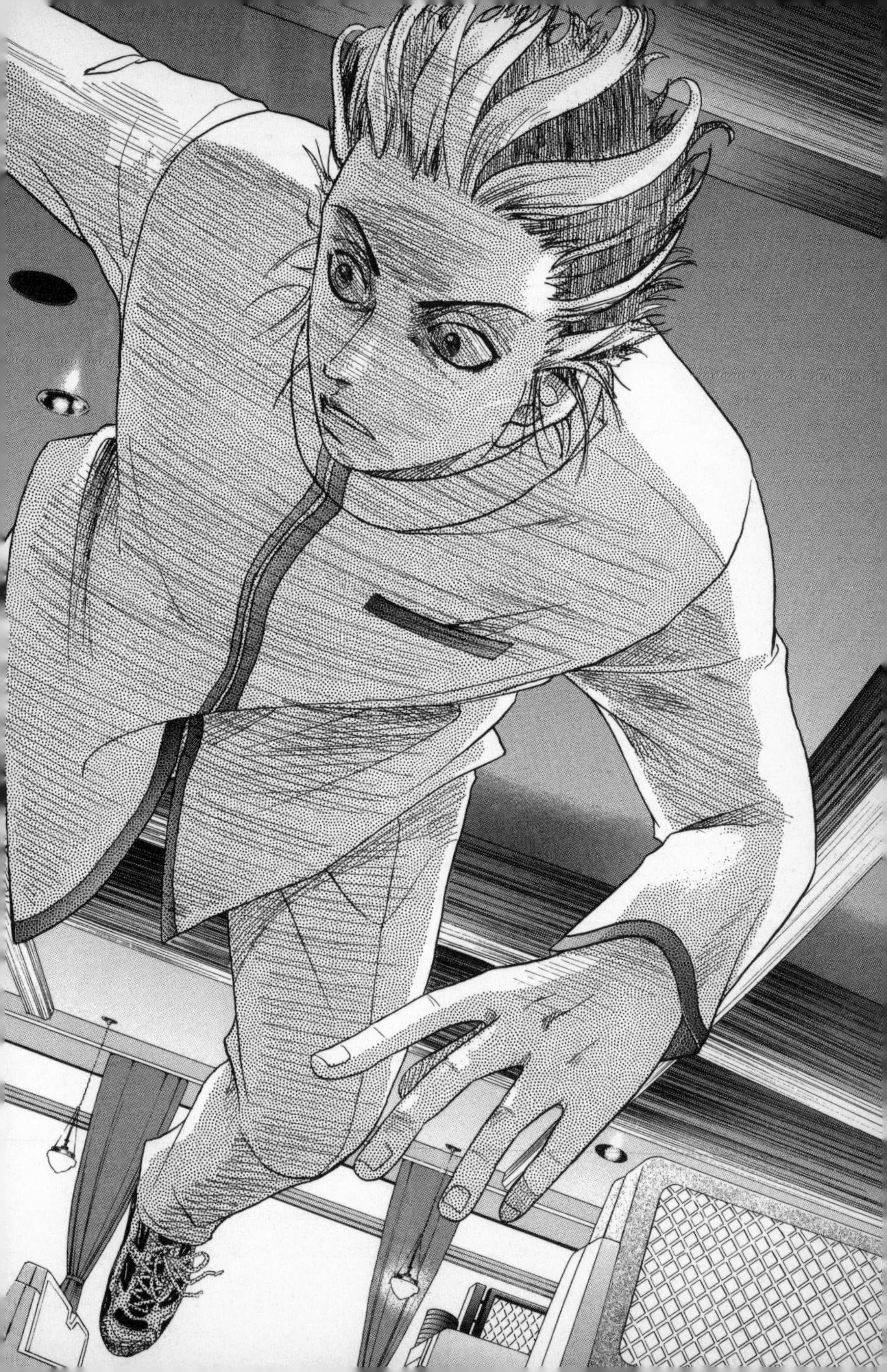

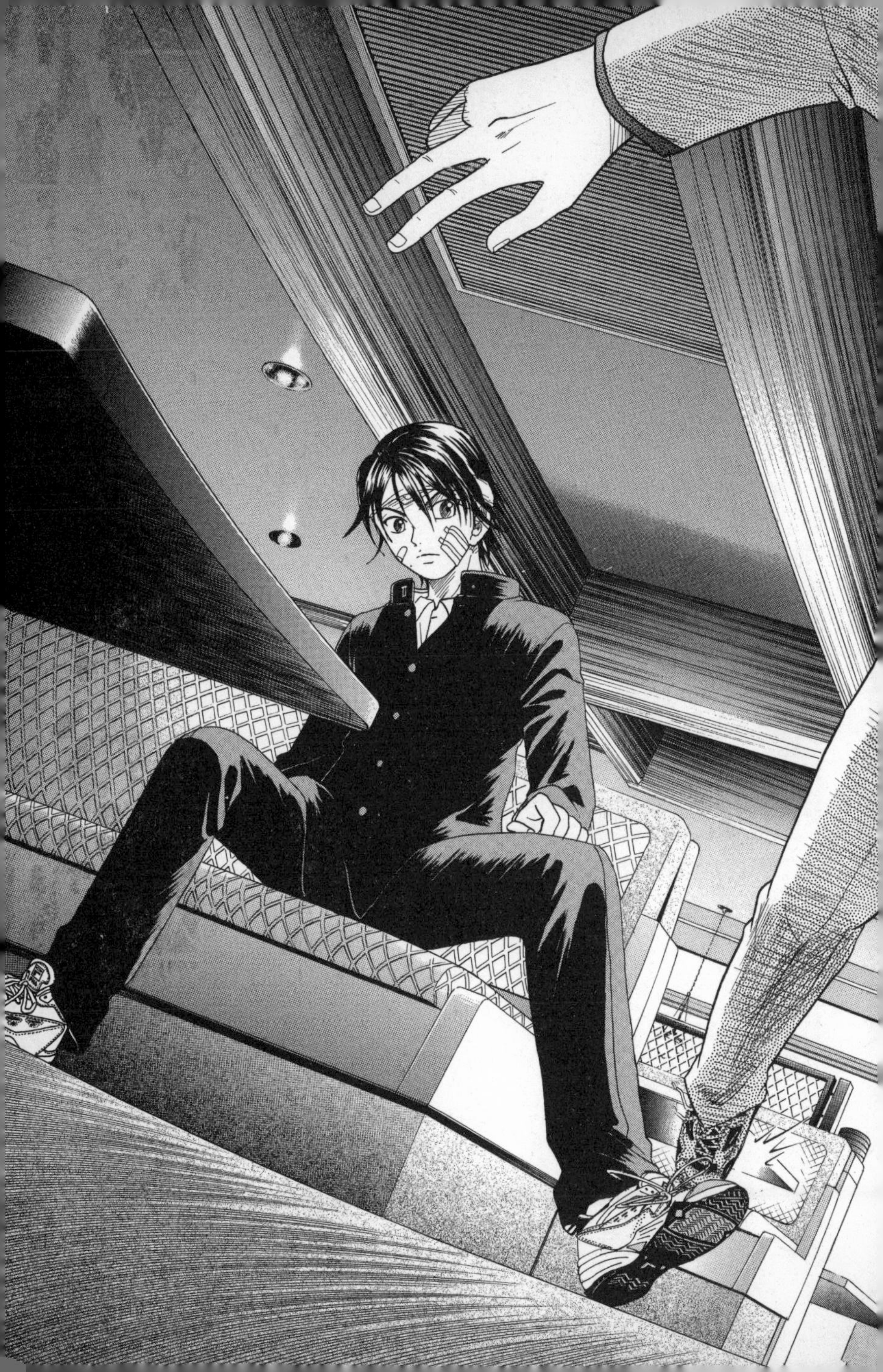

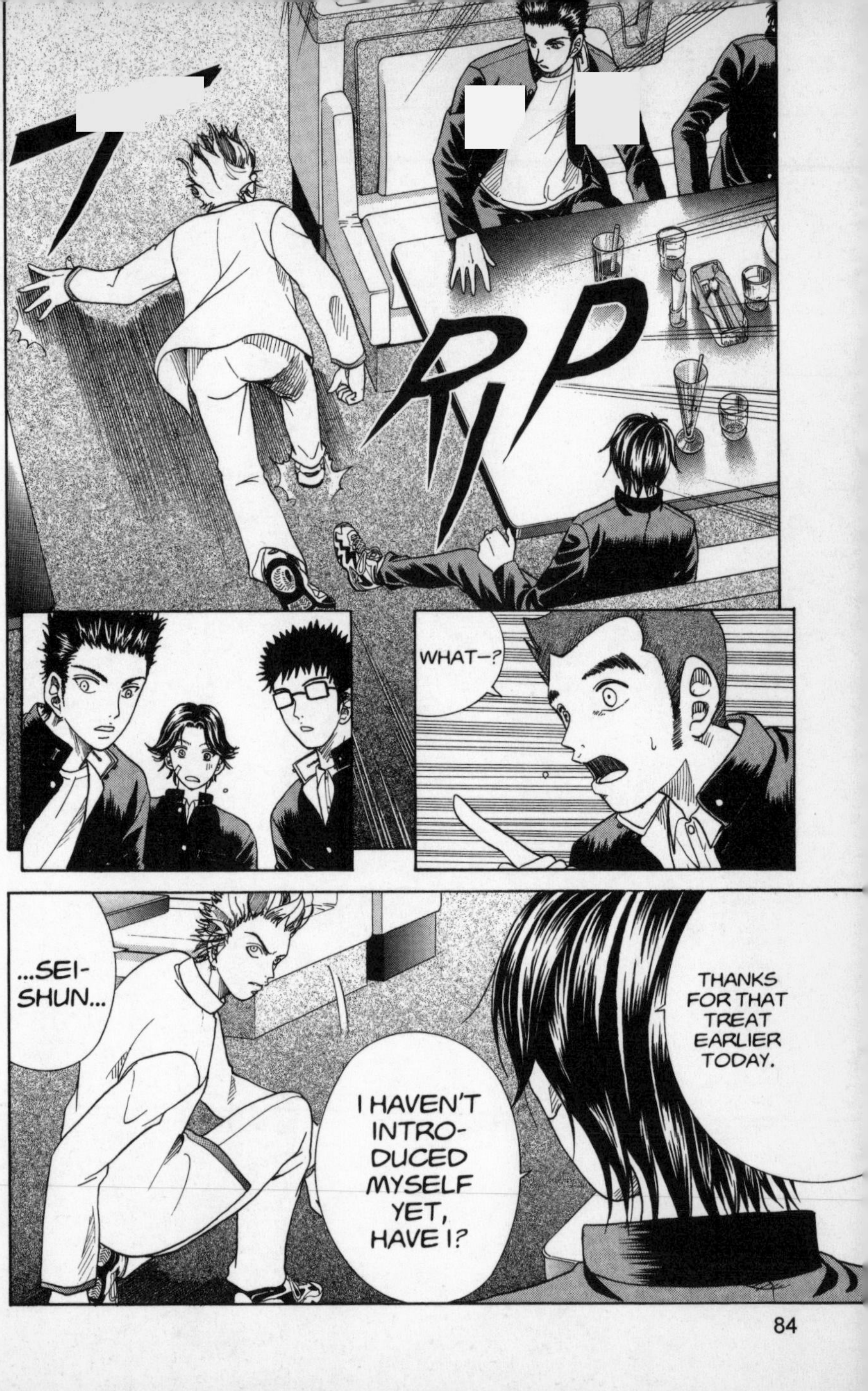
RIP
WHAT—?
THANKS FOR THAT TREAT EARLIER TODAY.
...SEI-SHUN...
I HAVEN'T INTRO-DUCED MYSELF YET, HAVE I?

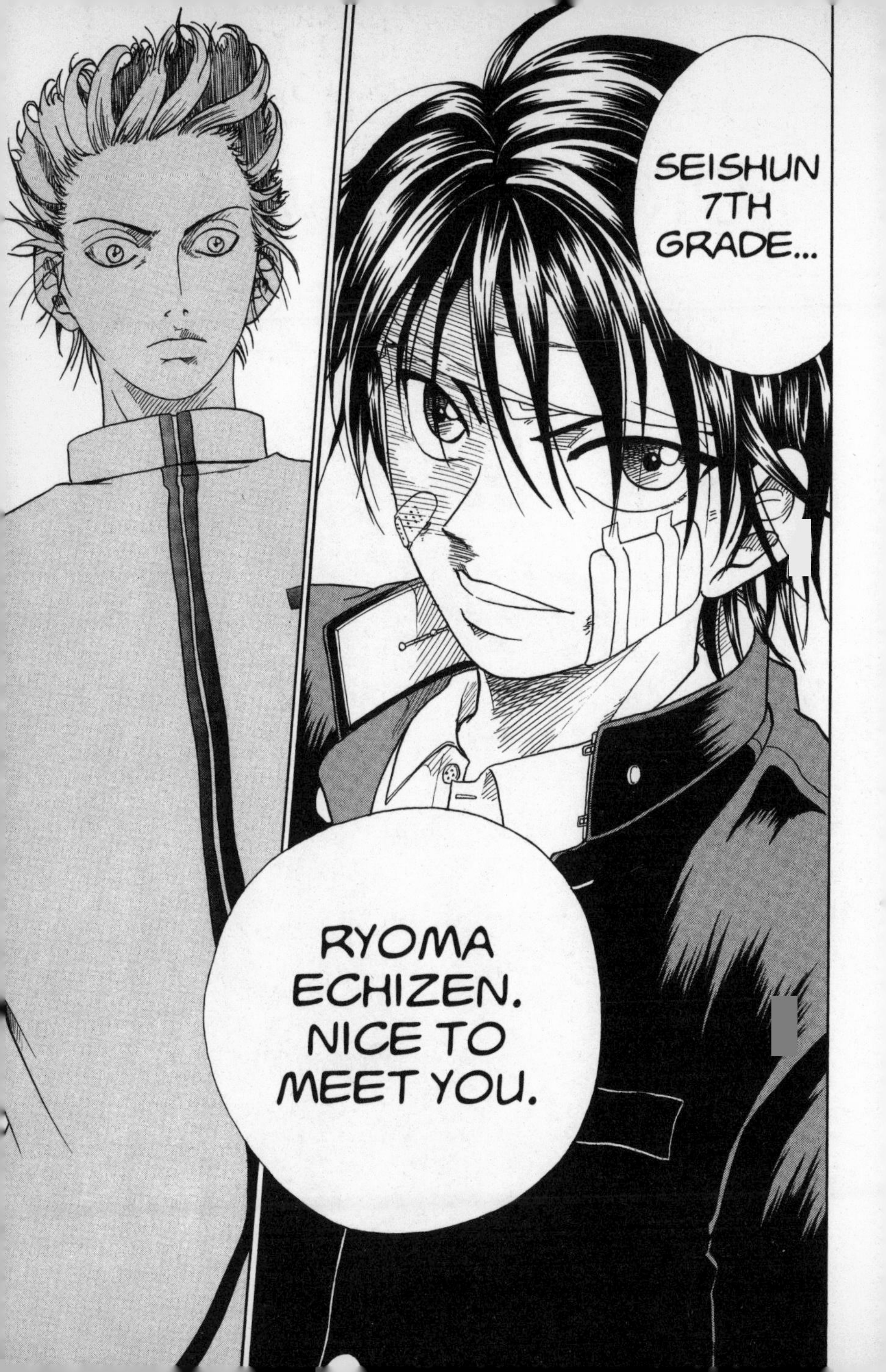
SEISHUN 7TH GRADE...
RYOMA ECHIZEN. NICE TO MEET YOU.

GENIUS 83:
FOR TOMORROW?!!

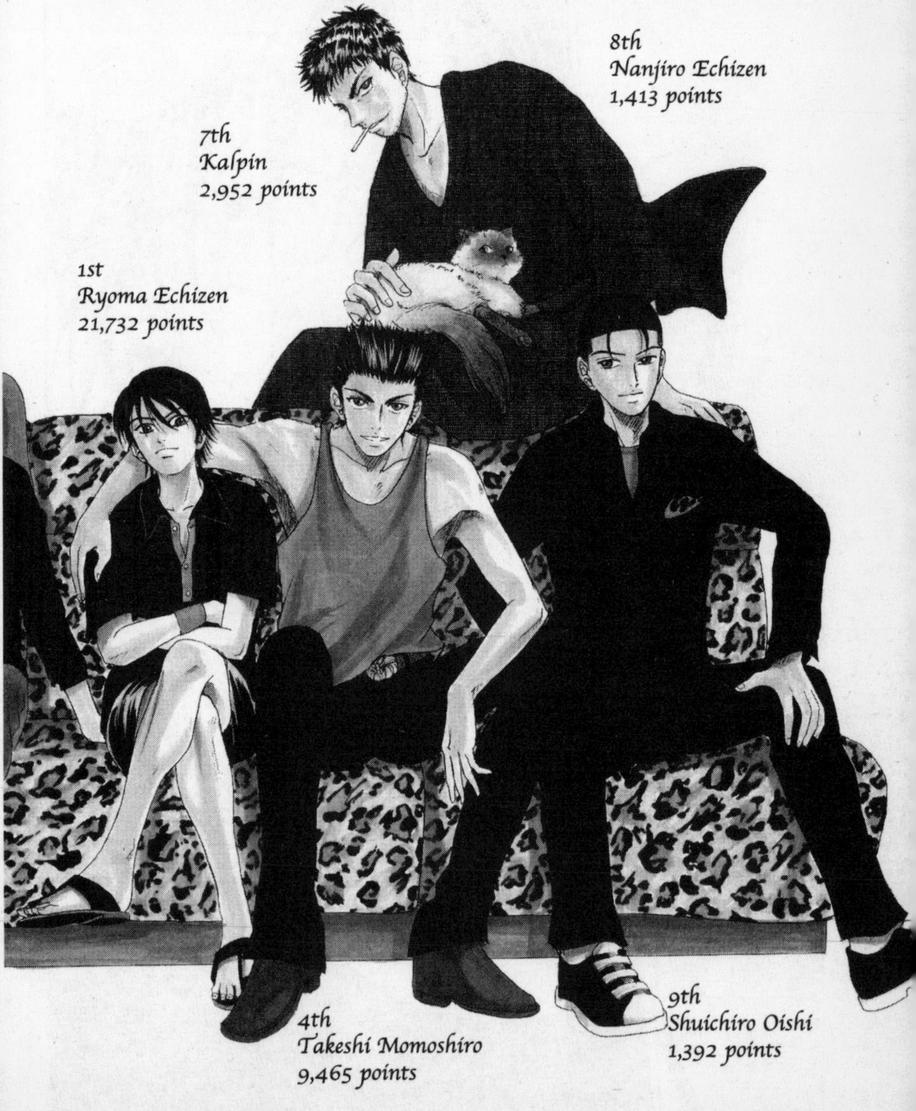
8th
Nanjiro Echizen
1,413 points
7th
Kalpin
2,952 points
1st
Ryoma Echizen
21,732 points
9th
Shuichiro Oishi
1,392 points
4th
Takeshi Momoshiro
9,465 points

1st Character Popularity Poll Results!!

(Note: Results were polled from *Weekly Shonen Jump* in Japan.)

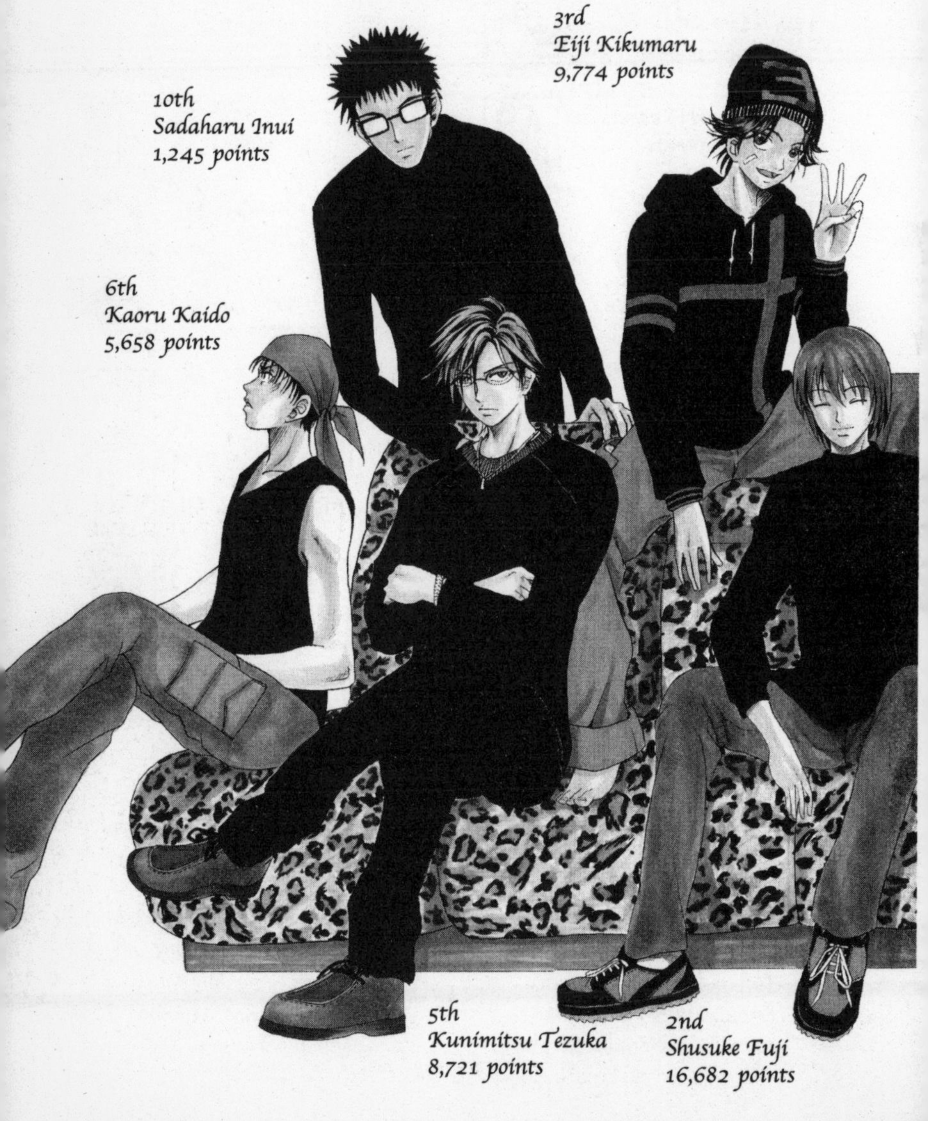
3rd
Eiji Kikumaru
9,774 points
10th
Sadaharu Inui
1,245 points
6th
Kaoru Kaido
5,658 points
2nd
Shusuke Fuji
16,682 points
5th
Kunimitsu Tezuka
8,721 points

11th Akira Kamio, 1,188 points

12th Sakuno Ryuzaki, 1,070 points

13th Shinji Ibu, 882 points

14th Takashi Kawamura, 764 points

15th Hajime Mizuki, 761 points

16th Atsushi Kisarazu, 555 points

17th Yuta Fuji, 512 points

18th Kiyosumi Sengoku, 468 points

19th An Tachibana, 423 points

20th Kachiro Kato, 306 points

21st Kippei Tachibana, 291 points

22nd Akaya Kirihara, 230 points

23rd Takeshi Konomi, 188 points

24th Sumire Ryuzaki, 159 points

Satsoshi Horio, 159 points

26th Shinya Yanagisawa, 142 points

27th Tetsu Ishida, 128 points

Keigo Atobe, 128 points

29th Katsuo Mizuno, 99 points

30th Genichiro Sanada, 89 points

31st Kabaji, 82 points
32nd Yumiko Fuji, 68 points
33rd Izumi, 54 points
34th Arai, 42 points
35th Yoshiro Akazawa, 38 points
Nanako, 38 points
37th Tomoka Osaka, 30 points
38th Sasabe family, 26 points
Kyosuke Uchimura, 26 points
Old man at Mitsumaru Sports, 26 points

41st Kachiro's father, 24 points
Masaya Sakurai, 24 points
Fukawa, 24 points
44th Mamoru Inoue, 10 points
45th Fudomine ex-coach Kichi Kuki, Suzuki of Gyokurin, Yanagi, Hayashi, Masaya Ikeda, Ryoma's mother, Saori Shiba, Koyanagi, etc.

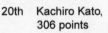

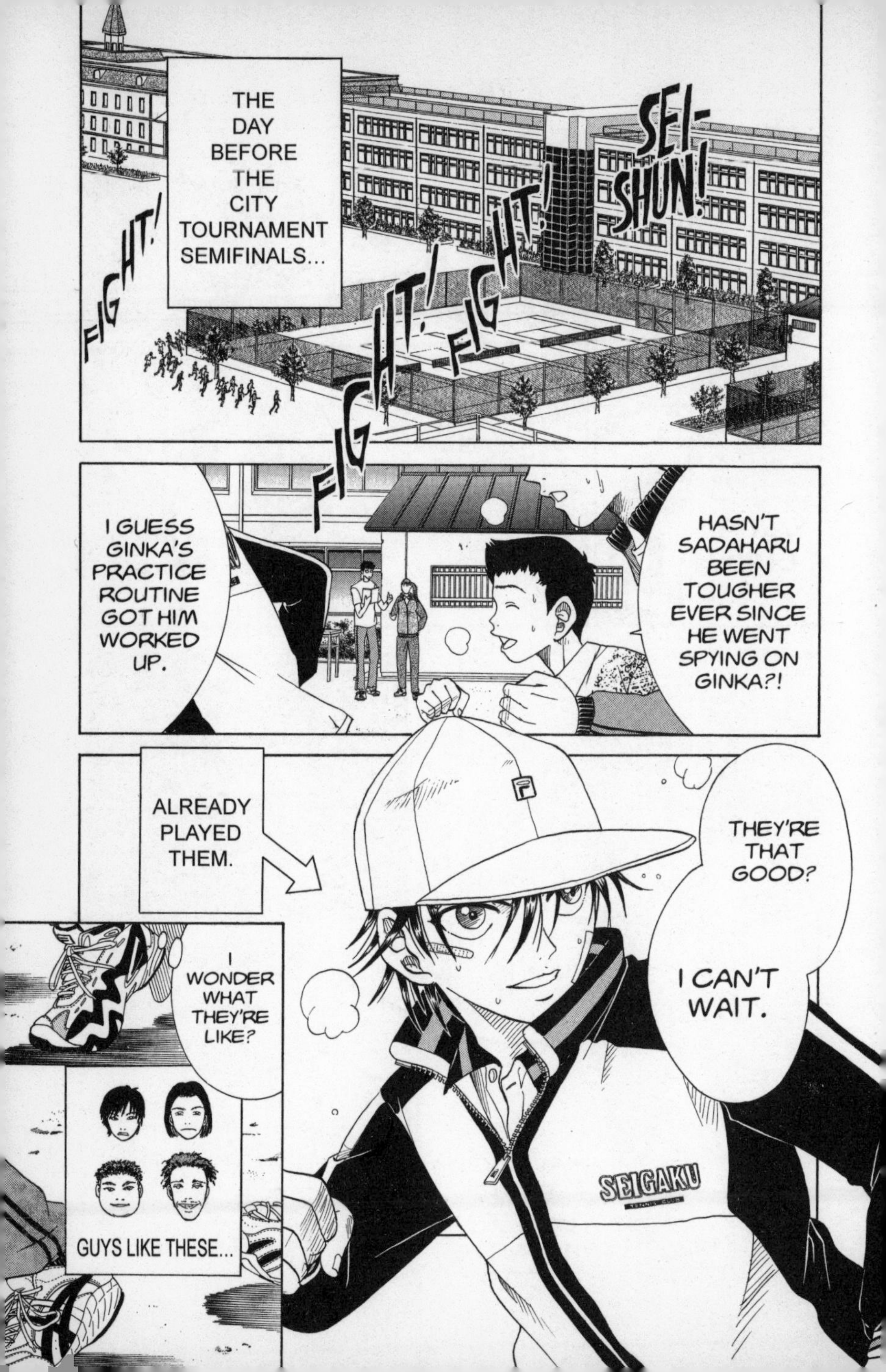
SEI-SHUN!
FIGHT!
FIGHT!
FIGHT!
THE DAY BEFORE THE CITY TOURNAMENT SEMIFINALS...
FIGHT!
HASN'T SADAHARU BEEN TOUGHER EVER SINCE HE WENT SPYING ON GINKA?!
I GUESS GINKA'S PRACTICE ROUTINE GOT HIM WORKED UP.
THEY'RE THAT GOOD?
I CAN'T WAIT.
ALREADY PLAYED THEM.
I WONDER WHAT THEY'RE LIKE?
GUYS LIKE THESE...
SEIGAKU

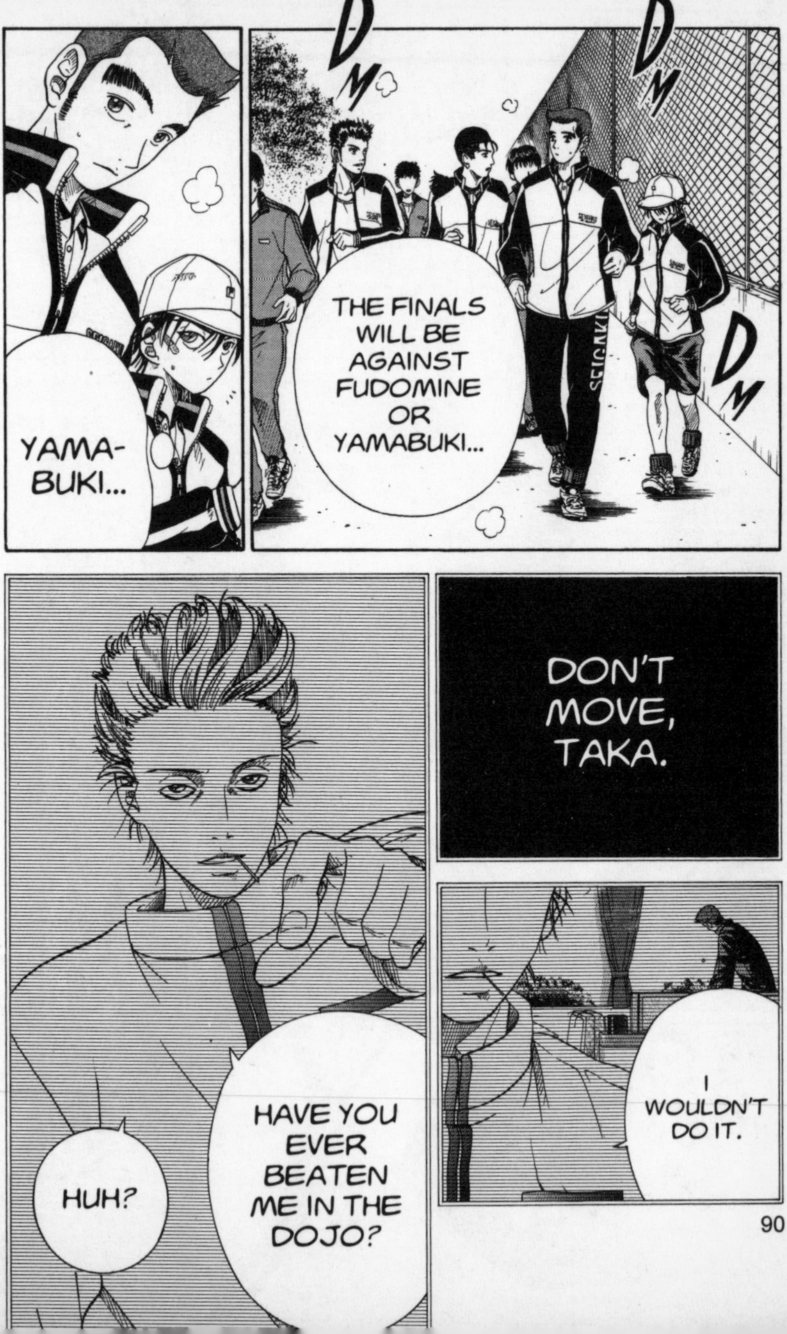

DM
DM
THE FINALS WILL BE AGAINST FUDOMINE OR YAMABUKI...
DM
YAMA-BUKI...
DON'T MOVE, TAKA.
I WOULDN'T DO IT.
HAVE YOU EVER BEATEN ME IN THE DOJO?
HUH?

READ THIS WAY

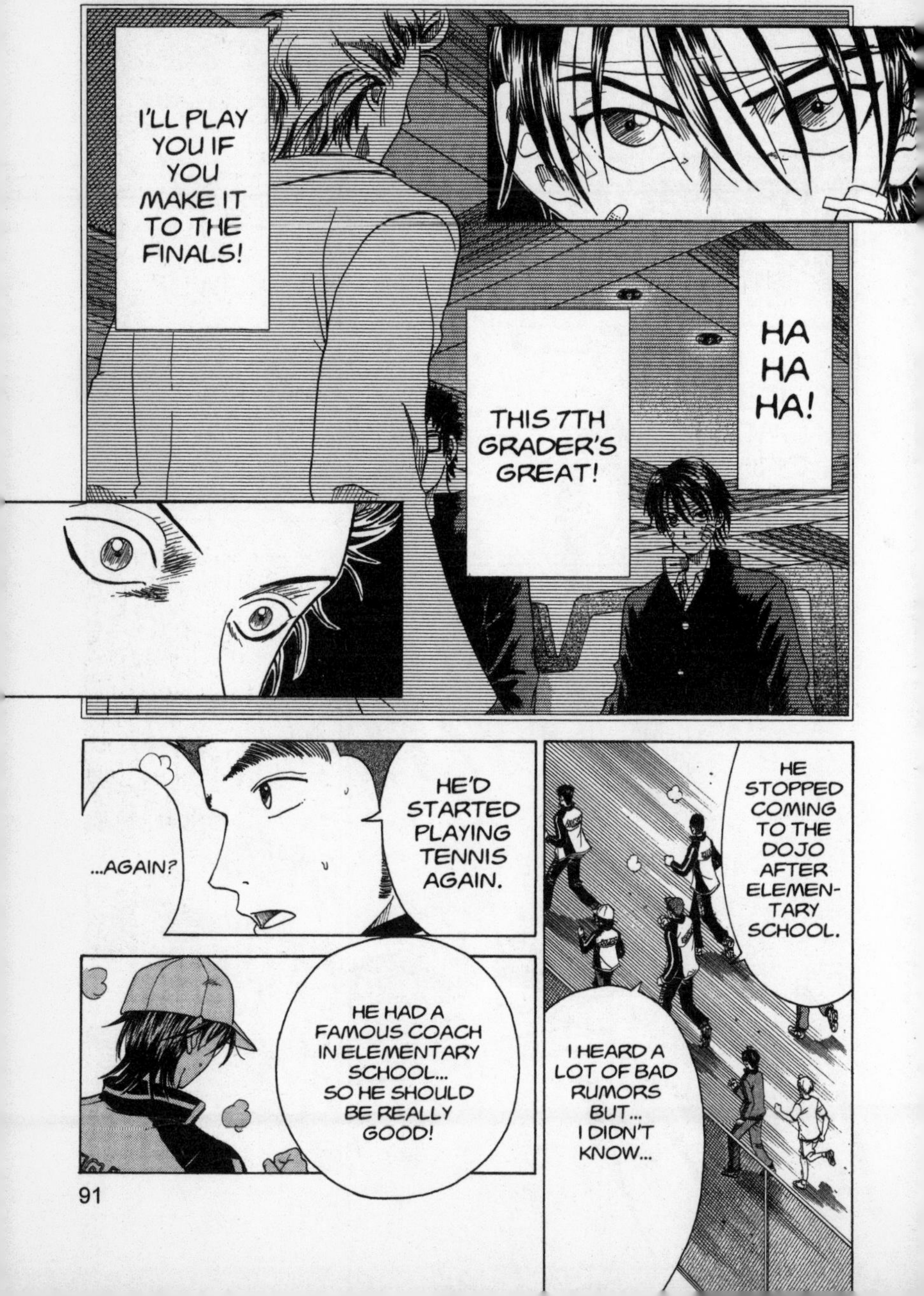
HA HA HA!
THIS 7TH GRADER'S GREAT!
I'LL PLAY YOU IF YOU MAKE IT TO THE FINALS!
HE STOPPED COMING TO THE DOJO AFTER ELEMENTARY SCHOOL.
I HEARD A LOT OF BAD RUMORS BUT... I DIDN'T KNOW...
HE'D STARTED PLAYING TENNIS AGAIN.
...AGAIN?
HE HAD A FAMOUS COACH IN ELEMENTARY SCHOOL... SO HE SHOULD BE REALLY GOOD!

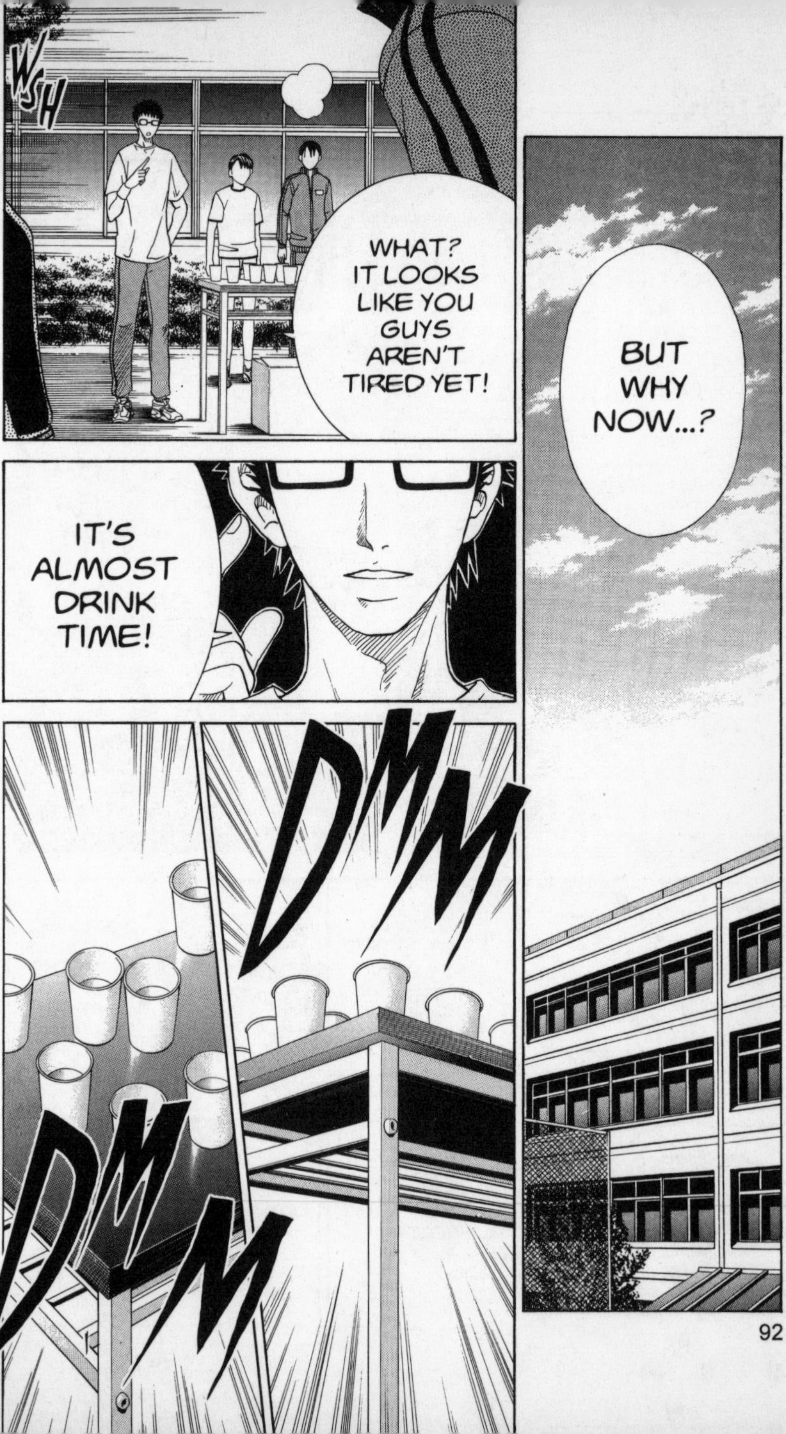
BUT WHY NOW...?
WSH
WHAT? IT LOOKS LIKE YOU GUYS AREN'T TIRED YET!
IT'S ALMOST DRINK TIME!
DMM
DMM

READ THIS WAY

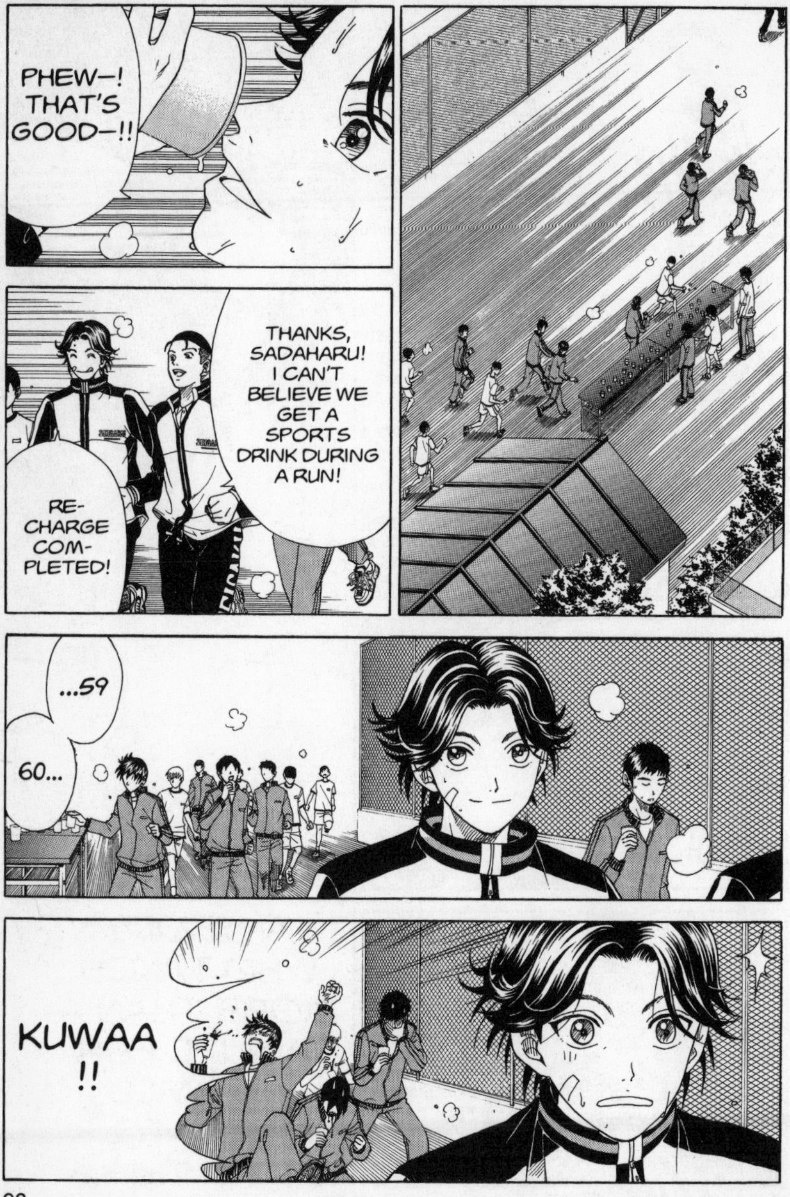
PHEW—! THAT'S GOOD—!!
THANKS, SADAHARU! I CAN'T BELIEVE WE GET A SPORTS DRINK DURING A RUN!
RE-CHARGE COM-PLETED!
...59
60...
KUWAA !!

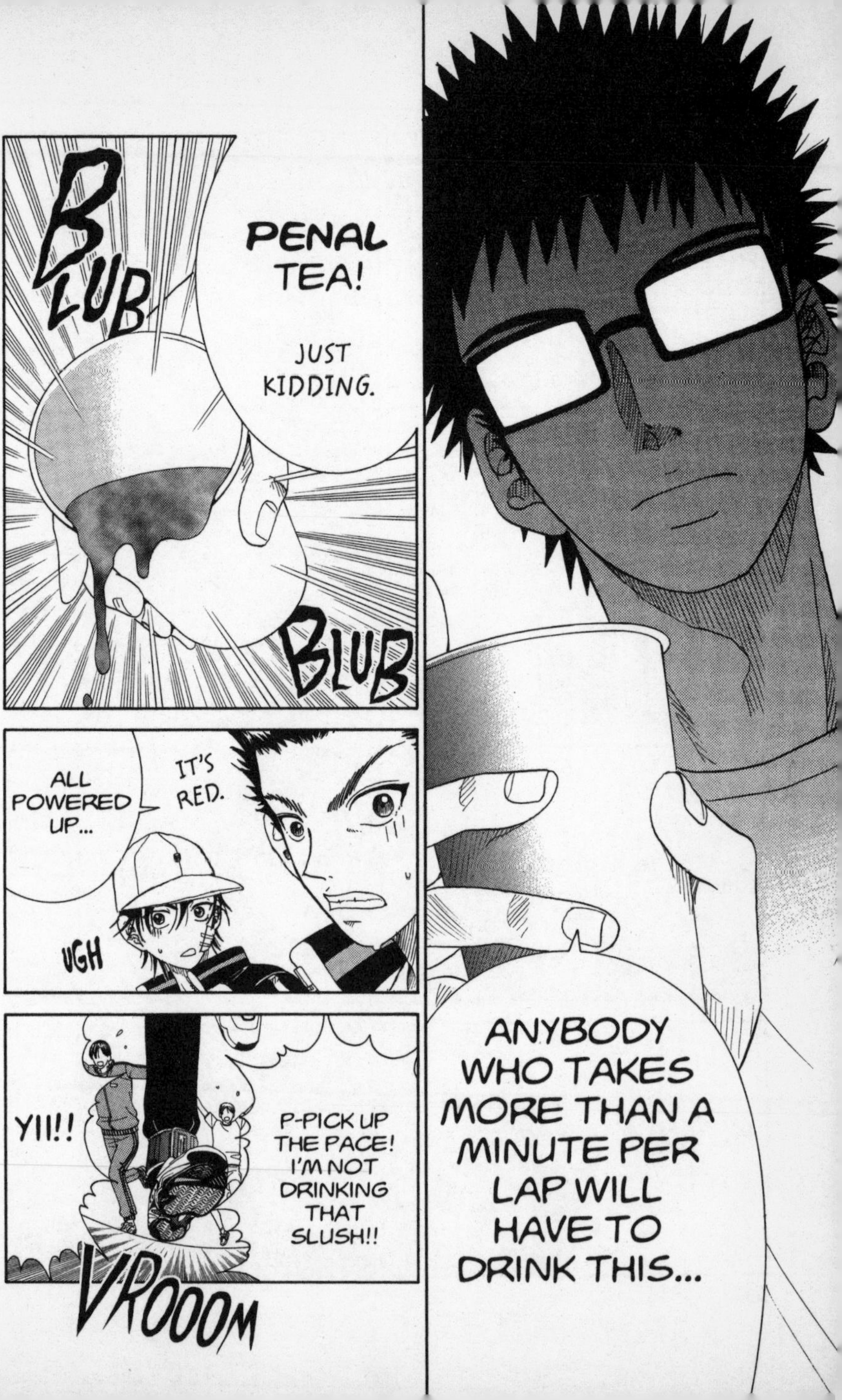
ANYBODY WHO TAKES MORE THAN A MINUTE PER LAP WILL HAVE TO DRINK THIS...
PENAL TEA!
JUST KIDDING.
BLUB
BLUB
IT'S RED.
ALL POWERED UP...
UGH
P-PICK UP THE PACE! I'M NOT DRINKING THAT SLUSH!!
YII!!
VROOOM

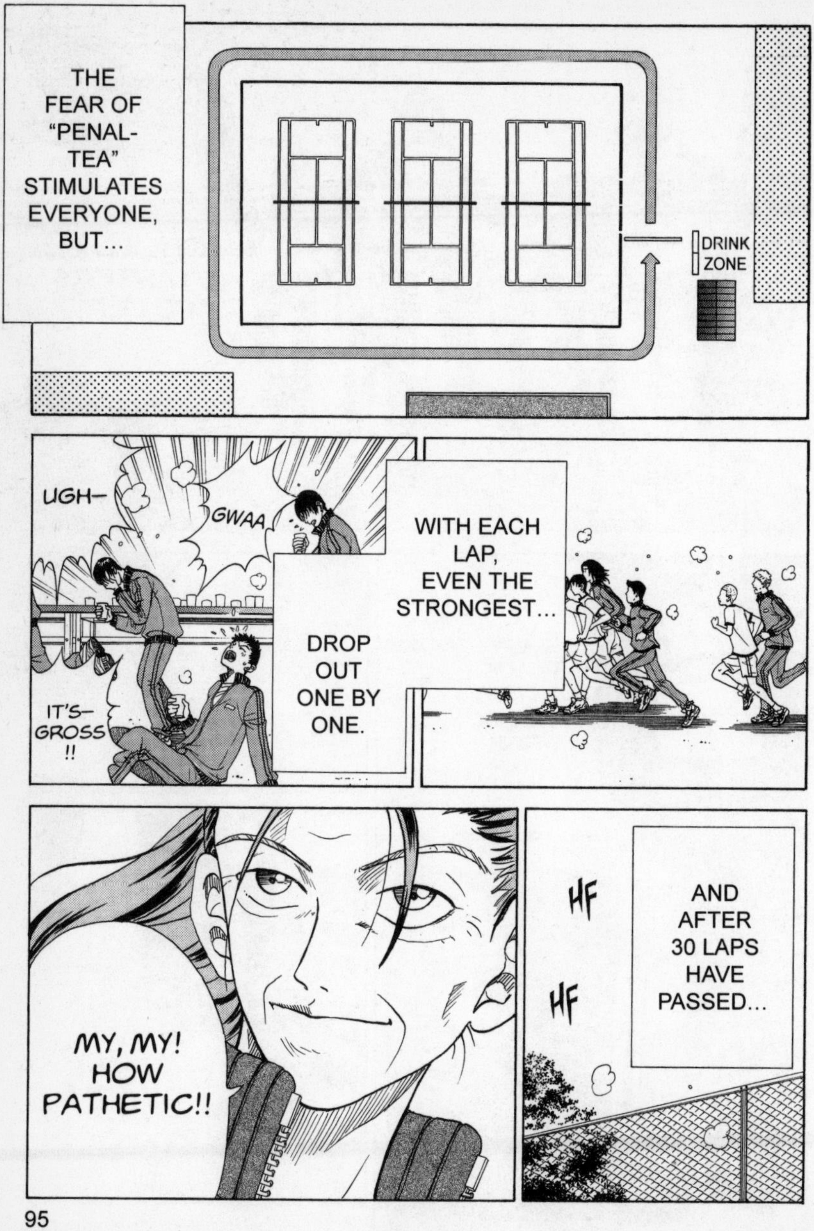
THE FEAR OF "PENAL-TEA" STIMULATES EVERYONE, BUT...
DRINK ZONE
WITH EACH LAP, EVEN THE STRONGEST...
DROP OUT ONE BY ONE.
GWAA
UGH—
IT'S— GROSS!!
AND AFTER 30 LAPS HAVE PASSED...
HF
HF
MY, MY! HOW PATHETIC!!

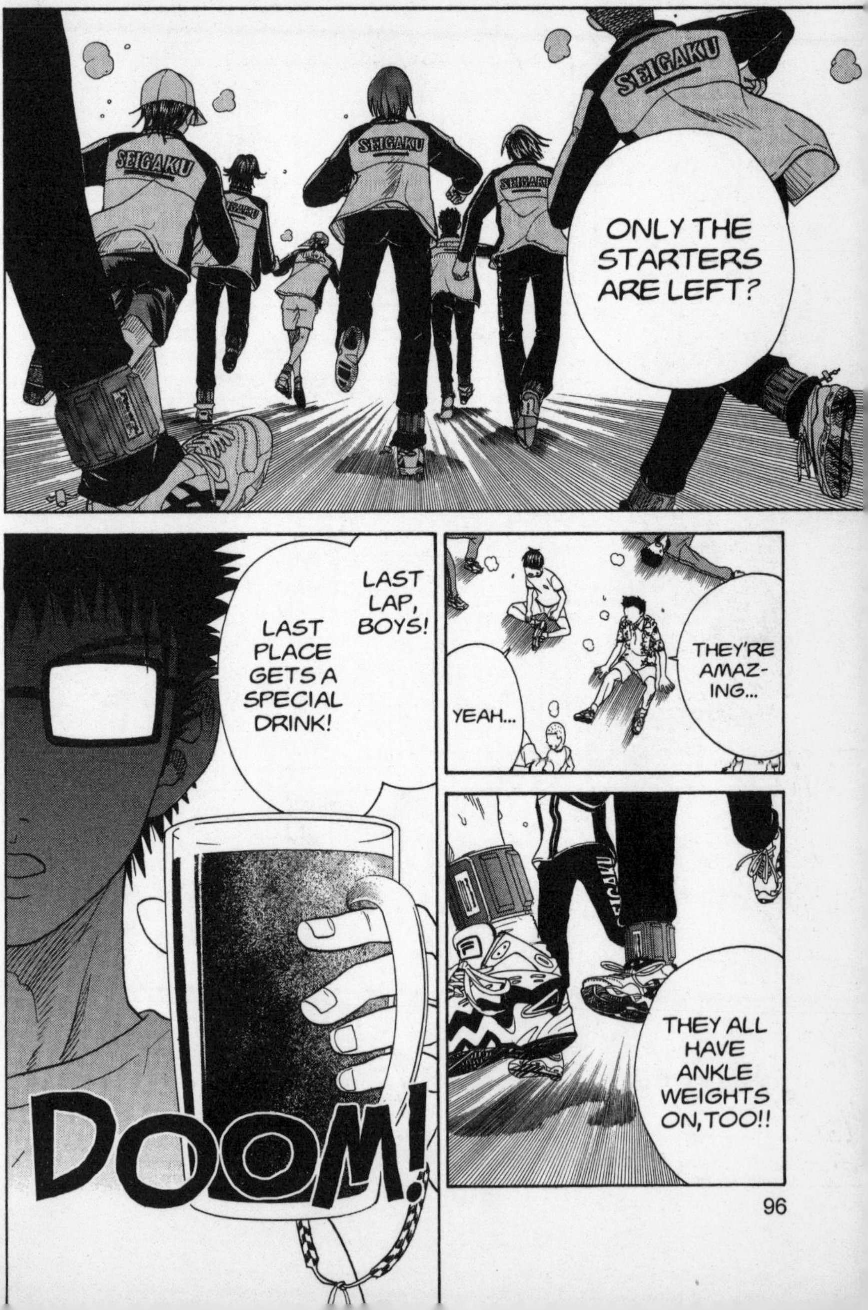
ONLY THE STARTERS ARE LEFT?
THEY'RE AMAZ- ING...
YEAH...
THEY ALL HAVE ANKLE WEIGHTS ON, TOO!!
LAST LAP, BOYS!
LAST PLACE GETS A SPECIAL DRINK!
DOOM!

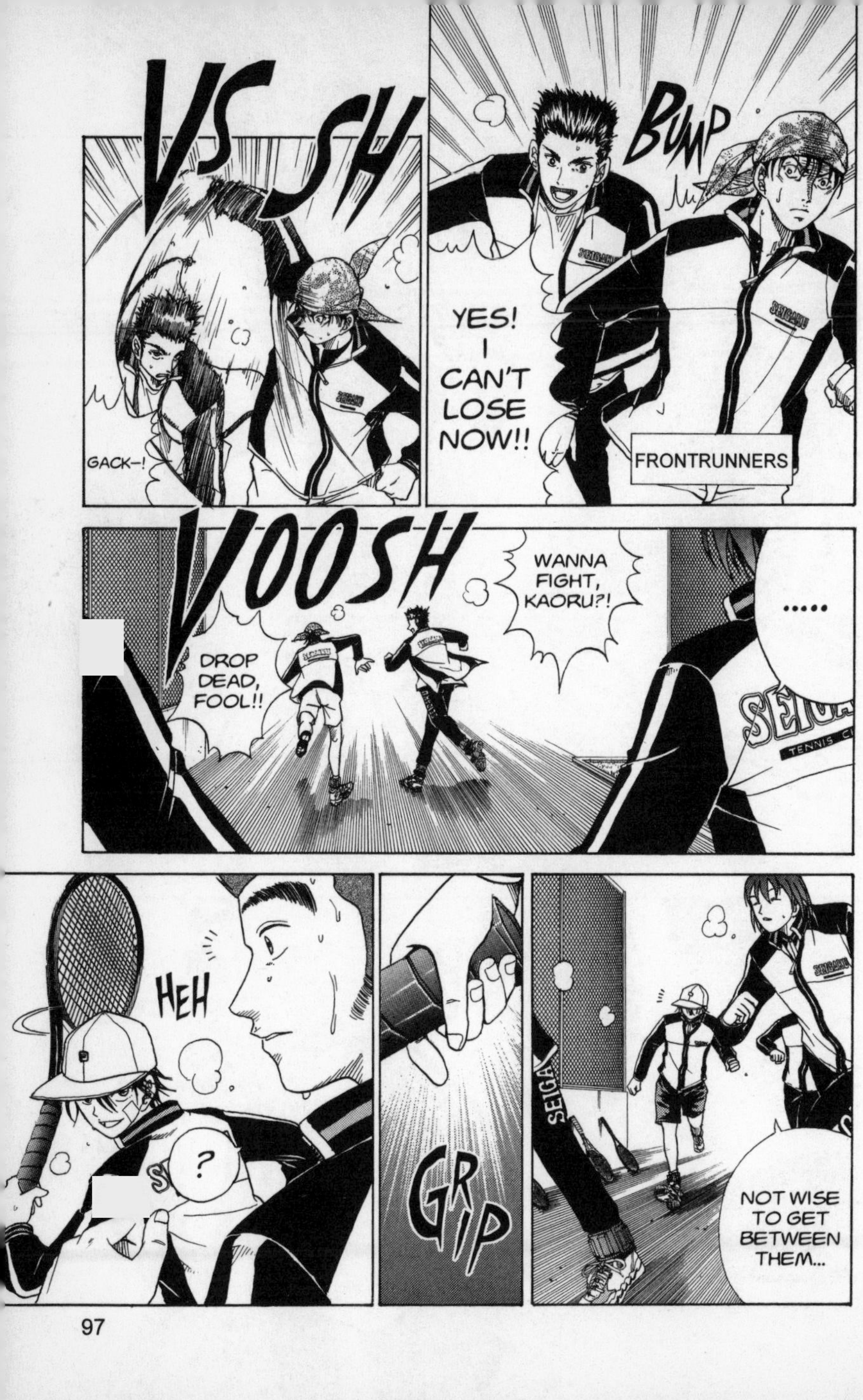
BUMP
YES! I CAN'T LOSE NOW!!
FRONTRUNNERS
VSSH
GACK-!
.....
WANNA FIGHT, KAORU?!
VOOSH
DROP DEAD, FOOL!!
NOT WISE TO GET BETWEEN THEM...
GRIP
HEH
?

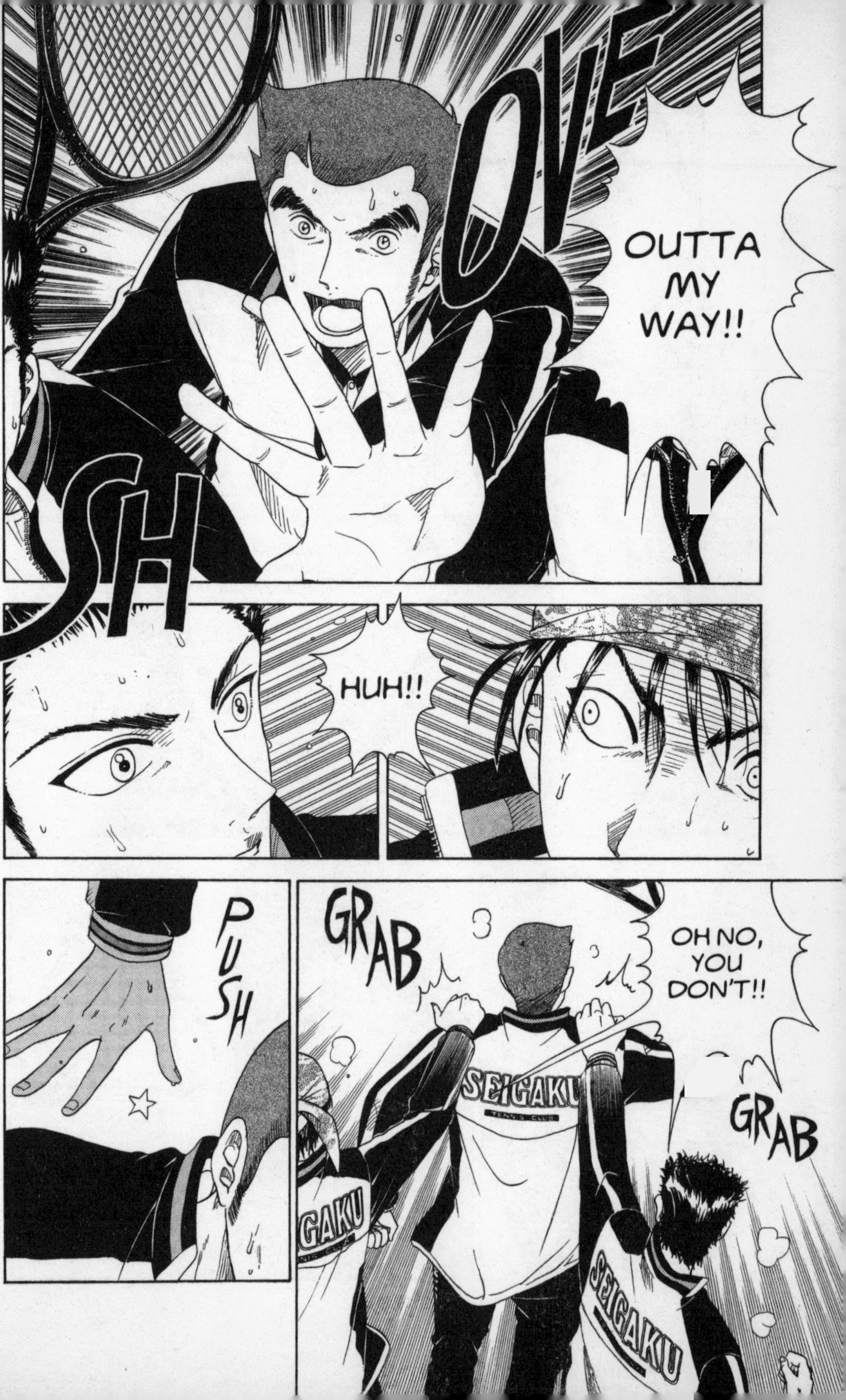
OVE
OUTTA MY WAY!!
SH
HUH!!
OH NO, YOU DON'T!!
GRAB
GRAB
PUSH

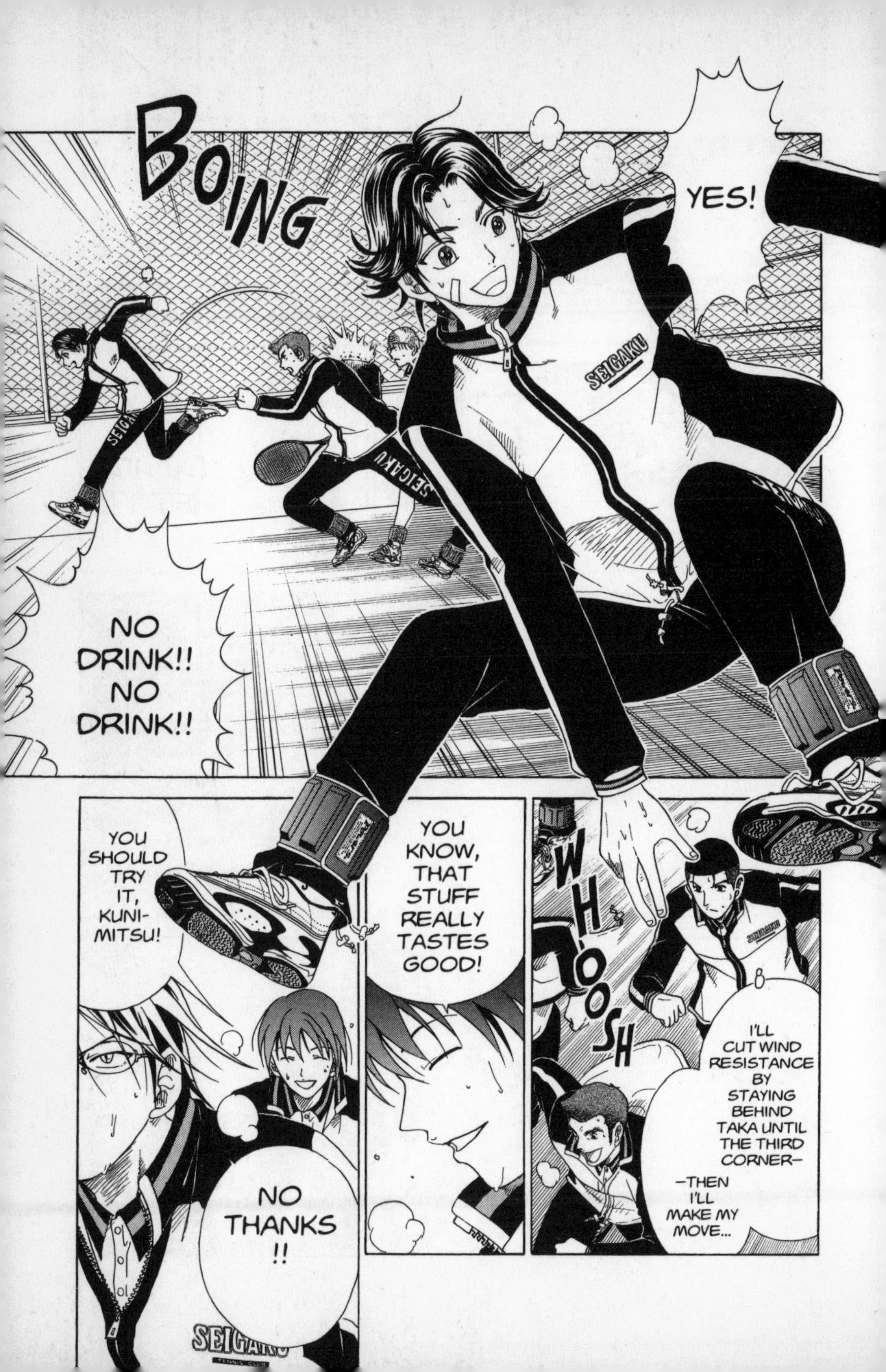
YES!
BOING
NO DRINK!! NO DRINK!!
WHOOSH
I'LL CUT WIND RESISTANCE BY STAYING BEHIND TAKA UNTIL THE THIRD CORNER—
—THEN I'LL MAKE MY MOVE...
YOU KNOW, THAT STUFF REALLY TASTES GOOD!
YOU SHOULD TRY IT, KUNI-MITSU!
NO THANKS !!

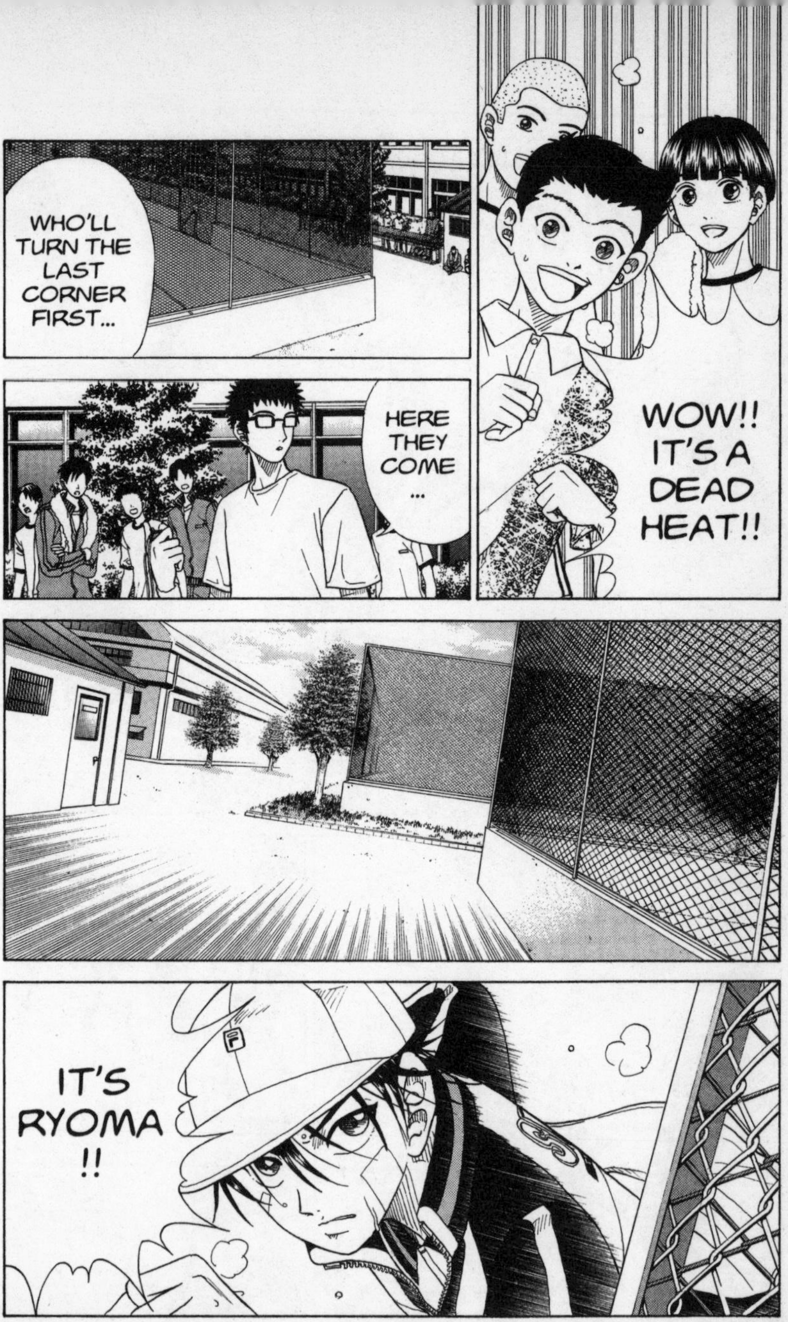
WOW!! IT'S A DEAD HEAT!!
WHO'LL TURN THE LAST CORNER FIRST...
HERE THEY COME ...
IT'S RYOMA !!

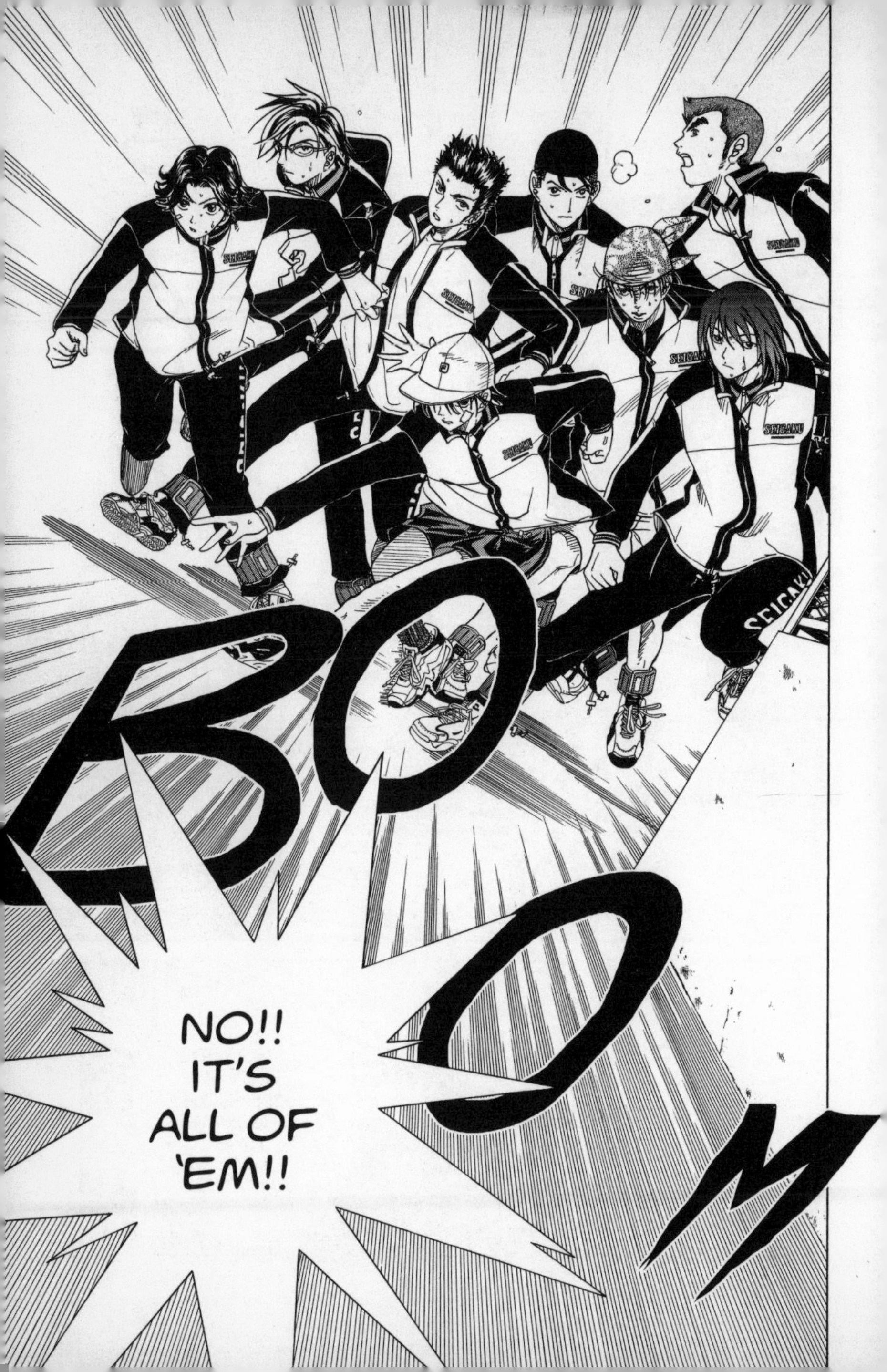
NO!! IT'S ALL OF 'EM!!
BOOM

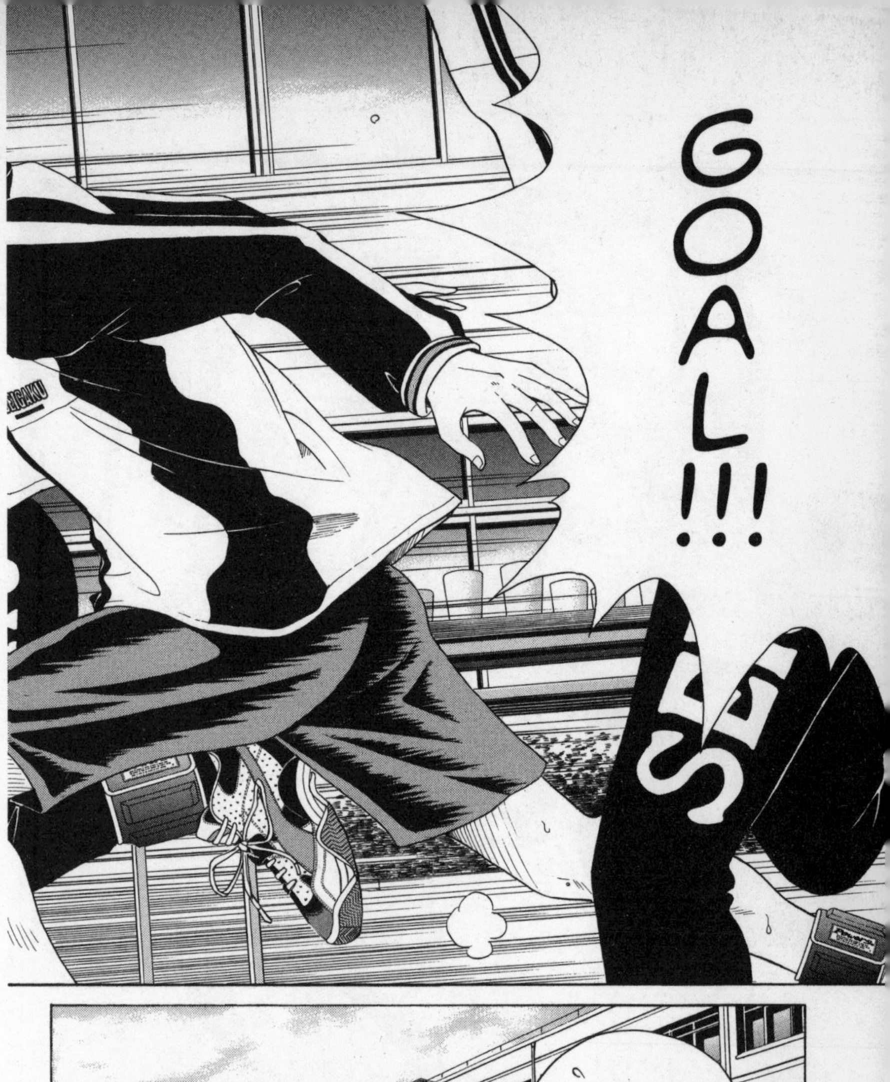
GOAL!!!
SEIGAKU

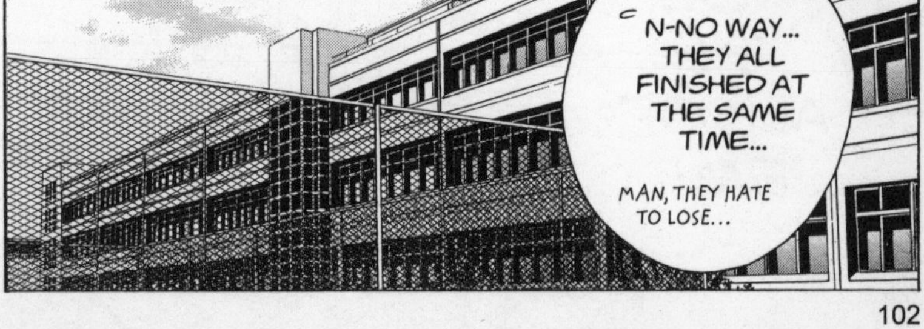
N-NO WAY... THEY ALL FINISHED AT THE SAME TIME...
MAN, THEY HATE TO LOSE...

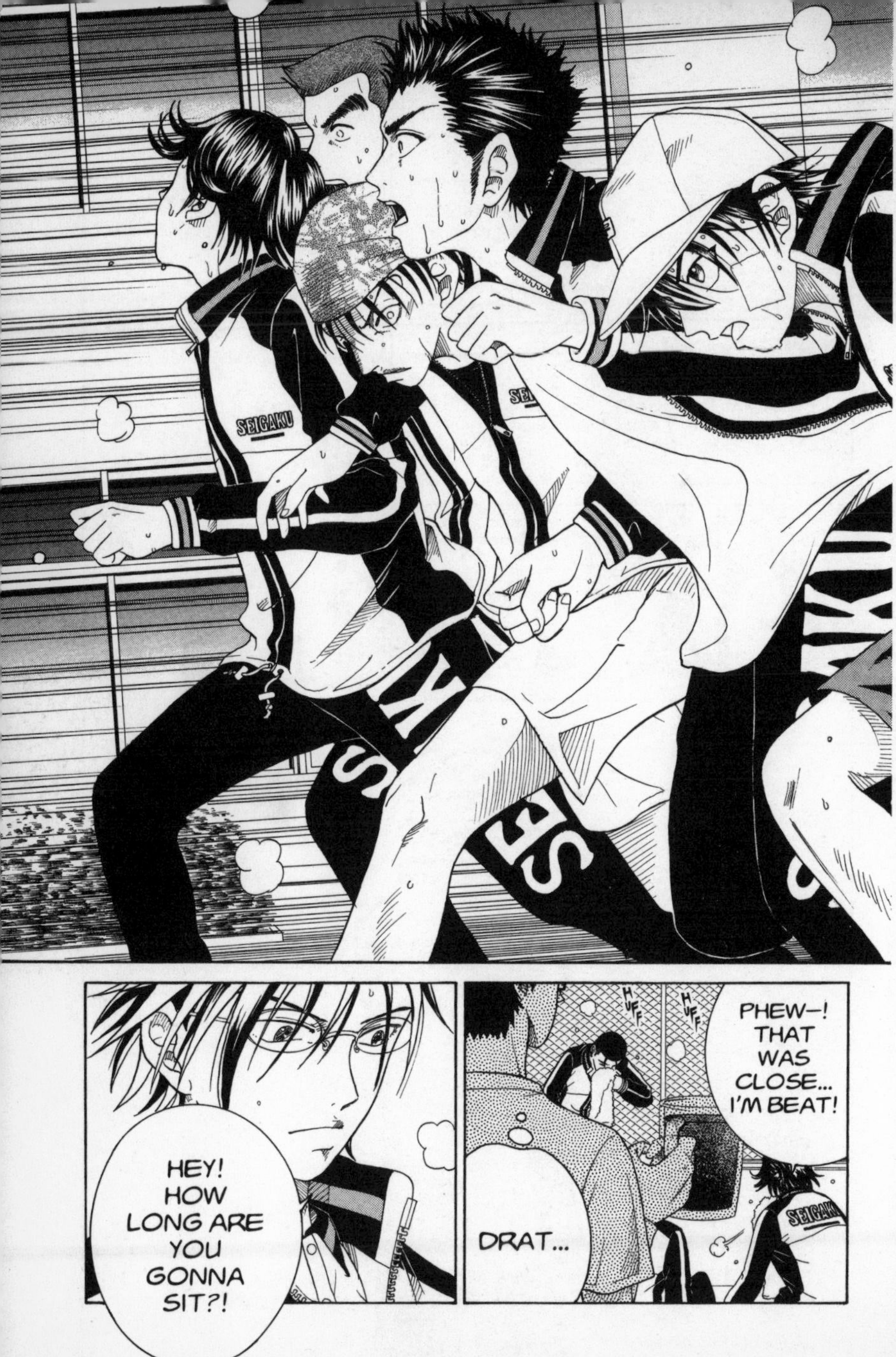
HUFF
HUFF
PHEW—! THAT WAS CLOSE... I'M BEAT!
DRAT...
HEY! HOW LONG ARE YOU GONNA SIT?!

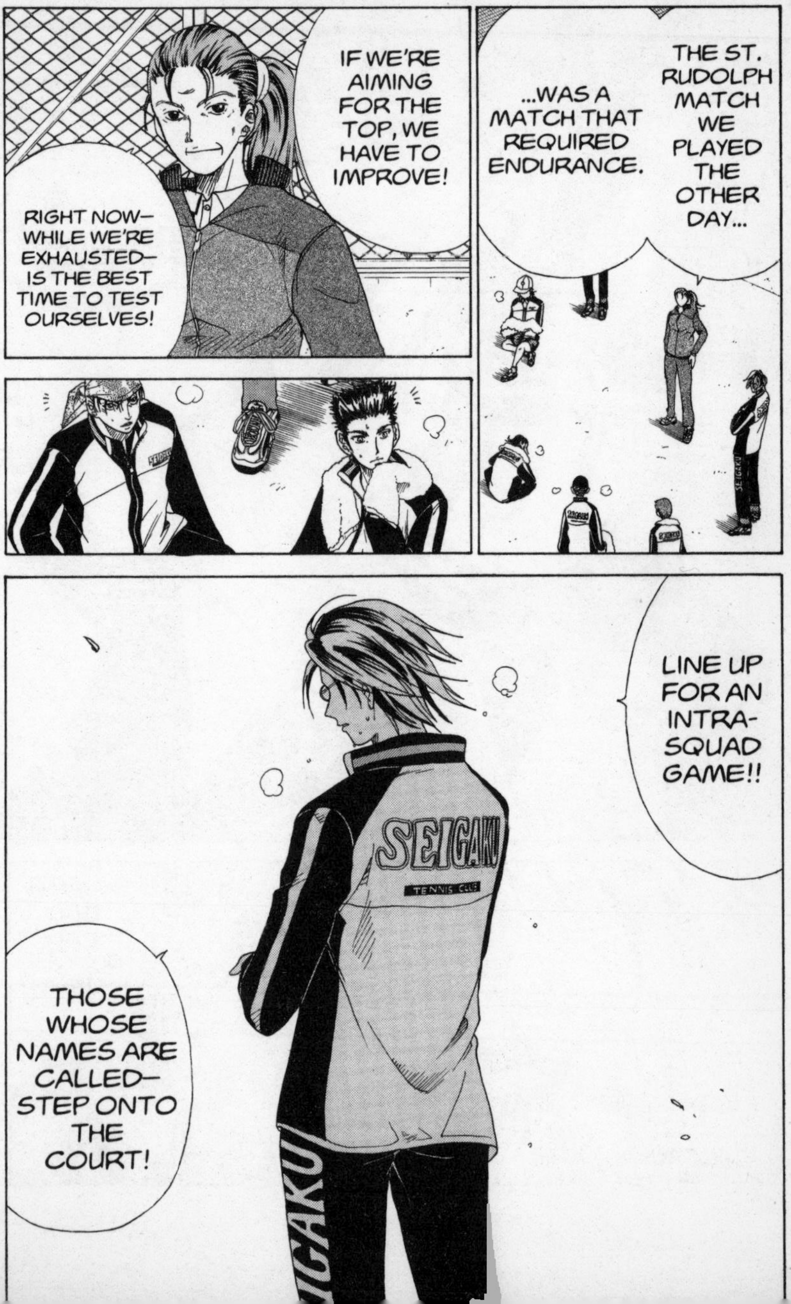
THE ST. RUDOLPH MATCH WE PLAYED THE OTHER DAY...
...WAS A MATCH THAT REQUIRED ENDURANCE.
IF WE'RE AIMING FOR THE TOP, WE HAVE TO IMPROVE!
RIGHT NOW—WHILE WE'RE EXHAUSTED—IS THE BEST TIME TO TEST OURSELVES!
LINE UP FOR AN INTRA-SQUAD GAME!!
THOSE WHOSE NAMES ARE CALLED—STEP ONTO THE COURT!
SEIGAKU
TENNIS CLUB

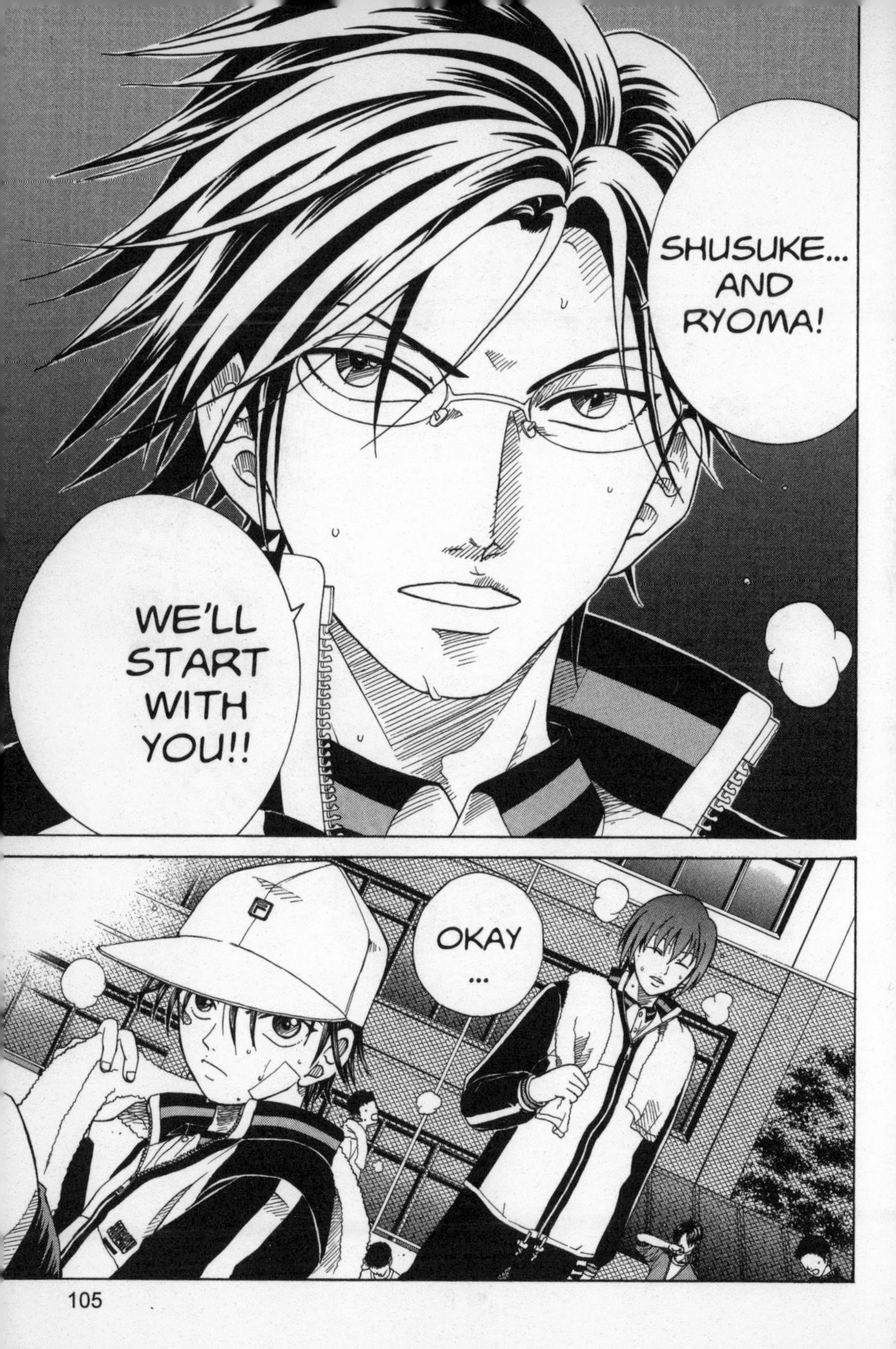
SHUSUKE... AND RYOMA!
WE'LL START WITH YOU!!
OKAY ...

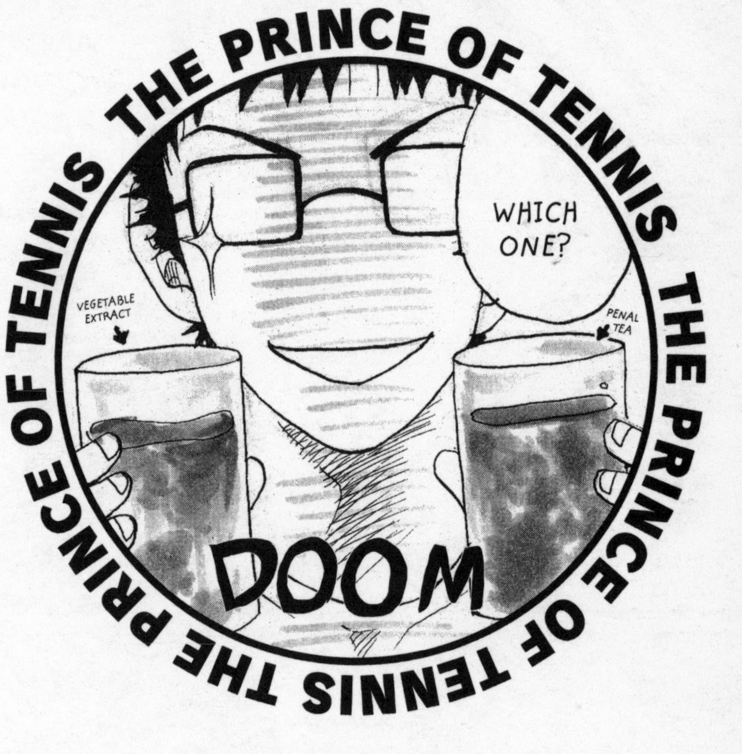
THE PRINCE OF TENNIS THE PRINCE OF TENNIS THE PRINCE OF TENNIS
WHICH ONE?
VEGETABLE EXTRACT
PENAL TEA
DOOM

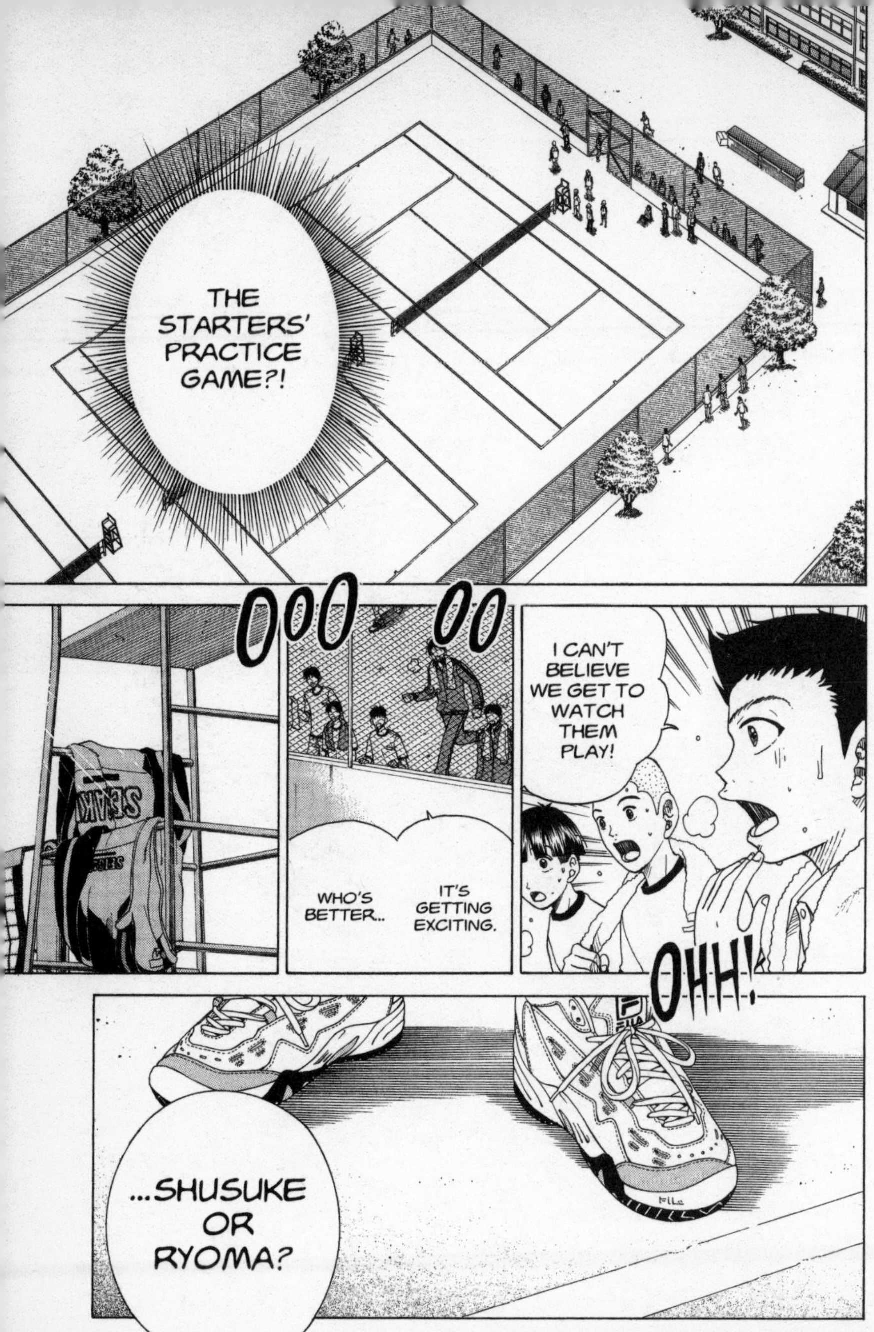
THE STARTERS' PRACTICE GAME?!
I CAN'T BELIEVE WE GET TO WATCH THEM PLAY!
OHH!
OOO OO
IT'S GETTING EXCITING.
WHO'S BETTER..
...SHUSUKE OR RYOMA?

GENIUS 84: PLAY FOR KEEPS

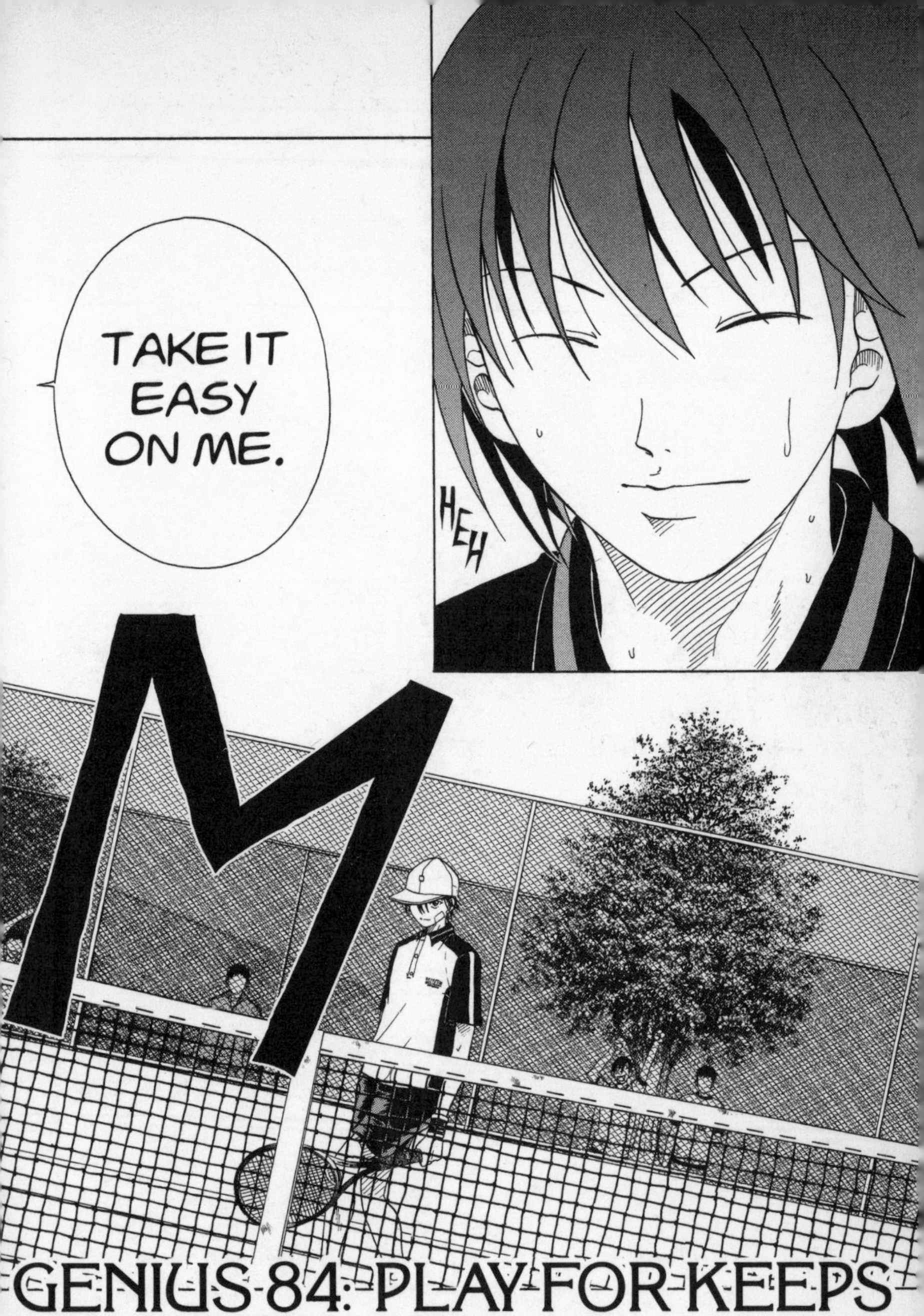
TAKE IT EASY ON ME.
HEH
M

GENIUS 84: PLAY FOR KEEPS

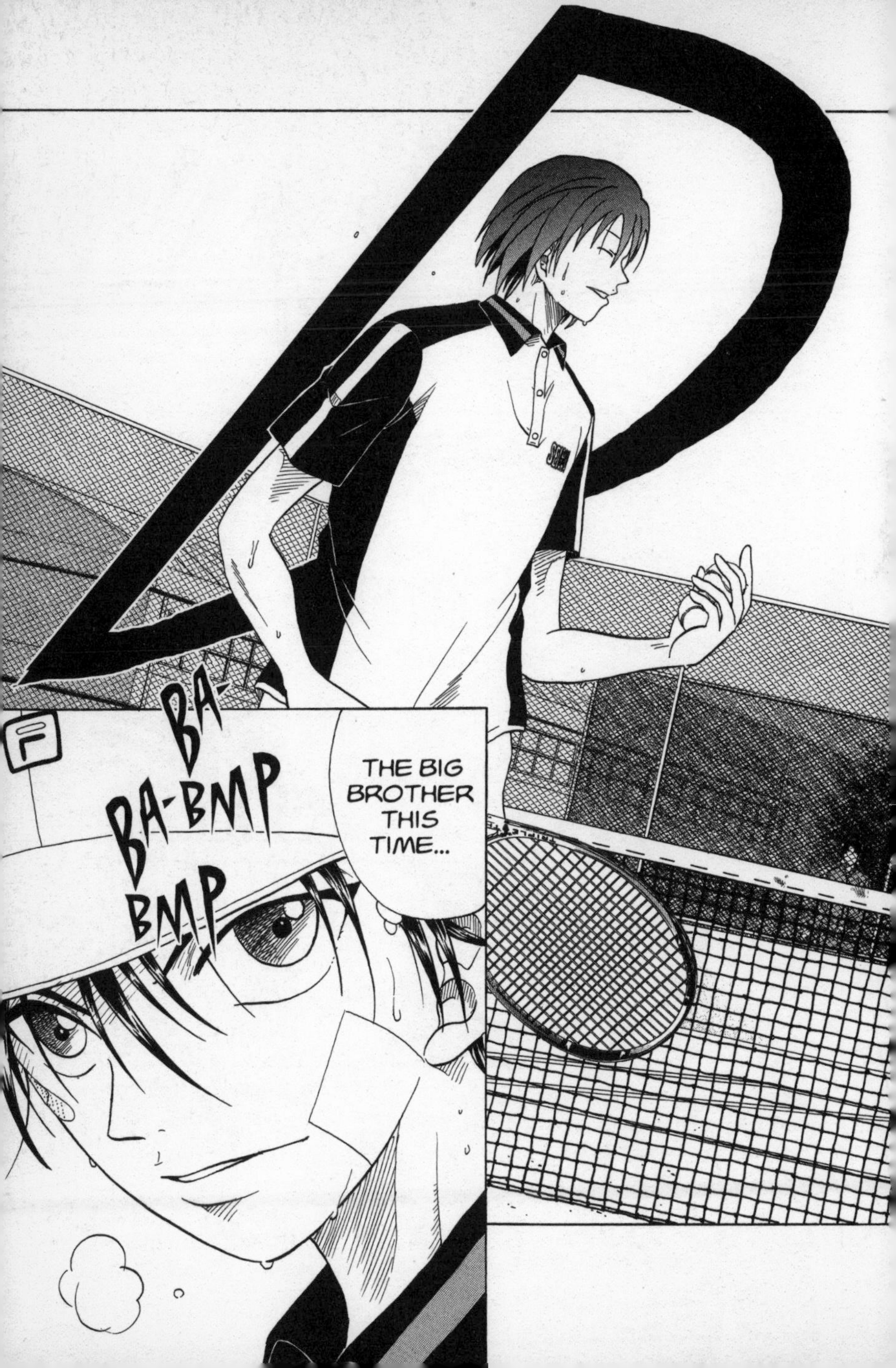
THE BIG BROTHER THIS TIME...
BA-BA-BMP BMP

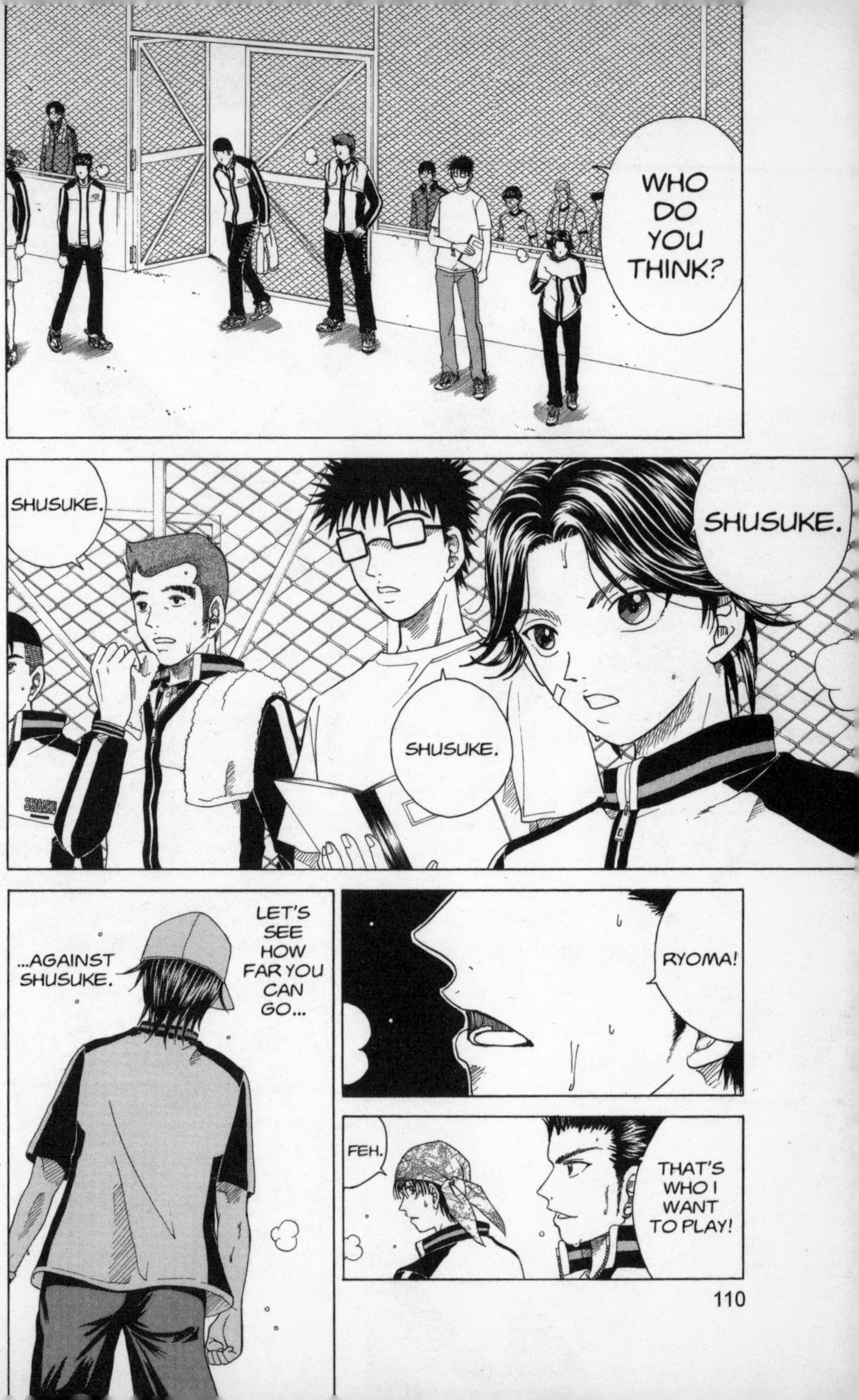
WHO DO YOU THINK?
SHUSUKE.
SHUSUKE.
SHUSUKE.
RYOMA!
THAT'S WHO I WANT TO PLAY!
FEH.
LET'S SEE HOW FAR YOU CAN GO...
...AGAINST SHUSUKE.

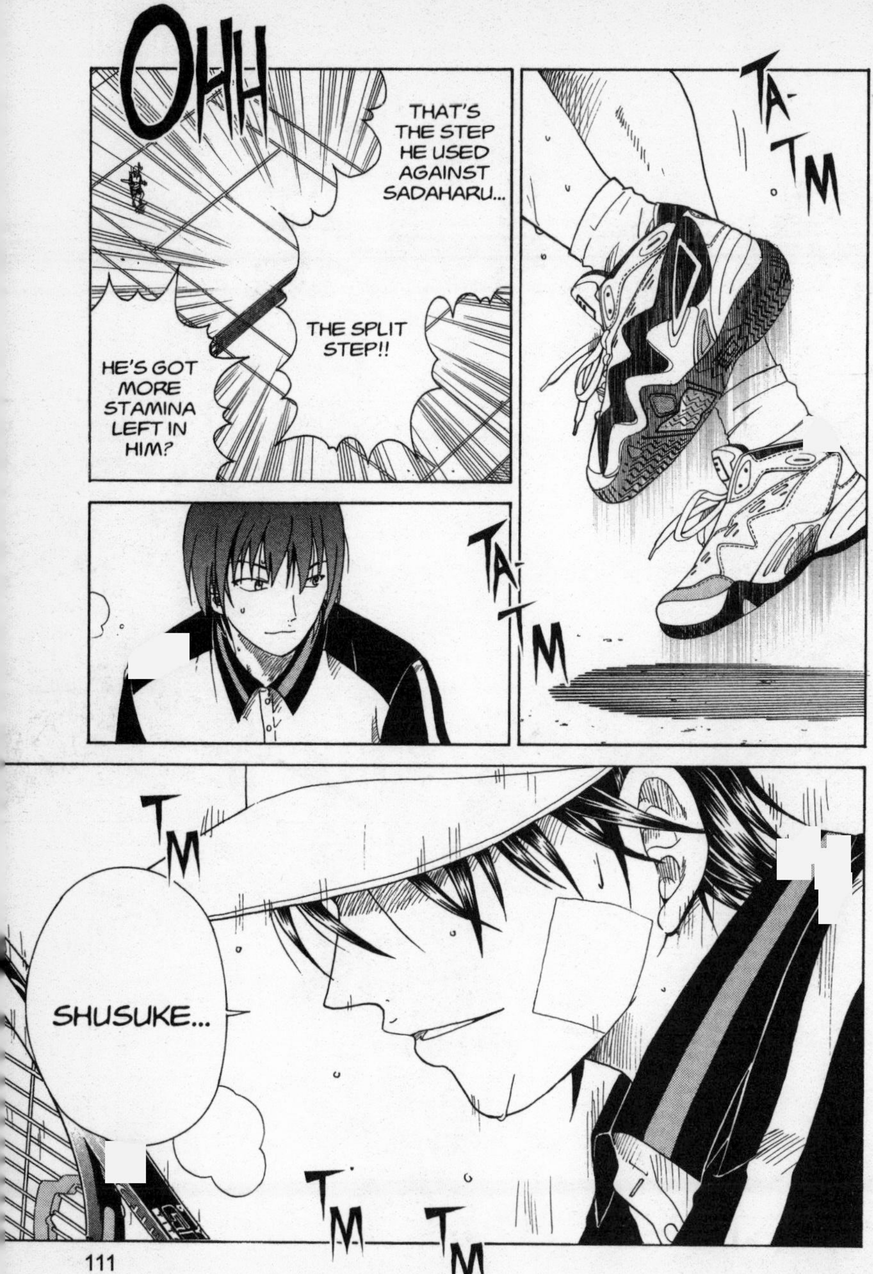
TA-TM
TA-TM
OHH
THAT'S THE STEP HE USED AGAINST SADAHARU...
THE SPLIT STEP!!
HE'S GOT MORE STAMINA LEFT IN HIM?
TM
SHUSUKE...
TM
TM

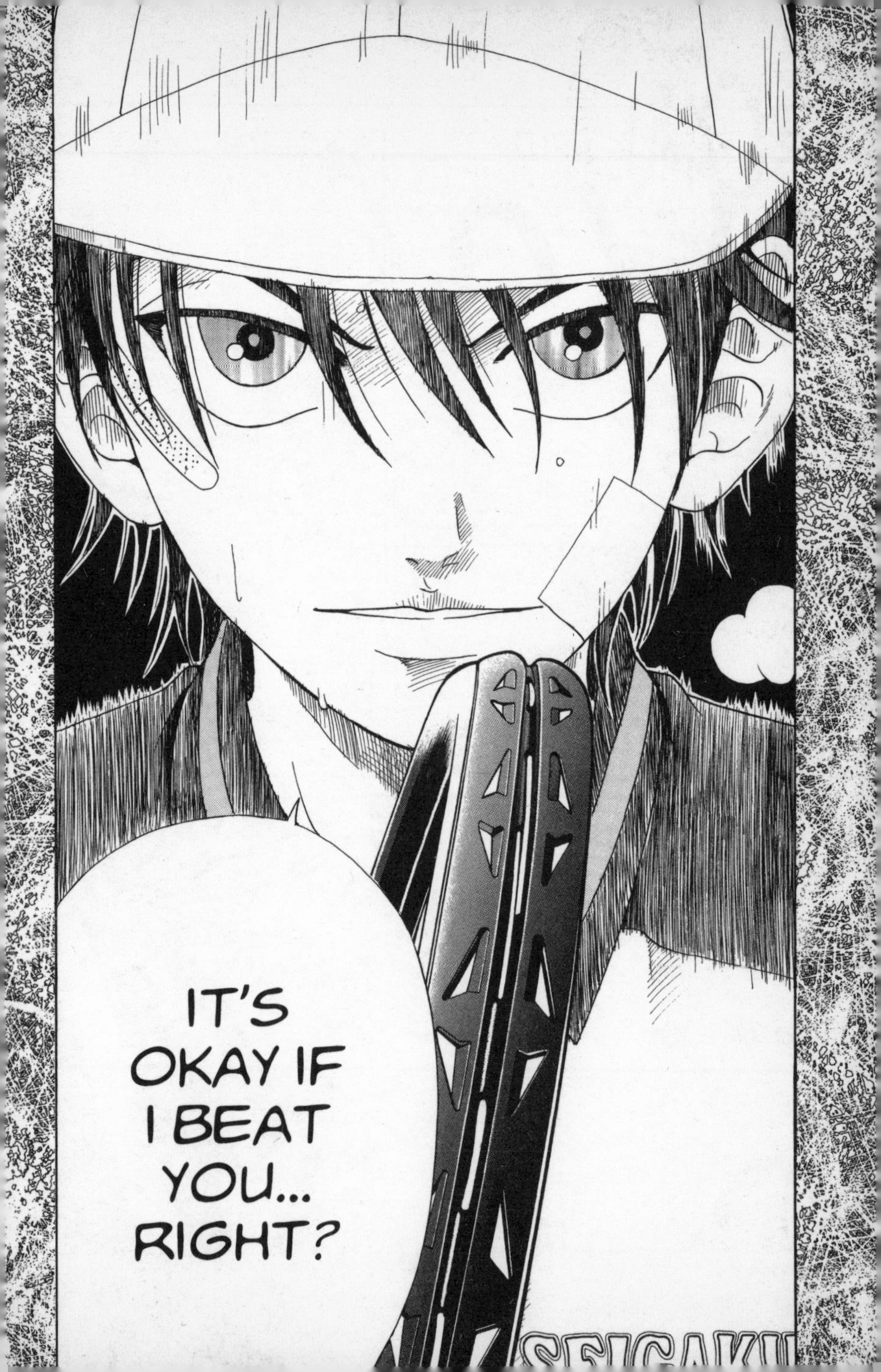
IT'S OKAY IF I BEAT YOU... RIGHT?

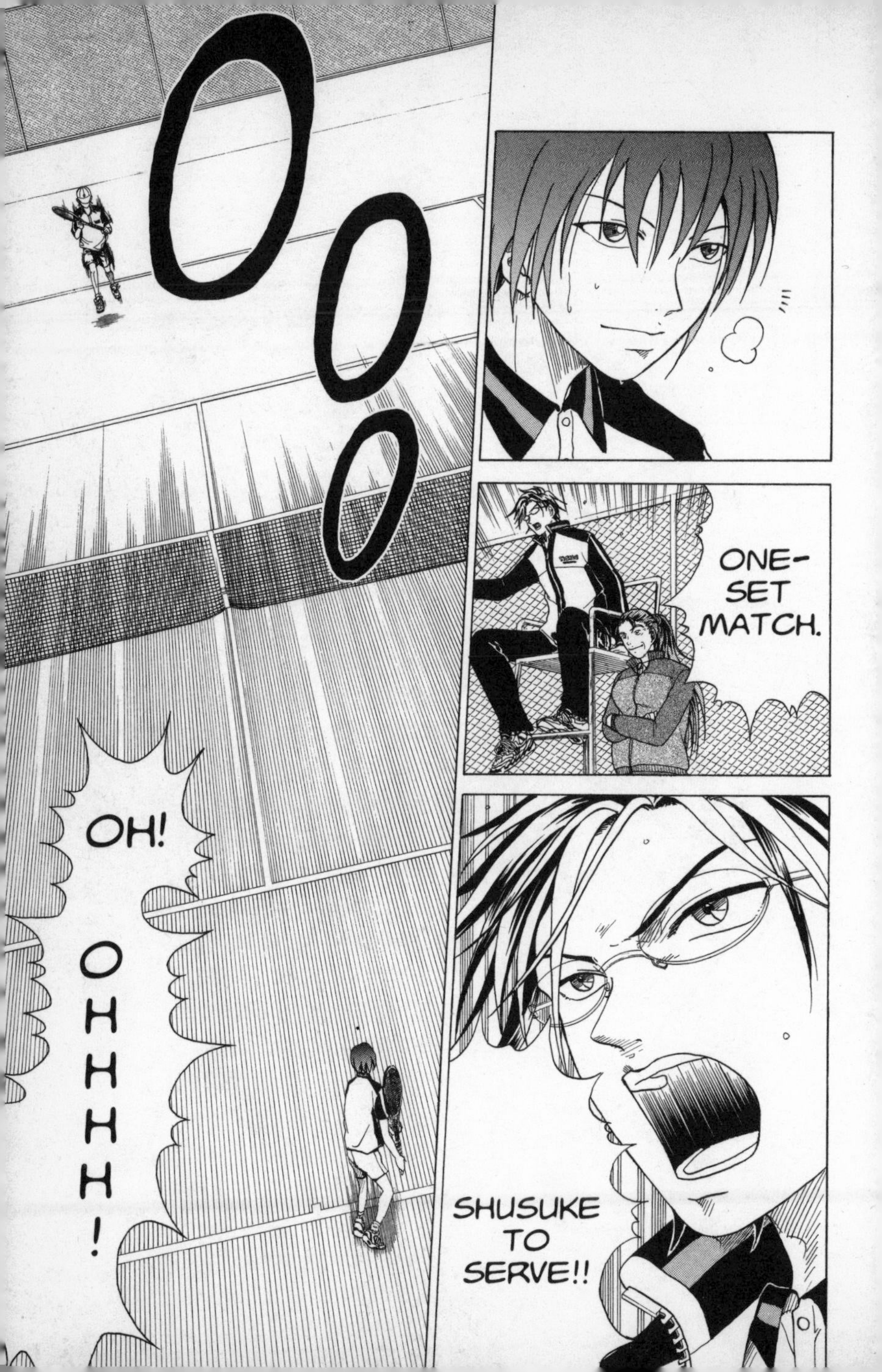
ONE-SET MATCH.
SHUSUKE TO SERVE!!
OOO
OH!
OHHHH!

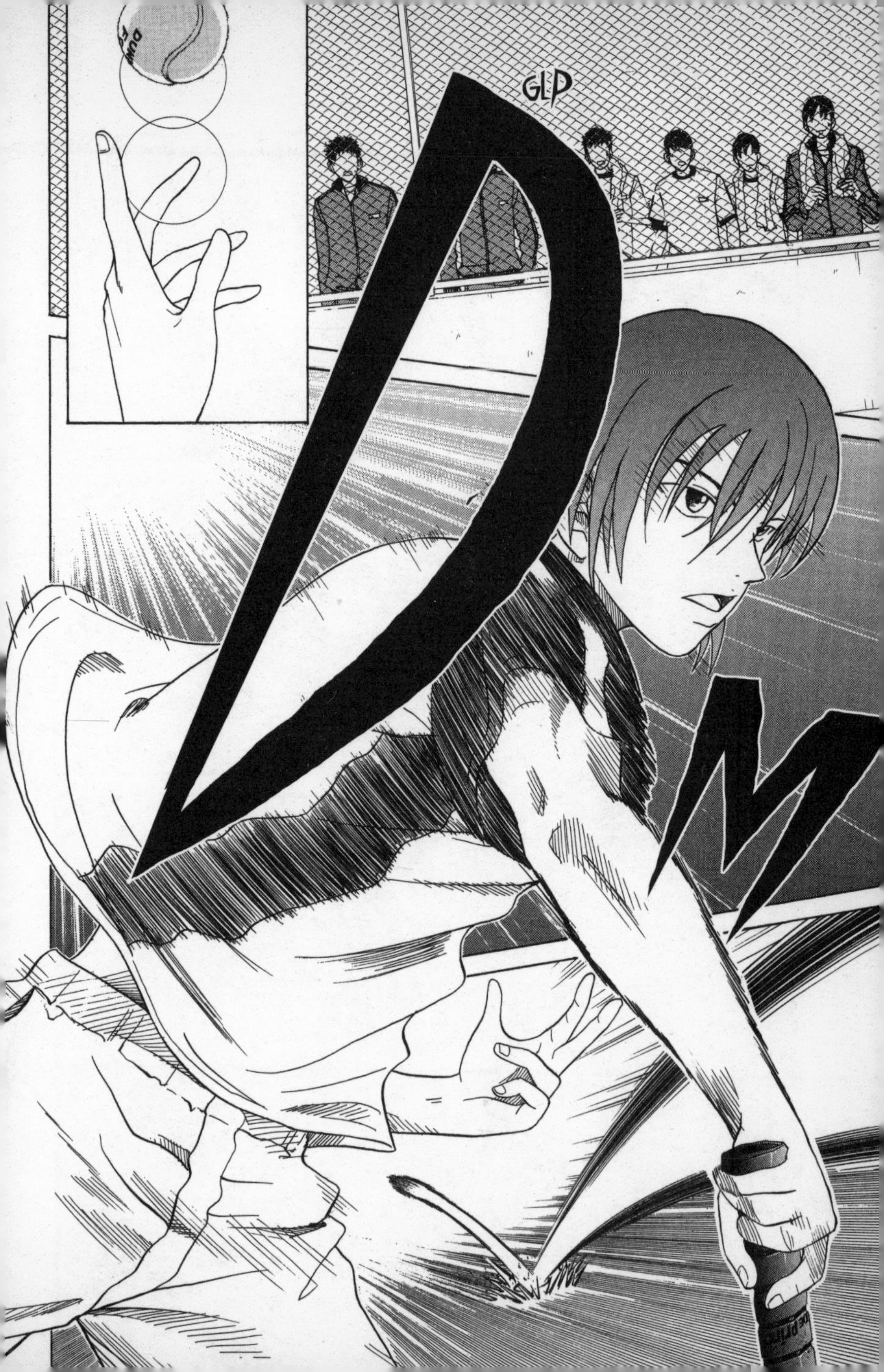
GLP
DM

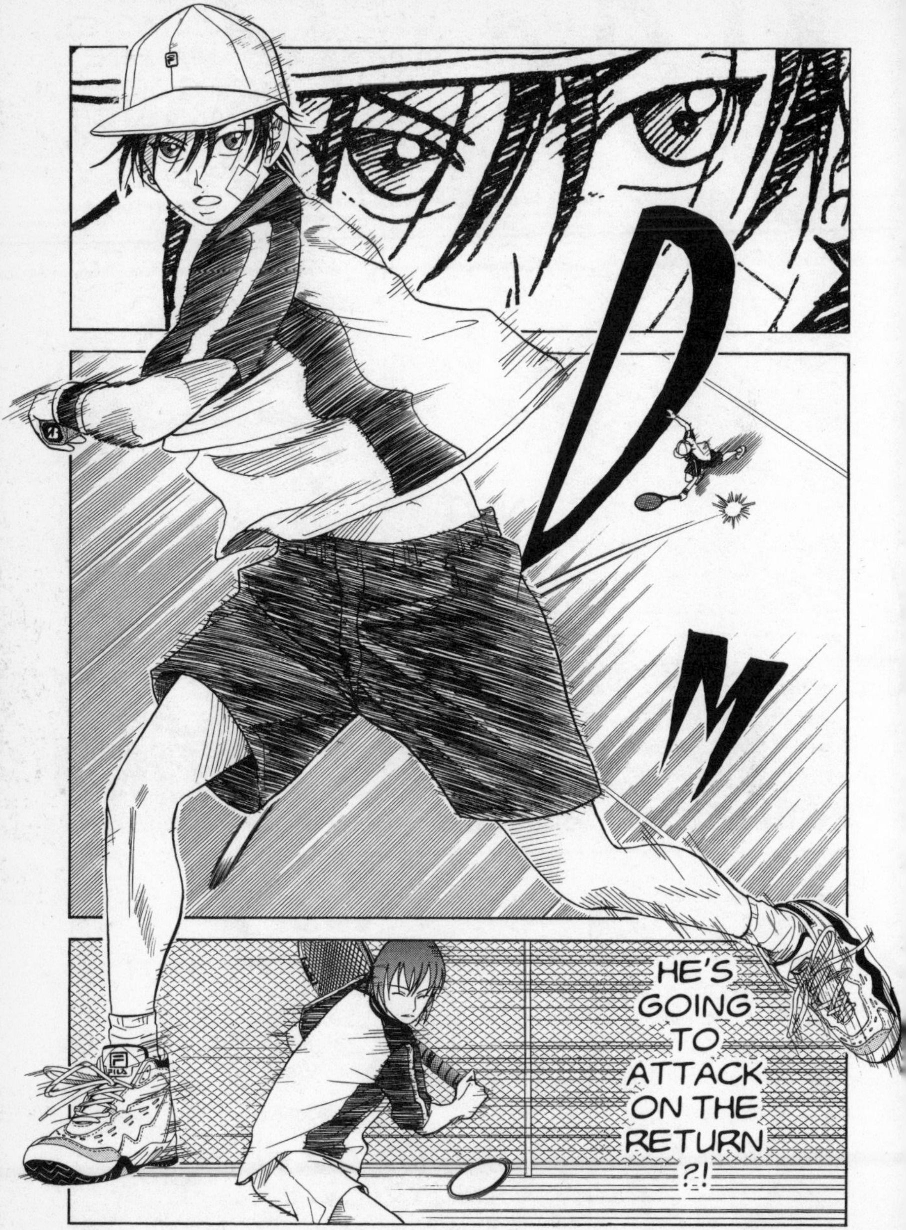
HE'S GOING TO ATTACK ON THE RETURN ?!

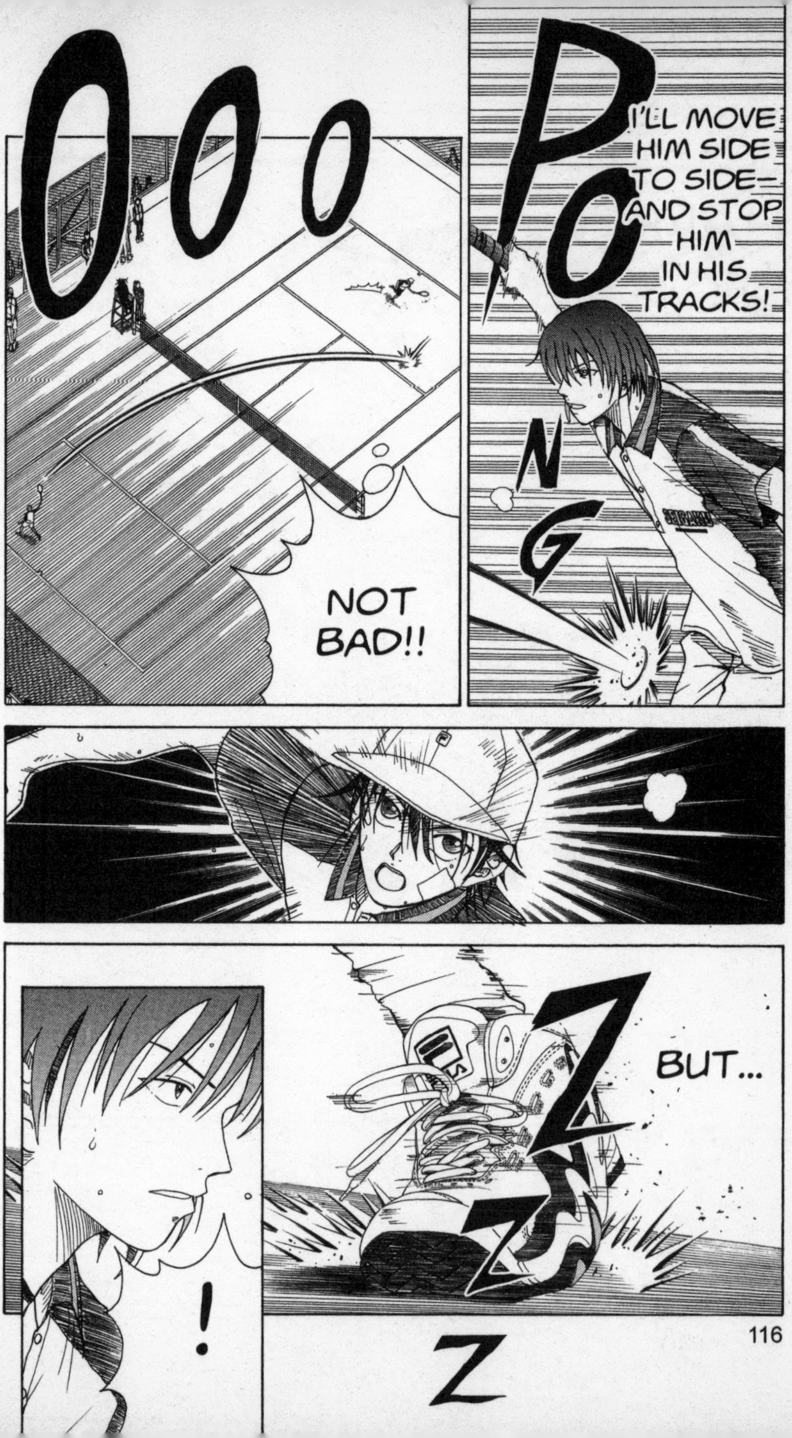
I'LL MOVE HIM SIDE TO SIDE—AND STOP HIM IN HIS TRACKS!
PONG
OOOO
NOT BAD!!
BUT...
ZZZ
!

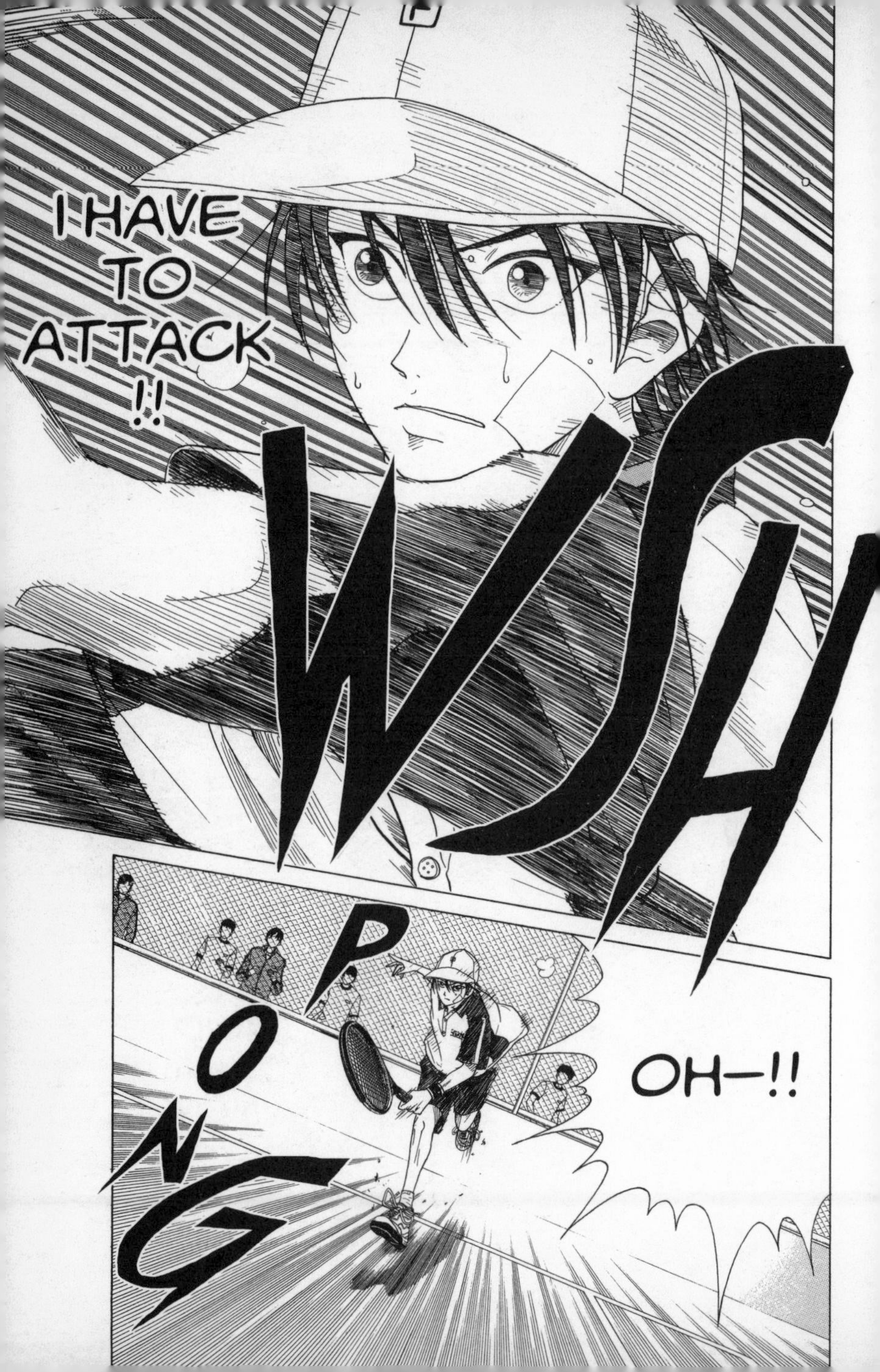
I HAVE TO ATTACK !!
WSH
OH—!!
PONG

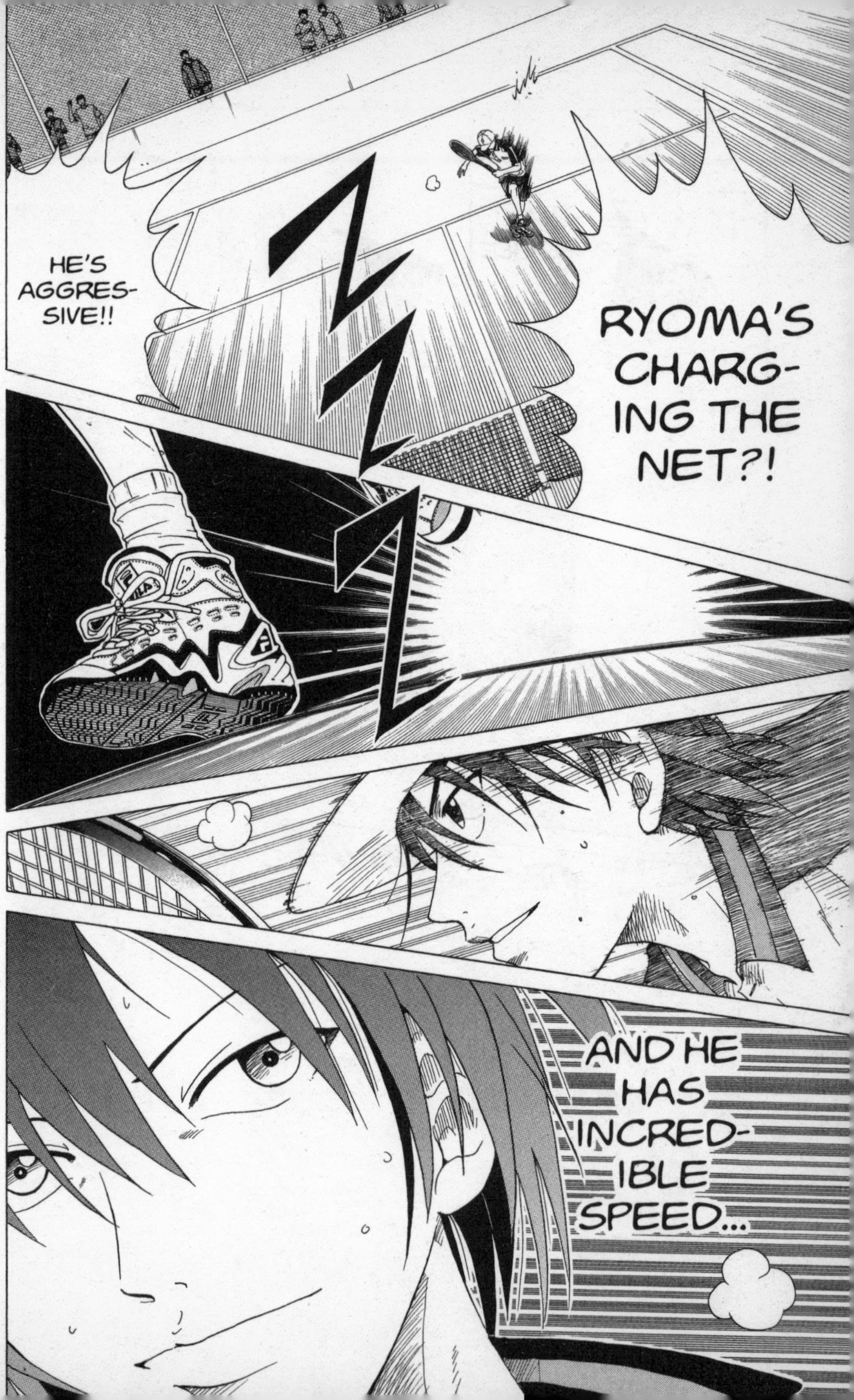
RYOMA'S CHARG-ING THE NET?!
HE'S AGGRES-SIVE!!
AND HE HAS INCRED-IBLE SPEED...

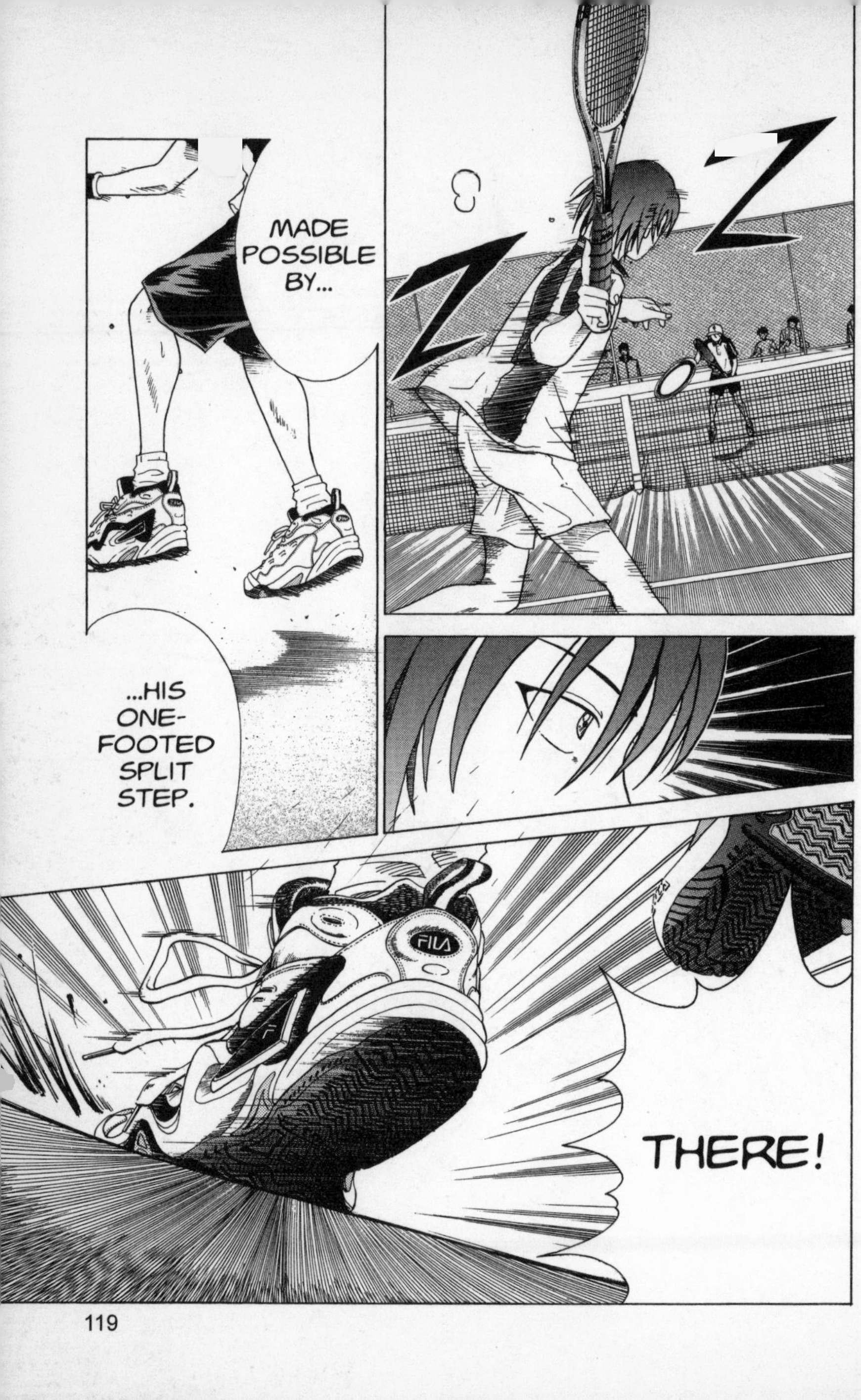
MADE POSSIBLE BY...
...HIS ONE-FOOTED SPLIT STEP.
FILA
THERE!

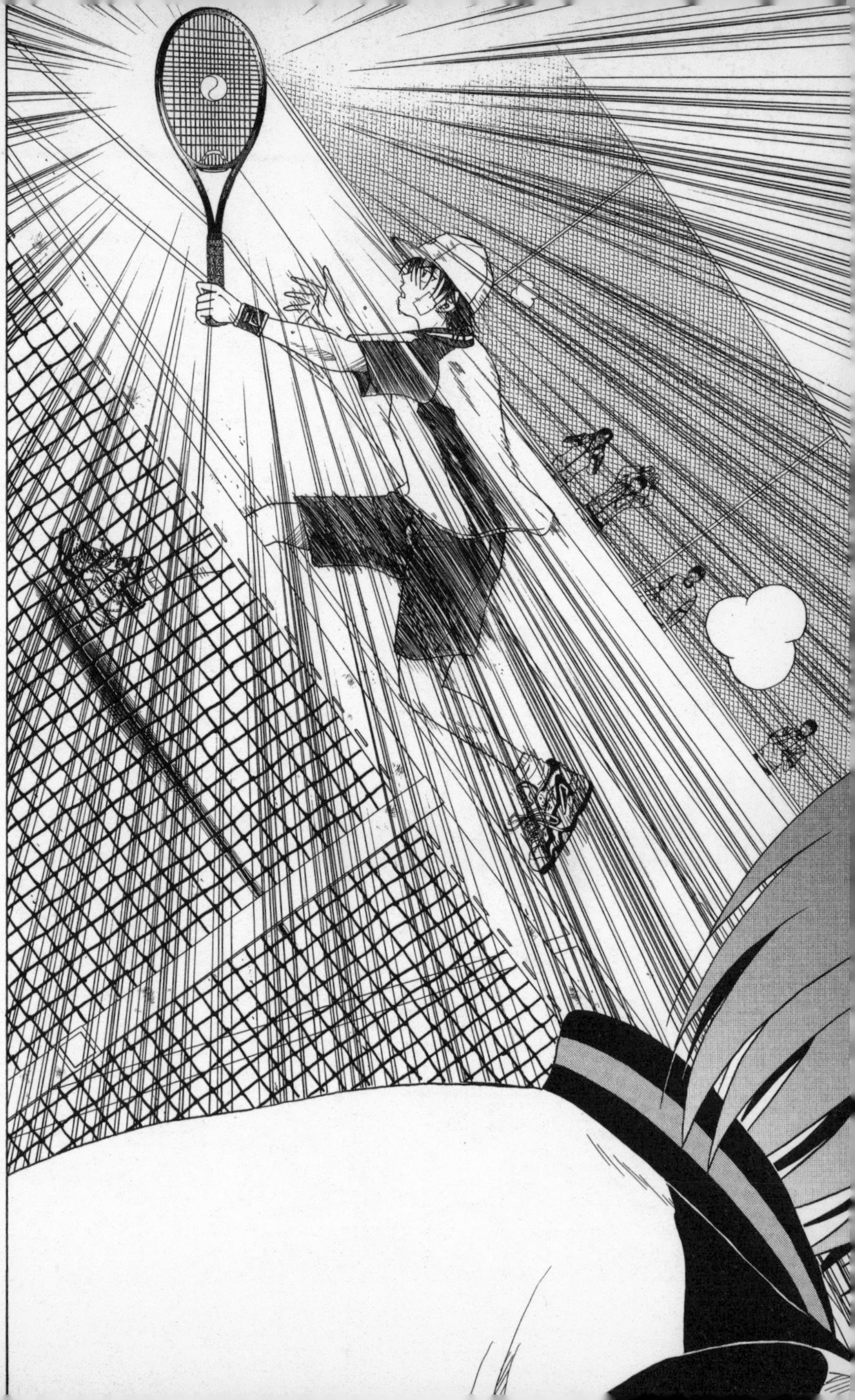

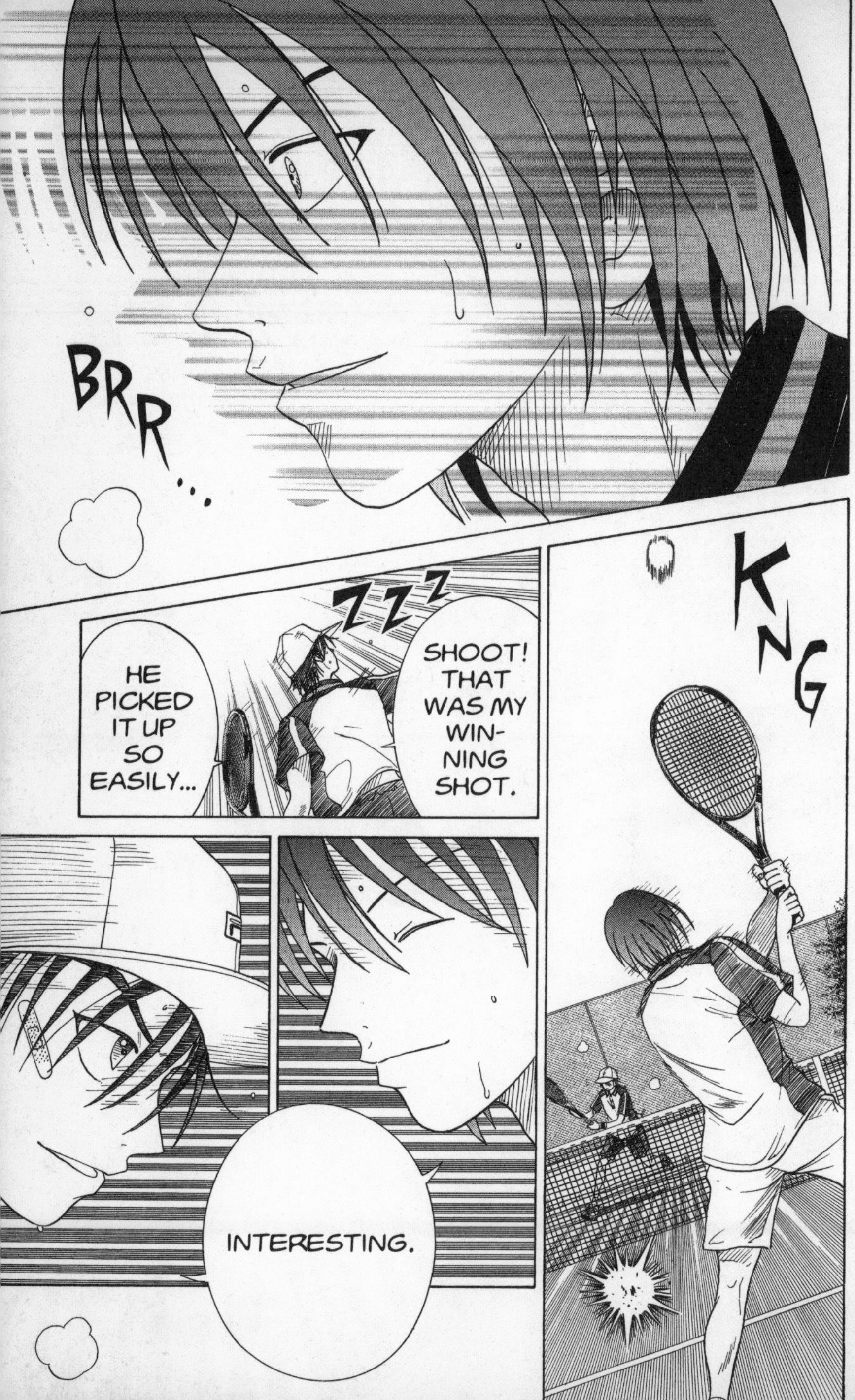
BRR...
KNG
ZZZ
SHOOT! THAT WAS MY WIN-NING SHOT.
HE PICKED IT UP SO EASILY...
INTERESTING.

I'LL CRUSH IT WITH MY DRIVE V!!

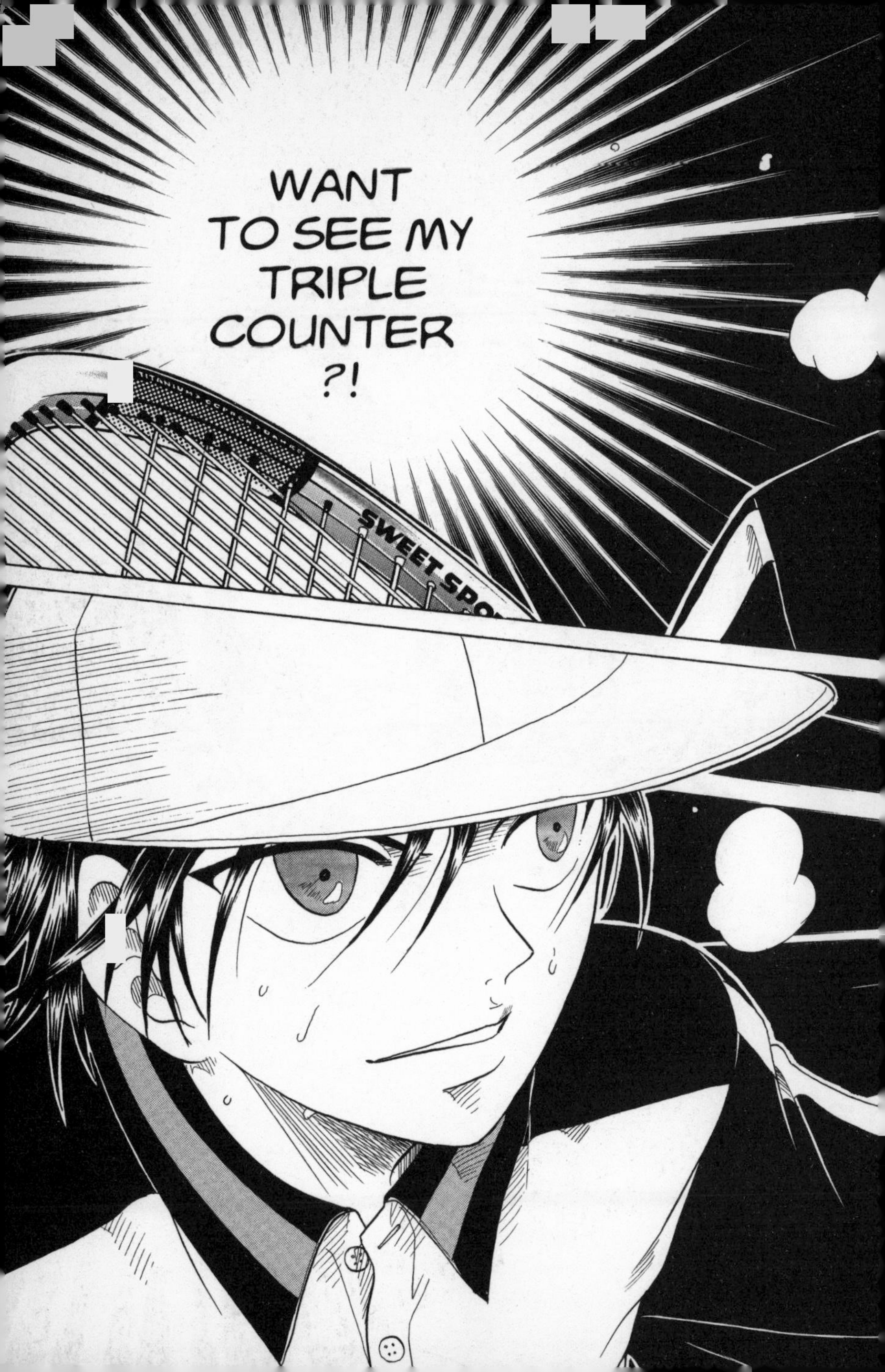
WANT TO SEE MY TRIPLE COUNTER ?!
SWEET SPOT

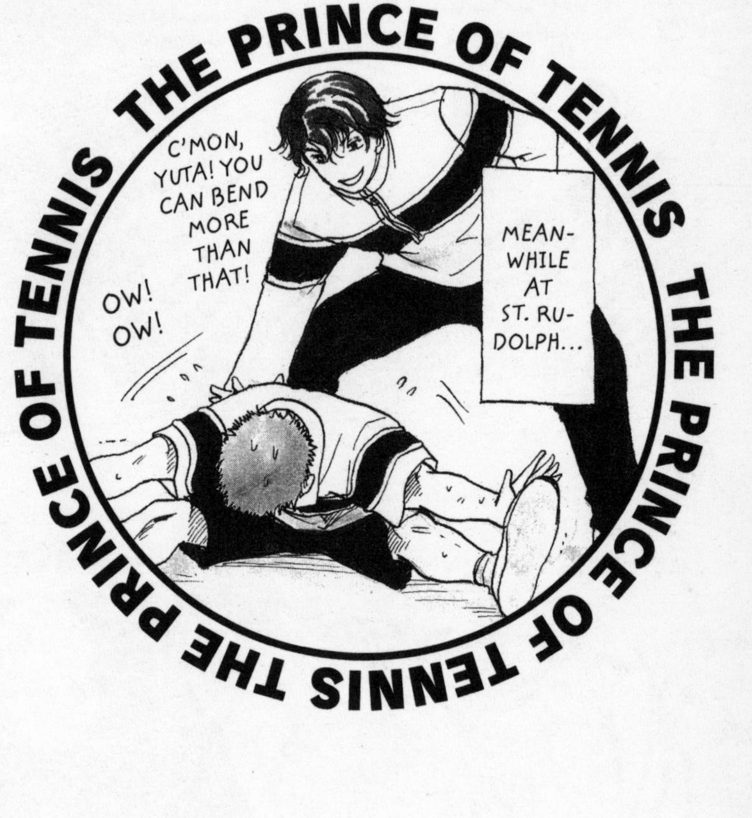
THE PRINCE OF TENNIS THE PRINCE OF TENNIS THE PRINCE OF TENNIS
MEAN-WHILE AT ST. RU-DOLPH...
C'MON, YUTA! YOU CAN BEND MORE THAN THAT!
OW! OW!

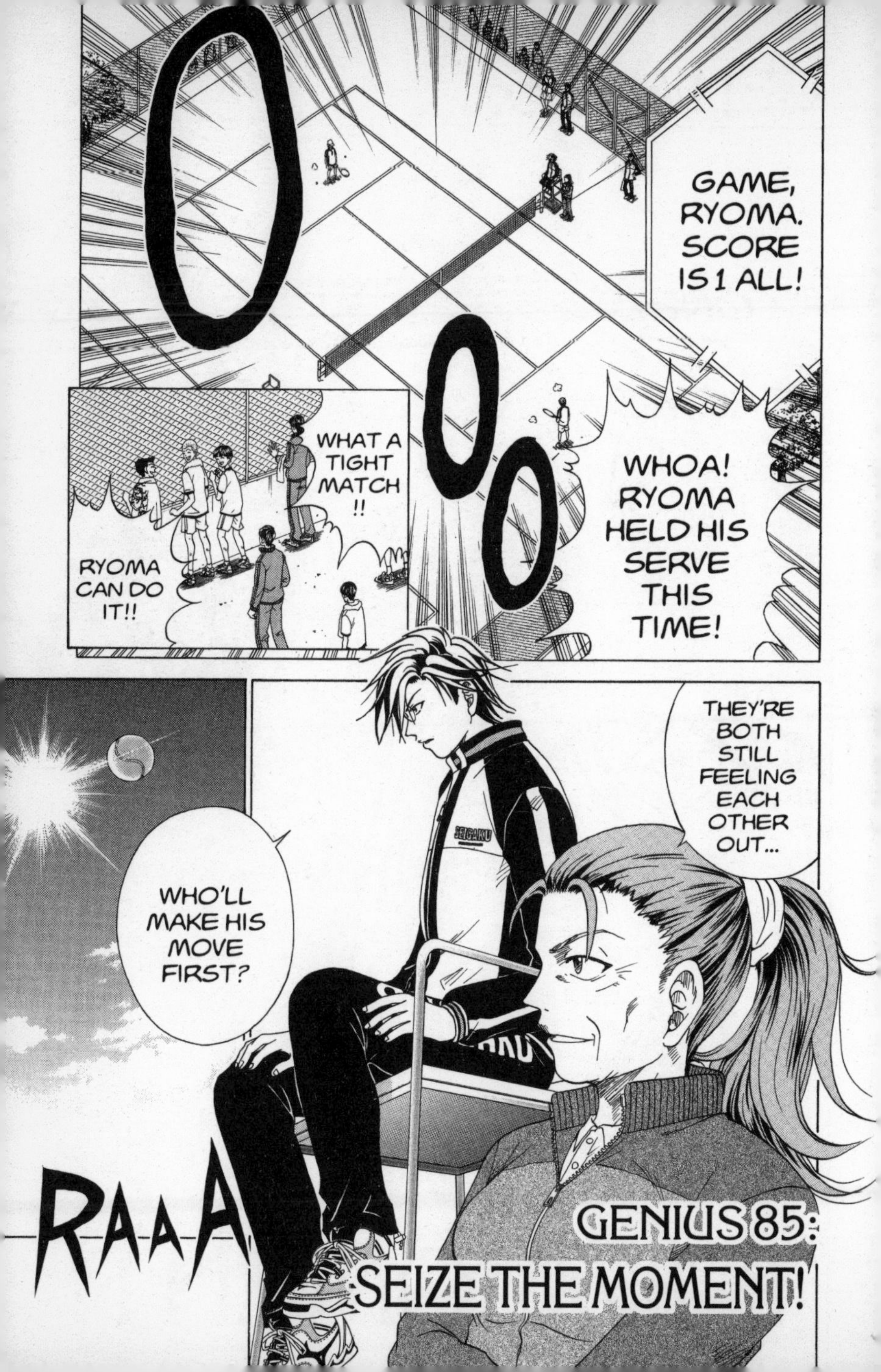
GAME, RYOMA. SCORE IS 1 ALL!
OOO
WHOA! RYOMA HELD HIS SERVE THIS TIME!
WHAT A TIGHT MATCH !!
RYOMA CAN DO IT!!
THEY'RE BOTH STILL FEELING EACH OTHER OUT...
WHO'LL MAKE HIS MOVE FIRST?
SEIGAKU
RAaA
GENIUS 85:
SEIZE THE MOMENT!

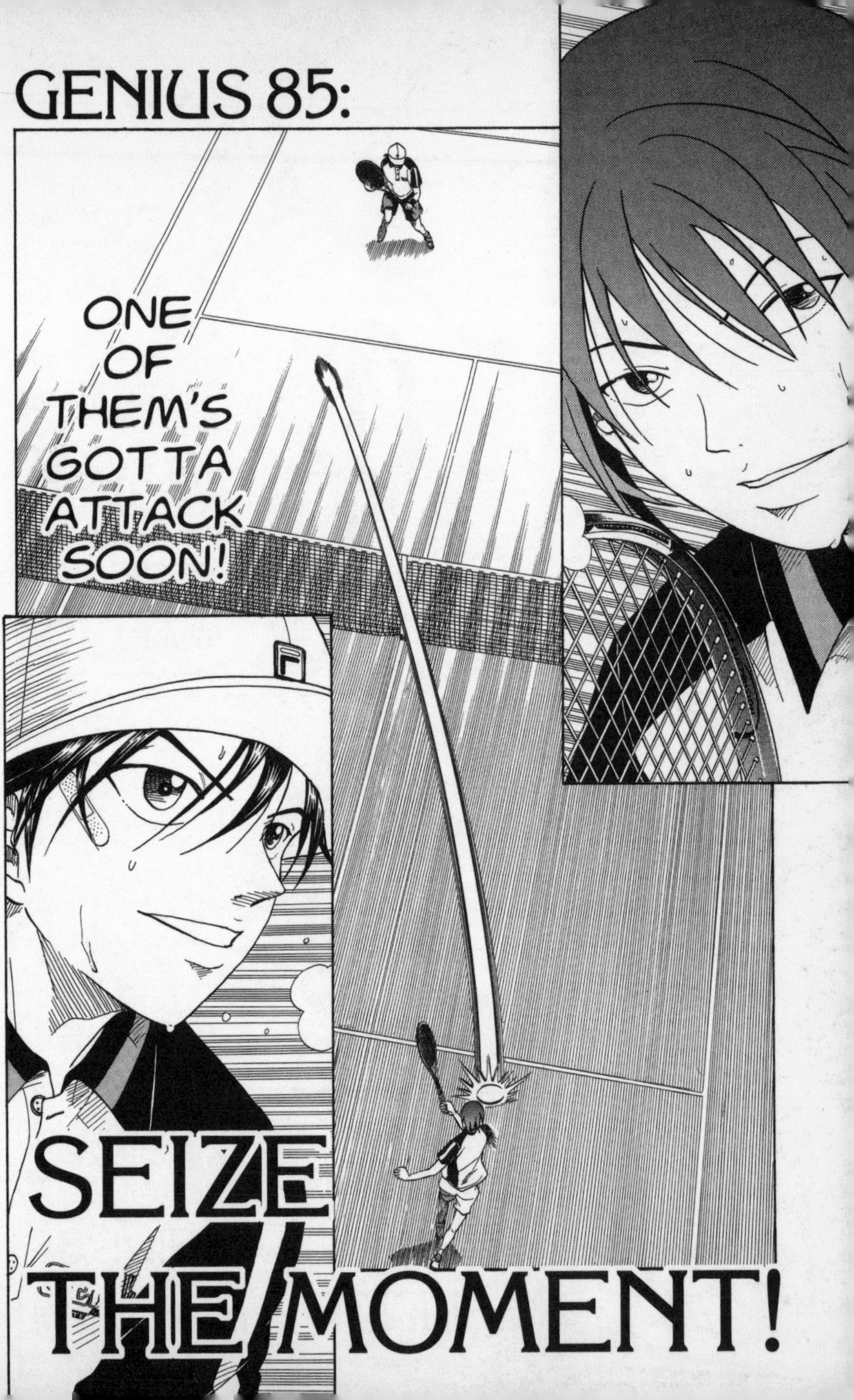
GENIUS 85:
ONE OF THEM'S GOTTA ATTACK SOON!
SEIZE THE MOMENT!

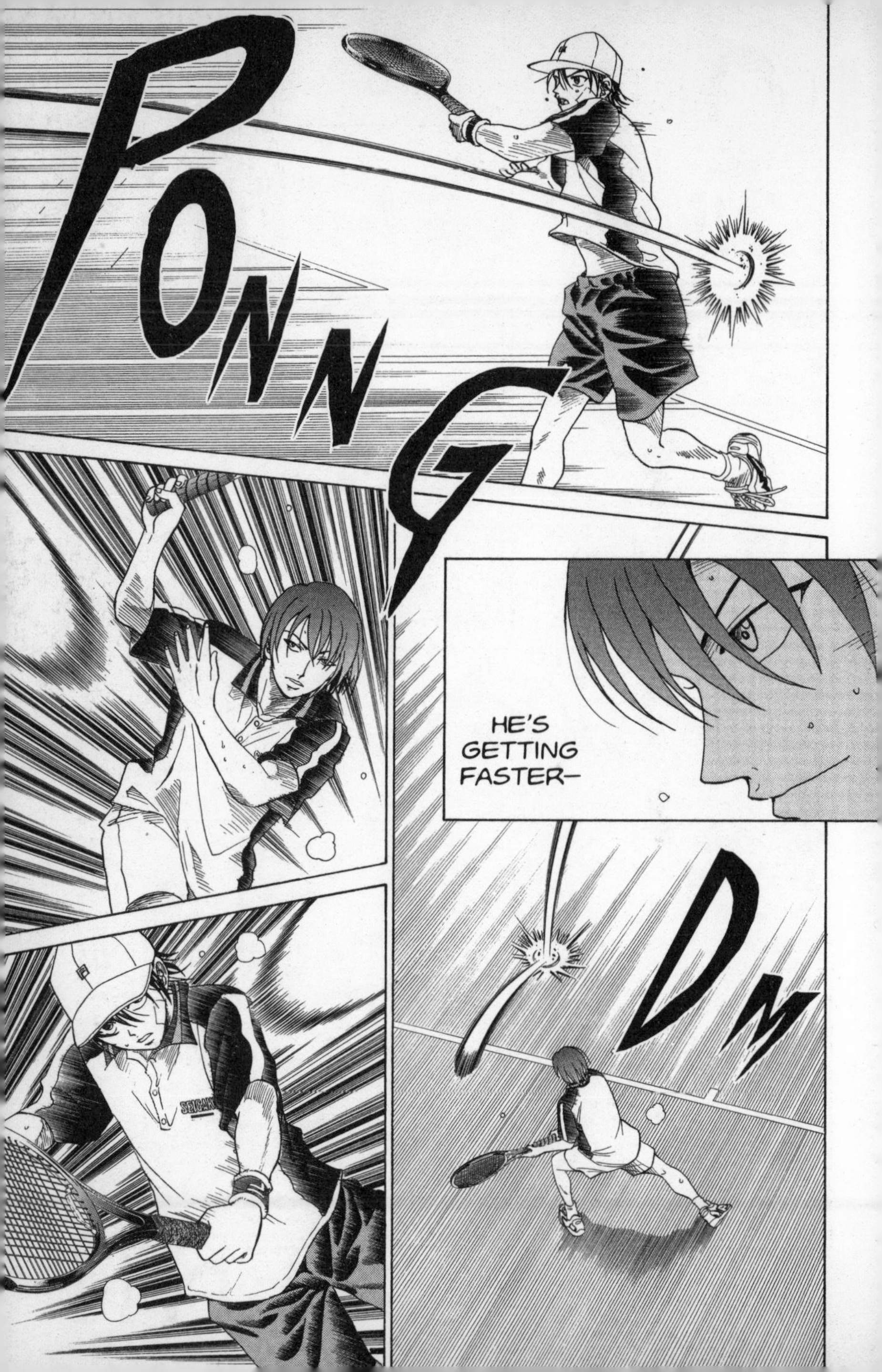
PONNG
HE'S GETTING FASTER—
DM

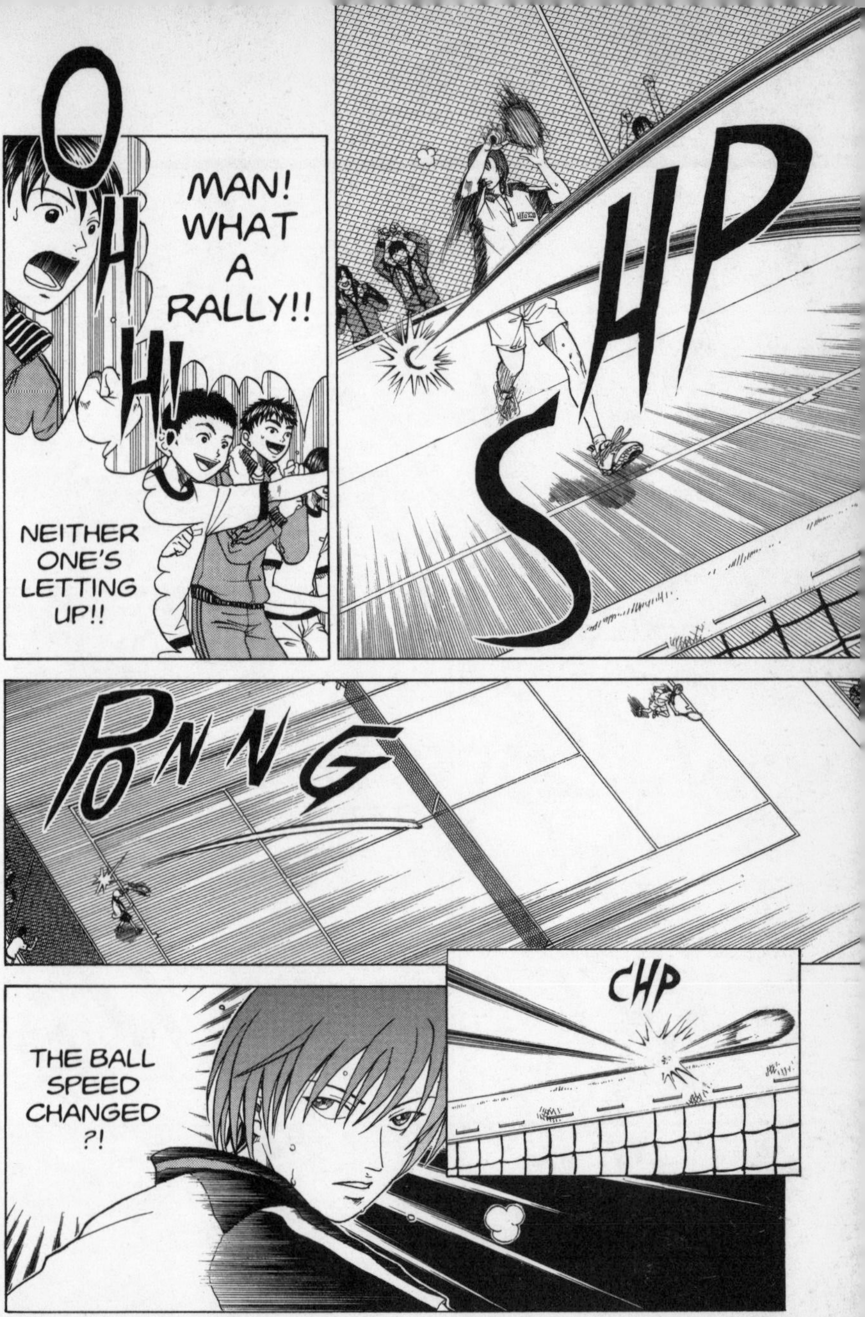
SHP
OHH!
MAN! WHAT A RALLY!!
NEITHER ONE'S LETTING UP!!
PONNG
CHP
THE BALL SPEED CHANGED ?!

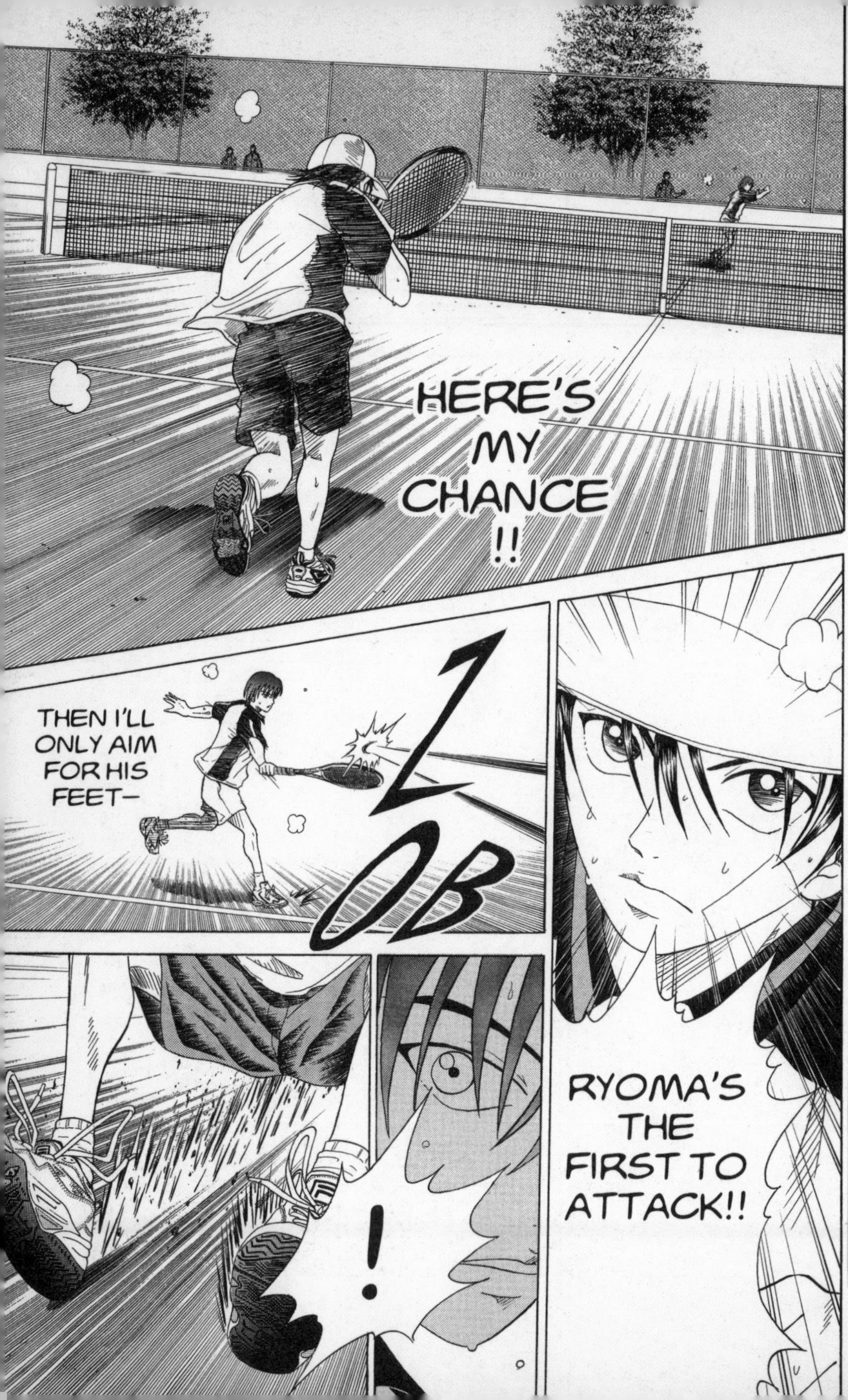
HERE'S MY CHANCE !!
RYOMA'S THE FIRST TO ATTACK!!
THEN I'LL ONLY AIM FOR HIS FEET–
ZOB
!

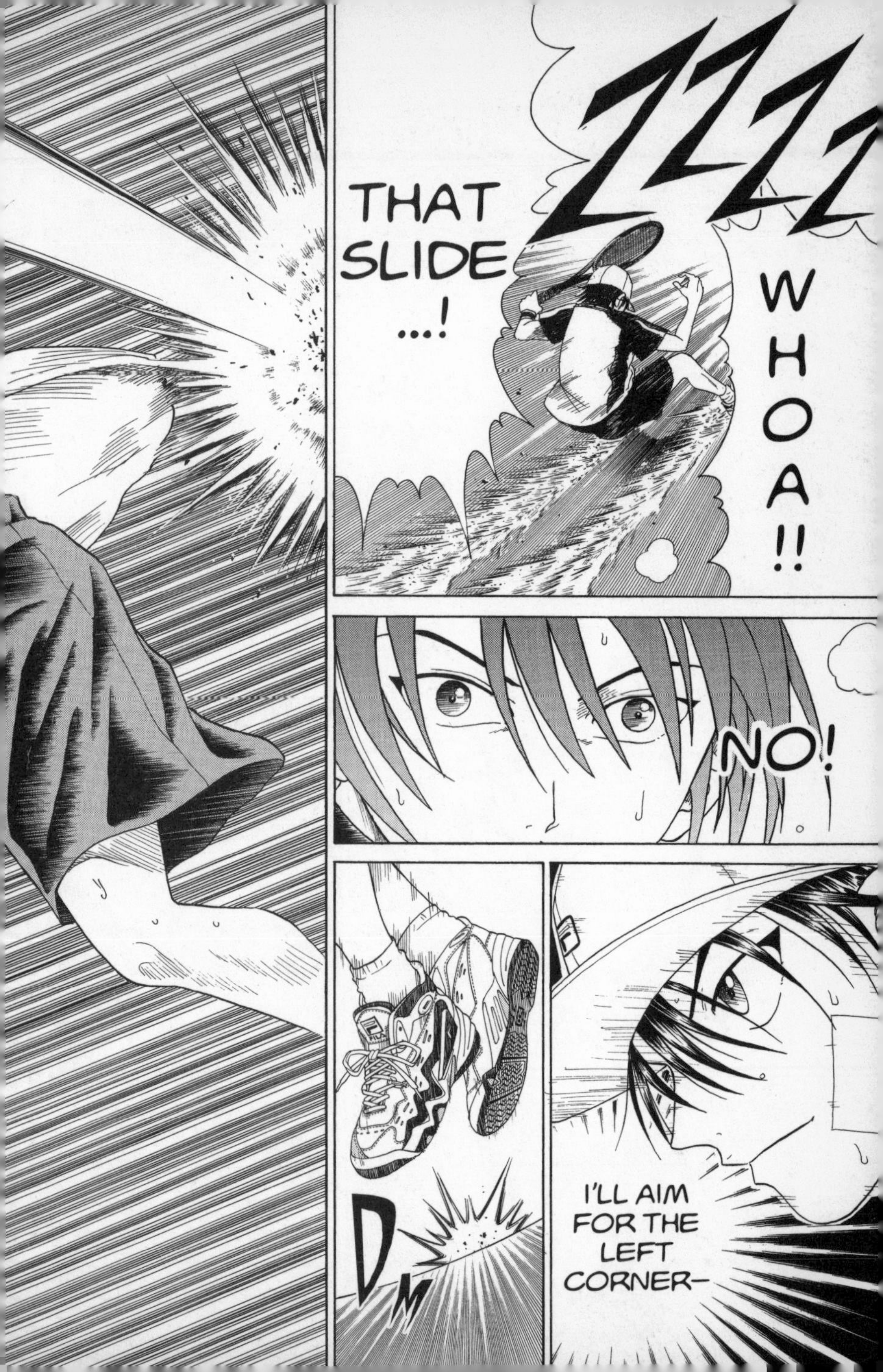
ZZZ
WHOA!!
THAT SLIDE ...!
NO!
I'LL AIM FOR THE LEFT CORNER–
DM

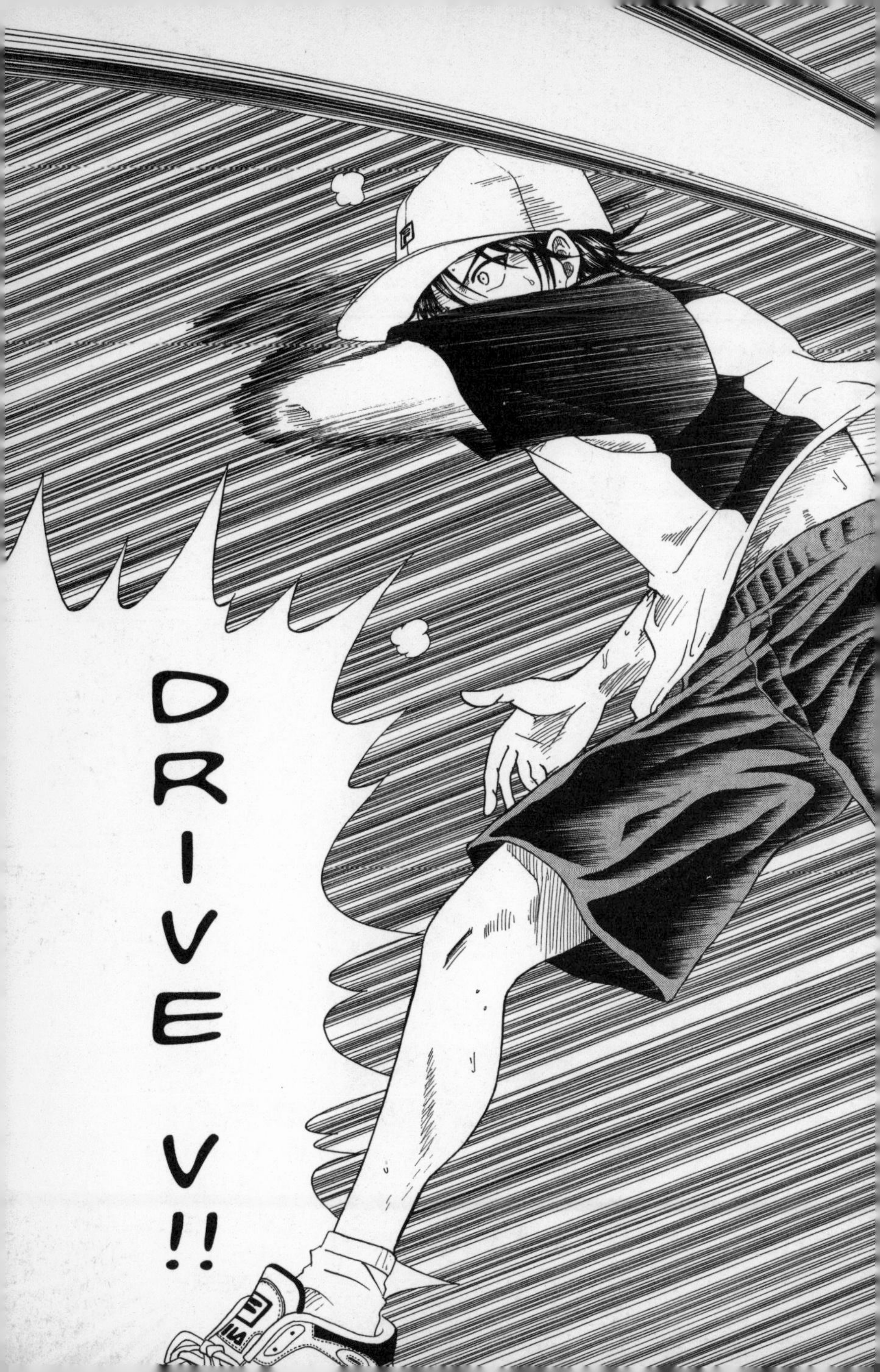
DRIVE V!!

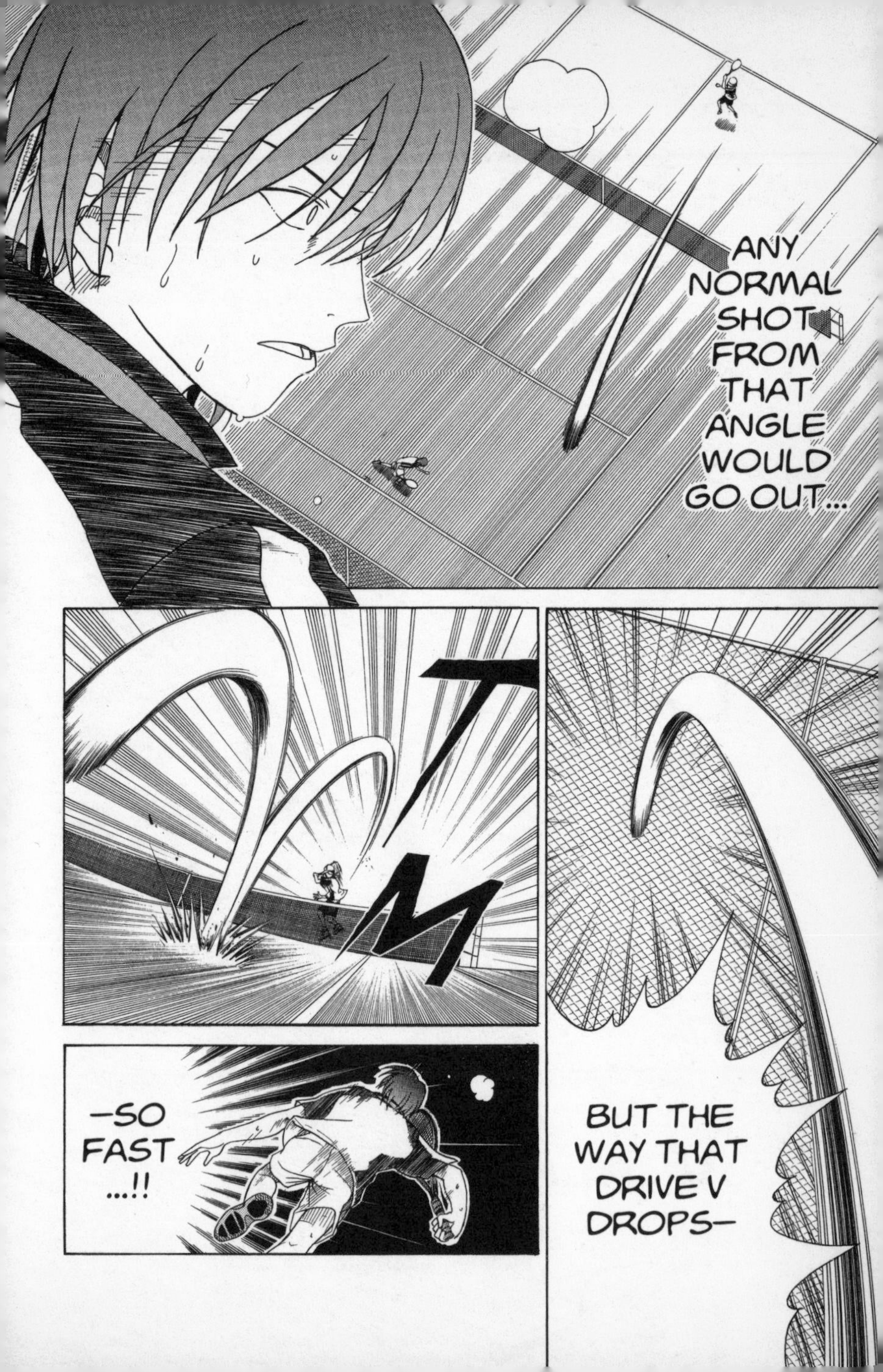
ANY NORMAL SHOT FROM THAT ANGLE WOULD GO OUT...
BUT THE WAY THAT DRIVE V DROPS—
TM
—SO FAST ...!!

READ THIS WAY

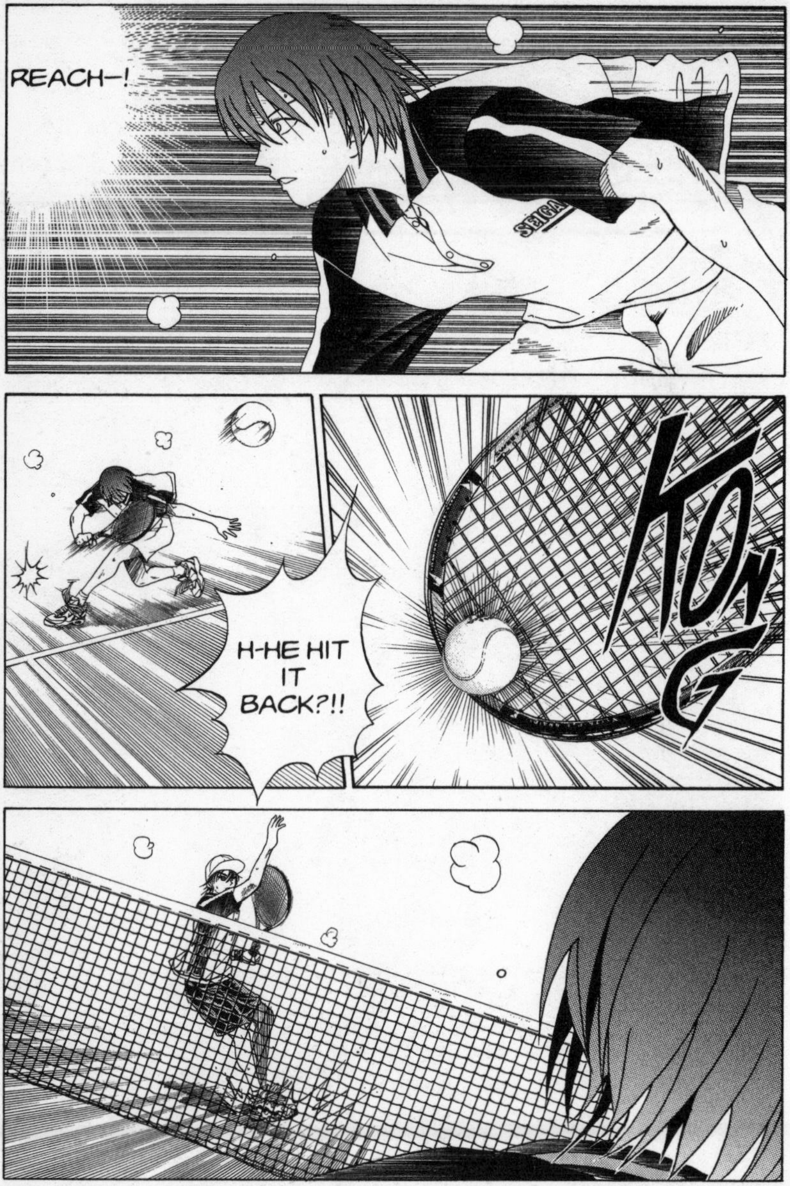
REACH—!
KONG
H-HE HIT IT BACK?!!

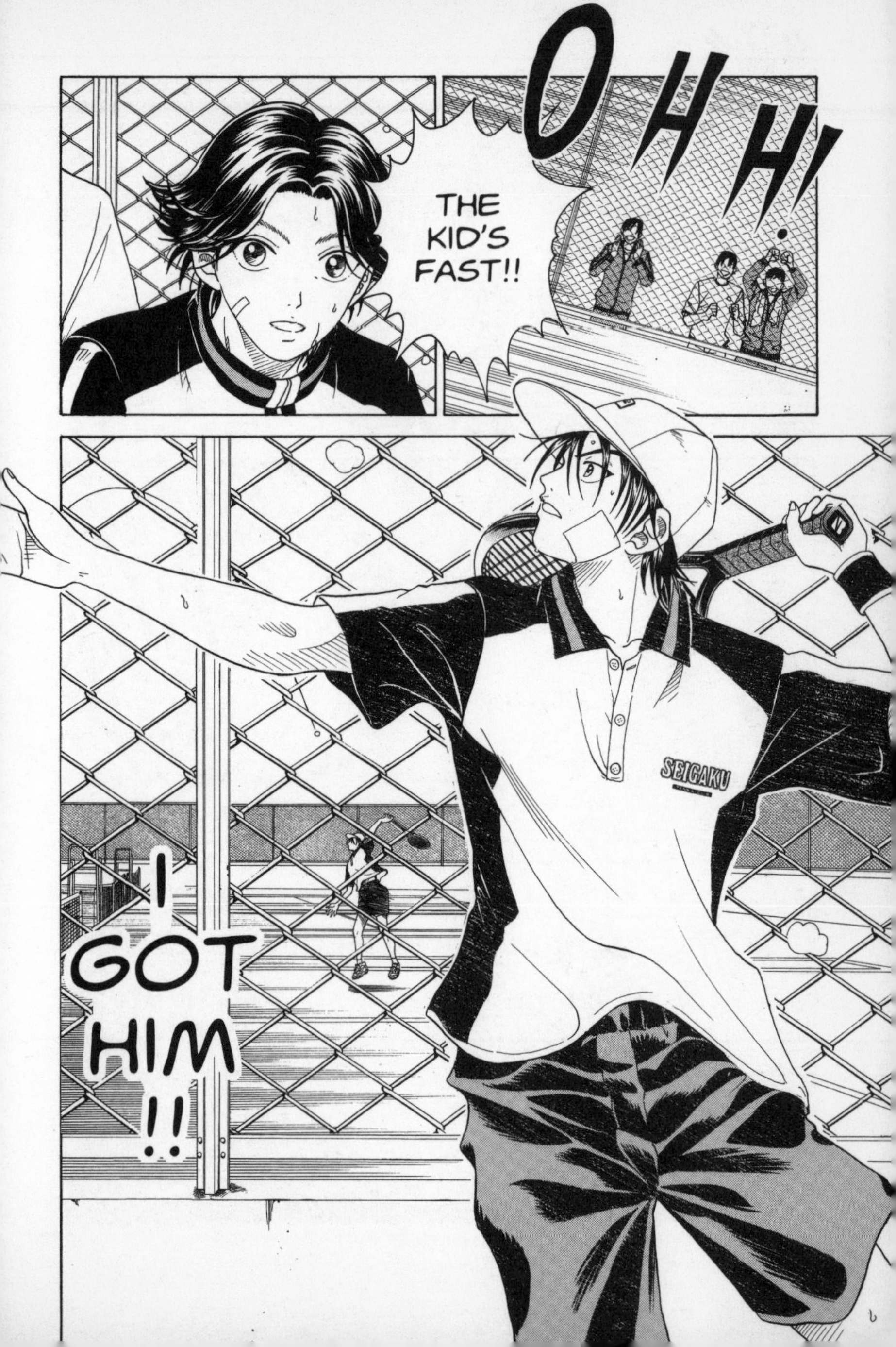
OHH!
THE KID'S FAST!!
I GOT HIM!!

READ THIS WAY

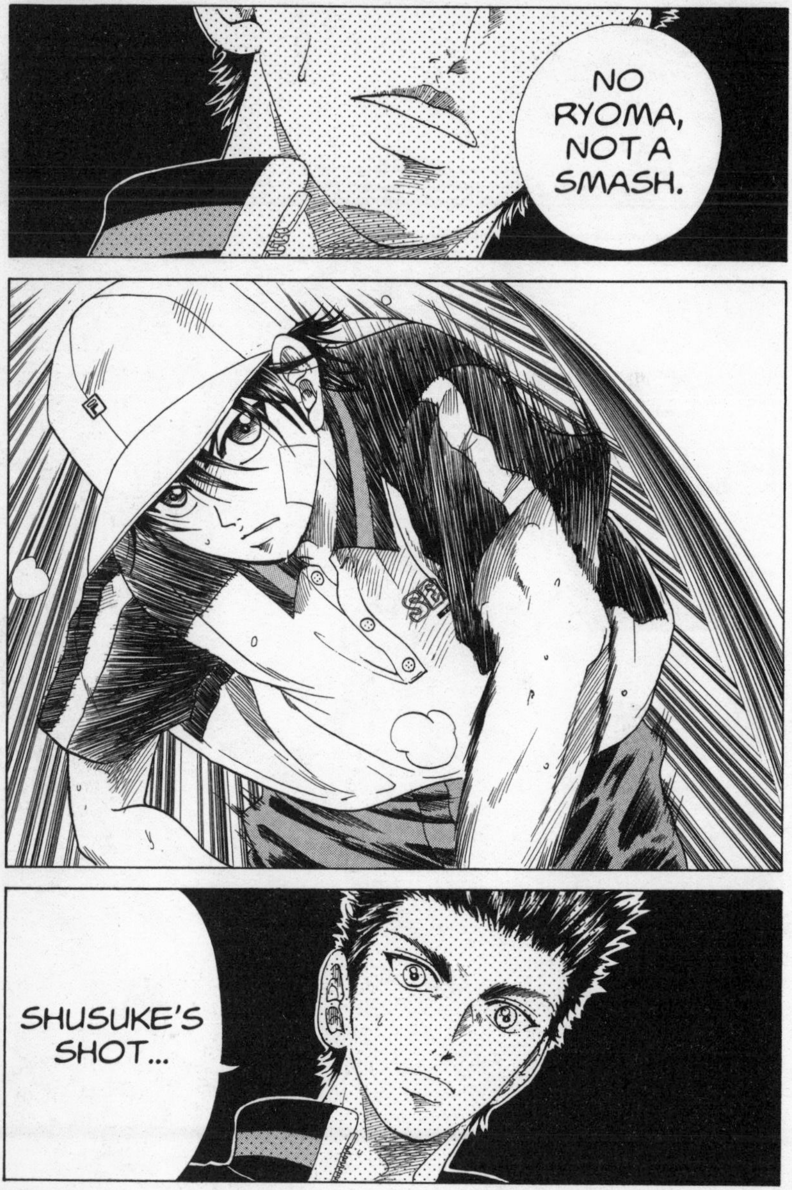
NO RYOMA, NOT A SMASH.
SHUSUKE'S SHOT...

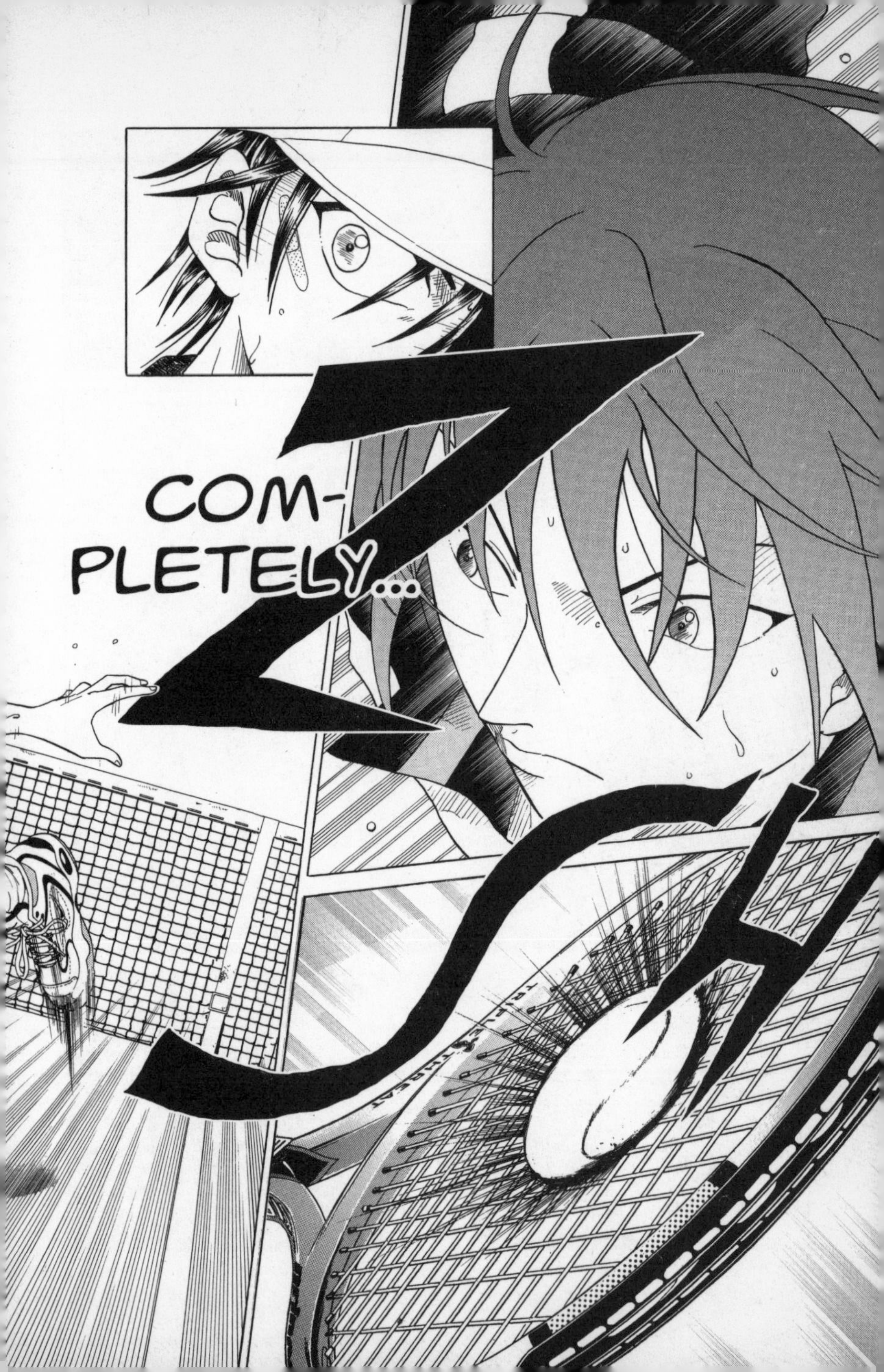
COM-
PLETELY...

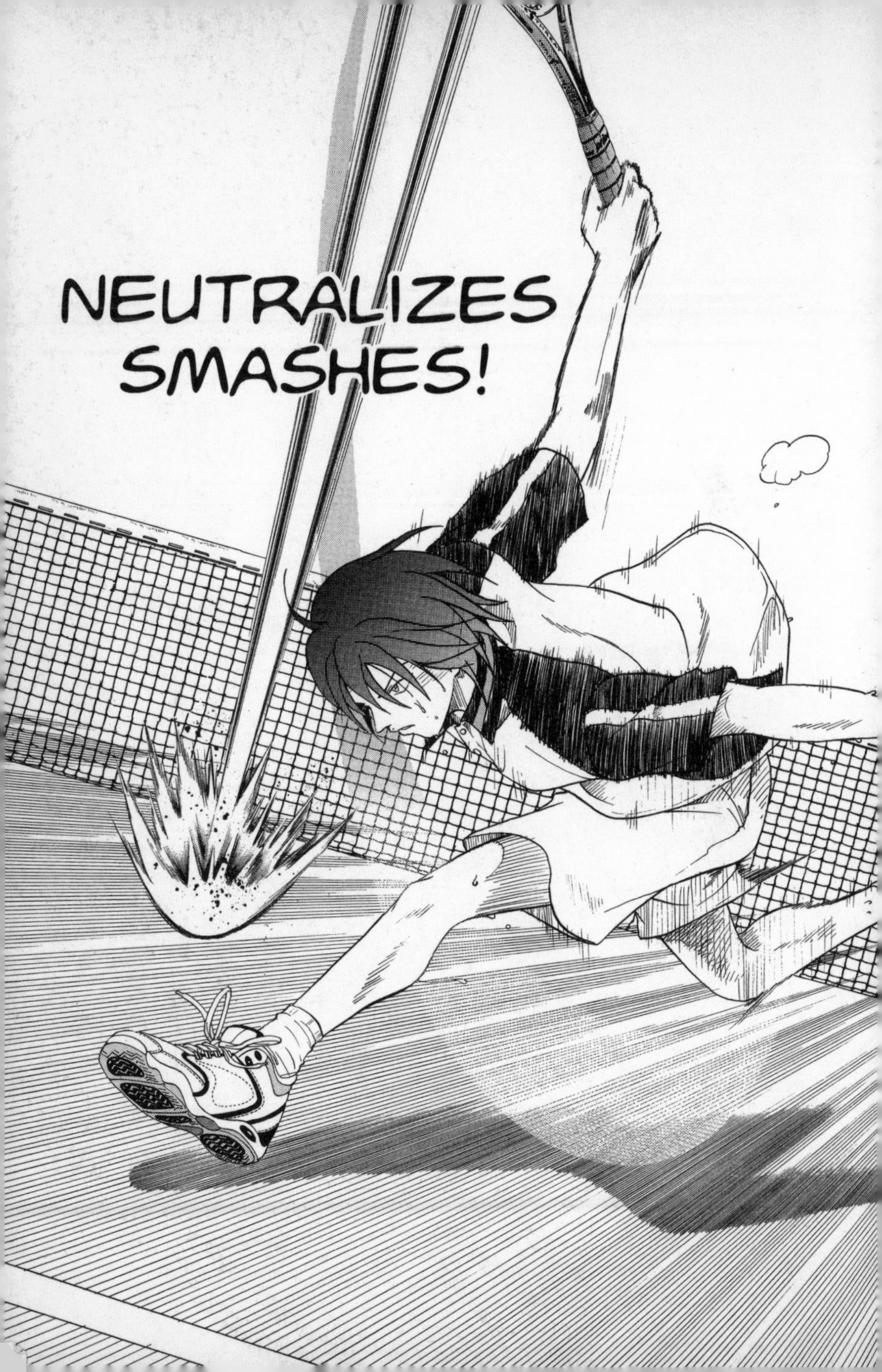
NEUTRALIZES SMASHES!

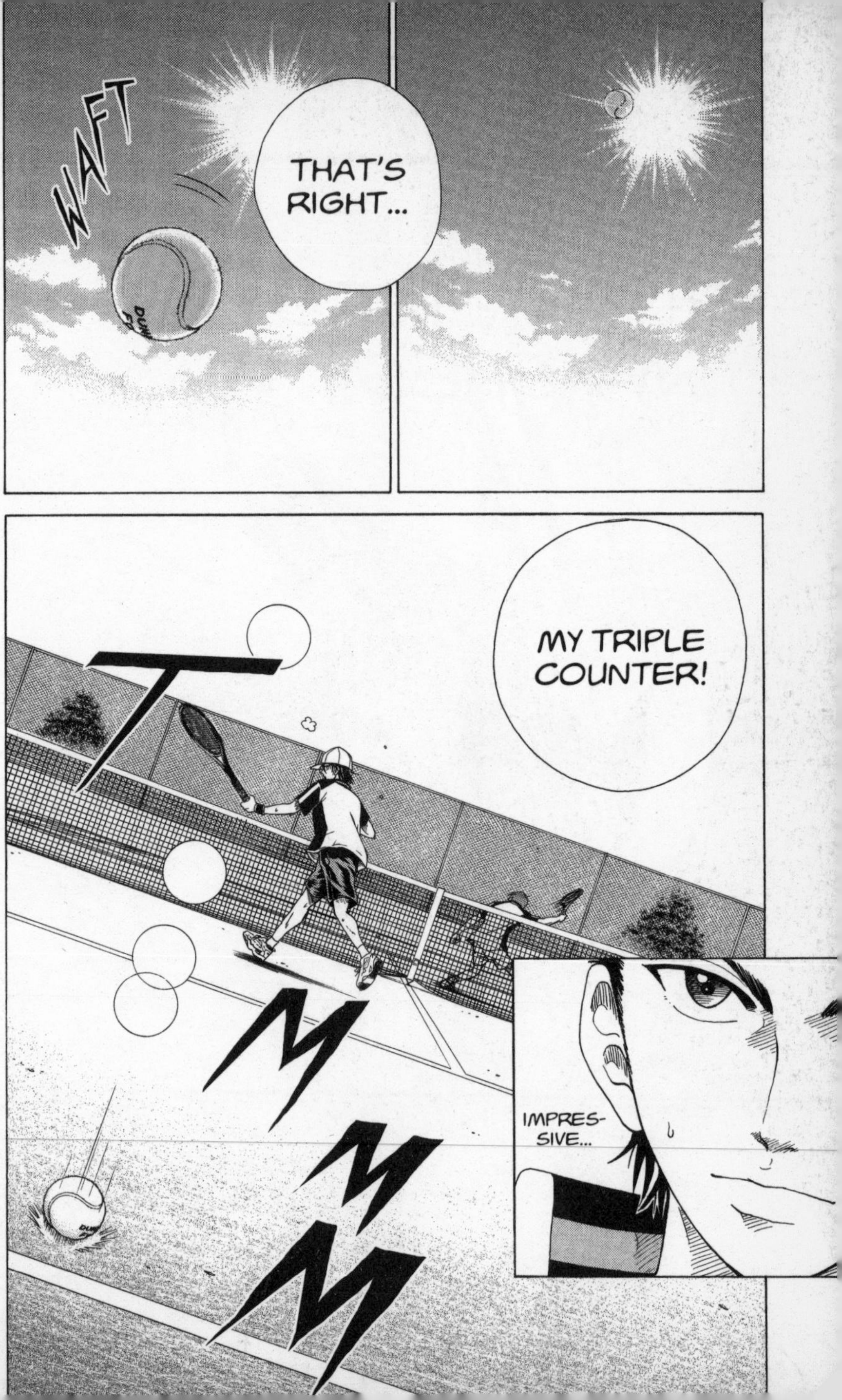
THAT'S RIGHT...
WAFT
MY TRIPLE COUNTER!
TMMM
IMPRES-SIVE...

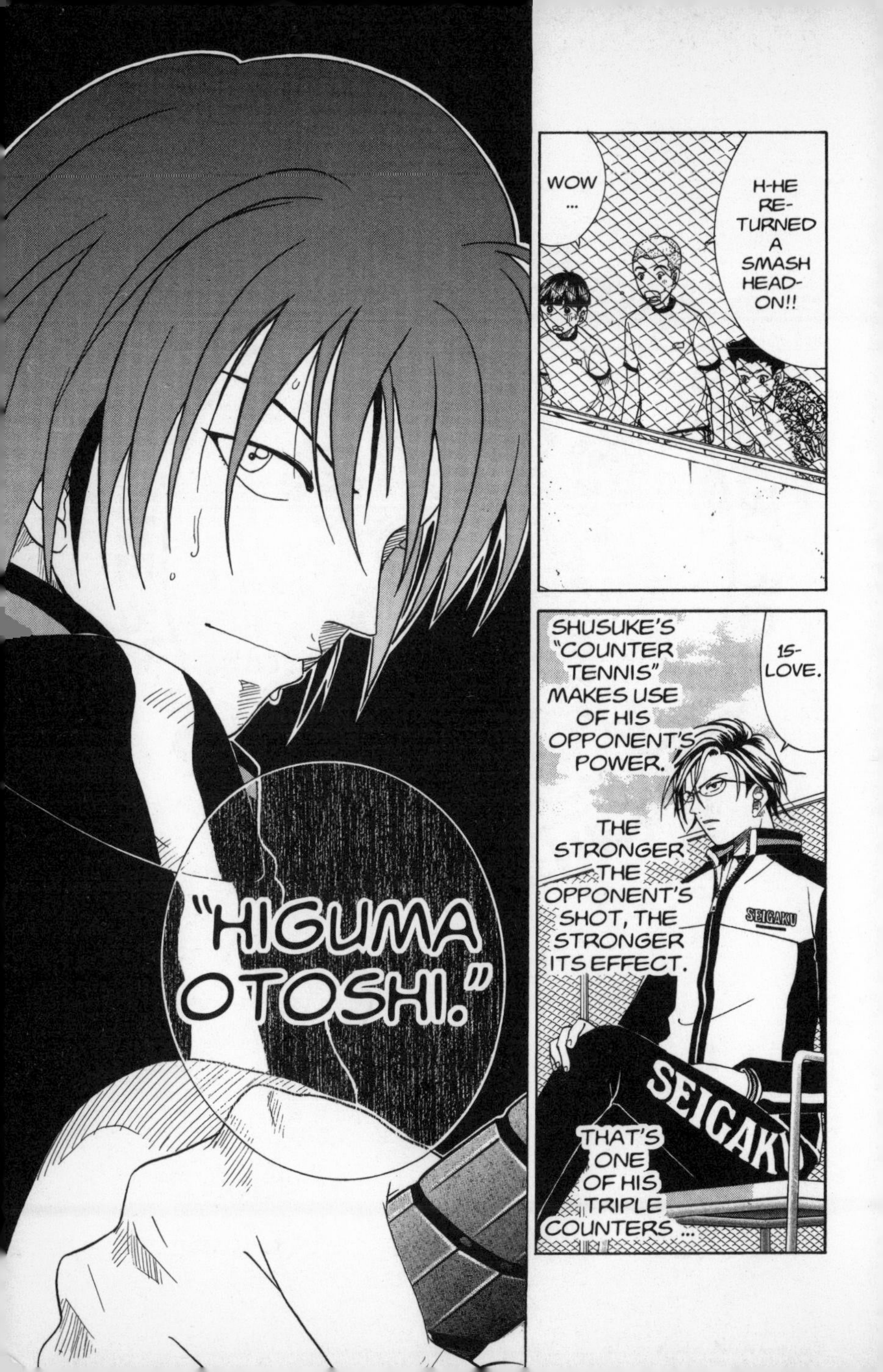
H-HE RE-TURNED A SMASH HEAD-ON!!
WOW ...
15-LOVE.
SHUSUKE'S "COUNTER TENNIS" MAKES USE OF HIS OPPONENT'S POWER.
THE STRONGER THE OPPONENT'S SHOT, THE STRONGER ITS EFFECT.
THAT'S ONE OF HIS TRIPLE COUNTERS ...
"HIGUMA OTOSHI."

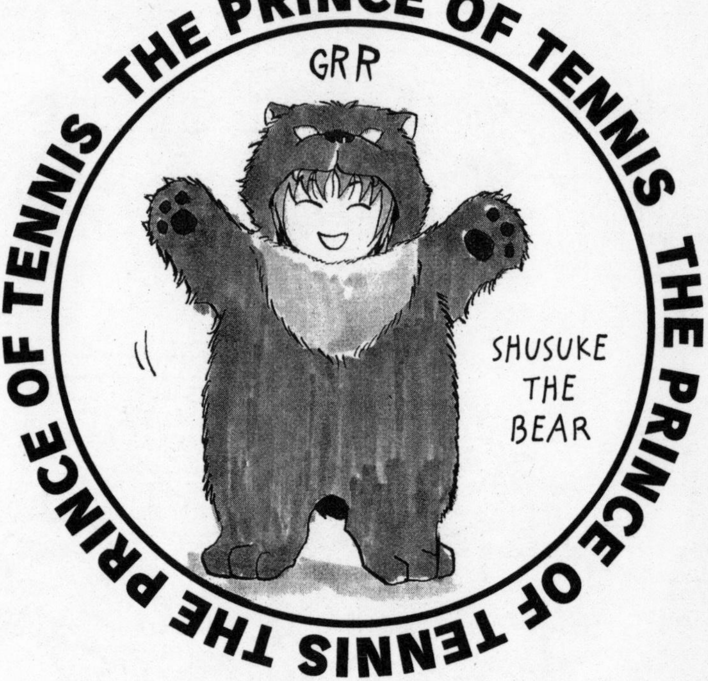
THE PRINCE OF TENNIS THE PRINCE OF TENNIS THE PRINCE OF TENNIS
GRR
SHUSUKE THE BEAR

GENIUS 86: CHALLENGE

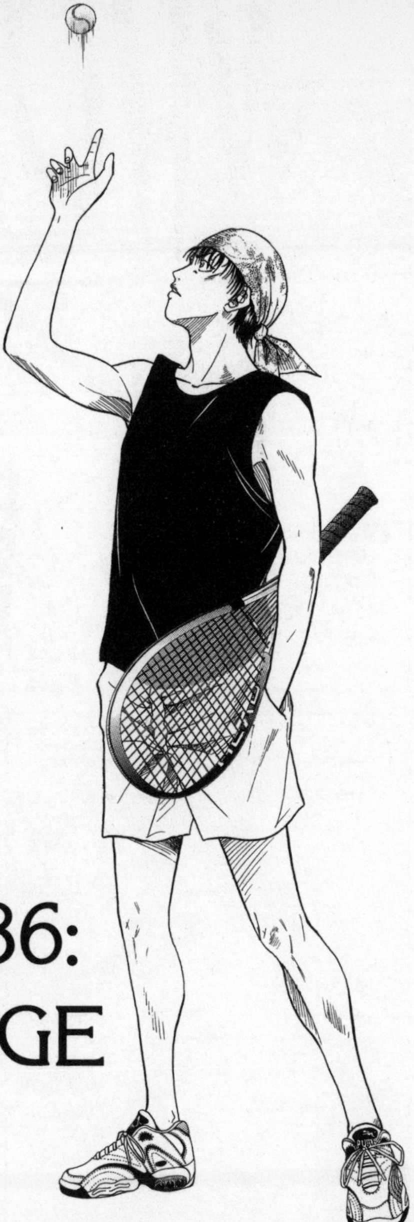

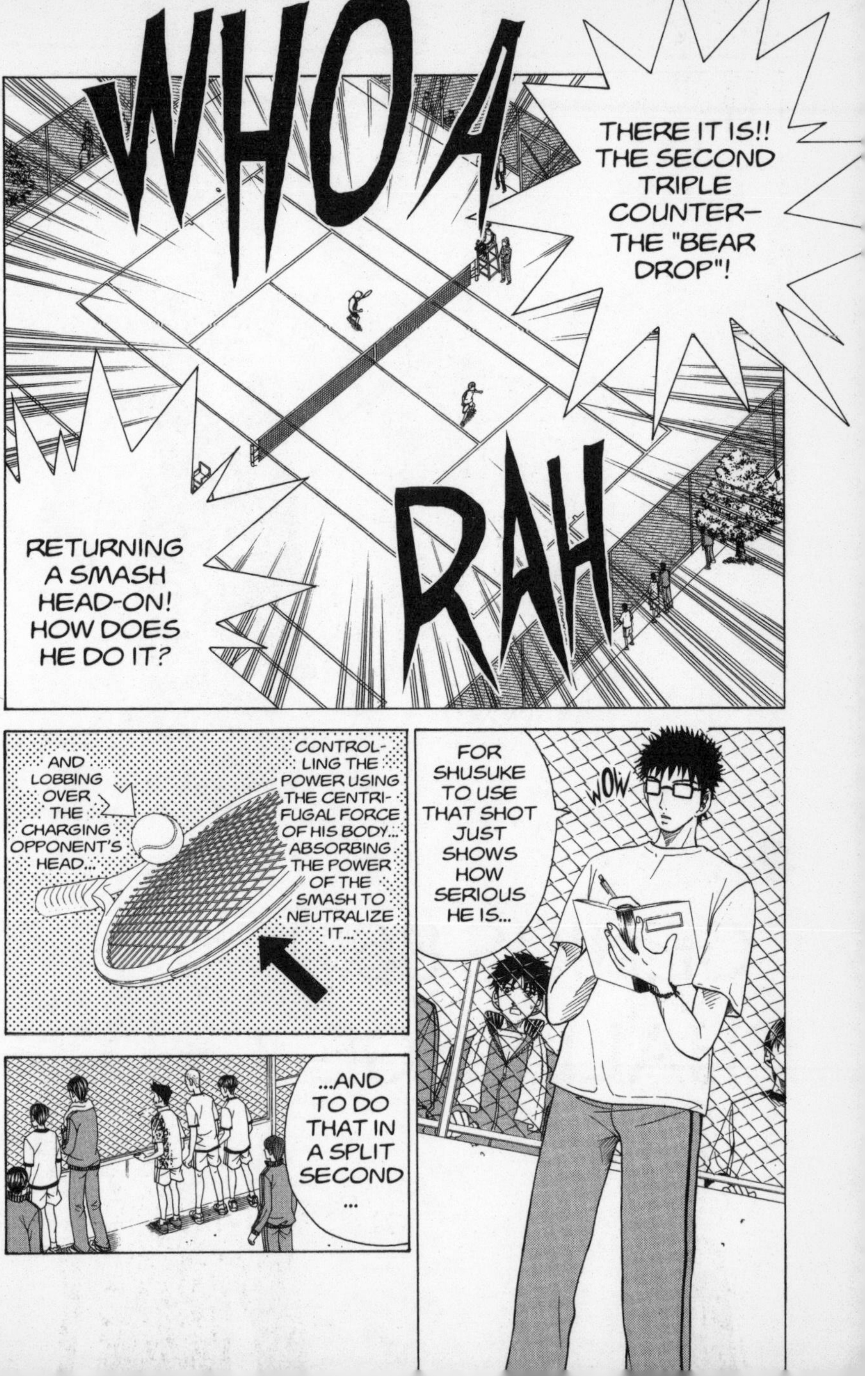
WHOA
THERE IT IS!! THE SECOND TRIPLE COUNTER– THE "BEAR DROP"!
RAH
RETURNING A SMASH HEAD-ON! HOW DOES HE DO IT?
WOW
FOR SHUSUKE TO USE THAT SHOT JUST SHOWS HOW SERIOUS HE IS...
CONTROL-LING THE POWER USING THE CENTRI-FUGAL FORCE OF HIS BODY... ABSORBING THE POWER OF THE SMASH TO NEUTRALIZE IT...
AND LOBBING OVER THE CHARGING OPPONENT'S HEAD...
...AND TO DO THAT IN A SPLIT SECOND ...

READ THIS WAY

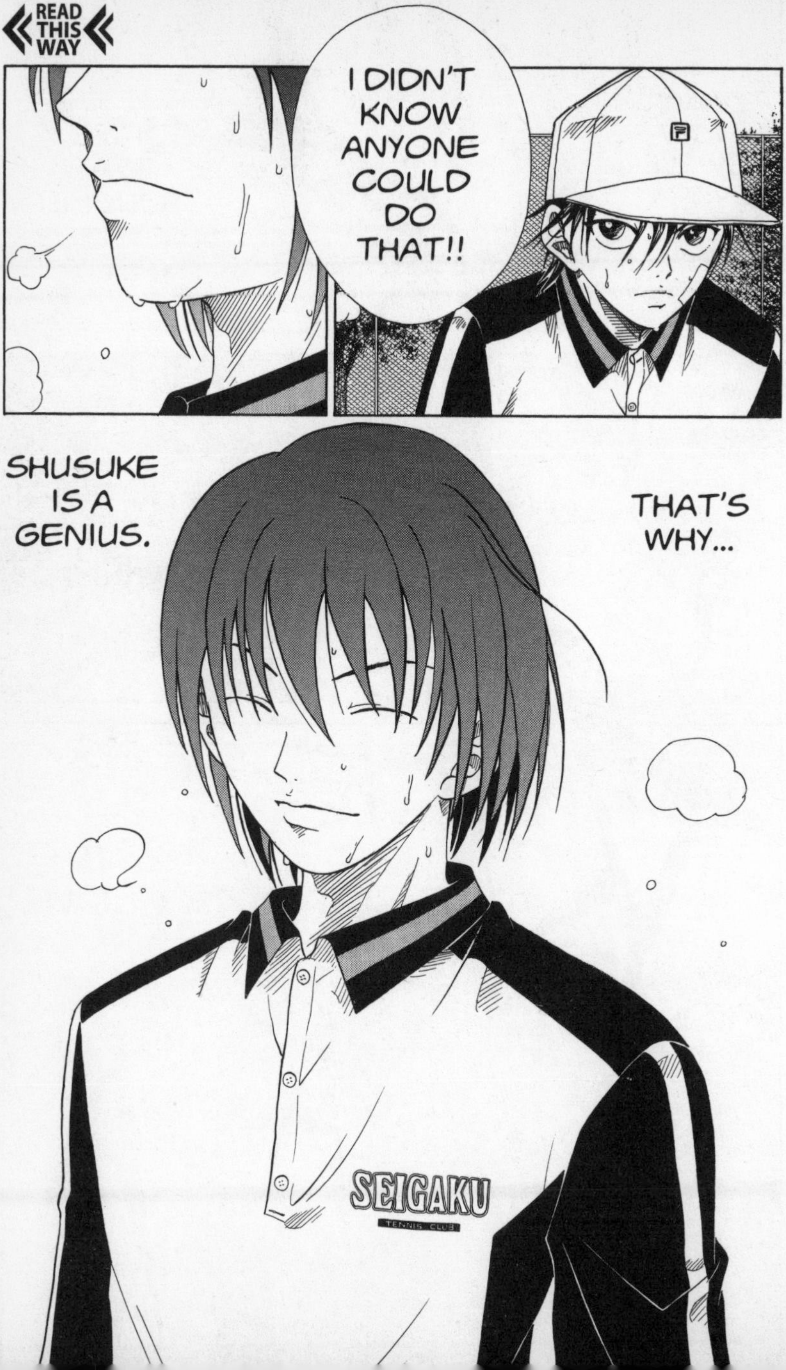
I DIDN'T KNOW ANYONE COULD DO THAT!!
SHUSUKE IS A GENIUS.
THAT'S WHY...
SEIGAKU
TENNIS CLUB

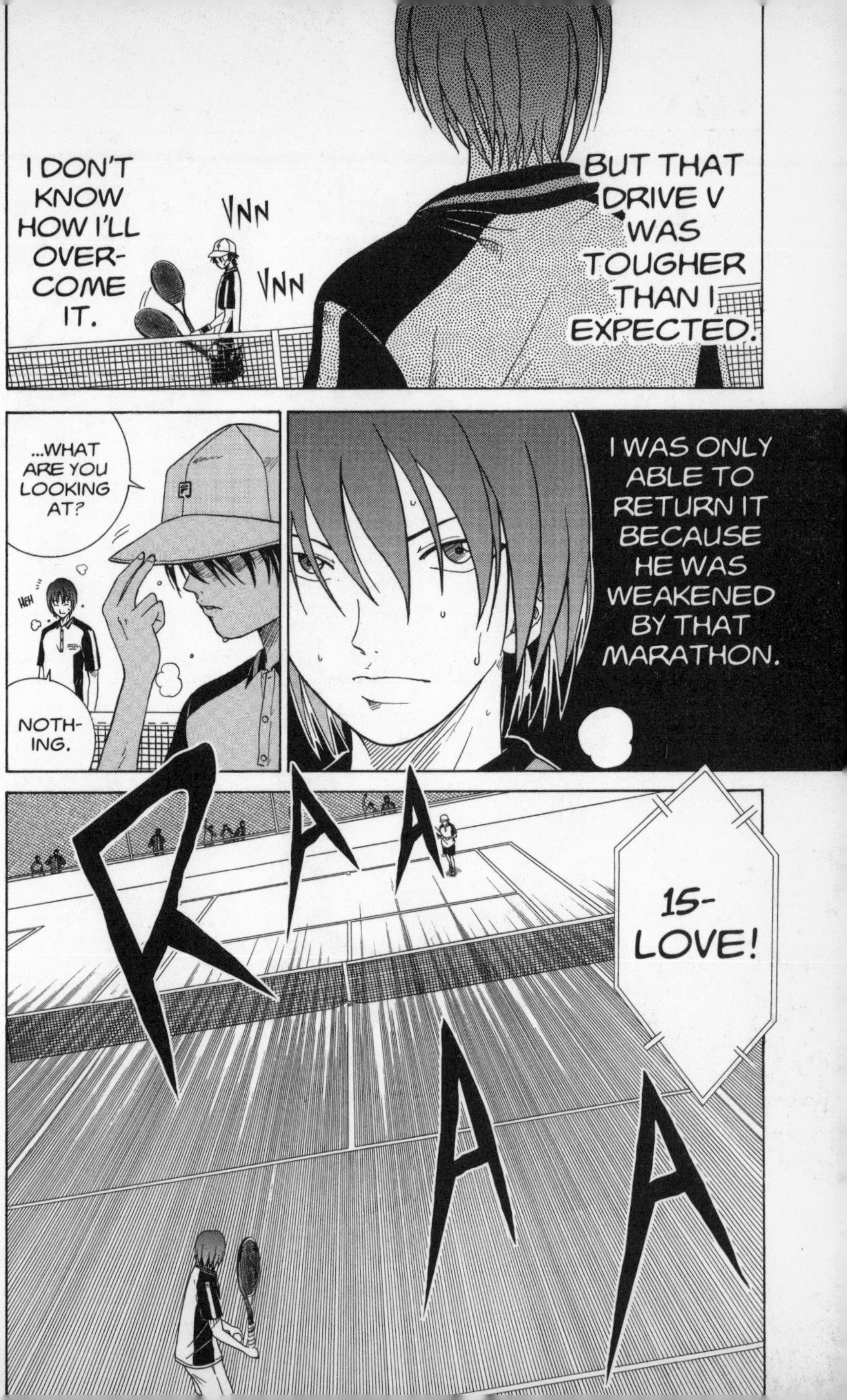
BUT THAT DRIVE V WAS TOUGHER THAN I EXPECTED.
VNN
VNN
I DON'T KNOW HOW I'LL OVER-COME IT.
I WAS ONLY ABLE TO RETURN IT BECAUSE HE WAS WEAKENED BY THAT MARATHON.
...WHAT ARE YOU LOOKING AT?
HEH
NOTH-ING.
RAAAA
15-LOVE!

READ THIS WAY

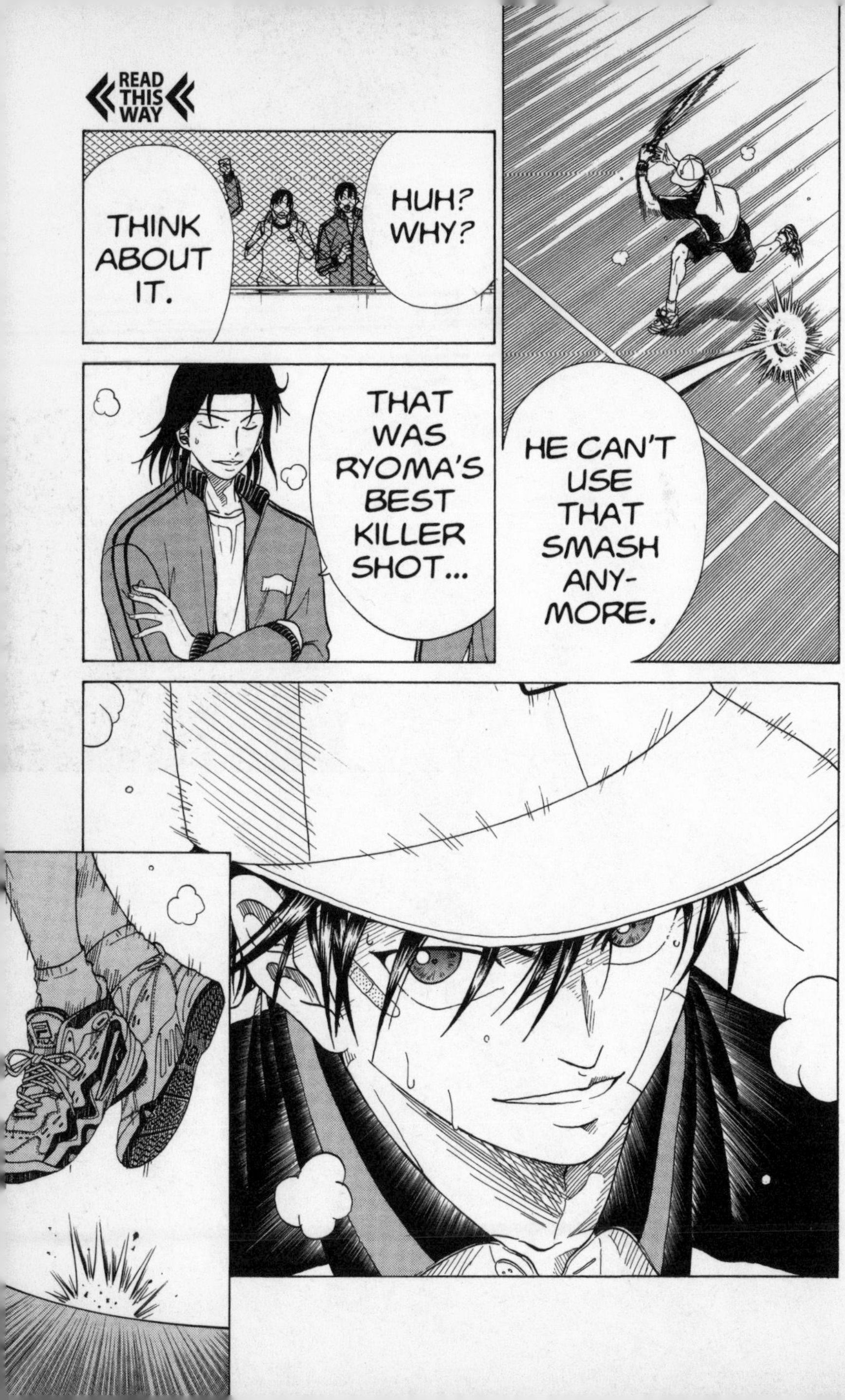
HE CAN'T USE THAT SMASH ANY-MORE.
HUH? WHY?
THINK ABOUT IT.
THAT WAS RYOMA'S BEST KILLER SHOT...

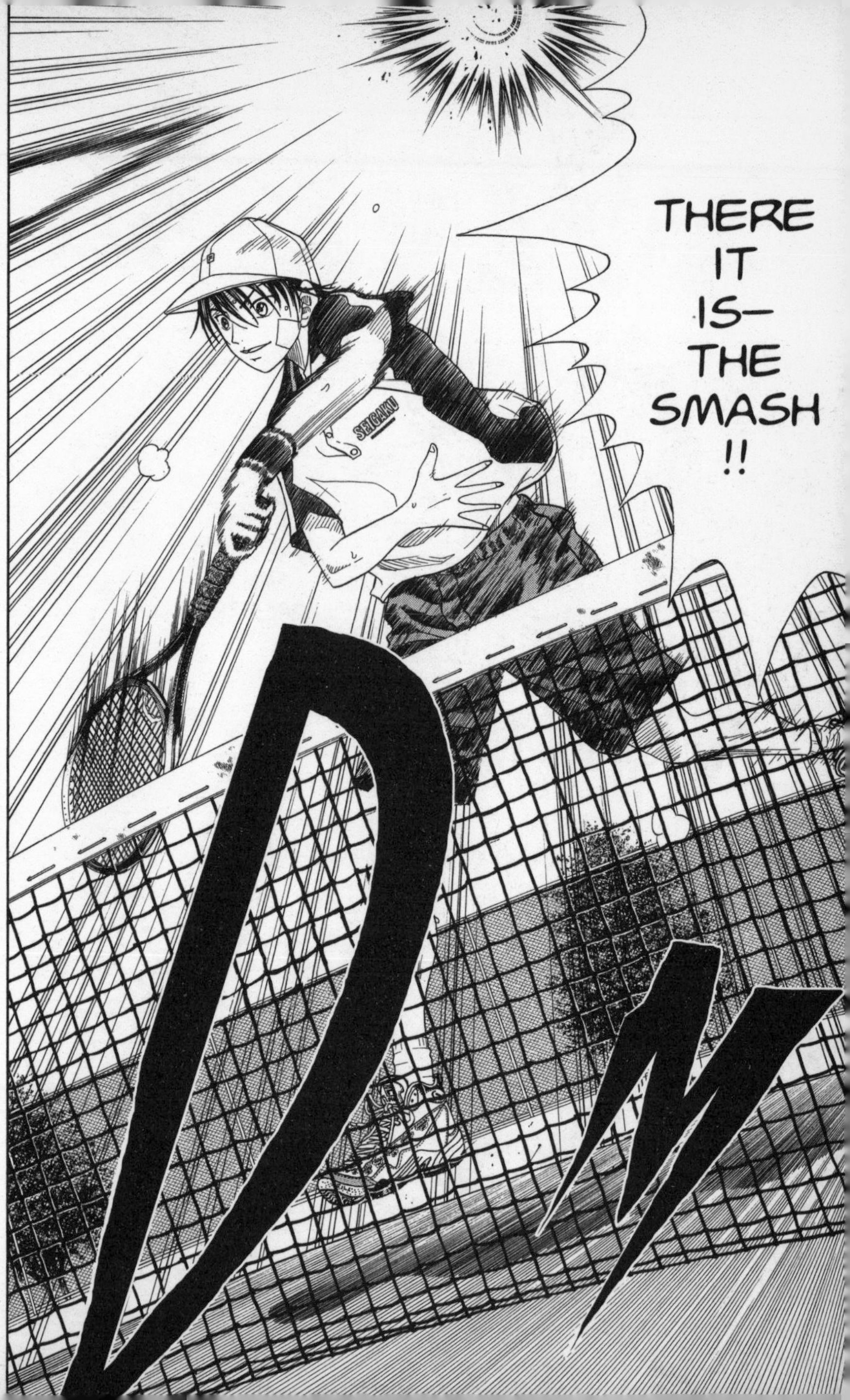
THERE IT IS—THE SMASH!!
SEIGAKU

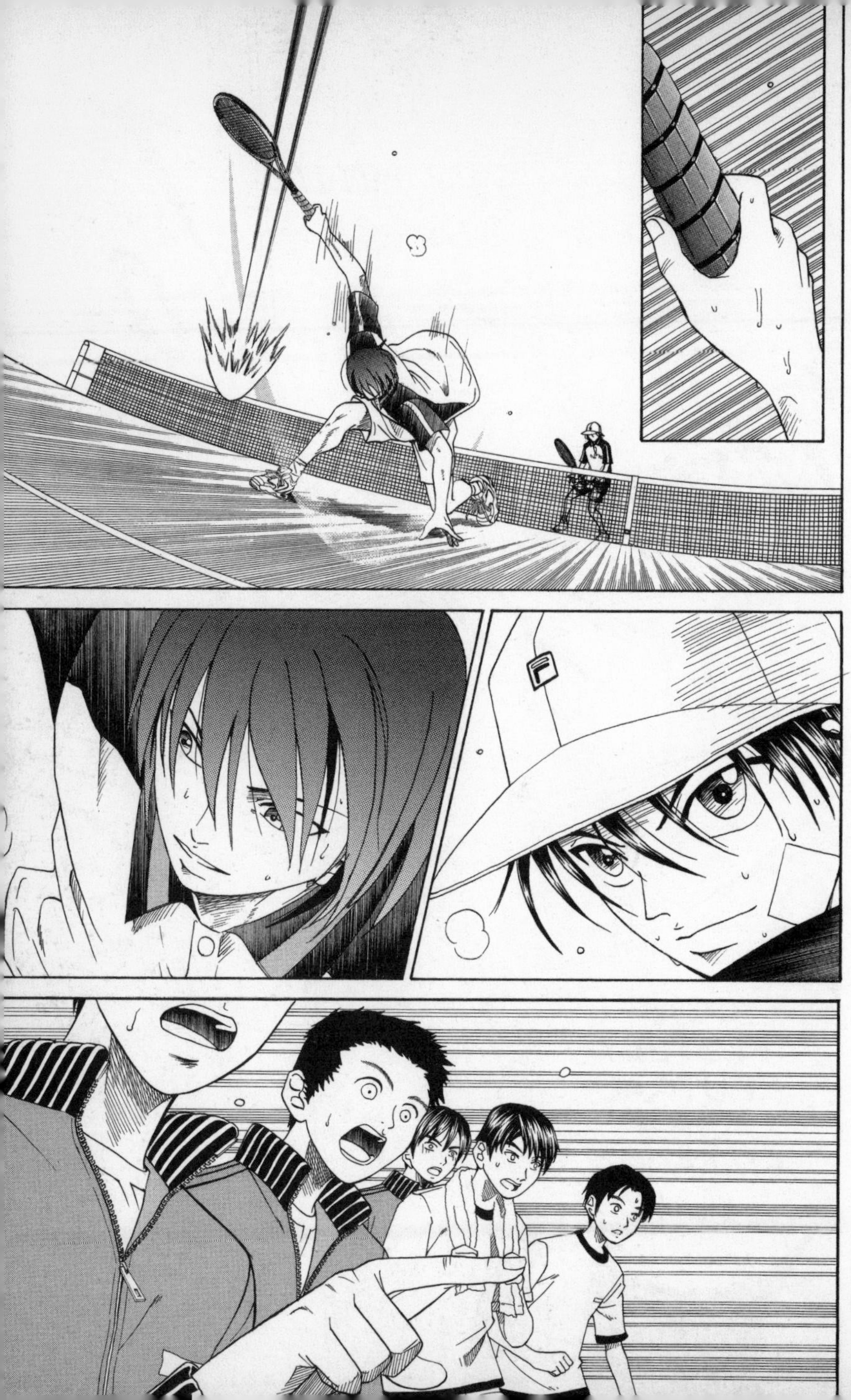

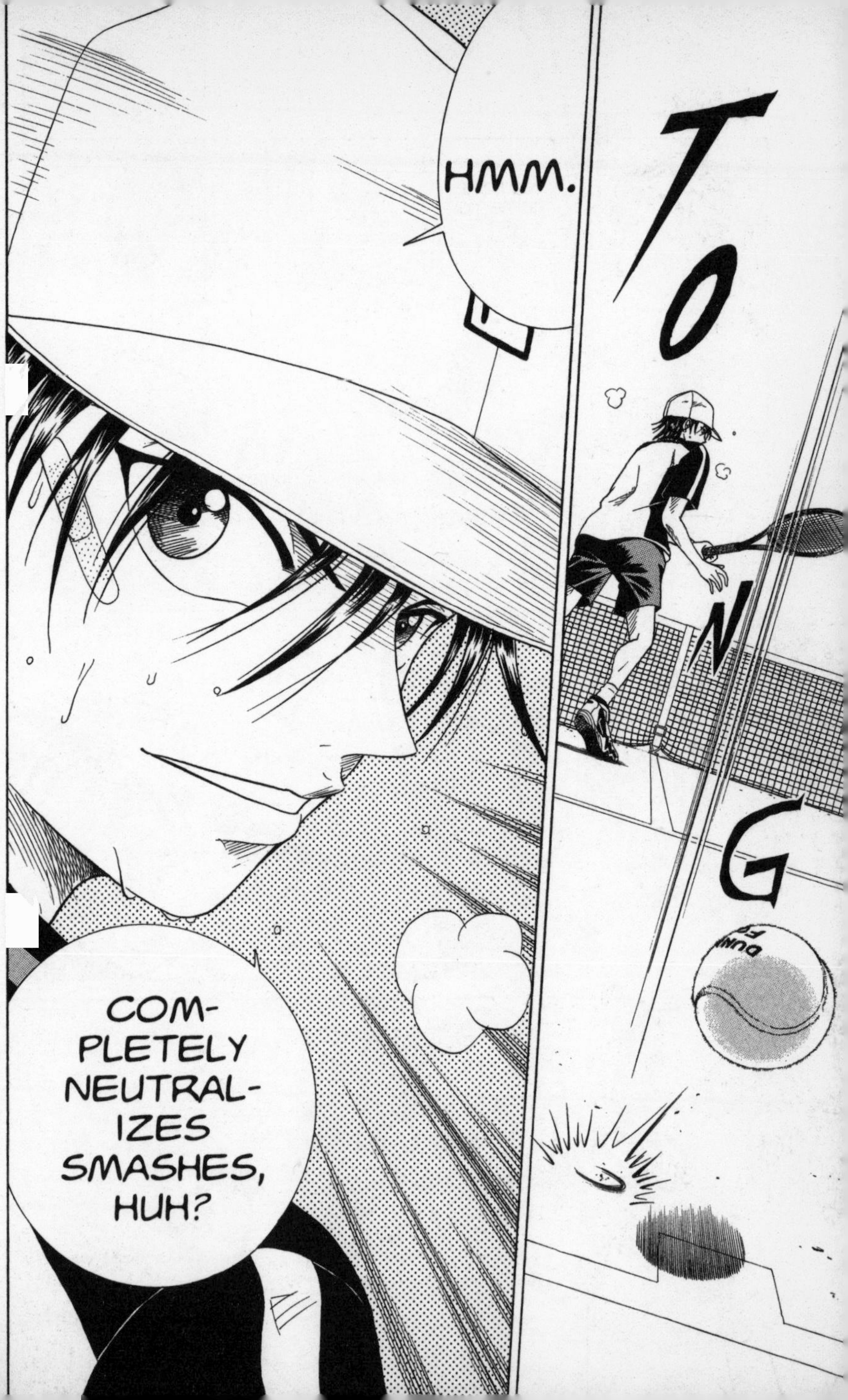
TONG
HMM.
COMPLETELY NEUTRALIZES SMASHES, HUH?

READ THIS WAY

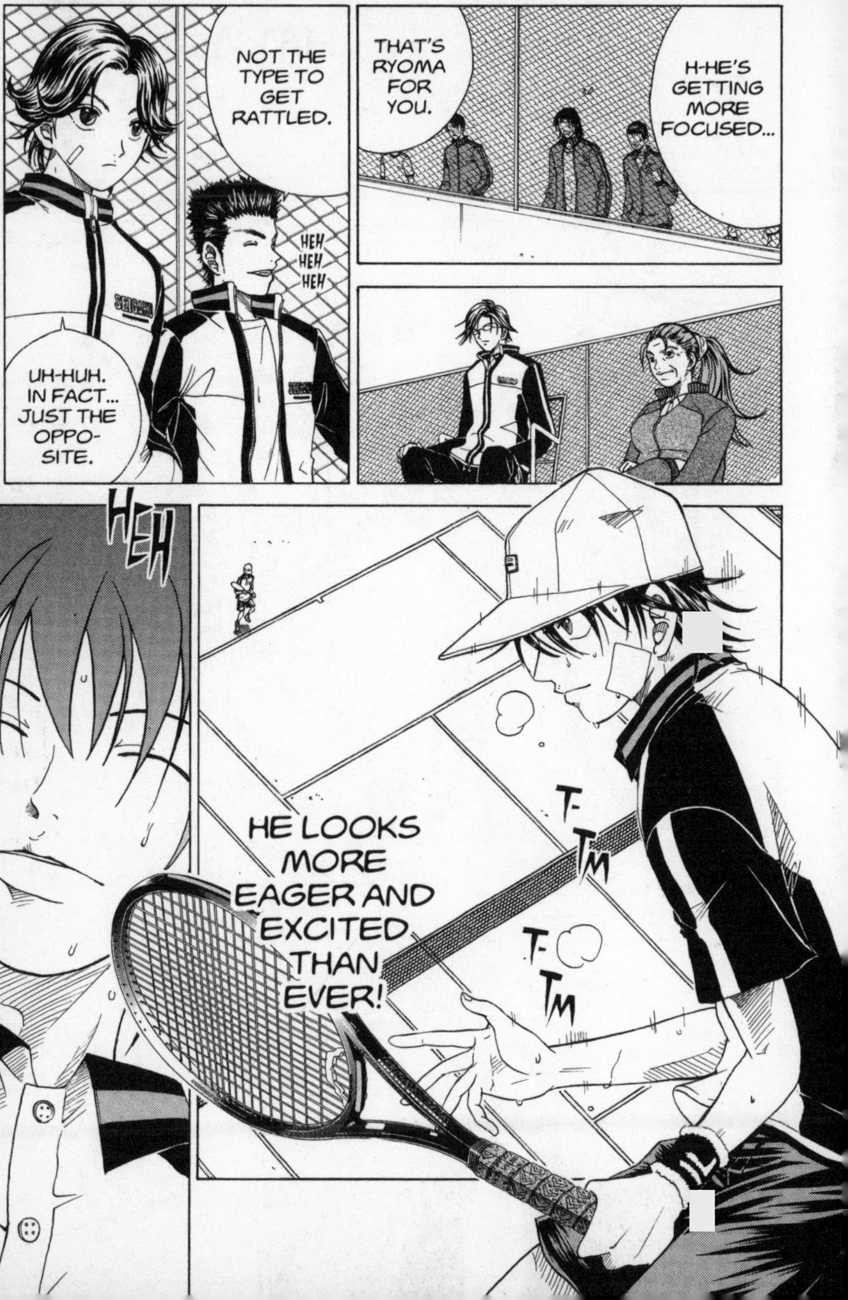

H-HE'S GETTING MORE FOCUSED...
THAT'S RYOMA FOR YOU.
NOT THE TYPE TO GET RATTLED.
HEH HEH HEH
UH-HUH. IN FACT... JUST THE OPPO-SITE.
T-TM
T-TM
HEH
HE LOOKS MORE EAGER AND EXCITED THAN EVER!

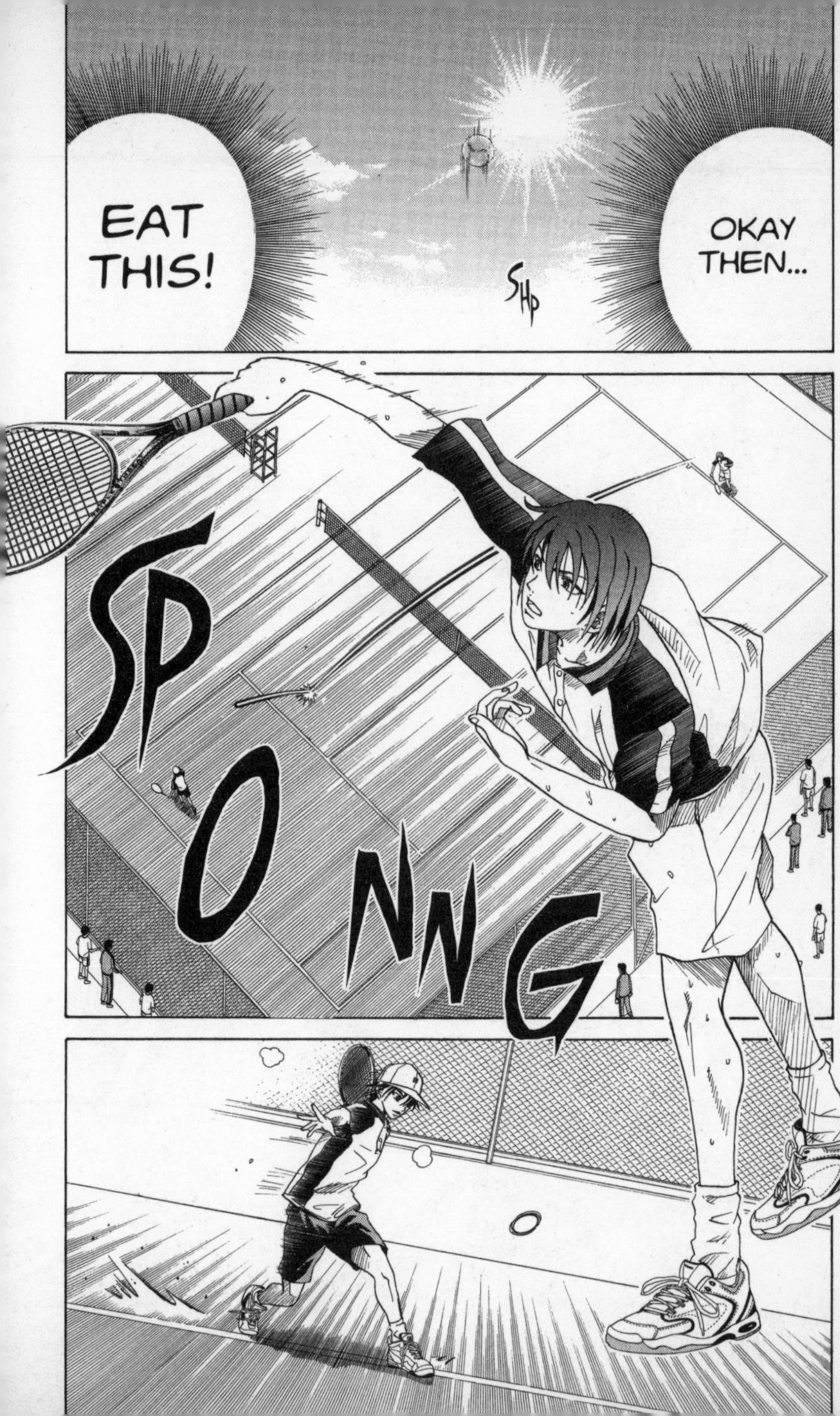
OKAY THEN...
EAT THIS!
SHP
SPONNG

READ THIS WAY

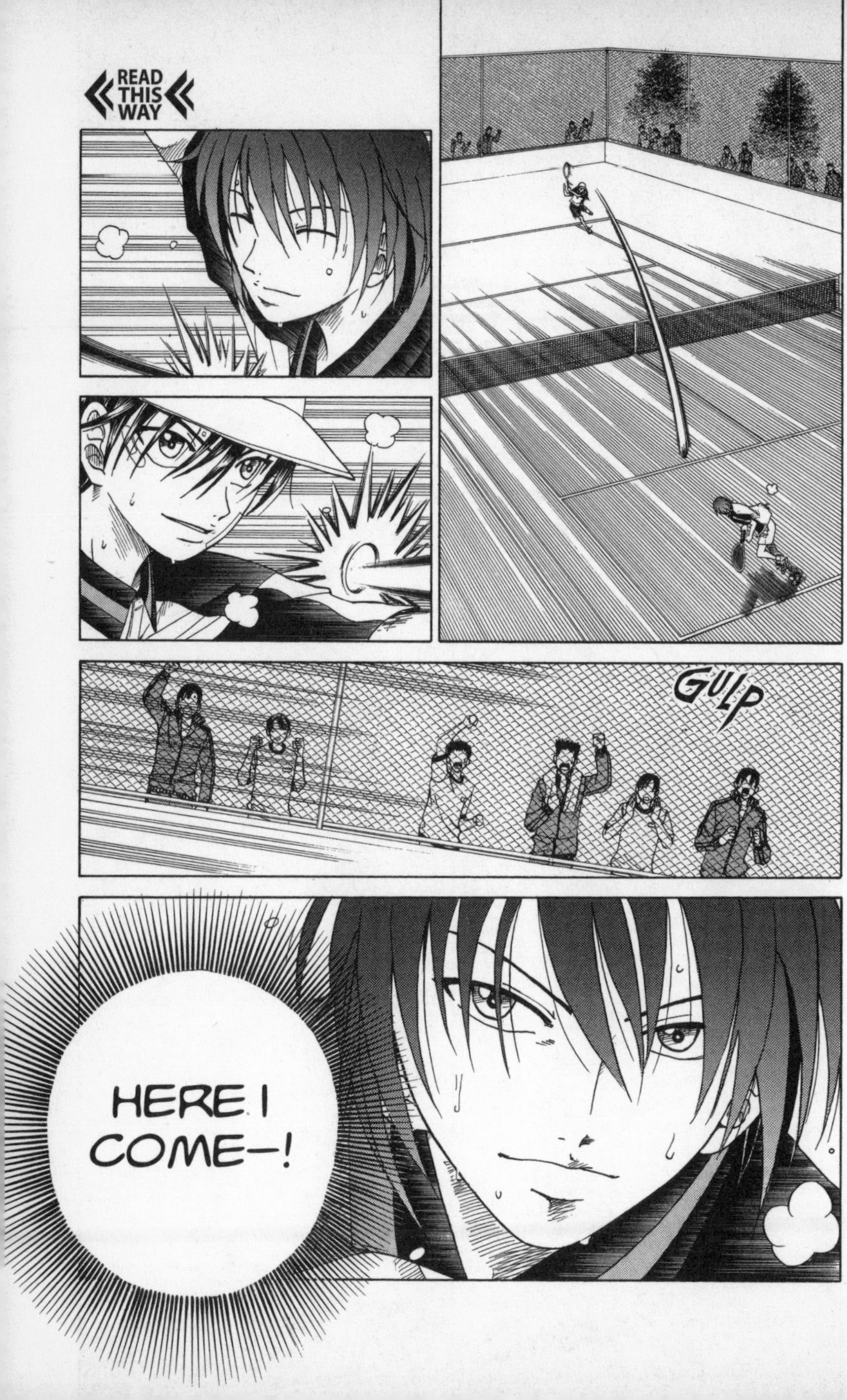
GULP
HERE I COME–!

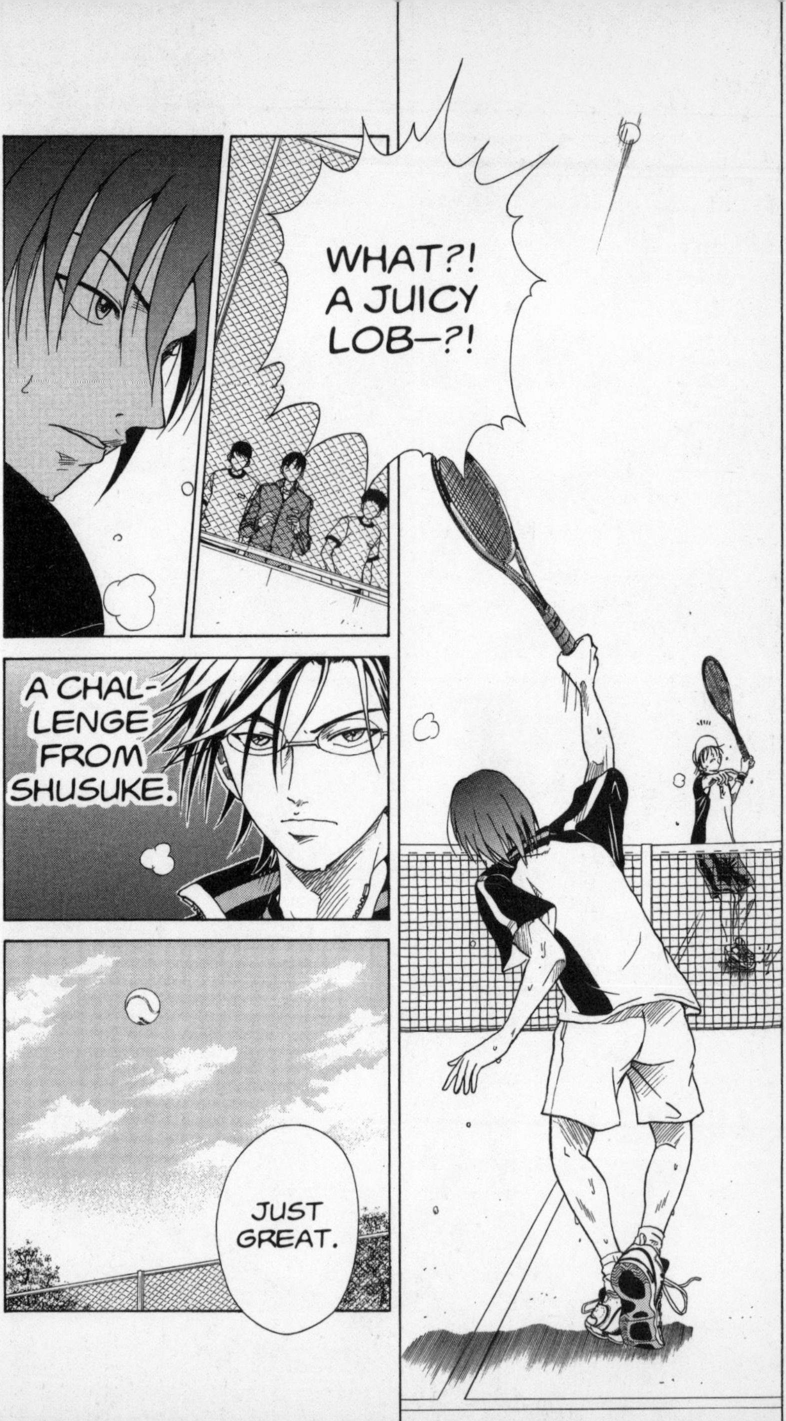
WHAT?! A JUICY LOB—?!
A CHAL-LENGE FROM SHUSUKE.
JUST GREAT.

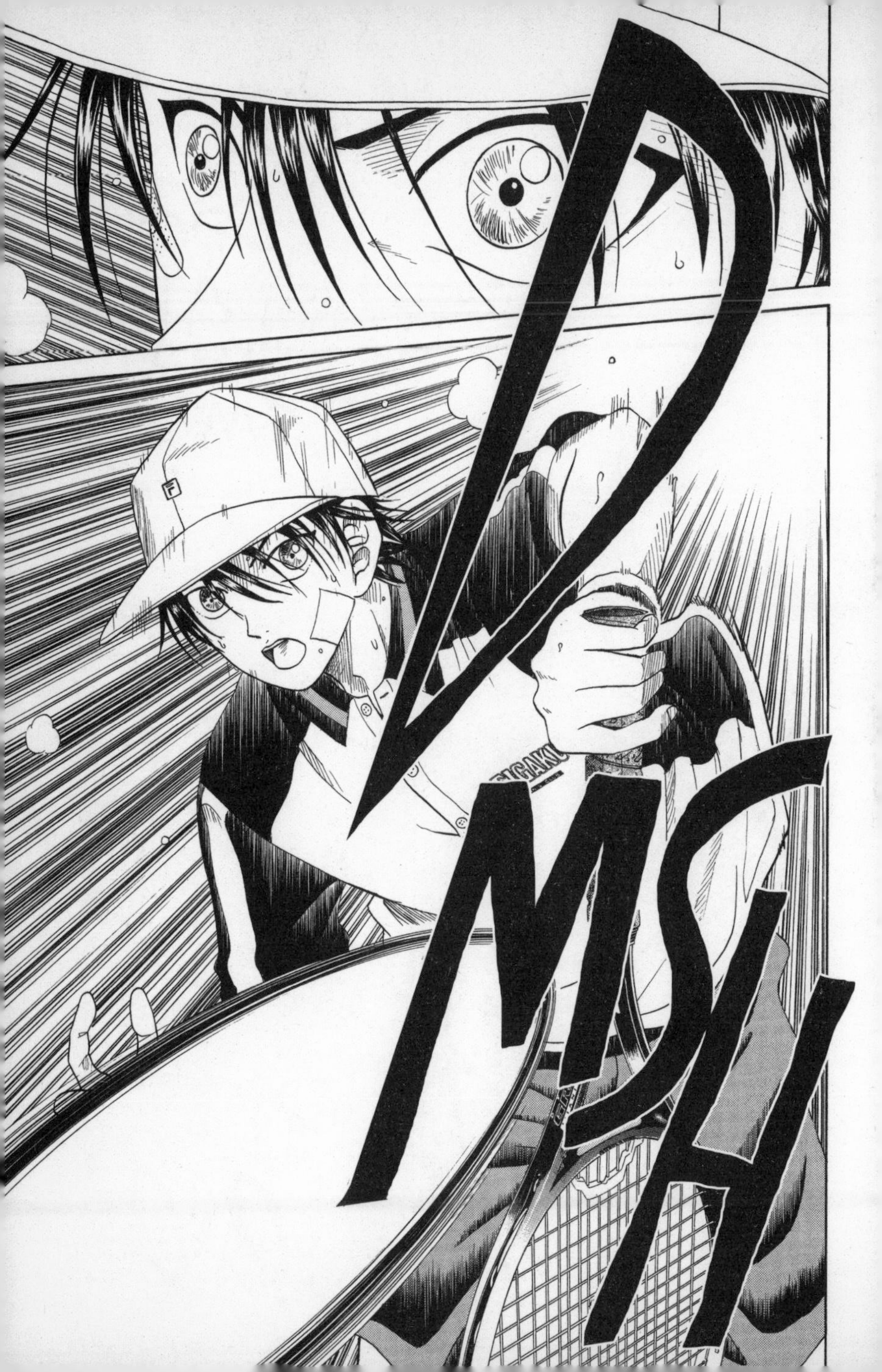

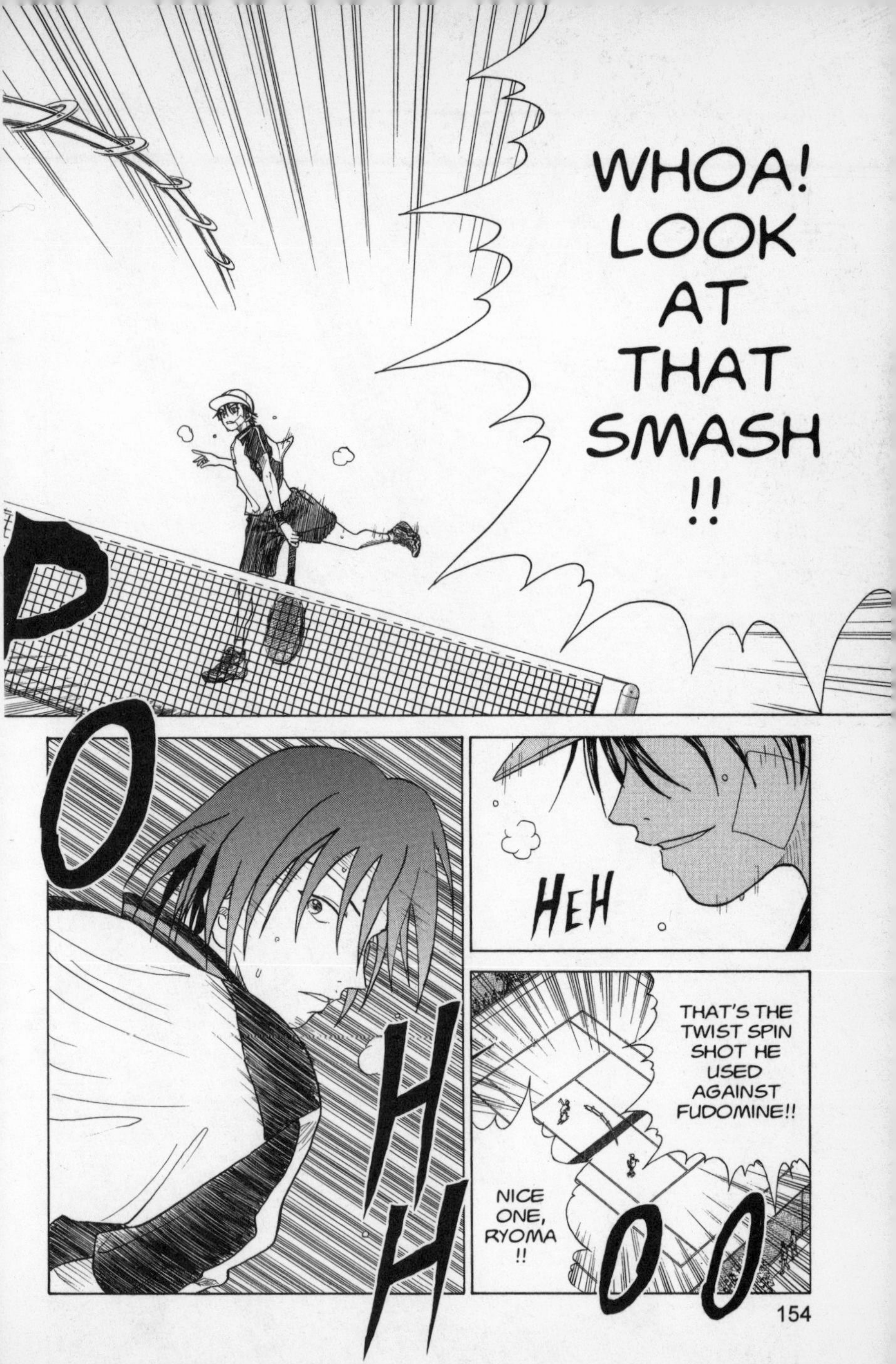
WHOA! LOOK AT THAT SMASH!!
DOHHOO
HEH
THAT'S THE TWIST SPIN SHOT HE USED AGAINST FUDOMINE!!
NICE ONE, RYOMA!!

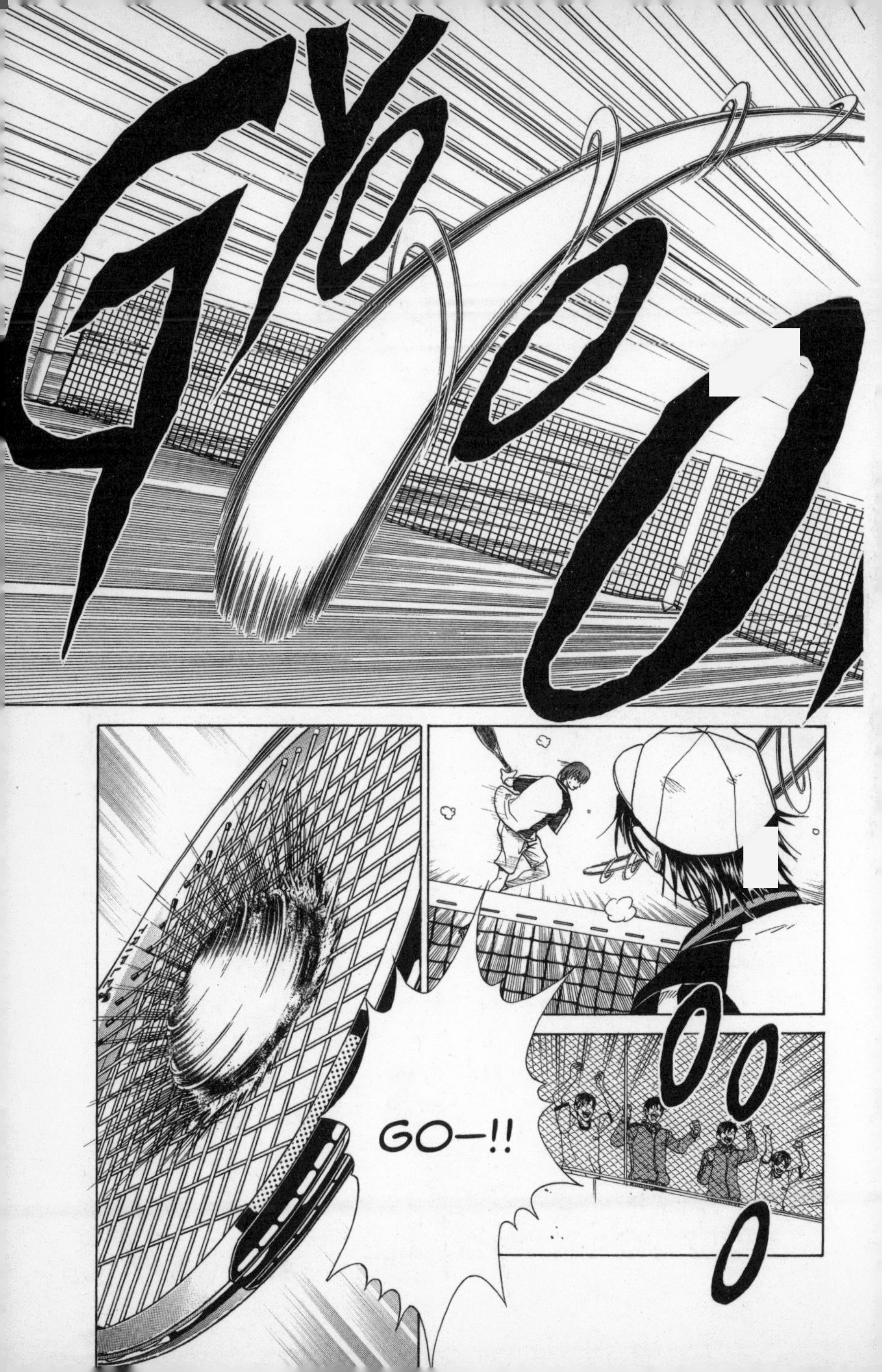
GO–!!

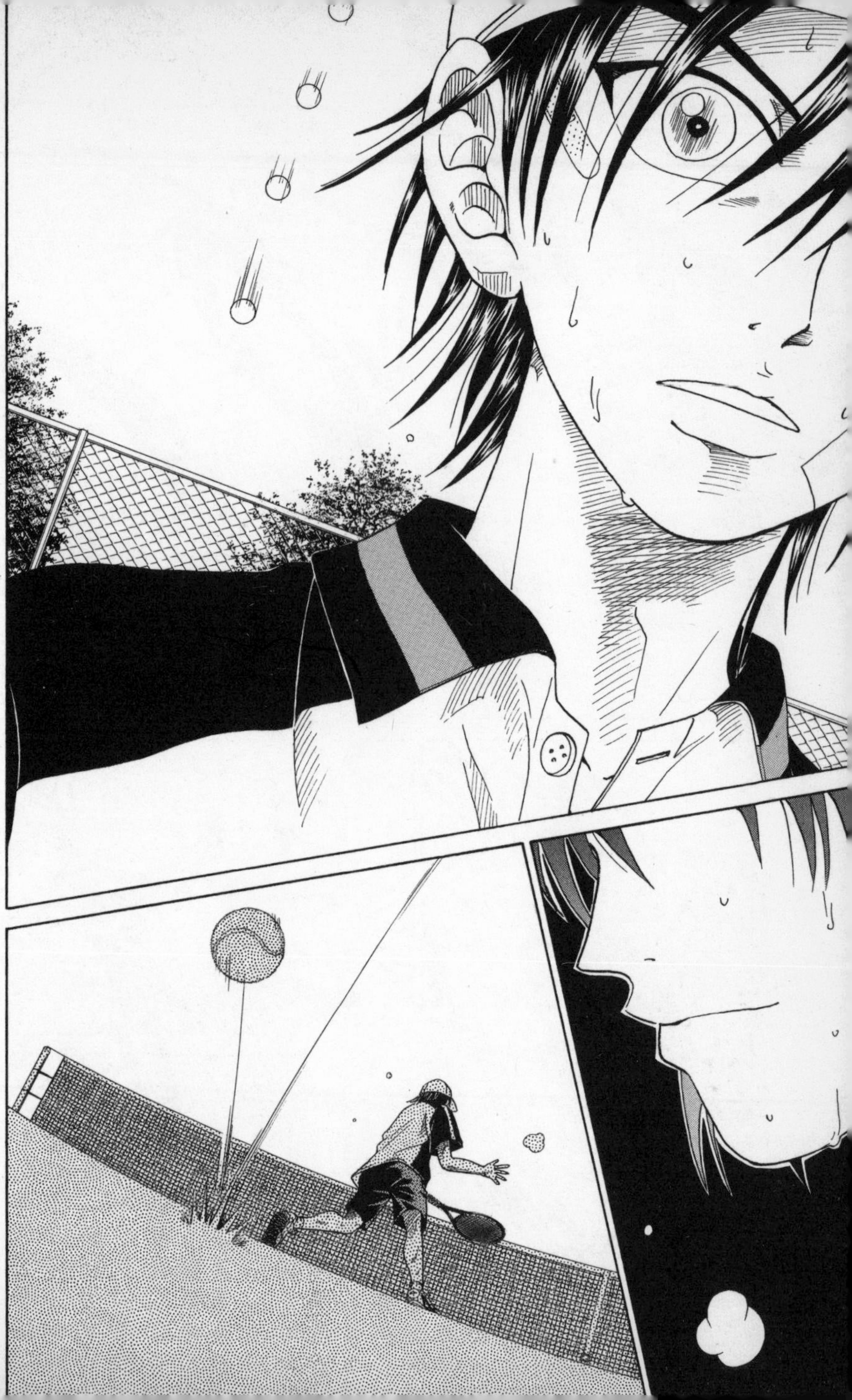

READ THIS WAY

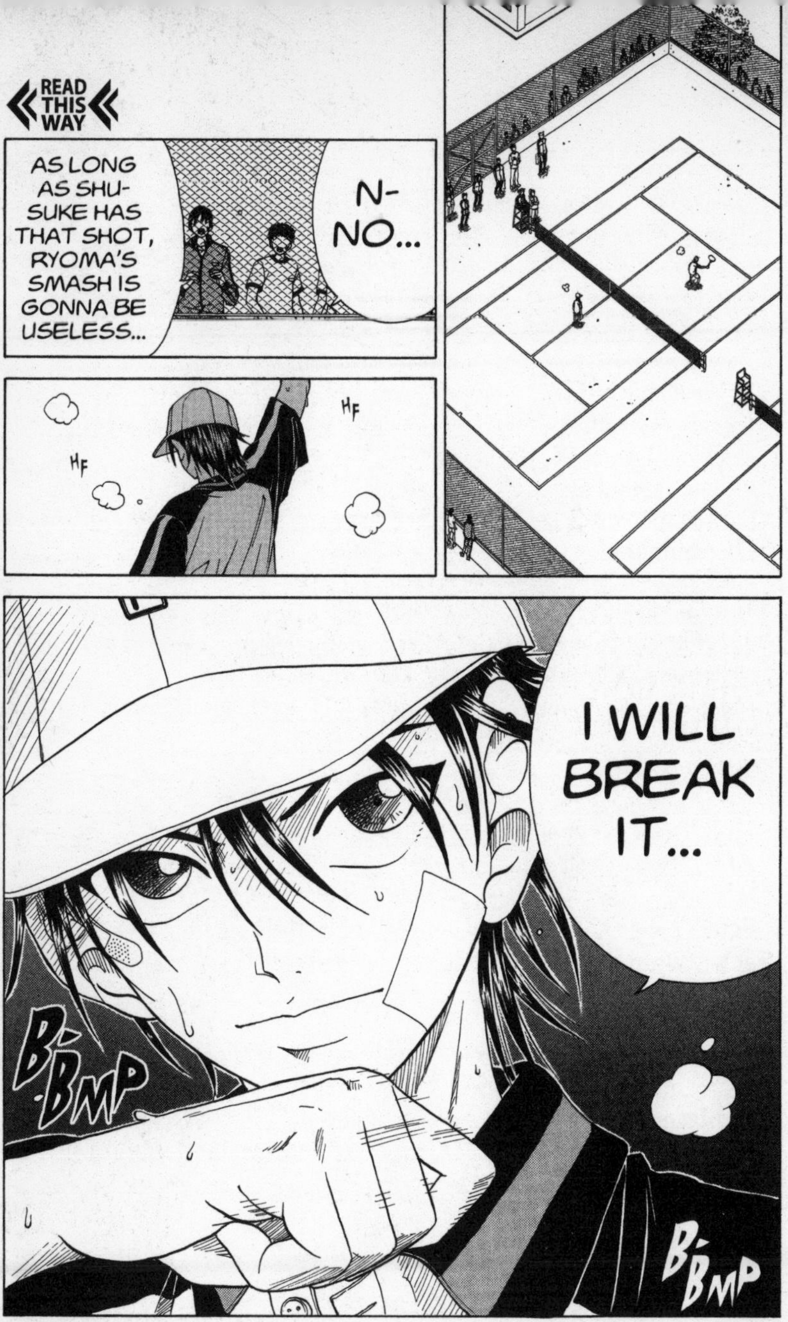

N-NO...
AS LONG AS SHUSUKE HAS THAT SHOT, RYOMA'S SMASH IS GONNA BE USELESS...
HF
HF
I WILL BREAK IT...
B-BMP
B-BMP

Thanks for reading volume 10 of *The Prince of Tennis*! With your support, this manga has reached double digits! I couldn't be happier. And now *The Prince of Tennis* will take a new turn...!

1. *The Prince of Tennis Fanbook* (over 300 pages) is on sale!!
I'm sure some of you remember the ad announcing "something" in Jump 2001, Issue 34. Well, here's the "something"! Usually, the author comes up with ideas for projects or takes requests from fans, but the editor and production crew are heavily involved with this one. (The editor came up with the project alone, in fact, and even I discovered it through the magazine!)
The fanbook includes fan contributions, color pictures, and facts about lots of schools, among other things—so please check it out! It will go on sale in early November 2001 as volume 10.5!!
(Ed. Note: *The Prince of Tennis* Volume 10.5 went on sale in Japan in 2001.)

2. And one more thing... *The Prince of Tennis* anime!
I just learned of it recently too (July), and I'm still surprised. At last Ryoma will actually move! I know I say this all the time, but...it wouldn't have been possible without your support! The details haven't been worked out yet, but by the time this volume goes on sale, I'm sure a lot will have been decided. Let's enjoy it together!

As of now, *The Prince of Tennis* is published in Thailand, Taiwan and Korea. And I get the pleasure of receiving fan letters from the locals and Japanese people living in those countries. (They go through the trouble of writing to me in Japanese. Well written, too!) Thank you very much.

Please keep supporting *The Prince of Tennis* and Ryoma. See you in the next volume!!

テニスの
王子様 ☆
T. KONOMI
2001.7.30.

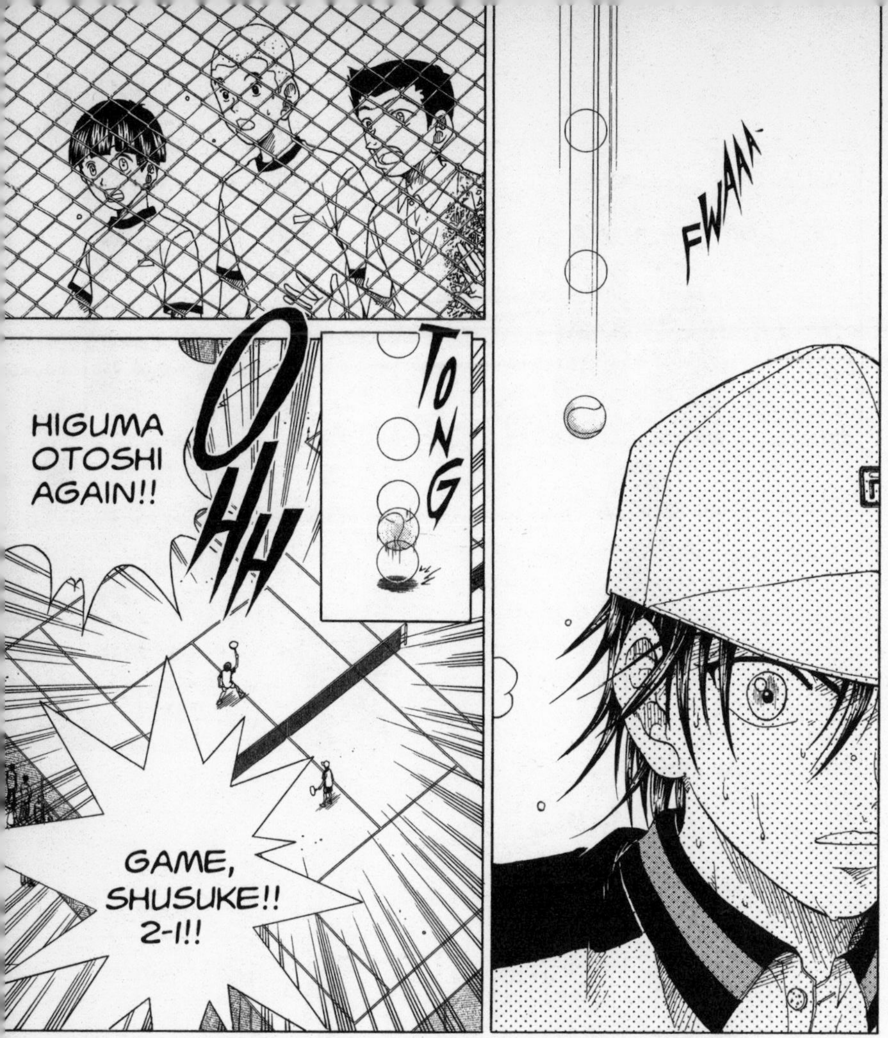
FWAAA
TONG
OHH
HIGUMA OTOSHI AGAIN!!
GAME, SHUSUKE!! 2-1!!

GENIUS 87: STUBBORN

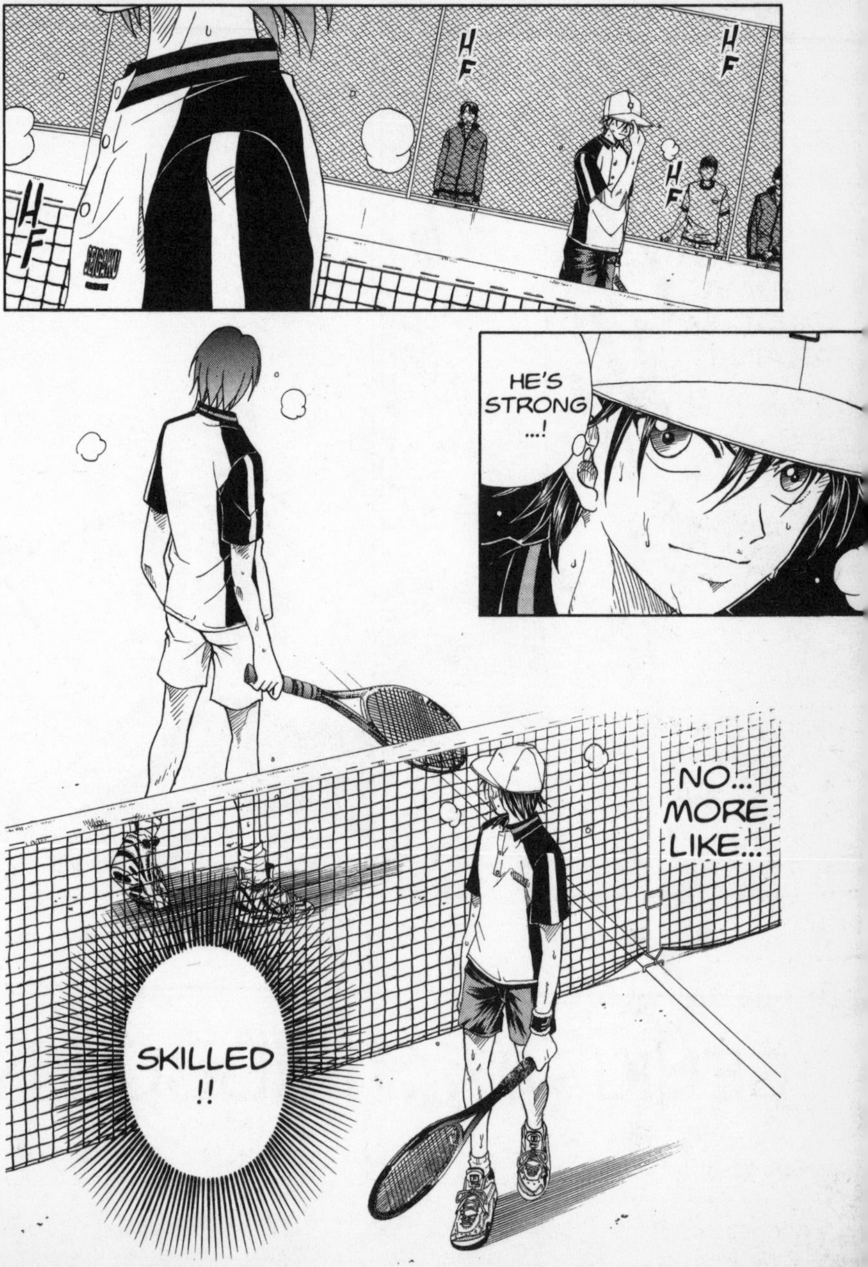
HF
HF
HF
HF
HE'S STRONG ...!
NO... MORE LIKE...
SKILLED !!

READ THIS WAY

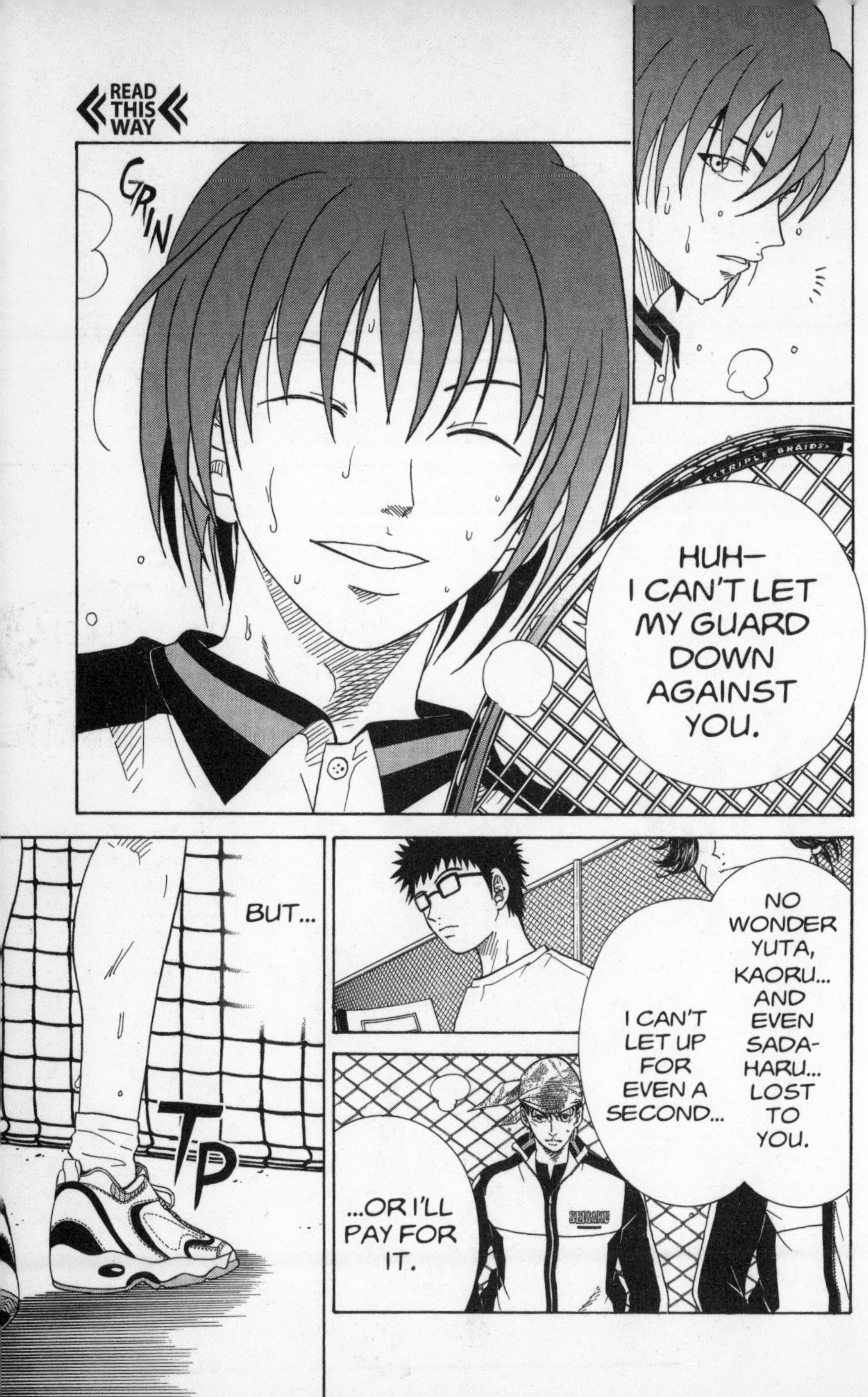
GRIN
HUH— I CAN'T LET MY GUARD DOWN AGAINST YOU.
NO WONDER YUTA, KAORU... AND EVEN SADA-HARU... LOST TO YOU.
I CAN'T LET UP FOR EVEN A SECOND...
...OR I'LL PAY FOR IT.
BUT...
TP

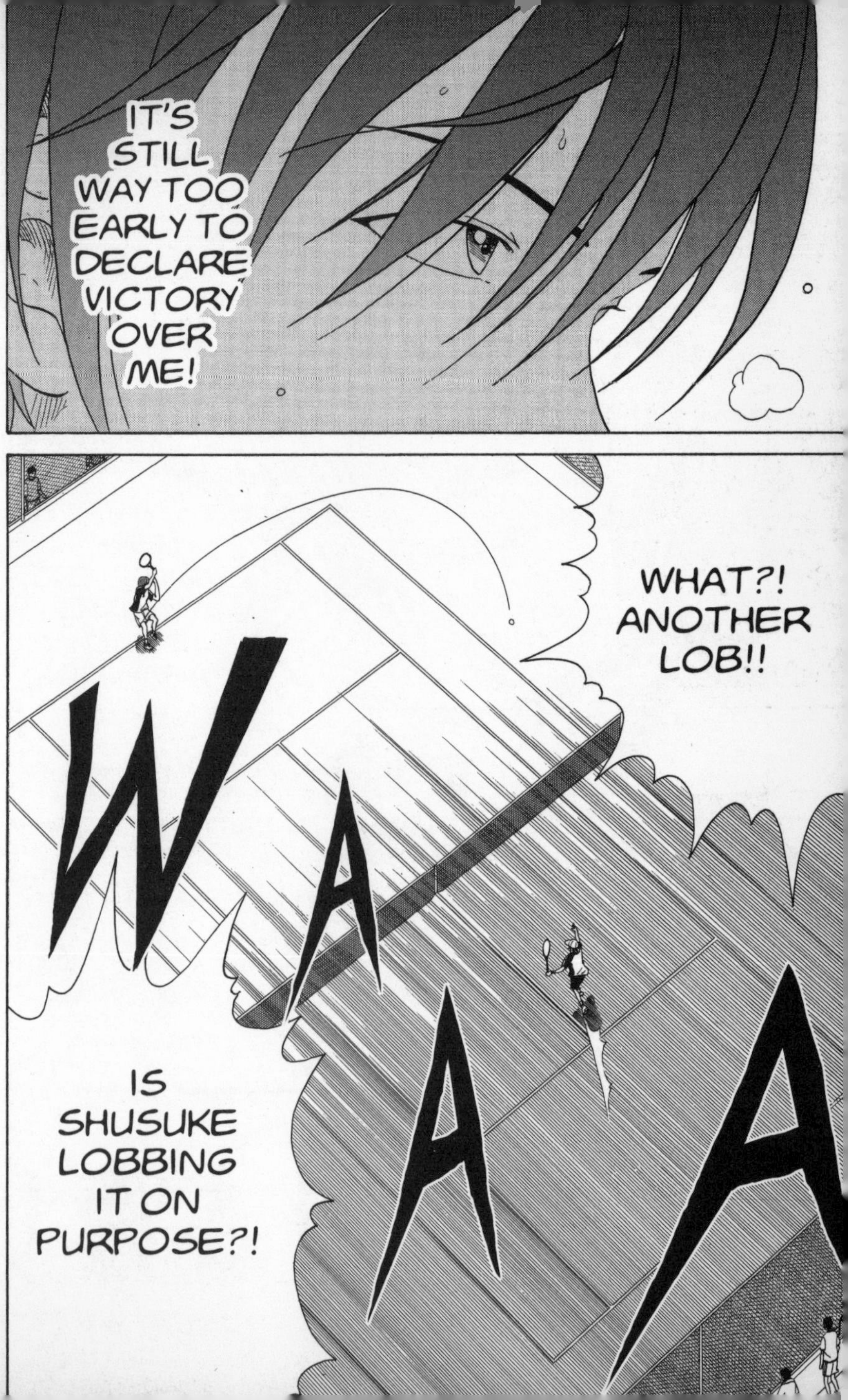
IT'S STILL WAY TOO EARLY TO DECLARE VICTORY OVER ME!
WHAT?! ANOTHER LOB!!
WAAA
IS SHUSUKE LOBBING IT ON PURPOSE?!

READ THIS WAY

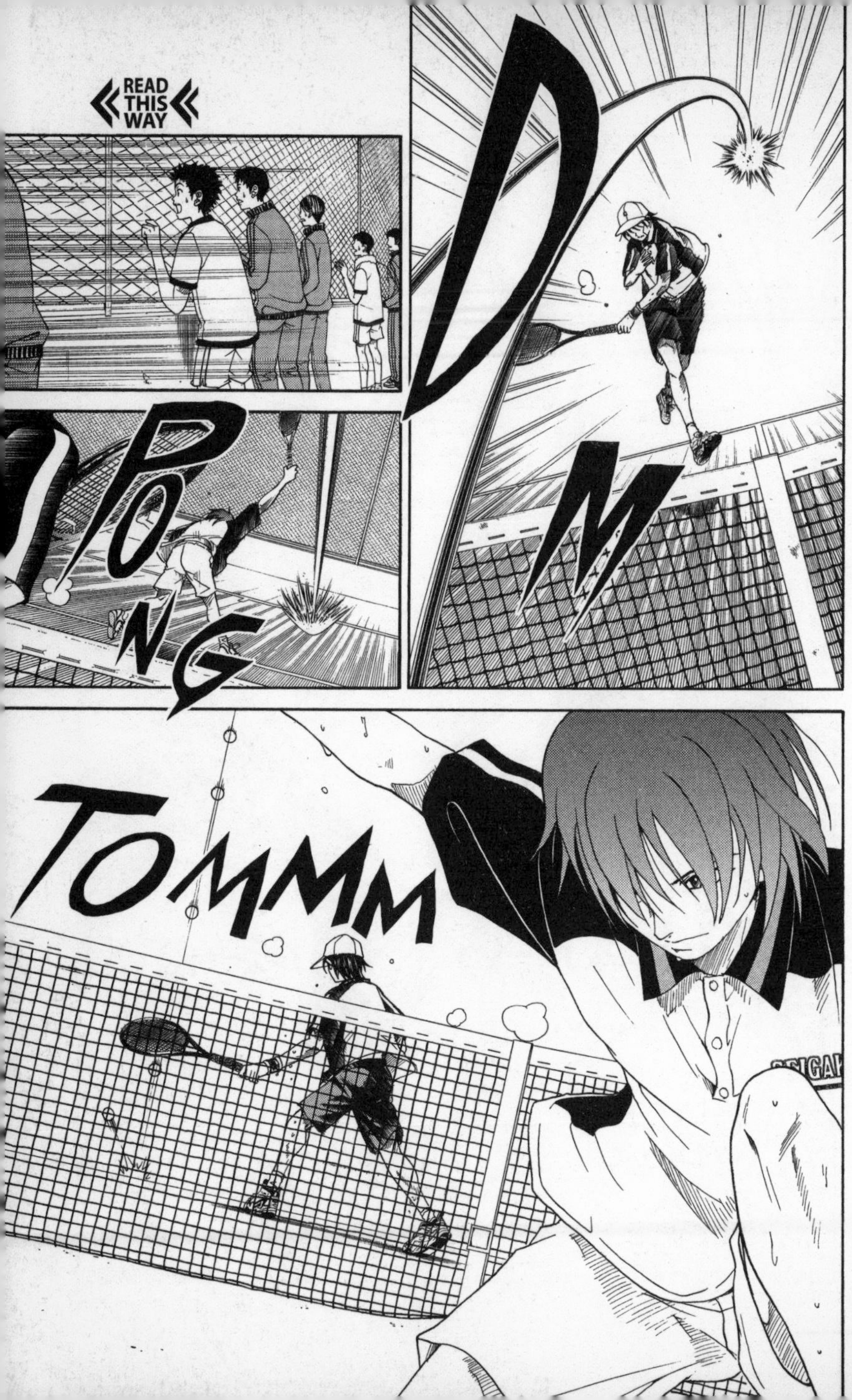
DM
PONG
TOMMM

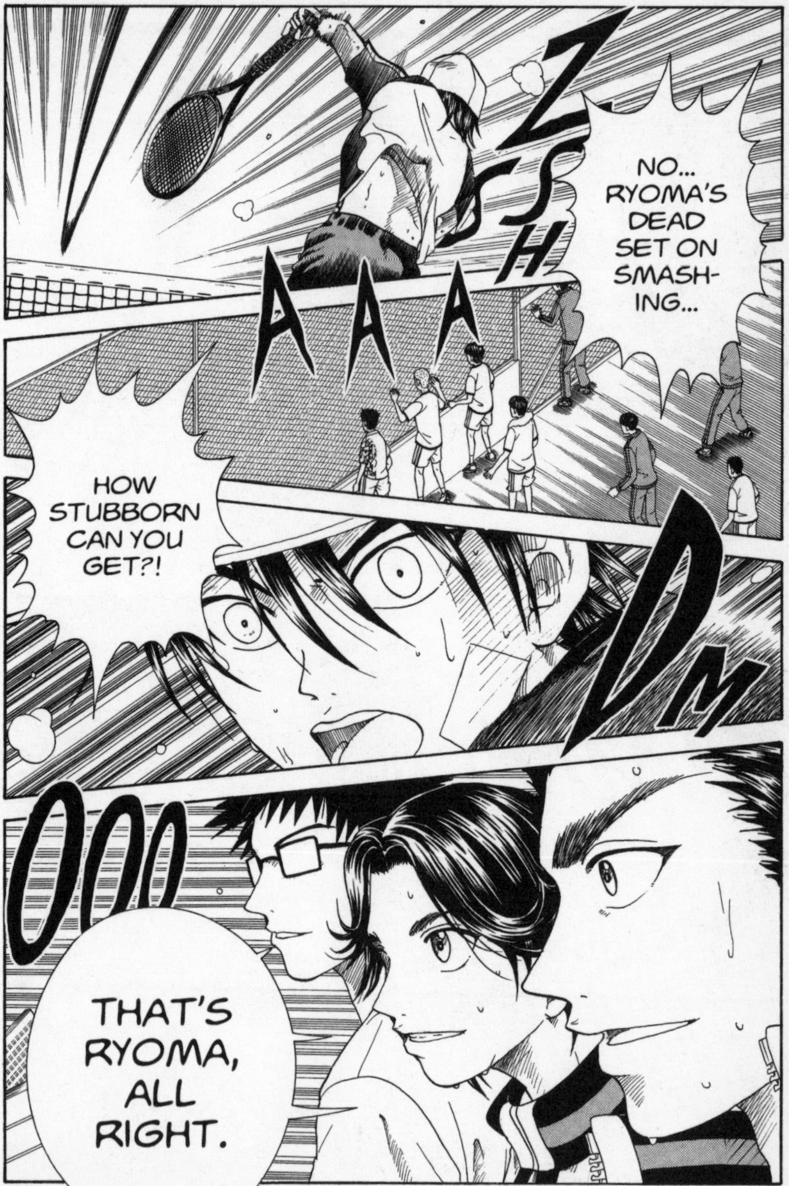
NO... RYOMA'S DEAD SET ON SMASH-ING...
ZSHAAA
HOW STUBBORN CAN YOU GET?!
DM
OOO
THAT'S RYOMA, ALL RIGHT.

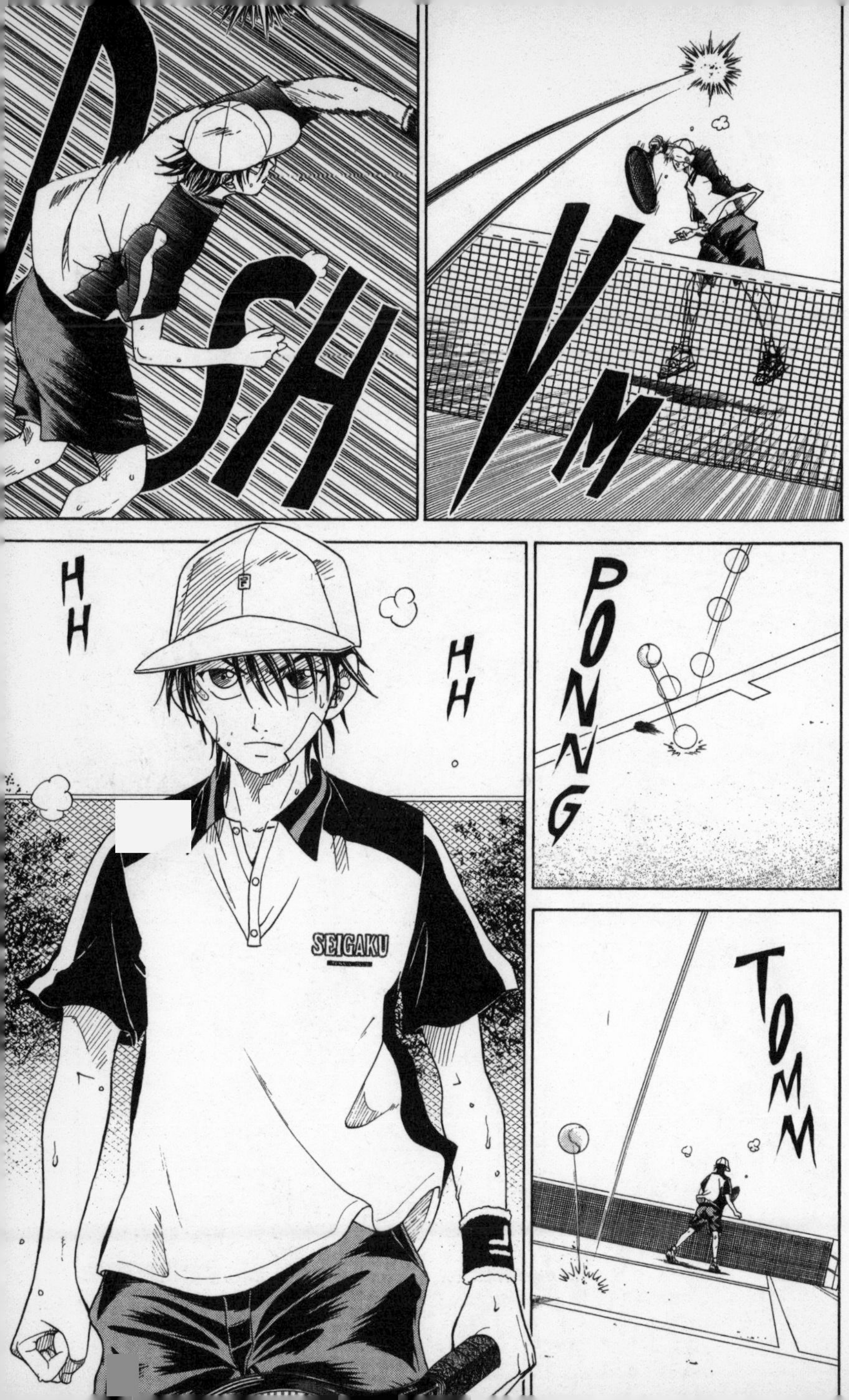
SHVM
DSH
PONNG
TOMM
HH
HH
SEIGAKU

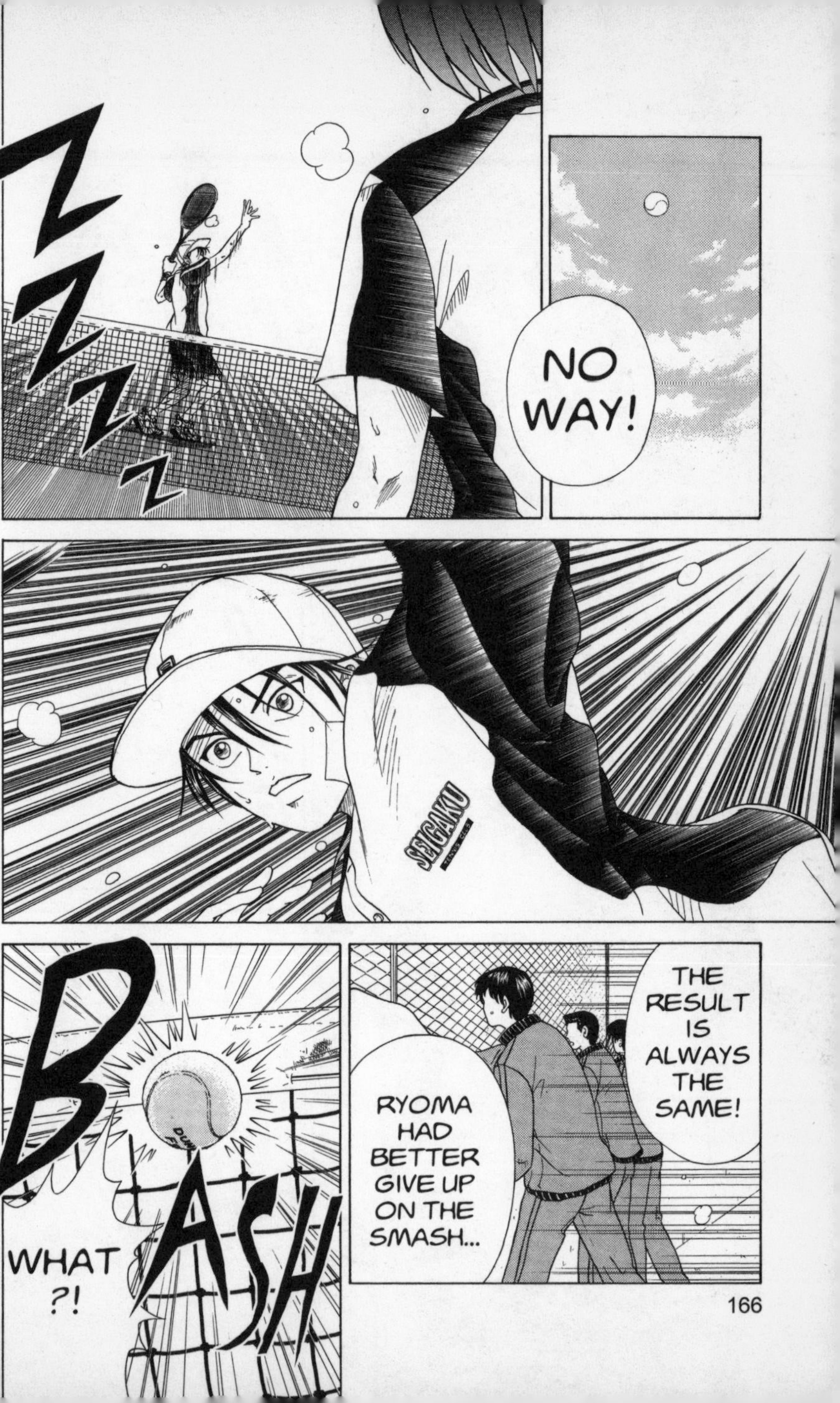
NO WAY!
ZZZZZ
SEIGAKU
THE RESULT IS ALWAYS THE SAME!
RYOMA HAD BETTER GIVE UP ON THE SMASH...
BASH
WHAT ?!

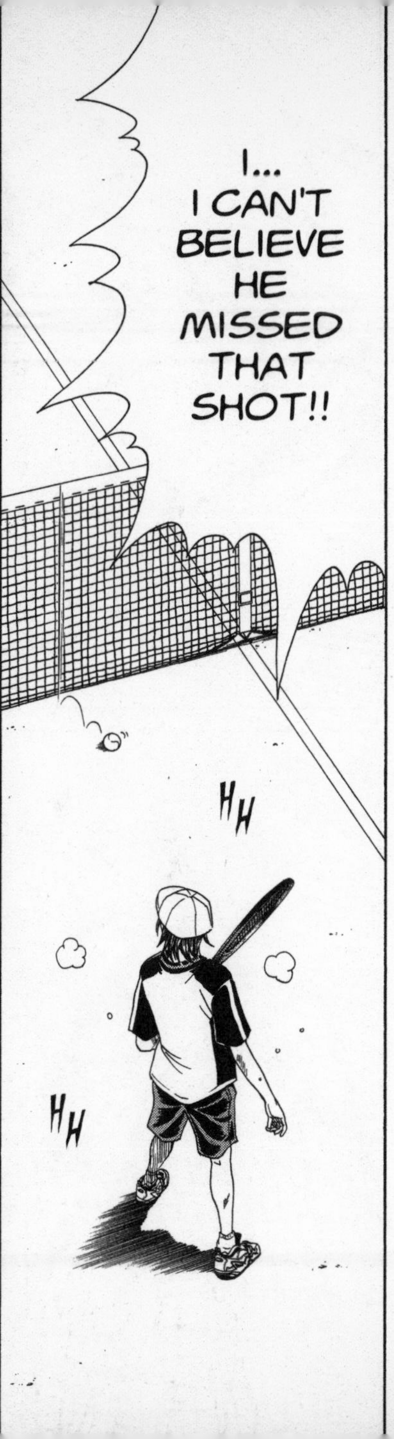
I... I CAN'T BELIEVE HE MISSED THAT SHOT!!
HH
HH

READ THIS WAY

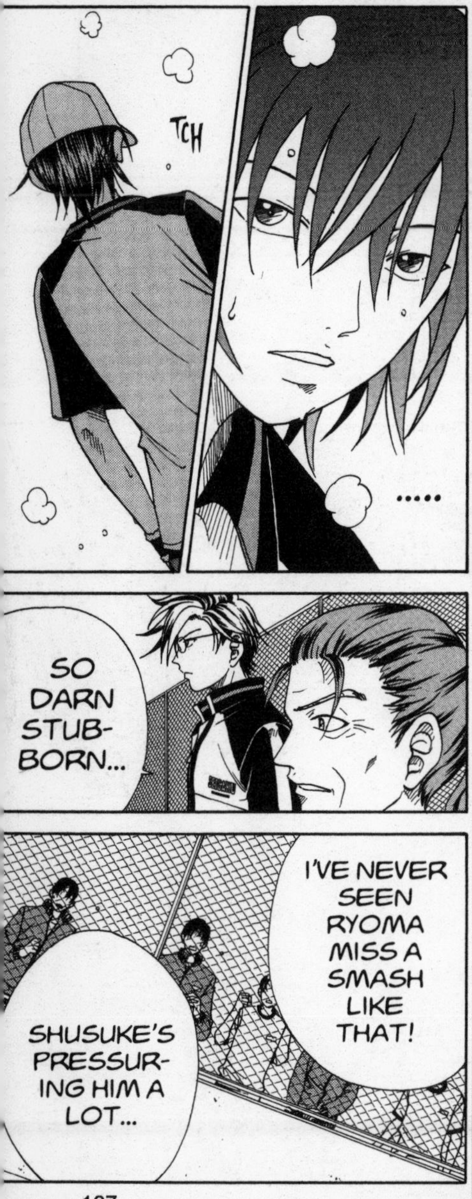
.....
TCH
SO DARN STUB-BORN...
I'VE NEVER SEEN RYOMA MISS A SMASH LIKE THAT!
SHUSUKE'S PRESSUR-ING HIM A LOT...

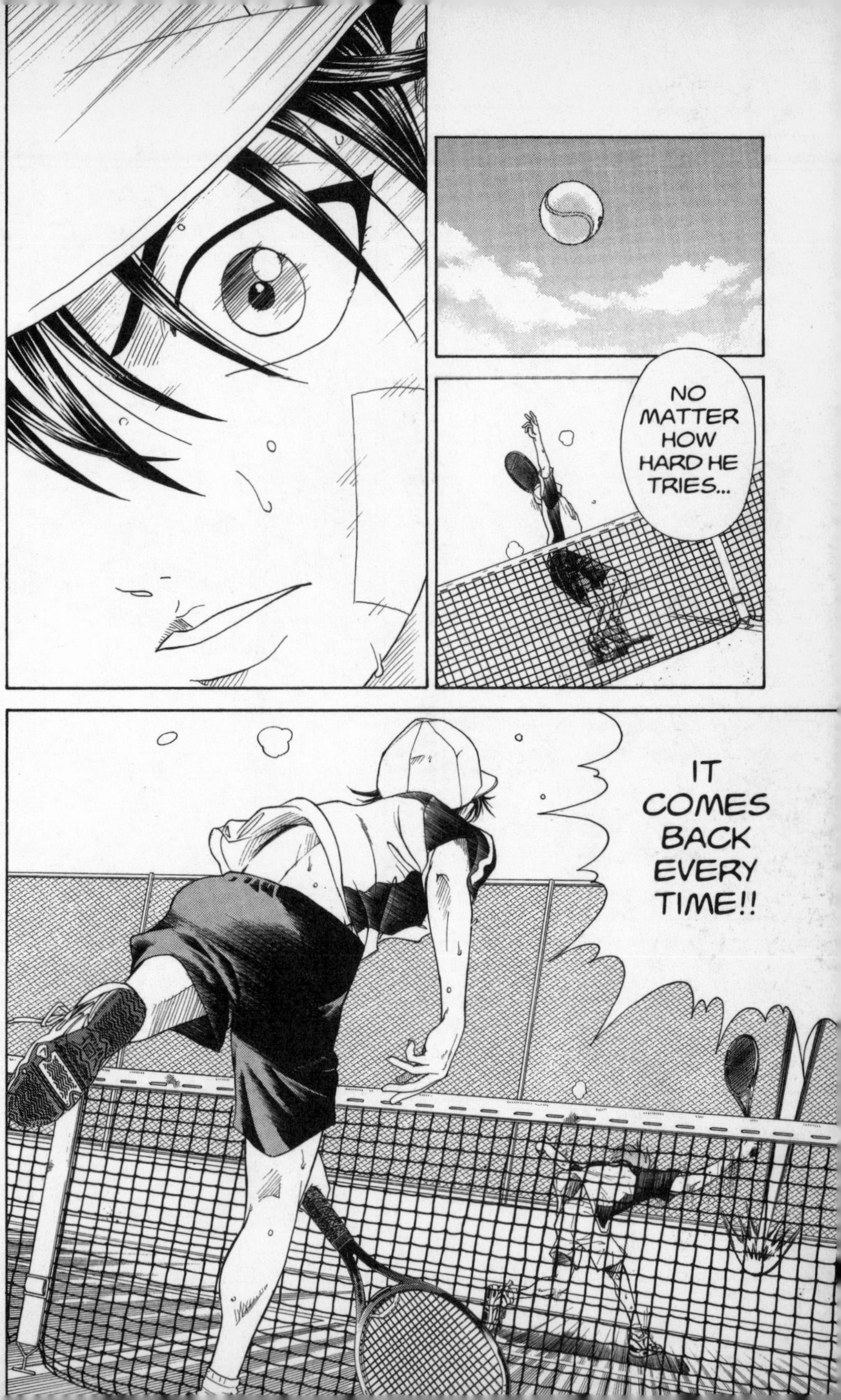
NO MATTER HOW HARD HE TRIES...
IT COMES BACK EVERY TIME!!

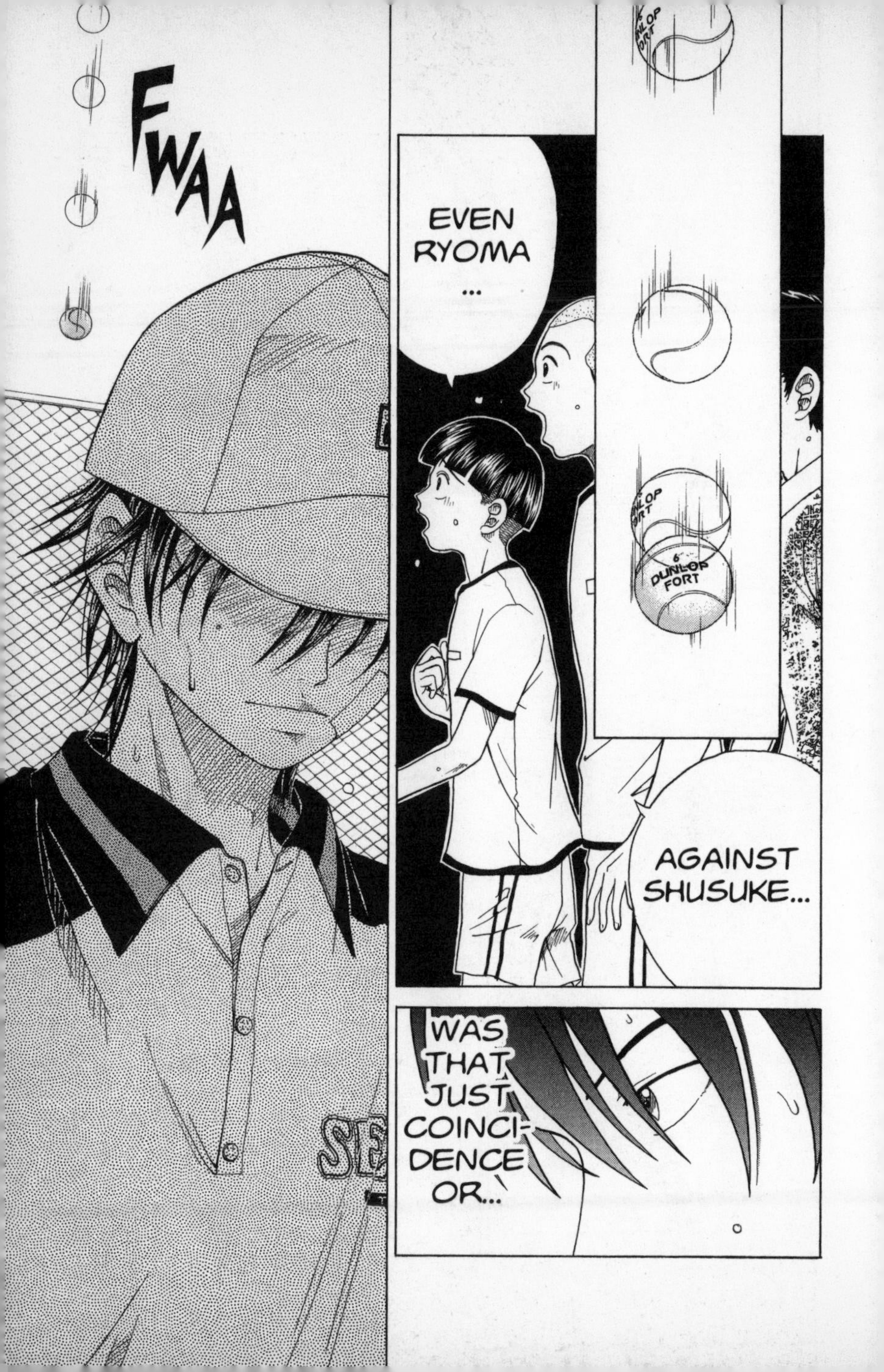
EVEN RYOMA ...
DUNLOP FORT
AGAINST SHUSUKE...
WAS THAT JUST COINCIDENCE OR...
FWAA

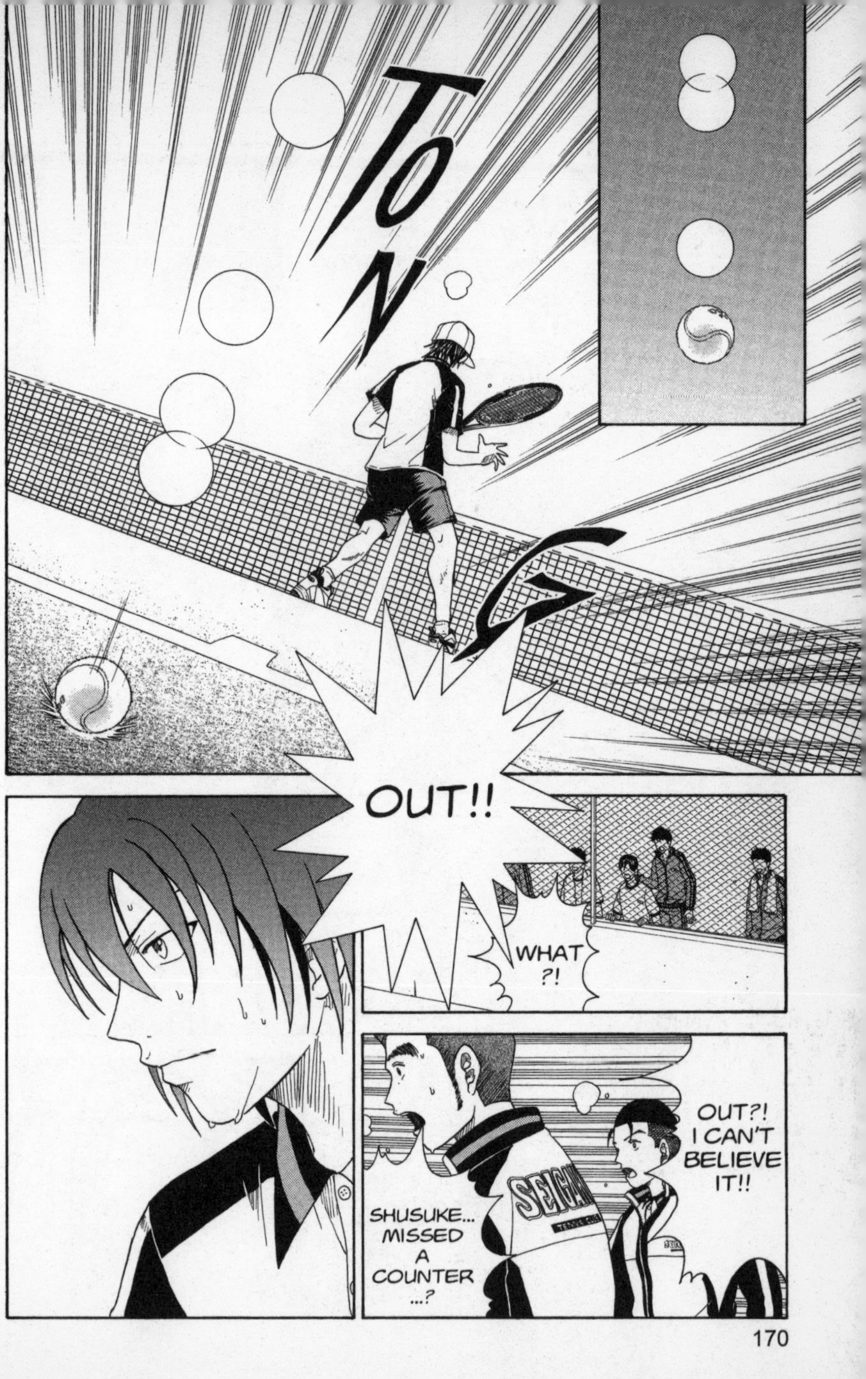
TONG
OUT!!
WHAT?!
OUT?! I CAN'T BELIEVE IT!!
SHUSUKE... MISSED A COUNTER...?

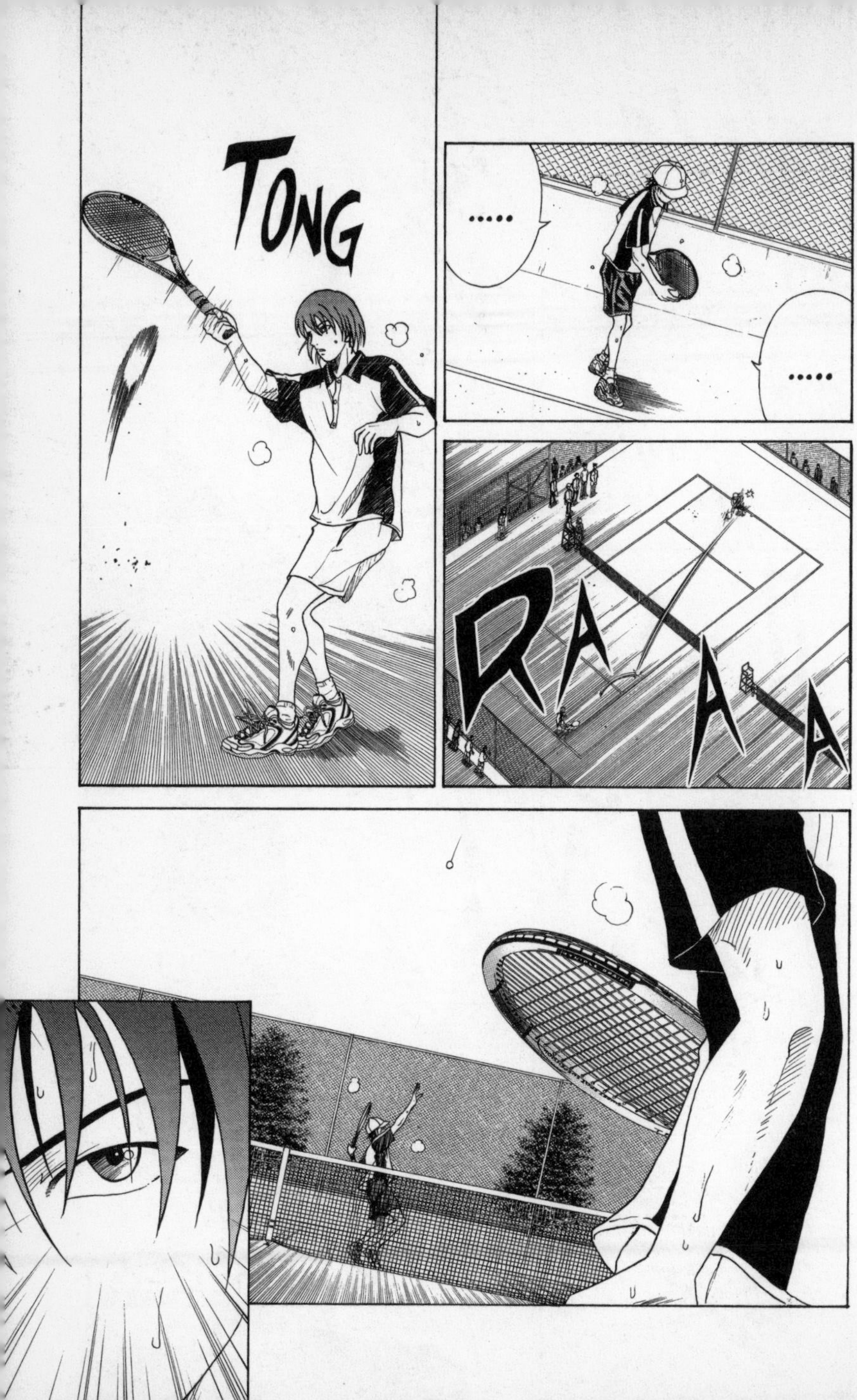
.....
.....
RAAA
TONG

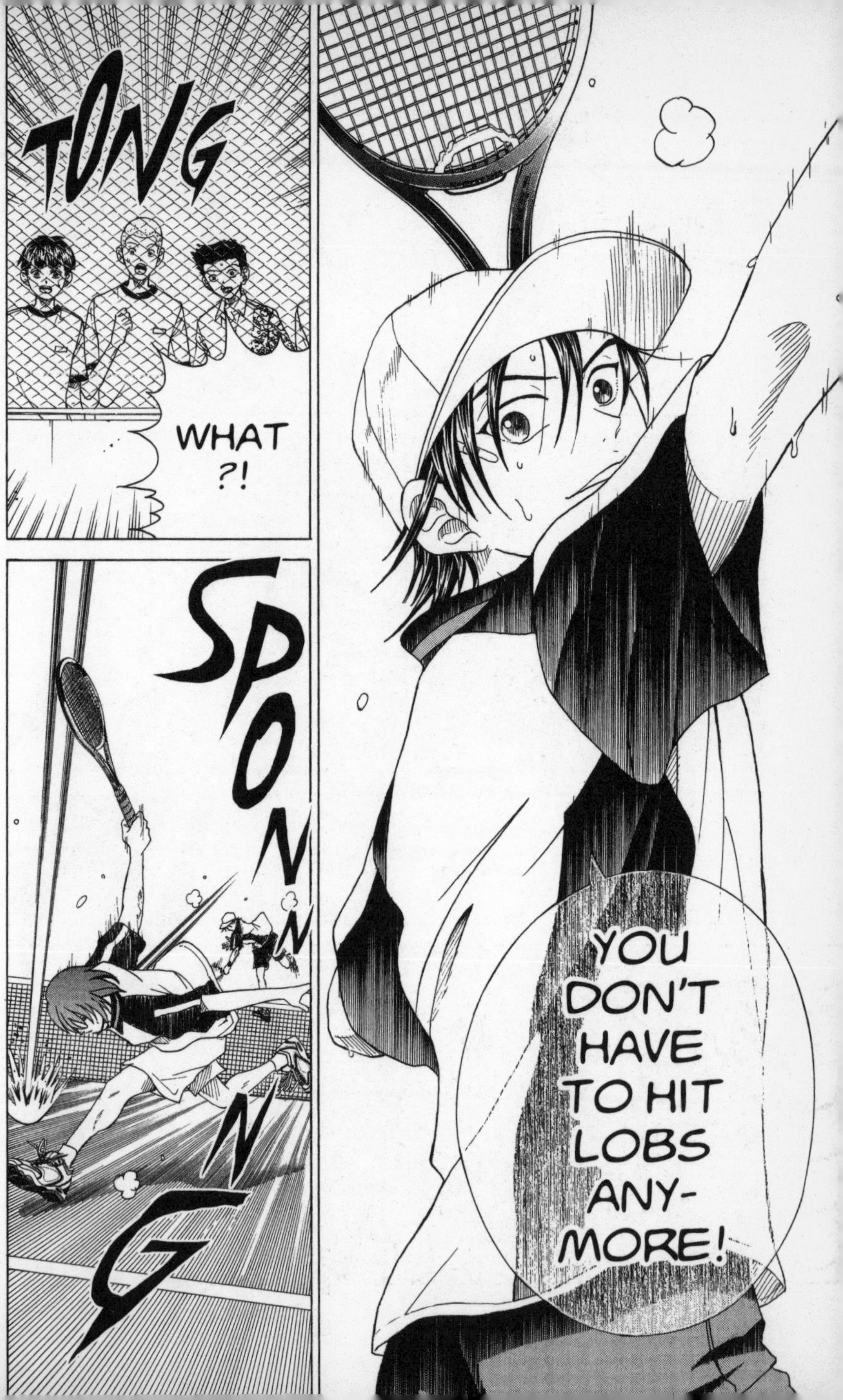
YOU DON'T HAVE TO HIT LOBS ANY-MORE!
TONG
WHAT ?!
SPONNNG

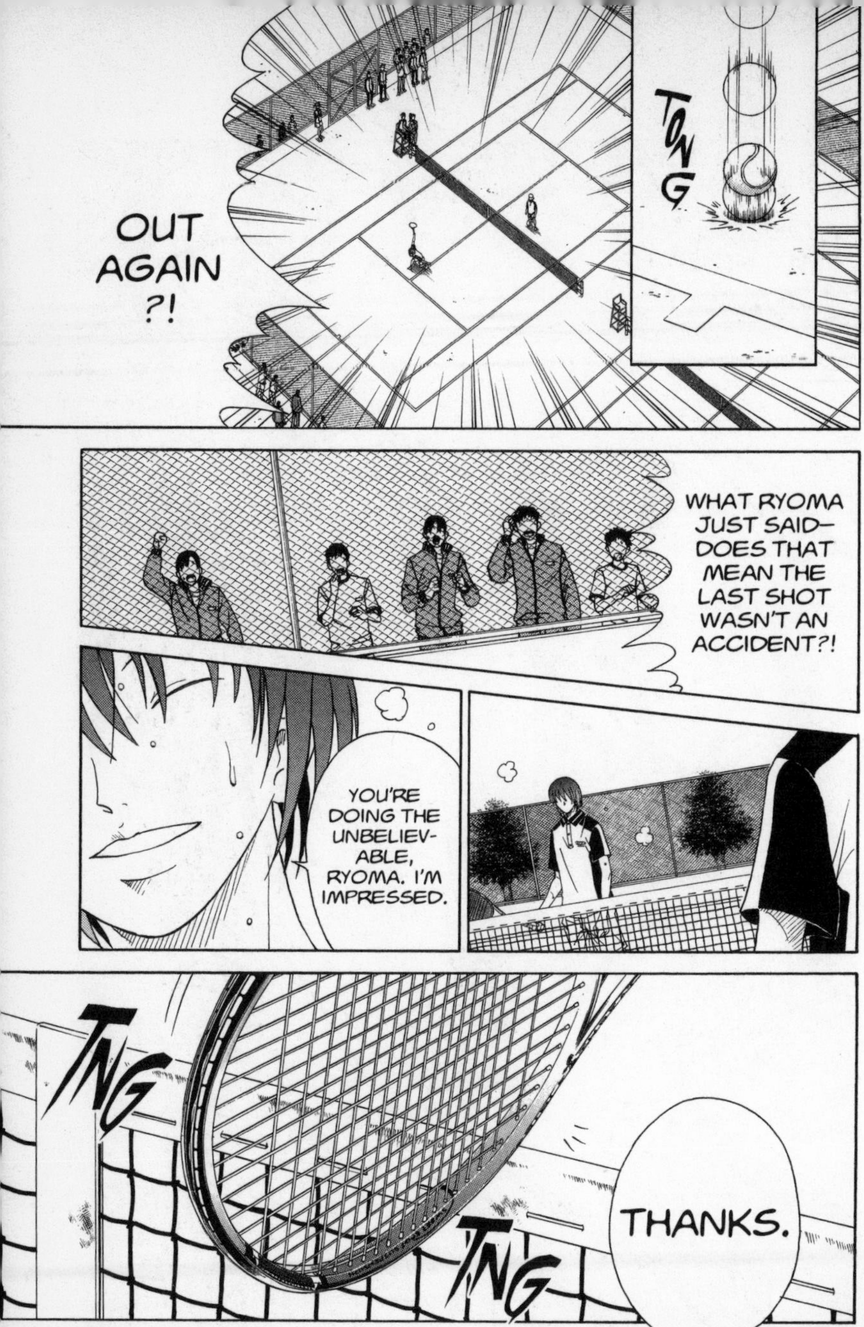
TONG
OUT AGAIN ?!
WHAT RYOMA JUST SAID— DOES THAT MEAN THE LAST SHOT WASN'T AN ACCIDENT?!
YOU'RE DOING THE UNBELIEV-ABLE, RYOMA. I'M IMPRESSED.
TNG
TNG
THANKS.

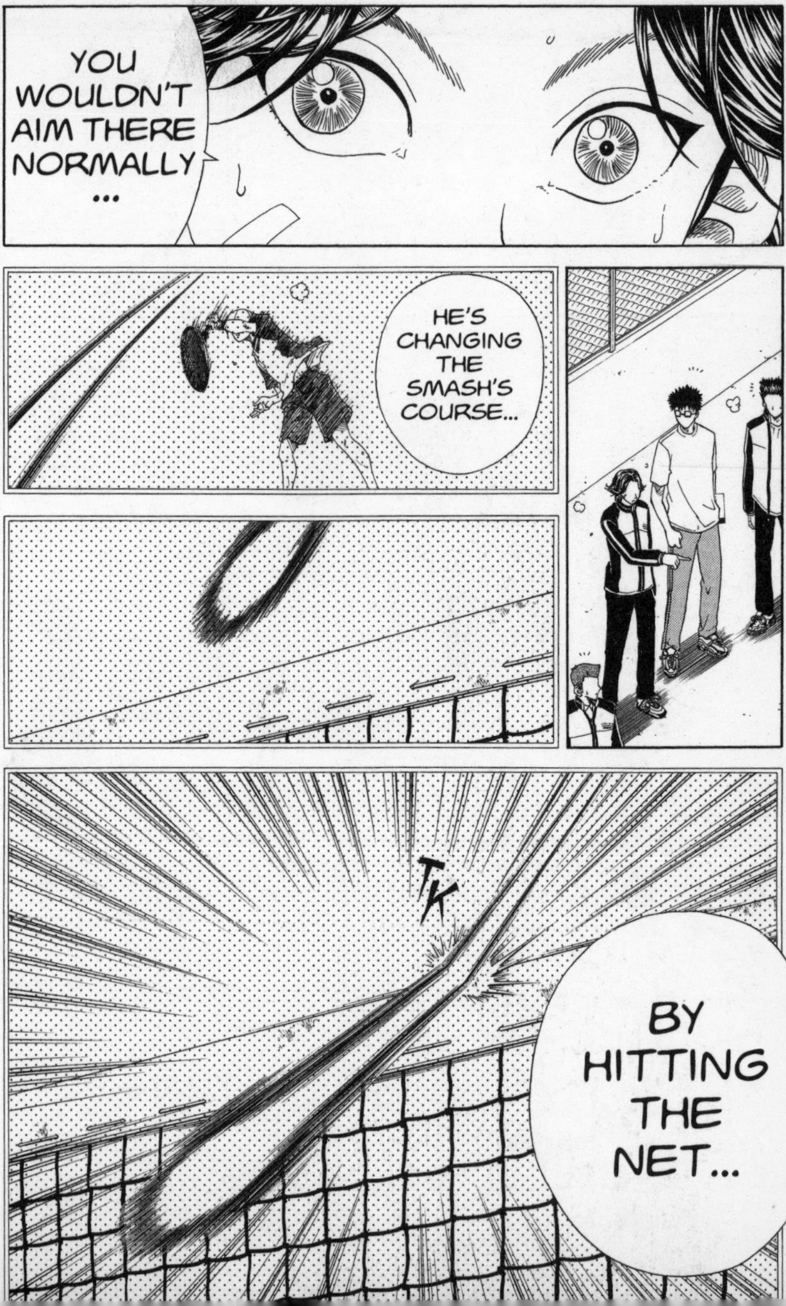
YOU WOULDN'T AIM THERE NORMALLY ...
HE'S CHANGING THE SMASH'S COURSE...
TK
BY HITTING THE NET...

READ THIS WAY

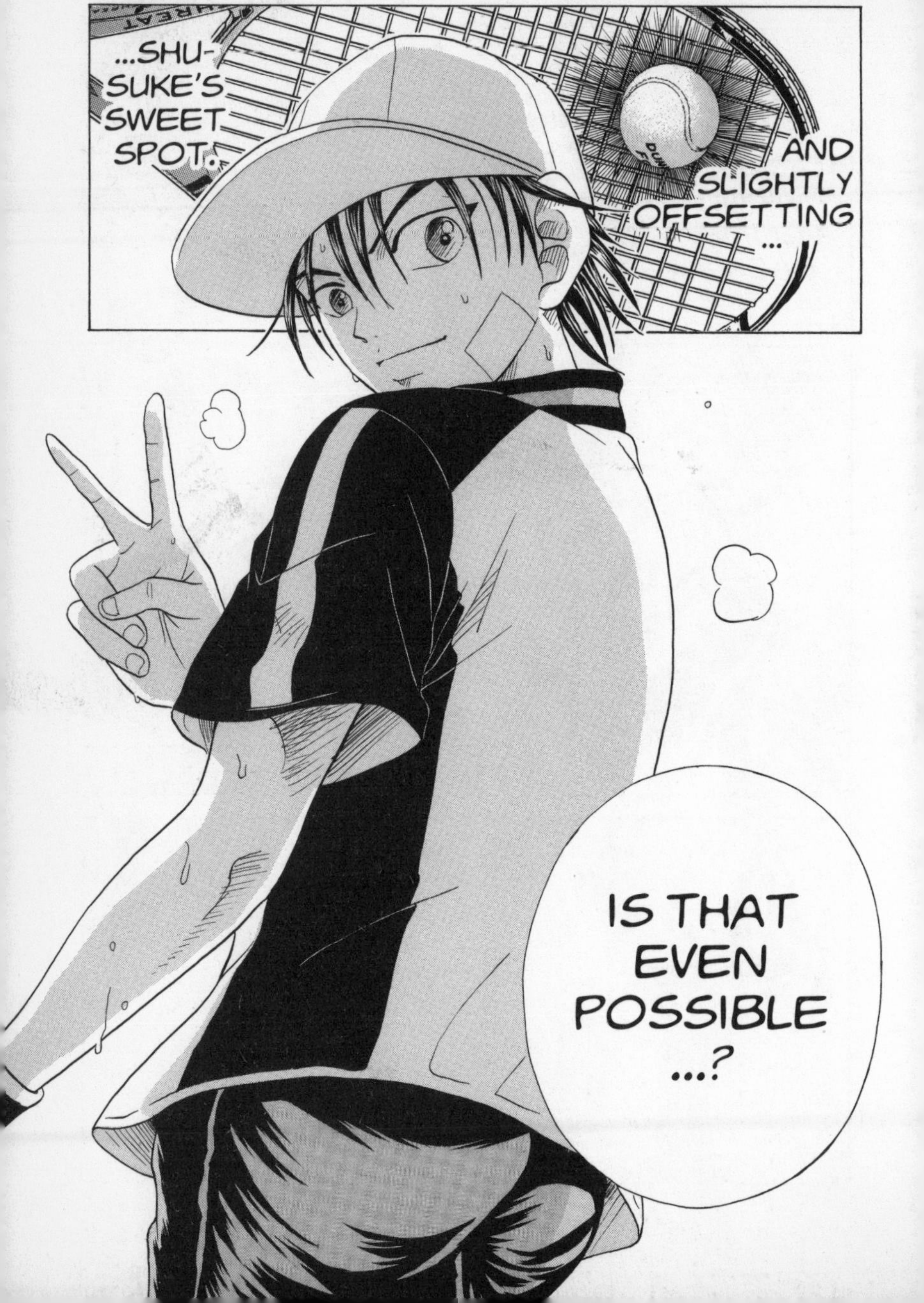
AND SLIGHTLY OFFSETTING ...
...SHU-SUKE'S SWEET SPOT..
IS THAT EVEN POSSIBLE ...?

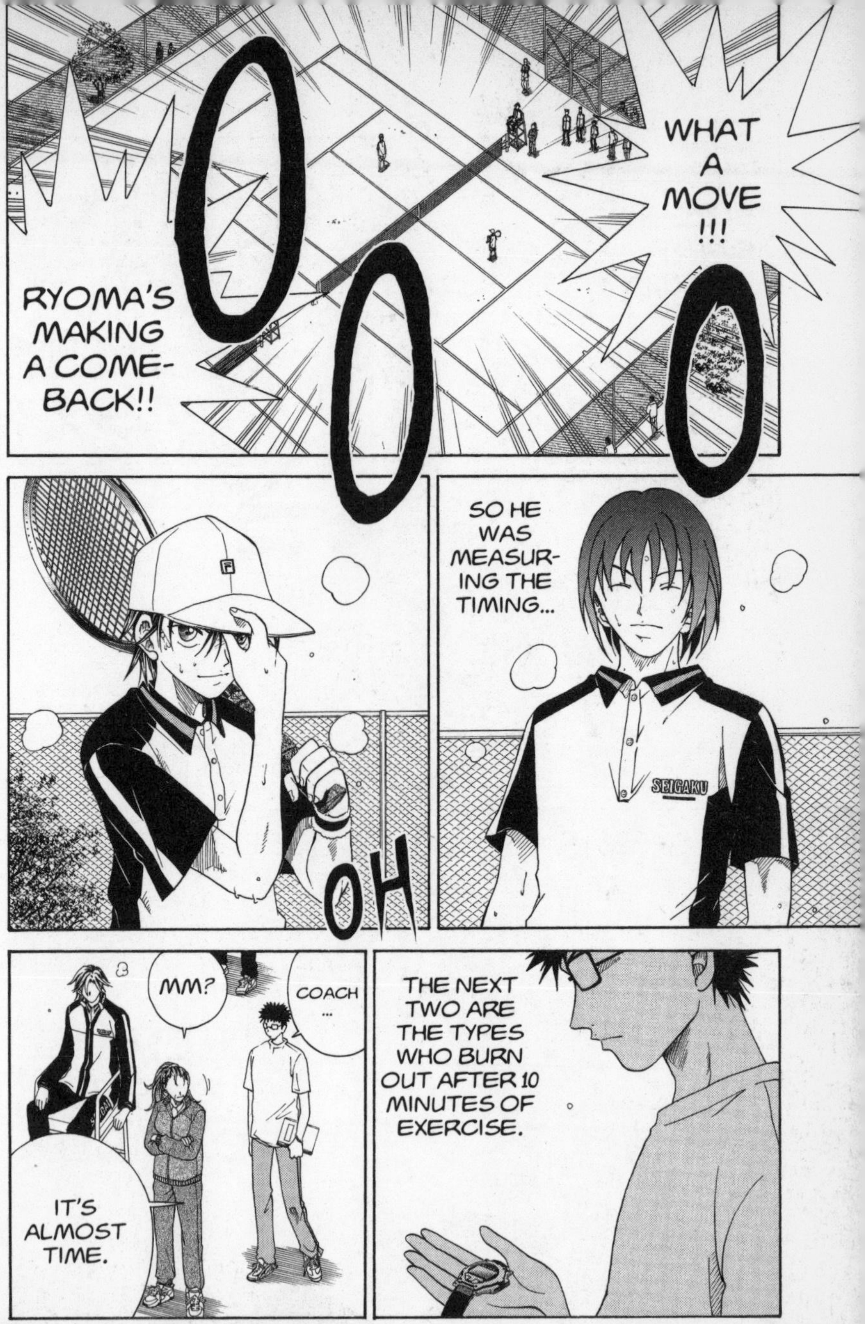
WHAT A MOVE !!!
RYOMA'S MAKING A COME-BACK!!
OOO
SO HE WAS MEASUR-ING THE TIMING...
OH
THE NEXT TWO ARE THE TYPES WHO BURN OUT AFTER 10 MINUTES OF EXERCISE.
COACH ...
MM?
IT'S ALMOST TIME.

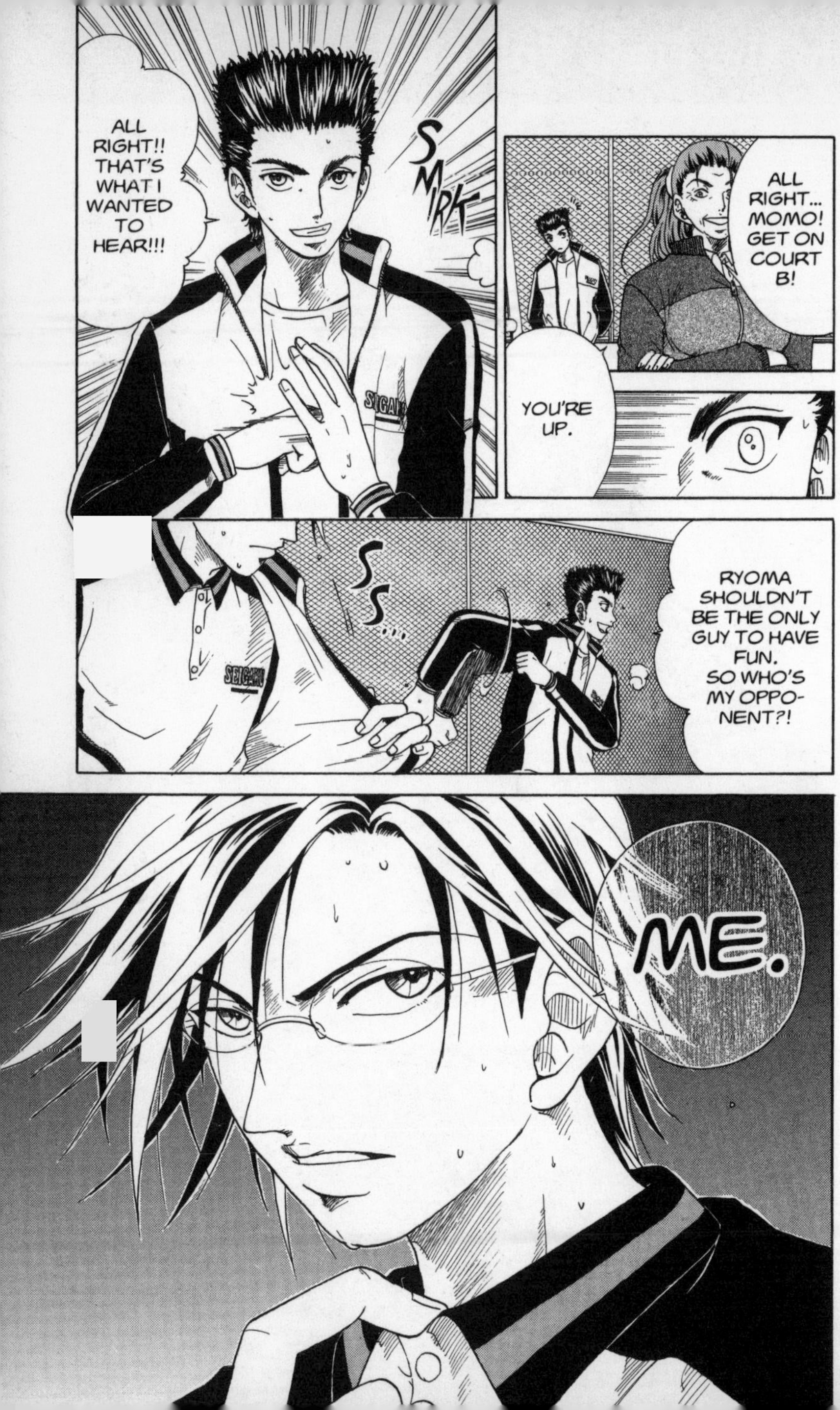
ALL RIGHT... MOMO! GET ON COURT B!
YOU'RE UP.
SMIRK
ALL RIGHT!! THAT'S WHAT I WANTED TO HEAR!!!
RYOMA SHOULDN'T BE THE ONLY GUY TO HAVE FUN. SO WHO'S MY OPPO-NENT?!
SS...
ME.

In the Next Volume...

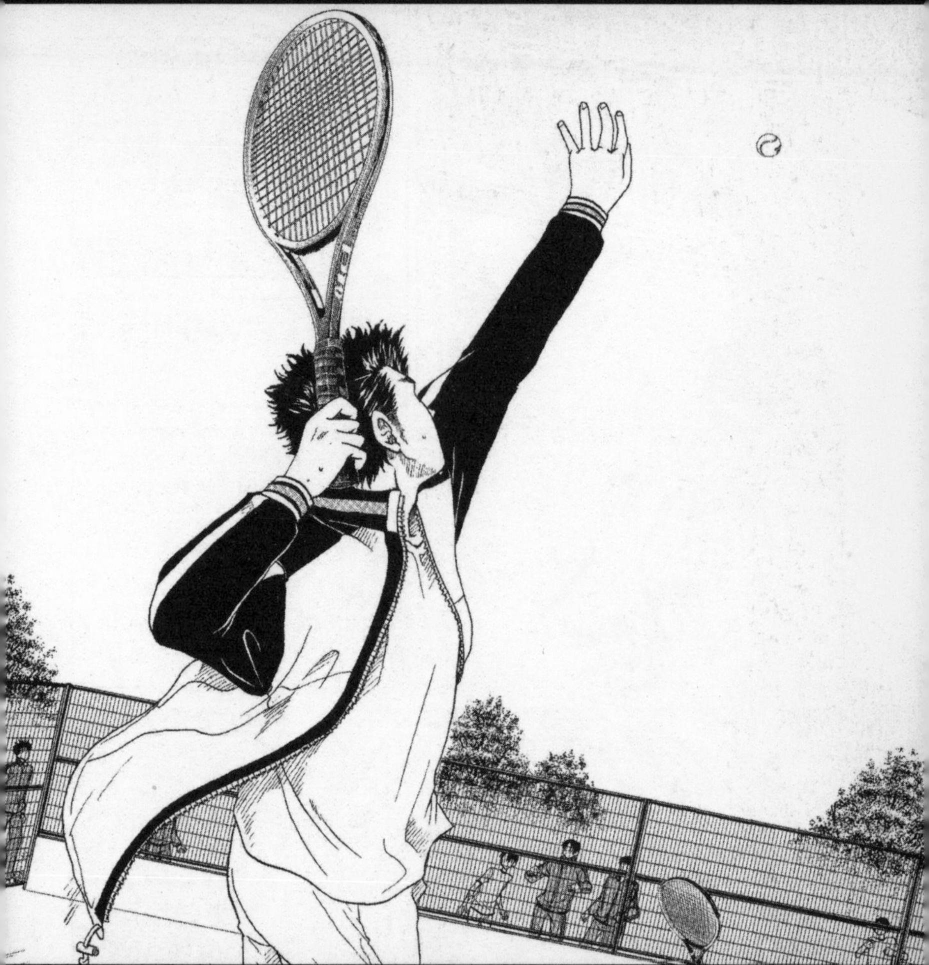

The road to the Nationals is paved with malicious intentions, and players from the competing teams come up with various styles and gimmicks to win. Find out how Seishun Academy's Momo fares against Sengoku's Kiyosumi, whose racket is strung way below the normal string tension!

Available Now!

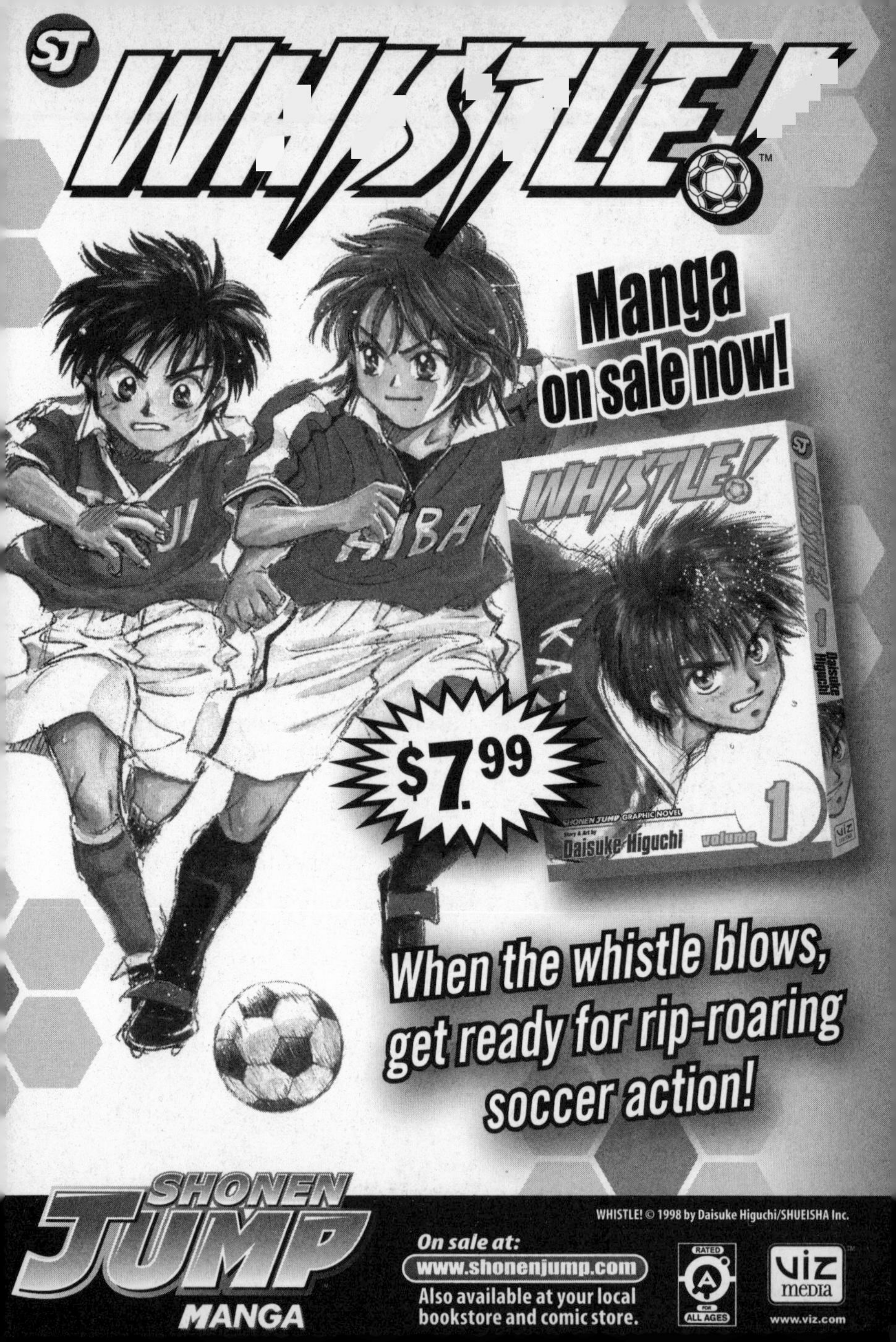
SJ
WHISTLE!™
Manga on sale now!
WHISTLE!
SHONEN JUMP GRAPHIC NOVEL
Story & Art by
Daisuke Higuchi
volume 1
$7.99
When the whistle blows, get ready for rip-roaring soccer action!
SHONEN JUMP MANGA
WHISTLE! © 1998 by Daisuke Higuchi/SHUEISHA Inc.
On sale at:
www.shonenjump.com
Also available at your local bookstore and comic store.
RATED A FOR ALL AGES
VIZ media
www.viz.com

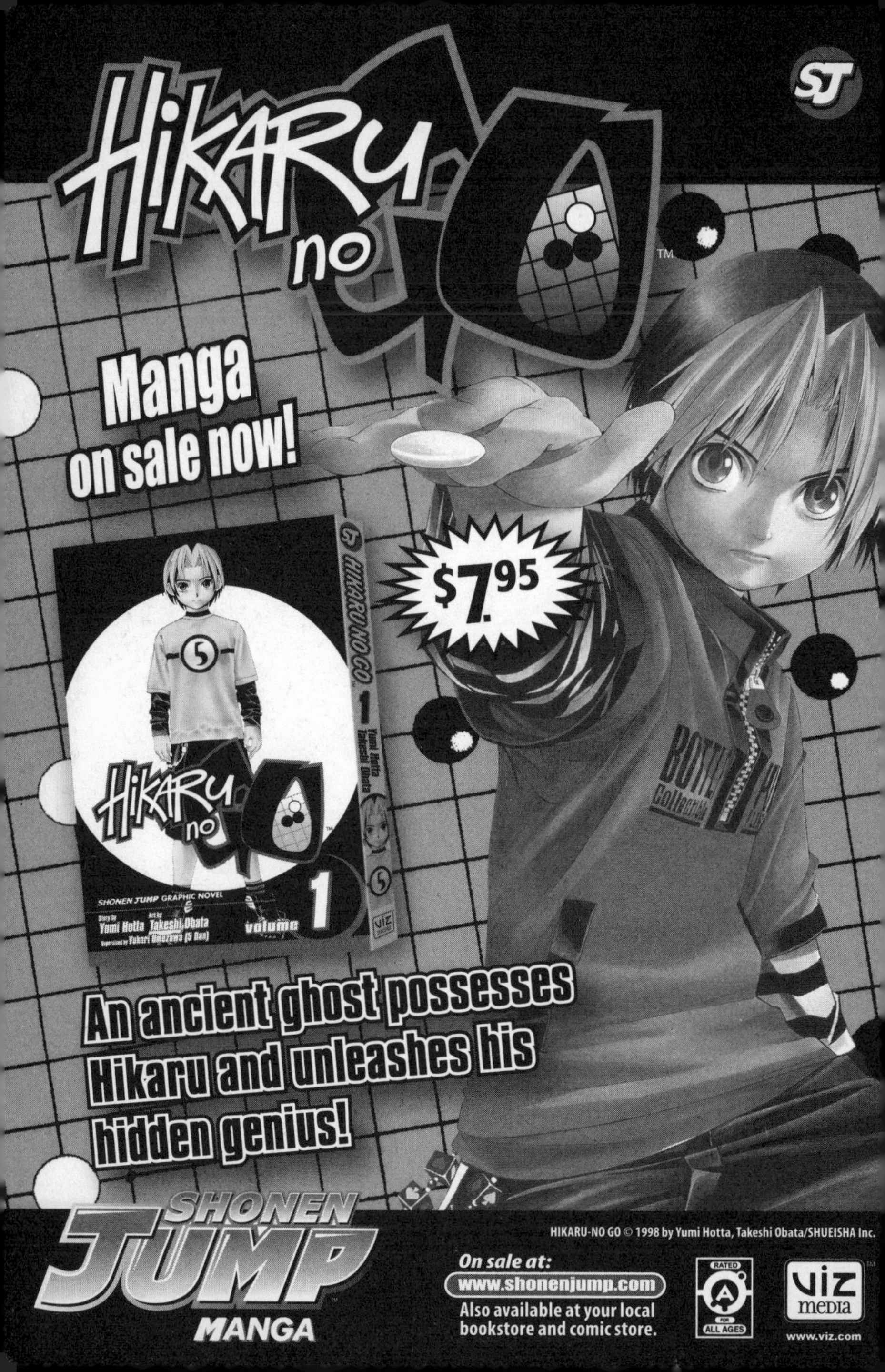
SJ
HIKARU no GO™
Manga on sale now!
$7.95
SHONEN JUMP GRAPHIC NOVEL
Story by Yumi Hotta Art by Takeshi Obata
Supervised by Yukari Umezawa (5 Dan)
volume 1
An ancient ghost possesses Hikaru and unleashes his hidden genius!
SHONEN JUMP MANGA
HIKARU-NO GO © 1998 by Yumi Hotta, Takeshi Obata/SHUEISHA Inc.
On sale at:
www.shonenjump.com
Also available at your local bookstore and comic store.
RATED A FOR ALL AGES
VIZ media
www.viz.com

Tell us what you think about SHONEN JUMP manga!

Our survey is now available online.
Go to: www.*SHONENJUMP*.com/mangasurvey

Help us make our product offering better!